1000

things to do in London for under £10

timeout.com

Published by Time Out Guides Ltd, a wholly owned subsidiary of Time Out Group Ltd.
Time Out and the Time Out logo are trademarks of Time Out Group Ltd.

© **Time Out Group Ltd 2009**

10 9 8 7 6 5 4 3 2

This edition first published in Great Britain in 2009 by Ebury Publishing
A Random House Group Company
20 Vauxhall Bridge Road, London SW1V 2SA

Random House Australia Pty Limited 20 Alfred Street, Milsons Point, Sydney, New South Wales 2061, Australia
Random House New Zealand Limited 18 Poland Road, Glenfield, Auckland 10, New Zealand
Random House South Africa (Pty) Limited Isle of Houghton, Corner Boundary Road & Carse O'Gowrie, Houghton 2198, South Africa

Random House UK Limited Reg. No. 954009

Distributed in USA by Publishers Group West
1700 Fourth Street, Berkeley, California 94710

Distributed in Canada by Publishers Group Canada
250A Carlton Street, Toronto, Ontario M5A 2L1

For further distribution details, see www.timeout.com

ISBN: 978-1-84670-090-3

A CIP catalogue record for this book is available from the British Library

Printed and bound by Firmengruppe APPL, aprinta druck, Wemding, Germany

The Random House Group Limited supports The Forest Stewardship Council (FSC), the leading international forest certification organisation. All our titles that are printed on Greenpeace approved FSC certified paper carry the FSC logo. Our paper procurement policy can be found at http://www.rbooks.co.uk/environment.

Time Out carbon-offsets all its flights with Trees for Cities (www.treesforcities.org).

Time Out Guides Limited
Universal House
251 Tottenham Court Road
London W1T 7AB
Tel + 44 (0)20 7813 3000
Fax + 44 (0)20 7813 6001
Email guides@timeout.com
www.timeout.com

Contributors Jessica Ablitt Sudbury, Dominic Addison, Sharif Ahmed, Edoardo Albert, Simone Baird, Alex Barlow, Paul Burston, Rachael Claye, Simon Coppock, Annie Dare, Amy Ellis, Anna Faherty, Mike Flynn, Grant Gillespie, Charlie Godfrey-Faussett, Hugh Graham, Sarah Guy, Derek Hammond, Ronnie Haydon, Kate Hutchinson, Serena Kutchinsky, Ben Lerwill, Jon Levene, Cathy Limb, Megha Mohan, Jenni Muir, Julie Pallot, Toby Pearce, Cath Phillips, Natasha Polyviou, Kate Riordan, Alan Rutter, Robin Saikia, Cyrus Shahrad, Andrew Shields, Bella Todd, Helen Walasek, Peter Watts, Patrick Welch, Sonia Zhuravlyova.

Interviews Nuala Calvi, Bella Todd, Sarah Thorowgood.

The Editor would like to thank Katerina Botsari, Simon Coppock, Grant Gillespie, Vincent White.

Maps London Underground map supplied by Transport for London.

Front and back cover by Heloise Bergman, Andrew Brackenbury, Tricia de Courcy Ling, Guy Hills, Jitka Hynkova, Britta Jaschinski, Olivia Rutherford, Ming Tang-Evans, Alys Tomlinson, Jonathan Perugia, Anthony Webb, Marzena Zoladz.

Photography by pages 3, 5 (bottom left), 7 (bottom right), 205, 208, 209 (middle & bottom left) Britta Jaschinski; pages 5 (top left), 35, 89, 124, 177, 236, 237, 309 Jonathan Perugia; pages 5 (top right), 28/29, 30/31, 37, 38, 90, 91, 123, 130/131, 134, 135, 194, 195, 201, 211 Olivia Rutherford; pages 5 (top & bottom middle), 9 (top), 53, 81, 106, 107, 143, 216, 230, 231, 233 Jitka Hynkova; pages 5 (bottom right), 7 (left), 105 (right), 141 (right) Haris Artimis; pages 7 (top right), 73 (bottom), 120, 175, 249 Andrew Brackenbury; page 9 (middle), 164 Michelle Grant; page 9 (bottom) Scott Wishart; pages 10/11, 26, 148, 150/151, 169, 185, 190/191 Alamy; page 13 Wellcome Images; page 18 Londonstills.com; page 19 newsteam.co.uk; page 33 National Maritime Museum, London; page 42 Neil Wissink; pages 48, 67, 77 Rob Greig; page 50/51 Alistair Muir; page 61 Libby Mor; pages 62, 63, 239 Tove K Breitstein; pages 70, 71, 264, 265, 303 Marzena Zoladz; page 73 (top) Abigail Lelliot; page 79 (top) Kate Peters; pages 79 (bottom right), 129, 167, 277 Alys Tomlinson; page 93 (left) WWT London Wetland Selena Sherid; page 93 (right) Werner Certh/ardea.com; page 95 Sarah Thorowgood; page 97 The Royal Parks; page 99 Tim Spicer; pages 100, 144, 157, 158, 159, 170/171, 197, 198 Elisabeth Blanchet; pages 105 (left), 108, 127, 209 (top left) 246 Ming Tang-Evans; page 109 Michael Franke; pages 110/111, 254, 290/291 Getty Images; page 133 Jon Furniss; page 147 www.gorminator.com; page 173 (top) Peter Garner; page 173 (middle) Sophie Lee; page 173 (bottom) Fung Wah-Man; page 193 www.britainonview.com; page 203 Adrian Pancucci; page 204 David Axelbank; page 209 (top left & bottom right) Rogan MacDonald; page 214 Richard Bryant/arcaid.co.uk; page 218 Stephen Dobbie; page 220 Tristram Kenton; page 221 Esme Appleton; page 227 Michael Cockerham; page 240 Heloise Bergman; page 242 Hayley Madden; page 245 Bernardo Doral; page 257 londonstills.com; page 268 Nick Ballon; page 269 Anthony Webb; page 276 (top & bottom right) Gemma Day; pages 294, 295 Tricia de Courcy Ling; page 306 Thomas Skovsende.

The following images were provided by the featured establishments/artists: pages 15, 42, 43, 47, 57, 69, 83, 87, 113, 122, 152, 153, 178, 187, 188, 206, 218, 221, 243, 248, 293, 297, 298.

Illustrations Ian Keltie, www.keltiecochrane.com.

Contents

ART FOR LESS

£4.95
WINSOR & NEWTON
COTMAN WATERCOLOUR
POCKETS SKETCHERS BOX
RRP £10.50

LESS THAN HALF PRICE

£7.95
WINSOR & NEWTON
WINTON OIL 200ML
TITANIUM WHITE
DOUBLE PACK
RRP £20.60

LESS THAN HALF PRICE

SPECIAL OFFER

£9.95
MOLESKINE
SKETCHBOOK
13X21CM
100 PAGES
RRP £12.95

£9.95
MOLESKINE
WATERCOLOUR
NOTEBOOK
9X14CM 200GSM
RRP £12.95

CASS VALUE

LESS THAN HALF PRICE

£6.50
FABER CASTELL
9000 8B-2H
12 DRAWING PENCILS
RRP £13.50

£8.50
REEVES 16x12
TRIPLE PACK CANVAS
RRP £23.97

LESS THAN HALF PRICE

SPECIAL OFFER

HALF PRICE

£9.95
CASS ART
HOG BRUSH PACK
SET OF 6
RRP £18.95

£3.95
DALER-ROWNEY OIL PASTEL
SET OF 24 RRP £10.25

£6.95
SEAWHITE A5
CONCERTINA
SKETCHBOOK
70 PAGES 140GSM

£4.95
LETRASET PROMARKER 5 SETS
RRP £9.95

LESS THAN HALF PRICE

£9.95
WINSOR & NEWTON
HENRY & WILLIAM
COLLECTION INK
SET OF 8X14ML
RRP £20.55

LESS THAN HALF PRICE

CASS PROMISE – CREATIVITY AT THE LOWEST PRICES. WE'RE CONFIDENT OUR PRICES CAN'T BE BEATEN

FLAGSHIP STORE: 66-67 COLEBROOKE ROW
ISLINGTON N1, 5 MINS FROM ANGEL TUBE, 020 7354 2999

ALSO AT: 13 CHARING CROSS RD WC2 (NEXT TO THE NATIONAL GALLERY), 24 BERWICK ST W1
220 KENSINGTON HIGH ST W8. ALL STORES OPEN 7 DAYS WWW.CASSART.CO.UK

ALL OFFERS SUBJECT TO AVAILABILITY AND PRICE CHANGE. PRICES VALID 01.01.09. CASS PROMISE. ASK INSTORE FOR DETAILS

about the guide

Telephone numbers

All phone numbers listed in this guide assume that you are calling from within London. From elsewhere within the UK, prefix each number with 020. From abroad, dial your international access code, then 44 for the UK, and then 20 for London.

Disclaimer

While every effort has been made to ensure the accuracy of information within this guide, the publishers cannot accept responsibility for any errors it may contain. Businesses can change their arrangements at any time so, before you go out of your way, we strongly advise you to phone ahead to check opening times, prices and other particulars.

Advertisers

The recommendations in *1000 Things to do in London for under £10* are based on the experiences of Time Out journalists. No payment or PR invitation of any kind has secured inclusion or influenced content. The editors select which venues and activities are listed in this guide, and the list of 1,000 was compiled before any advertising space was sold. Advertising has no effect on editorial content.

Let us know what you think

Did we miss anything? We welcome tips for 'things' you consider we should include in future editions and take note of your criticism of our choices. You can email us at guides@timeout.com.

Leighton House Museum
and Linley Sambourne House

Two remarkable historic houses in Kensington

18 Stafford Terrace - Linley Sambourne House

18 Stafford Terrace is a unique and beautifully preserved late Victorian townhouse with almost all of its original décor and furnishings. The house is a time capsule offering a glimpse into late-Victorian life.

Visits are by guided tours only. Weekend afternoon tours are led by a costumed actor.
Wednesdays 11.15am and 2.15pm
Saturdays and Sundays 11.15am, 1pm, 2.15pm, 3,30pm
Adult £6, Concession £4, Under 18s £1. Booking recommended on 020 7602 3316
18 Stafford Terrace, London W8 7BH
www.rbkc.gov.uk/linleysambournehouse

Leighton House Museum
Re-opening in Winter 09/10

Home of the eminent artist Frederic, Lord Leighton, the house is preserved as a remarkable and opulent tribute to Victorian aesthetics. The celebrated Arab Hall, based on the 12th century Palace of La Zisa at Palermo, is decorated with Leighton's collection of over 1,000 Syrian tiles.

The museum's collection includes paintings by Leighton and his contemporaries Burne-Jones, Millais, Alma-Tadema and Albert Moore. One of the UK's most remarkable buildings of the 19th century, Leighton House re-opens to the public in winter 09/10 after extensive restoration and refurbishment works.

Leighton House Museum, 12 Holland Park Road, London W14 8LZ
www.leightonhouse.co.uk 020 7602 3316

Introduction

London is a famously – some might even say reassuringly – expensive city. A place that consistently tops highest cost of living charts and which people from out of town save up to visit. There's no denying the fact that a martini at Claridge's or a box at the Royal Opera House will set you back considerably more than ten pounds – and that's probably the way it should be. Some things *are* worth paying a lot for. Yet despite the high rents and other costly living expenses, there is also a wealth of entertainment on offer in the city that's free – or at least attainable for less than a tenner.

When we set about compiling a list of ideas, it soon became clear that we were not going to be short of suggestions. For starters, since the great national museums threw open their doors for free after the millennium, it's been possible to spend days wandering the capital soaking up culture without paying a penny – once you've bought your travelcard. But even travelling through the city can be part of the floor show – head upstairs on a double decker bus with Peter Watts (*see p278*) and you'll see what we mean, and happy is the child that bags the front seat on a driverless DLR train (*see p238*). Then there are the hundreds of other art galleries and museums to visit, walks to take, performances to see (including opera in Covent Garden), bargains to buy, food to eat and even cocktails to sip – all for less than £10. You can use the thematic index (*see p315*) for inspiration and the A-Z one (*see p310*) if you are looking for something specific.

It's true that sometimes a little ingenuity is required to keep things ticking along for less than a tenner – we're not above a well-placed blag in the interests of research (*see p156*) – and there are some things in this book that would not be here if it weren't for the generosity of the people that run them (for some special deals, *see p221* and *p266*). But, as you'll quickly discover with the help of this book, London's full to bursting with gloriously cheap thrills. Grab a crisp ten pound note and start exploring.

Sarah Thorowgood, Editor

1

Refresh yourself in Battersea Park
Here's hoping for a repeat of summer 2006 when the mercury hit 36° centigrade and London's fountains became more than just decorative attractions. If the heatwave comes, you'll be relieved to know that the fountains in Battersea Park – the largest of any London park – spring into life at least once every hour.

2 Take tea in the British Museum

You could have a cuppa in one of the museum's various cafés, but if you have some spare time why not enjoy the free 'Way of Tea' session instead? This demonstration of the Japanese tea ceremony takes place in Room 92 roughly once a fortnight. There's also a terrific programme of free gallery talks, which are often focussed around the current blockbuster exhibition. Many of them are also timed just right (at 45 minutes) for a lunch break. Check the website for specific dates and details of all events.
British Museum *Great Russell Street, WC1B 3DG (7323 8000/www.britishmuseum.org).*

3 Buy Chinese food in Chinatown

Head to New Loon Moon (9 Gerrard Street, W1D 5PL, 7734 3887) – a labyrinth of pan-Asian delights – for an unrivalled range of products from different countries including China, Thailand, Vietnam, Korea, India, Japan, Indonesia, the Philippines, Malaysia and even Burma. Try fresh gai lan (crystal pears), Thai pea aubergines or huge, spiky jackfruit sold by the slice. Loon Fung (42-44 Gerrard Street, W1D 5QG, 7437 7332, www.loonfung.com) is one of the only oriental supermarkets in this part of town to have a butcher's counter – pork shin bones and chicken feet are offered alongside more traditional cuts. See Woon Hong (18-20 Lisle Street, WC2H 7BA, 7439 8325, www.see woo.com) is good for fresh vegetables and cured Chinese meats, while the Good Harvest Fish Market (65 Shaftesbury Avenue, W1D 6LH, 7734 4900) is London's (only) answer to the Chinese 'wet market' and is best for live seafood – crabs, lobsters and razor clams, for instance – as well as sashimi-grade salmon, tuna and seabass.

4 Go falcon-watching on the South Bank

The Royal Society for the Protection of Birds (RSPB) isn't all about red kites, golden eagles and puffins – high profile species living in remote sanctuaries. From July to September, you'll find Society volunteers toting telescopes next to the Millennium Bridge just outside Tate Modern. The RSPB's Richard Bashford told us that their plan is 'to approach people and say "would you like to see a falcon", then give them binoculars and information and point them up to where they're perched up on top of the Tate Modern chimney, post breeding.' Find out more at www.rspb.org.uk/brilliant/sites/tate.

5 Get something for nothing...

... at friendly monthly tombola bash Something for Nothing held at Dream Bags/Jaguar Shoes (34-36 Kingsland Road, E2 8DA, 7729 5830, www.jaguarshoes.com). Amid the playful indie-electro tunes of local DJs, free fashion swag from labels like American Apparel, Lee, Dr Martens and Cheap Monday are given away to grateful drinkers. Arrive at 7pm, take a ticket and wait for your number to be called out – then claim your loot.

6 See London through Nelson's eye

Situated in the south-west corner of Trafalgar Square, the Trafalgar Hotel's small rooftop bar (2 Spring Gardens, Trafalgar Square, SW1A 2TS, 7870 2900) overlooks the lions, the fountains, the general melée – and Nelson on his column. Up here you get pretty much the same view of the city as the great Admiral standing 170 feet up in the air. The bar serves a range of drinks (many of which cost less than a tenner), but is only open in the summer months and may be closed for private parties – phone ahead to check before you visit.

7 Be grateful for modern medicine

The Wellcome Collection explores the connections between medicine and art through its three spaces. Upstairs, exhibits drawn from 19th-century explorer Sir Henry Wellcome's findings include a 14th-century Peruvian mummy, a used guillotine blade, Napoleon's toothbrush and a wickedly bladed torture chair. Next door, is 'Medicine Now', which contains some startling modern art on medical themes (a realistic sculpture of a man disappearing into the folds of his own obese stomach, for example). Downstairs, the series of temporary exhibitions get better and better: *Skeletons* – a forensic analysis of ancient bones from the Museum of London storerooms – was one of our favourite recent shows.

Wellcome Collection *183 Euston Road, NW1 2BE (7611 2222/www.wellcomecollection.org).*

8 Drink to George Orwell in the Fitzroy Tavern

This lively West End boozer first secured its reputation as a literary salon in the 1920s when it provided a bolt- and watering-hole for Fitzrovia's more outré residents, including Augustus John, Jacob Epstein and Aleister Crowley. Queen of Bohemia Nina Hamnett could also be found sprawled over the bar here, trading anecdotes of her numerous adventures with Picasso in exchange for drinks. In the '50s, regulars included Dylan Thomas, George Orwell, Soho raconteur Julian McLaren-Ross and there was even the occasional visit from Lawrence Durrell when he was in the country. The Sam Smith pub still wears its history with pride – head downstairs to the Writers' and Artists' Bar, find yourself a cosy wooden booth and toast London's former literary glories.

Fitzroy Tavern *16A Charlotte Street, W1T 2LY (7580 3714)*

Wellcome Collection

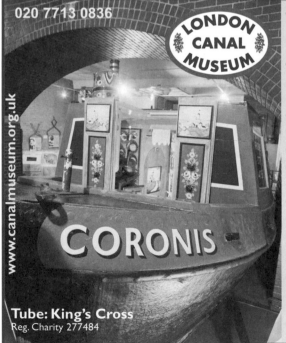

A few of my favourite things

9-13

Russell Kane, comedian

If you want to see some good comedy on the cheap, the best place to go is the Greenwich venue Up The Creek (302 Creek Road, SE10 9SW, 8858 4581, www.up-the-creek.com) on a Sunday night. It's just a little local place, but the standard of comedy is always high and it'll only cost you a fiver to get in. Another favourite of mine is the Fat Tuesdays Comedy Night at the Salmon and Compass (58 Penton Street, N1 9PZ, 7837 3891, www.salmon andcompass.com). If you are lucky you'll sometimes see people like Frank Skinner and Eddie Izzard popping in to try out their new material.

You can't do much better than walk the half mile or so through the centre of Covent Garden to look at the jugglers, human statues and street performers – it's like a constant free theatre show out there. The other day when I was there, I saw some people having a paella cook-off. If you get a drink at the Punch and Judy pub (40 The Market, The Piazza, WC2E 8RF) you can look down on proceedings from the upper level and have a laugh at the City types getting drunk and falling over.

Something that I really love doing is going on what I call a 'human safari'. You have to head out at about 11pm, having drunk no more than one bottle of wine – you need to be lubricated but relatively sober for this – then take a tuk tuk along Great Newport Street and through Chinatown and Leicester Square. I can guarantee that you will never see such a brilliant snapshot of humanity. Every stage of inebriation and emotion will be on display – from first love right the way through to animosity and violence.

There are lots of cool places to go to see films in London, but I think that the Ritzy (Brixton Oval, Coldharbour Lane, SW2 1JG, 0871 704 2065, www.picturehouses.co.uk) is really something special. As well as having tickets for £6.50 and live music for free in the café upstairs, it's also in a beautiful old building, all the movie timetables are written up on chalkboards and the staff really know their stuff. Plus it's in the heart of Brixton so it has a really great atmosphere.

I love food, and because I'm a bit hyperactive I can eat massive quantities of it without penalty. At the Stockpot (18 Old Compton Street, W1D 4TN, 7287 1066) you can get two courses, like sausage and mash and apple pie and ice-cream, for example, plus a drink, for under a tenner. It's the perfect place to go if you love British cooking – and if you feel like gorging yourself.

14

Take pleasure in the Palace on Bankside

As recently as the 1960s, the Bishop of Winchester's Palace on Bankside was little more than a rumour, hidden away behind Victorian warehouse walls. But now its tumbledown walls and high rose window once again add some spiritual frisson, as well as some 13th-century gravitas, to Clink Street. In the 15th and 16th centuries, Bankside was the focal point for fun in London – and who better to control the theatrical shenanigans, the dog-tossers, bear-baiters and prostitutes (aka 'Winchester geese', *see p264*) than the right honourable Bishop himself? Oh for the days when this 'private retreat from the pressures of medieval governance' featured not only 'a prison, a brewhouse and a butchery' but also the more wholesome delights of a 'tennis court, bowling alley and pleasure gardens'. No wonder the area was known as the 'Liberty of the Clink'.

Winchester Palace *(www.english-heritage.org.uk).*

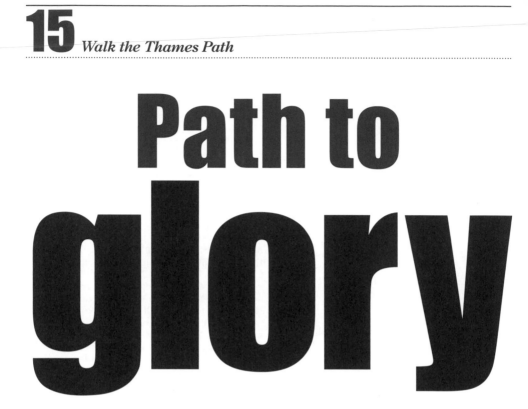

Path to glory

Cath Phillips packs some plasters and walks the Thames Path – all the way from the Thames Barrier to Hampton Court Palace.

The pain set in just past County Hall. The sunlight was bouncing off the water, the Houses of Parliament resplendent in the afternoon sun, and the riverside café did a mean cappuccino. But my feet were suffering: the blisters on my ankles had started to bleed, my toes were red and raw, and a strange puffy swelling had appeared on the underside of one foot. Perhaps we could call it a day, nip round the corner to Waterloo station and get the tube home? Fat chance. We were on a mission: to walk the Thames Path through London, all 36 miles of it from the Thames Barrier to Hampton Court Palace, over one weekend, and no way was the little matter of bleeding blisters going to stop us. At least I'd got some plasters and a spare pair of socks. And it was only another 23 miles to go.

It was a bright Saturday morning at the beginning of October. We'd started at 9am, meeting at North Greenwich tube station at the top of the desolate Greenwich Peninsula, next to the 02 Centre. From there it was a bus ride to the Thames Barrier, the official 'end' of the Thames Path, which starts 184 miles away at the river's source in the Cotswolds. For us it was the beginning, however, because we were walking east to west. You can do it in either direction, of course, but we had an overnight stop in Barnes and anyway it somehow seemed more appropriate to walk west – away from the city into the countryside, the sunset and the glories of a splendid palace.

Few people walk great distances in London. Walks tend to be short and practical: to and from the tube station or bus stop, to the shops, perhaps a Sunday stroll around a park if you're lucky. There are other long-distance paths within the capital (the Capital Ring, the

London Loop, the Green Chain Walk), but the Thames Path takes you through the heart of London, not the outskirts; it reveals the ever-changing nature of the city, from the industrial east through the seats of power in the built up centre to the increasingly rural west; and it's a brilliant way to reclaim the Thames, that great thoroughfare that defines the city yet is often ignored by its inhabitants.

You don't need a map as there are are signposts all along the route, but it's worth taking the three (free) mini guides to the London stretch of the Thames Path National Trail. You can download them from the publications section of www.nationaltrail.co.uk/thamespath or order them from Managers of the Thames Path National Trails Office (Environment & Economy, Holton, Oxford OX33 1QQ, 01865 810224). The brochures are written west to east, but they're just as useful in the opposite direction if you want sights pointed out to you, historical information and, crucially, for helping you decide which side of the river to walk on. You have no choice at the extremities, but from Greenwich to Teddington Lock the path straddles both sides of the river and it's possible to zigzag via the numerous bridges. Swapping sides gives a different perspective, but there are also lengthy and irritating detours that are best avoided, when the path is forced away from the water's edge and goes all round the houses (literally, in some instances) before getting back on course. Other essential equipment should include proper hiking boots and thick socks for cushioning, plasters, water and raingear. Binoculars are useful too.

The first ten miles, to Tower Bridge, were easy. From the shiny silver pods of the Thames Barrier to genteel Greenwich, it's a bleak but thrilling landscape of industrial decay, the path hugging the shoreline past scrapyards, derelict wharves, heaps of aggregate and mysterious metal structures dangling over the water. Rusting shopping trolleys are visible in the mud at low tide, and signs of life are few, bar the solitary Anchor & Hope pub and the occasional dog walker. In the 17th century pirates' corpses were hung in cages at the tip of the peninsula as a deterrent to other pirates; later it became an industrial stronghold, dominated by works for guns, ships, steel, metal, cement and gas, and therefore heavily polluted. Nowadays, the Greenwich Ecology Park, rows of colourful new apartment blocks and the David Beckham Football Academy signal the area's transformation – but it's still got a long way to go.

> ## 'The path reveals the ever-changing nature of the city: from the industrial east, through the seats of power to the increasingly rural west.'

Just past the O2 Centre is Antony Gormley's sculpture *Quantum Cloud*, a tangle of metal rods that gradually reveals the outline of a human figure. A sweet, heavy stench hangs in the air: Tate & Lyle's refinery still processes a million tonnes of sugar a year here. The brick towers of the Greenwich Power Station loom dramatically over the diminutive Trinity Hospital almshouses, founded in 1613; beyond lies the stately Royal Naval College and tourist shops of Greenwich, an ideal place for a coffee break.

At Greenwich, you can continue along the south bank, through Deptford and Rotherhithe, or traverse the Thames via the Greenwich Foot Tunnel and walk through the Isle of Dogs and Wapping. It's one or the other; there's no alternative river crossing until you reach Tower Bridge. We chose the southern route, ducking and diving around historic Rotherhithe, with changing views of the higgledy-piggledy apartment blocks and gleaming high-rises of Canary Wharf opposite as the river bends around the Isle of Dogs.

There's an awkward detour at Pepys Park in Deptford (look out for the Thames Path signs or you'll get lost). Then comes Deptford Strand, site of Henry VIII's Royal Dockyards – Drake's Steps mark the point where Francis Drake was knighted by Elizabeth after his circumnavigation of the globe in the Golden Hind. The docks here, once the heart of Britain's seafaring ambitions – whalers left for the Arctic from Greenland Dock – are now used by watersports enthusiasts and yachting types. Occasional danger signs warn of 'Slippery Steps. Sudden Drop. Deep Water.' Surrey Docks Farm, a ramshackle oasis with its goats, pigs, donkeys and café, is another handy refreshments stop. As the river bends to the west, you get the first glimpse of Tower Bridge.

Perhaps surprisingly, the section from Tower Bridge through the heart of the city and the tourist hotspots of the Tower of London, HMS Belfast, Shakespeare's Globe, Tate Modern, the South Bank Centre and the London Eye is the least interesting for the purposes of this mission. Inevitably, this is the most crowded part of the walk and it was hard to retain a sense of purpose and an air of adventure as we struggled through hordes of sightseers and office workers on their lunch break. (The northern bank, along the edge of the City, Victoria Embankment and Charing Cross, is quieter.) Eventually the throngs petered out beyond Westminster Bridge.

We crossed to the north at Lambeth Bridge (to avoid lengthy detours in Vauxhall and around the dilapidated hulk of Battersea Power Station), then crossed back again at Chelsea Bridge to take in leafy Battersea Park. We then yo-yoed once more to the north over Albert Bridge and wandered past assorted houseboats and gleaming yachts at Chelsea Harbour,

followed by a seemingly endless array of swanky new riverside apartment blocks to get to Wandsworth Bridge. By now it was getting dark and we were dog-tired; perhaps the reason that we made the mistake of continuing on the north side and had to endure a tedious longcut around the grounds of Fulham's private Hurlingham Club, before hitting Putney Bridge. We crossed the Thames once more.

From here, the most direct route to Barnes was a couple of miles, but we were walking next to the river and at this point it does one of its great meandering loops up to Hammersmith Bridge and then south again. At least the hard, foot grinding tarmac turned to gravel after the boathouses of Putney, and the tree-lined path was tranquil and increasingly pretty at we headed behind the London Wetland Centre, past playing fields and the Leg o' Mutton nature reserve. Finally, the humps of Barnes Bridge signalled the end of day one. A stiff drink, a hot bath and an early night swiftly followed. We weren't up early the following morning.

Day two started well. The stretch from Barnes to Richmond on the south bank is particularly idyllic. (It also avoids a rambling detour through the backstreets of uninteresting Brentford and, if you're counting miles – which of course we were – the southern route is more than two miles shorter than the northern one.) Trees line the gravel path, which hugs the water's edge, curving past cottages, various pubs, the Budweiser brewery at Mortlake (the smell of hops in the west countering the sugar in the east) and a glitzy, glassy housing development just before Kew Pier and Bridge.

The weather was bright and sunny and ducks and swans paddled by on the water, keeping out of the way of the heaving rowers. Then a lovely green vista opened up as the path skirted the edge of the Royal Botanic Gardens and the Old Deer Park. It was low tide, and foxes were playing on the foreshore opposite; beyond we could see lion-topped Syon House amid the grassy expanse of Syon Park. Then came pretty Richmond Lock, Twickenham Bridge and, shortly afterwards, the White Cross pub and the smart riverside frontage of Richmond. We stopped for coffee, cake and a breather at the café nestled under the bridge.

Just after Richmond lies one of the most picturesque parts of the Thames. The buildings disappear and there's the long sweep of Petersham Meadows (where cows still graze) and a little island midstream. Handsome 17th-century Ham House on the south bank faces off against 18th-century Marble Hill House on the north (a foot ferry runs between the two). Himalayan balsam has colonised the riverbank here; it's an invasive exotic, but it's hard to resist squeezing the seedcases – which pop satisfyingly, as if alive – thus spreading it further. Then comes a series of playing fields, nature reserves and, finally, Teddington Lock.

As well as the lock (which is crammed with pleasure boats in summer), there's a weir, a summer café and footbridges to Teddington proper. The lock marks the end of the tidal Thames; from this point the river takes on a placid and unhurried air, very different from the turbulent highs and lows Londoners are used to. This is also where the path loses its double-sided character. It runs on the south bank through a grassy hinterland as far as Kingston, then you have to cross to the northern bank, following the sweeping edge of Hampton Court Park to Henry VIII's glorious Tudor palace.

Just three miles to go. Trees and bushes dangled in the water, swans floated gently past a marina; the houses of Thames Ditton across the water the only reminder that we weren't in the heart of the country. But the light was fading, and an autumnal chill had descended making our legs feel heavy and stiff. Even the gravel towpath was getting too hard underfoot, so we hobbled, staggered and stumbled on the grassy verge until the long brick wall and ornate gates of Hampton Court Palace came into view. The sense of achievement was profound and – not capable of much more – we fell into the nearest pub for a celebratory pint.

On the train home (Hampton Court station is 30 minutes from Waterloo), despite aching limbs and bleeding feet, we were already planning to do it all again, this time from west to east, filling in the gaps we'd missed this time.

16-19

Decode Da Vinci

'In London lies a knight a Pope interred…' reads the clue in Dan Brown's *The Da Vinci Code* which leads our heroes to the 'Pantheonically pagan' round nave at the 12th-century Temple Church off Fleet Street (Temple, EC4Y 7BB). There are spooky, lifelike memorial effigies of Knights arrayed in the Round, where the order once held their secret initiation rites. But the hunt swiftly moves on to Westminster Abbey (20 Dean's Yard, SW1P 3NY), where fans will find Isaac Newton's tomb complete with the orb mentioned in the next part of the clue, although on a quiet day the Chapter House may feature a distinct lack of flying cryptex cylinders, gunplay and/or damsels in distress. It turns out that Alexander Pope ('A Pope', geddit?) read Newton's funeral eulogy.

Code devotees will also enjoy the crucifixion mural by Jean Cocteau (like Da Vinci, allegedly Grand Master of the Priory of Sion) in the Notre Dame de France church off Leicester Square (5 Leicester Place, WC2H 7BX). The surreal 1950s mural features much occult symbolism, from disguised pentagrams through John the Baptist handsigns to a black sun casting black rays into the sky.

But top of the hit list has to be the hulking art deco Freemasons Hall (60 Great Queen Street, WC2B 5AZ, www.ugle.org.uk), in Covent Garden – especially as it isn't common knowledge that tours are freely available. Highlights at the hall include a wealth of magickal, inexplicable regalia, walls and paraphernalia strewn with Egyptian, Hebrew and esoteric symbolism – and the 2,000-seater Grand Temple. It's stacked with Zodiacal signs, a depiction of Solomon's architect Hiram, symbols for Faith, Hope, Charity and Jacob's Ladder. There are also celestial and terrestrial globes, all-seeing eyes, charioteers and 'five-pointed stars'. Other items in the collection include the various belongings of other notable masons such as Winston Churchill and Edward VII.

20 Get behind the scenes at London Transport Museum's depot

London Transport Museum has a secret horde at its depot in Acton. Normally this is closed to the public but the treasure trove of unused exhibits opens occasionally for a themed weekend so that the public can have a peek – a treat that includes its working model layouts of London's transport network. You can ride on the depot's miniature railway – there are steam as well as electric trains – or take a trip on full-size heritage vehicles, including the 1950s prototype of the Routemaster bus (the RM1).
London Transport Museum Depot *2 Museum Way, 118-120 Gunnersbury Lane, W3 8BQ (7565 7298/www.ltmuseum.co.uk). £10.00, under-16s free.*

21 Ask 'Can you tell what it is yet?' at Heavy Pencil

Ever innovative, the ICA holds various themed nights in its bar as well as a rolling programme of contemporary art exhibitions. One such night is Heavy Pencil, a once-a-month event (check website for dates) that invites some of the UK's best illustrators to draw live just for the pleasure and fascination of the drinkers in the bar. Inspired, and accompanied by their favourite music, the artists' doodles are projected onto the bar's walls.
Institute of Contemporary Arts *The Mall, SW1Y 5AH (7930 3647/www.ica.org.uk).*

22 Make space in your diary for Open House weekend

Block out the third weekend of September and spend it visiting some of the more than 700 places – buildings of every conceivable size and type – that you can't visit the rest of the year. And, what's more, they are *all* free. See www.openhouse.org.uk for details.

Head for the hills

Alexandra Palace, N22
Alexandra Palace is famous for its splendid Victorian architecture and ice skating rink, but the view is a similarly big draw. Framed by a low brick wall and ornamental railings, and dotted with pay-per-view machines, the vista encompasses everything from the leafy Victorian terraces of Crouch End and Wood Green to the City glitter of the Gherkin. The view from below, looking back at the flamboyant 'Ally Pally', is equally majestic.

Brockwell Park, SW2
A short walk from the mean streets of Brixton, leafy Brockwell Park is worlds away in feel. Wandering amid the ancient trees, postcard lakes and gentle hills, you may feel like you're in the shires, but turn northwards and take in the vista – the Gherkin, the London Eye, Tower 42 – and suddenly the city meets the country.

Denmark Hill, SE5
Formerly Dulwich Hill, Denmark Hill was rechristened in honour of Queen Anne, wife of Prince George of Denmark, who lived on the east side. The Fox on the Hill pub stands on the site of the 'Fox under the Hill', the only building in the area shown on John Cary's 1786 map.

Forest Hill, SE23
This sleepy southern suburb is best-known for the eccentric Horniman Museum. It's a gem, to be sure, but the view from the park behind will leave an equally lasting impression – the City shimmering in the distance, rising above a canopy of leafy green.

Greenwich Park, SE10
It's quite a steep hike up to the summit of Greenwich Park from the river but the sweat is well worth it. As well as the genteel views of the Royal Park spread out before you, there's a host of graceful structures to take in on the way: from Wren and Hawksmoor's baroque Old Royal Naval College through to Inigo Jones's Queen's House and on up to the Royal Observatory. The view from the top looking back across the river is breathtaking (*see p190*).

Muswell Hill, N10
The site of a spring that was thought to have healing properties and named 'Mossy Well', Muswell Hill was a place of medieval pilgrimage. Later on, its impressive views over the Thames and Lea Valleys made it a popular rural retreat until – back in 1896 – key estates were bought by developer James Edmondson. He built new houses and shopping arcades, effectively creating a London suburb from scratch.

Parliament Hill, NW3
At the top of the wild and woody Hampstead Heath, you are a long way from the urban grit, but Parliament Hill offers a true natural high within the city. The extraordinary vista provides a medley of London's greatest landmarks – the Gherkin, the London Eye, the Houses of Parliament, St Paul's – and many harder-to-spot highlights.

Primrose Hill, NW3
The name sounds incredibly romantic, and the view from the top of Primrose Hill is just that. On a warm summer evening, this spot is a mecca for loved-up couples – it's the perfect cheap date in a neighbourhood of millionaires. London is laid out before you and its buildings are helpfully identified on a plaque. Visual highlights include Regent's Park and its zoo, the London Eye, and a couple of modernist icons: the BT Tower and Centrepoint.

Shooters Hill, SE18
At 433 feet, Shooters Hill is the highest point in south London. During the Middle Ages the lofty position was a favourite with archers and highwaymen took it to their hearts in the 17th century (because it was on the route of the mail coaches that ran between London and Dover). There was a gallows at the bottom of the hill, and the bodies of the hanged were displayed on a gibbet at the summit, close to where the Victorian gothic water tower now stands.

32-33

Ring church bells

If you thought bellringing was just a simple matter of pulling on a rope, think again. It's an art form, one that requires precision, a degree of physical exertion and team work. The current technique, known as change ringing, was developed in the 17th century. Don't expect to be able to ring perfectly straight away; there are plenty of practice sessions around London that welcome beginners. For more details, check out www.mcaldg. org.uk We particularly recommend St John at Hackney (Lower Clapton Road, E5 0PD, www.stjohn-athackneychurch. org.uk, Mondays) and St Mary Abbots Kensington (Kensington High Street, W8 4HN, www.stmaryabbots church.org, Thursdays).

34-44 Take your time in London's bookshops

For some, there are few retail joys more unalloyed than an afternoon spent in a bookshop. And, with many now offering seating, and in some cases, cafés, it's become one of the capital's classic budget activities. Here are just a few of our favourite browsing haunts.

Borders

Borders may be the enemy of independent bookshops but forgive us: the big, bad American chain deserves an honourable mention for its browsing potential. Not only does it have a vast selection of books and magazines, you can also snuggle up on a sofa or armchair, read to your heart's content and staff won't bat an eyelid. There's a Starbucks franchise on the first floor of this branch.
120 Charing Cross Road, WC2H 0JR (7379 8877).

Biblion

Biblion is the literary equivalent of Portobello Road. Comprising 50 to 60 booksellers, who congregate during the week in Grays Antiques Market, near Bond Street, it stocks around 20,000 rare, second-hand and antiquarian books – a permanent bookfair. Specialities include illustrated works, children's and travel books, titles on glass, modern first editions and finely bound volumes. And if that doesn't keep you occupied, there's a free gallery dedicated to book-related art.
1-7 Davies Mews, W1K 5AB (7629 1374/www.biblion.co.uk).

Bolingbroke

After more then 27 years in business, Bolingbroke is now as much a local communications hub as it is a bookshop. Stock is varied and includes interesting titles from publishers such as Eland and Persephone. Oh, and there's also a steam engine installation.
147 Northcote Road, SW11 6QB (7223 9344/www.bolingbrokebookshop.co.uk).

Crockatt and Powell

The bookshop on Lower Marsh near Waterloo now has a new branch in Chelsea where there's a dedicated children's room (which means that it should be quieter in the rest of the shop). You can take any of the relatively small but well chosen selection of books (mainly history, biography, philosophy and literary fiction) into the garden to read at your leisure.
345 Fulham Road, SW10 9TW (7351 3468/www.crockattandpowell.com).

Daunt Books

A wonderful place to while away a few hours, Daunt Books is housed in a beautiful Edwardian building, complete with oak balconies, viridian walls, conservatory ceiling and a stained-glass window. The back room boasts a travel section extraordinaire but Daunt is also a good all-round bookshop: staff are well-read and dedicated, and their carefully curated picks – the best literary fiction, biography, children, design and cookery books – are dotted throughout the rest of the store.
83-84 Marylebone High Street, W1U 4QW (7224 2295/www.dauntbooks.co.uk).

the Café

Foyles

Daunt Books

Foyles

The big daddy of independent bookshops, Foyles is a London legend and a browsers' best friend. Size does matter here: 56 specialist subjects are spread across five floors. Fiction is a forte, as are music, sport, film and gay interest. Enhancing the contemplative mood is Ray's Jazz Café, on the first floor.
113-119 Charing Cross Road, WC2H OEB (7437 5660/www.foyles.co.uk).

Hatchards

London's oldest bookshop has a refined air, but it's not too stuffy for browsing. On the contrary, the old-school charm is particularly conducive to drifting off into a literary reverie. Biography, politics, travel and fiction are strengths, and keep your eyes peeled for famous authors – the shop regularly gets in bigwigs for signings.
187 Piccadilly, W1J 9LE (7439 9921/ www.hatchards.co.uk).

London Review Bookshop

In the heart of Bloomsbury, the London Review Bookshop oozes intellectual gravitas, as you'd expect from a shop owned by the esteemed periodical. If you need inspiration, you'll find it here: the impeccable selection includes politics, current affairs, history, philosophy and poetry. Walk through an archway into the adjoining London Review Cake Shop, a charming café adorned with original art.
14 Bury Place, WC1A 2JL (7269 9030/ www.lrbshop.co.uk).

Magma

In some ways, design books are the ideal genre for browsing – lots of eye candy and minimal reading required. Magma is the motherlode of look-at-me coffee table books and glossy style magazines, featuring cutting-edge design, architecture and graphics. In fact, the shop's objective is to blur the boundary between bookshop and exhibition space, so quiet contemplation is highly appropriate.
117-119 Clerkenwell Road, EC1R 5BY (7242 9503/www.magmabooks.com).

Skoob

At Skoob you'll stumble across out-of print gems, cult classics, obscure biographies and forgotten best-sellers. There are some 60,000 titles spread across 2,500 square feet and every subject under the sun is represented: from philosophy, biography, maths and science to languages, literature and criticism, art, history, economics and politics.
Unit 66, the Brunswick, WC1N 1AE (7278 8760/ www.skoob.com).

Stanfords

If Daunt whets your appetite for travel, Stanfords will trigger a case of full-blown wanderlust. The shelves are bursting with books on every country, city, highway and byway. Pick up a book, a map and a latte and get planning your dream trip in the small ground floor café.
12-14 Long Acre, WC2E 9LP (7836 1321/ www.stanfords.co.uk).

45-52

Look for John Soane (and find him in a telephone box)

One of Britain's greatest and most innovative architects, Sir John Soane (1753-1837) was a national treasure by the time of his death and his wonderfully idiosyncratic home, now the Sir John Soane's Museum (13 Lincoln's Inn Fields, WC2A 3BP, 7405 2107, www.soane.org), was bequeathed to the nation by Act of Parliament.

Soane believed in 'the poetry of architecture' and used his house as a testing ground for his ideas on light and space. He was a great collector, so the house is full of ingenious space-saving touches – like the panels hung with paintings that unfold from the walls. The downstairs is packed with antiquities, architectural models and art; above ground, in airy contrast, light streams through top-lit ceilings and is reflected off mirrored inserts.

But there's more to Soane than his museum – London is still full of his architectural influences. His most important commission (and the building he was most proud of) was the Bank of England. An established architectural masterpiece, it's all the more shocking that most of it was torn down after World War I.

But Soane's powerful perimeter wall remains and his first major work, the Bank Stock Office, has been reconstructed inside the Bank's Museum (Threadneedle Street, EC2R 8AH, 7601 5545, www.bankofengland.co.uk).

Purchased as Soane's country retreat in 1800, Pitzhanger Manor (Walpole Park, Mattock Lane, W5 5EQ, 8567 1227) was soon remodelled according to the architect's ideas of design and decoration and features his trademark curved ceilings and inset mirrors. Acquired by Ealing Council in 1900, the house became a library. Today the library has gone and the building has been restored to showcase Soane's work. Set in lovely Walpole Park, an extension houses a contemporary art gallery.

Dulwich Picture Gallery (Gallery Road, Dulwich, SE21 7AD, 8693 5254, www.dulwich picturegallery.org.uk) was an unlikely outcome of 18th-century European politics. Art dealers François Bourgeois and Noel Desenfans spent years gathering a spectacular assemblage of art for the King of Poland. But by 1795 Poland was partitioned, the King was kingdomless and so had no need of a royal collection. With no takers for the pictures, Bourgeois willed them to Dulwich College in 1811, stipulating that his friend Sir John Soane design a building to display them and that it be open to the public. What Soane built has been described as the most beautiful art gallery in the world and was an inspiration for countless later architects.

Set in a little Regency enclave, St Peter's Walworth (76 Tatum Road, SE17 1QR, 7703 3139) is the best preserved of Soane's three London churches, with its slim dome-topped tower, austere brick façade and Ionic portico. Its crypt is a masterful example of 19th-century brickwork. At his Holy Trinity Church opposite Great Portland Street Station (Marylebone Road, NW1 4DU), you'll have to attend a church service to see the interiors; St John's Bethnal Green (Cambridge Heath Road, E2 6NB) has been remodelled following damage in 1870 and World War II, but for Soane groupies, it's still worth a visit.

A final must-see is Soane's tomb in the atmospheric setting of St Pancras Gardens, behind St Pancras Station. Originally erected by Soane for his wife, the monument inspired the design of one of Britain's most iconic structures: Giles Gilbert Scott's K6 series of red telephone boxes.

53 *Smoke a shisha...*

Shisha, hubbly bubbly, hookah, nargileh… the names vary but the waterpipe itself is pretty much the same throughout the Middle East. London's weather may not be so congenial but there are many places where you can still sit with a friend and watch the world drift by while savouring some apple tobacco and perhaps a mint tea. The Hookah Lounge on Brick Lane is one such place; a shisha of apple tobacco here costs just £6.95.
Hookah Lounge *133 Brick Lane, E1 6SB (7033 9072).*

54 *...or snort snuff*

Meanwhile, downstairs in the confines of basement cabaret venue CellarDoor in the West End, they thoughtfully offer nicotine addicts a variety of flavours of snuff so that they don't have to go outside for a cigarette. As they put it, it's 'immeasurably less anti-social than smoking and, if only someone had the foresight to ban it, infinitely cooler than coke'.
CellarDoor *Zero Aldwych WC2E 7DN (7240 8848/www.cellardoor.biz).*

55 Play skittles at the Freemasons Arms...

No, don't even mention ten-pin bowling in the same breath. That commercial, sanitised version has little to do with the ancient game and its descendent, London Skittles, which is not so much played as venerated by the Hampstead Lawn Billiard and Skittle Club. The game uses nine pins and a cheese – the wooden discus players use to knock down the pins – and involves such intricacies as the 'flying fornicator' (a cheese with bad spin) and the dreaded 'Gates of Hell' pin formation that takes expert felling. Few skittle alleys remain in London, but it's still being played, much as it has been since 1934, in the cellar at the Freemasons Arms in Hampstead. Come along on club night or book the alley for a group of friends – an experienced club member will provide help and equipment.
Freemasons Arms *32 Downshire Hill, NW3 1NT. To arrange a game contact the club at www.londonskittles.co.uk.*

56-59 ...or throw things at a 'piglet'

The Balls Brothers wine bar (Hay's Galleria, Tooley Street, SE1 2HD, 7407 4301, www.balls brothers.co.uk) runs a free pétanque pitch in the middle of the shopping arcade near London Bridge and this essential French pastime has proved such a success that there's now an annual lunchtime tournament in summer. Games are also played in the square outside the Prince of Wales pub (48 Cleaver Square, SE11 4EA, 7735 9916), at the Surprise pub (16 Southville, SW8 2PP, 7622 4623), and on a pitch near the Chevening Road entrance to Queen's Park in north-west London (8969 5661).

The game requires no prior experience and can be played on equal terms by young and old, male and female, drunk and sober (although in France the players tend to be old, male and drunk). Each of three teams or individuals has two 'boules', which they must throw in turns as near as possible to the golf ball-sized cochonnet (literally 'piglet'). The player or team whose boule is closest to the cochonnet wins. *Voilà!*

60 *Get around town on a clipper*

When you look at the river these days it's full of traffic – and we don't just mean day tripping cruisers. The speedy and sleek catamaran service, Thames Clippers (7001 2222, www.thames clippers.com), largely designed for commuters, is still going strong since its launch in 1999.

61 Check out 1930s gadgets at Eltham Palace

In the Domesday survey of 1086 the manor of Eltham is recorded as being in the possession of William the Conqueror's half-brother. Its estate was one of the country's largest and, for nearly six centuries, most frequented royal residences (Henry VIII spent much of his boyhood at Eltham). Gradually, however, it fell into decay, becoming a humble farm after the Civil War. In the 1930s super-rich society couple Stephen and Virginia Courtauld built a house adjoining the 1470s Great Hall. Their new home boasted the very latest in ultra-modern art deco design and was packed with mod-cons of the day including synchronous clocks that received a time signal direct from Greenwich; loudspeakers that piped music through all the rooms of the ground floor; a private internal telephone exchange; and a centralised vacuum cleaner system. The light-filled circular entrance hall is jaw-droppingly, cinematically glamorous, and exploring the luxurious rooms – with their wood panelling, built-in furniture, abstract carpets and decorative plaster reliefs – is enough to make Jeeves and Wooster fans swoon with delight. Even the couple's pet lemur, Mah-Jongg, enjoyed caged sleeping quarters decorated with bamboo forest murals. The extensive grounds, carefully restored to a 1930s design and complete with sunken rose garden and a rock garden with water cascades, are also well worth a wander. Admission costs £8 (£6.50 reductions).

Eltham Palace *Court Yard, SE9 5QE (8294 2548/www.elthampalace.org.uk).*

62 Play tennis for free

With some London boroughs charging nearly a tenner for an hour's worth of play, it's no wonder we're a little light on tennis talent here in the UK. Fortunately, thanks to the Tennis for Free organisation (55 Thornhill Square, N1 1BE, www.tennisforfree.com, 0870 011 3733), there's now no excuse for not becoming the next Andy Murray or Tim Henman. Visit their website for a list of council courts at which you can play for free.

63 Enter the Great Spitalfields Pancake Race

The pancake race is said to date back 500 years to the time when a woman, cooking at home, heard the church bells calling people to confession and ran out of her hovel, still holding her frying pan. Fast forward to the present, and there are a number of races held in London every Shrove Tuesday to mark this historic (and, let's be honest, quite possibly entirely fabricated) event. Among the best is the Great Spitalfields race: teams of four, often in fancy dress (anything from Captain Jack Sparrow to a giant bright green squid) toss pancakes as they run. Phone in advance if you want to take part (it's all done for the charity London Air Ambulance) and you'll have to bring your own frying pan (pancakes are provided). Alternatively, just show up if all you're after is the sight of daft costumes darting down the streets and pancakes hitting the pavement. There are engraved pans not only for the race winners but also for the best dressed tosser, so come imaginatively attired.

Great Spitalfields Pancake Race
7375 0441/www.alternativearts.co.uk.

64 Read a play with a playwright

If you like your theatrical experiences interactive, then get yourself along to the Write to Play events (07973 120 270, www.inthesame boat.org.uk) hosted each month by a different modern playwright (recent writers have included Mark Ravenhill and Simon Stephens). They talk about their style and method before taking questions from the audience and – if you are so inclined – you can join in the reading of an extract from one of their plays. Tickets cost £5 and the venues change each month, so check the website for further details.

65 Explore Mars, or launch your own space probe

At the forefront of astronomy for over three centuries, the Royal Observatory now houses London's only public planetarium. Designed by architects Allies and Morrison, the RIBA-award winning concrete cone of the planetarium is clad with almost 250 bronze plates, welded together to look like a single piece. Positioning of the planetarium is minutely precise: the sloping southern side of the cone points towards the north celestial pole and pole star, the angle of the slope is the same as the degree latitude of the Royal Observatory (51° 28' 4") and the reflective glass top of the cone is sliced at an angle parallel to the celestial equator. Inside, thanks to digital laser technology, you can explore the surface of Mars or experience the life and death of a star with Hollywood-style special effects. Each adventure is introduced by an astronomer who sticks around to field post-show questions. It's also worth saving some time for the interactive galleries upstairs where you can design and launch your very own space probe.

Royal Observatory & Planetarium *Blackheath Avenue, Greenwich Park, SE10 8XJ (8312 6565/ www.nmm.ac.uk/astronomy). Planetarium £6.*

66 Mix booze and art at Dr Sketchy's Anti Art School

Say what you want about cocaine, but the drug of choice for any artist worth their price tag has always been alcohol – a fact not lost on the organisers of Dr Sketchy's Anti Art School. This monthly craft salon manages to tuck life drawing and neo-burlesque into the same bed for a heady coitus of booze-soaked carnal whimsy. Founded in New York in 2005, this alterna-art party now has franchises in over 40 cities worldwide. Each differs in their level of conservatism – or lack thereof, some go for full nudity – but the London branch, organised by proud Chelsea Art School drop-out Ruka Johnson, follows the same format as the original: semi-naked luminaries of the burlesque scene strike unconventional poses for a happily gender-balanced class of wannabe Renoirs. Led by an irreverent host, sketchers – or 'art monkeys' – compete in various drawing contests throughout the evening, our favourite being a challenge to interpret the model as a domestic appliance. At the end awards are handed out; prizes for the best work are, of course, bottles of alcohol – and lots of it.

Dr Sketchy's Anti Art School *various venues (www.drsketchylondon.co.uk).*

Royal Observatory & Planetarium

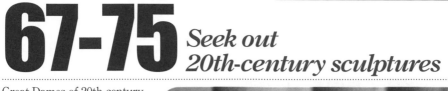

Great Dames of 20th-century sculpture, abstract Barbara Hepworth and figurative Elisabeth Frink, have various works sited all over the city – link them together and you've got a great day's sculpture stroll. Start your trail at Kenwood House on Hampstead Heath. After a cuppa and a scone in the tea room, in the grounds you'll find Hepworth's Monolith (*Empyrean*) from 1953, still standing proud.

Then head south-east to find Dame Elizabeth's first major public commission, *Blind Man and his Dog* (1957), at the Bethnal Green end of Roman Road. Next, it's a short hop on the Central line to St Paul's to see her *Shepherd and Sheep* (1975) in Paternoster Square, a naked man herding four Attic-looking ovine forms. Further along the Central line, near Oxford Circus, Hepworth's *Winged Figure* (1963) adorns the Holles Street façade of John Lewis on Oxford Street.

A quick walk through Mayfair to Grosvenor Square is rewarded by Frink's winged bronze bald American eagle (1986), which sits atop the World War II Eagle Squadron memorial. Head on south to find her *Horse and Rider* (1975), inspired by the stallions of the Camargue, now surrounded by the tables and chairs of Caffé Nero on Dover Street. Next, hop on a bus to Knightsbridge to see the beaten copper panels, entitled the *Four Seasons* (Frink, 1961), adorning the Jumeirah Carlton Tower Hotel on Cadogan Place.

From here, head south-west to Battersea Park, for Hepworth's lakeside *Single Form* (1961). It's a smaller version (about 10 feet tall) of her monumental piece for the United Nations in New York. Finally, die-hard Hepworth should trek out to Dulwich Park to see her *Two Forms* (Divided Circle), commissioned in 1970 by the Greater London Council.

A different league

Andrew Shields gets his kicks with some cheap footie thrills.

Why pay £54 to sit behind a pillar at White Hart Lane? Or £30 to be shoehorned into Loftus Road in a plastic seat designed for a six-year-old? Professional football clubs know they have a near-stranglehold over the emotions of their fans, but control of their wallets is less secure. It's no surprise that with cash tight but the pull of live football as strong as ever, more and more supporters are acquainting themselves with London's non-league scene.

If you're used to the Premier League and are contemplating getting your fix at a lower level, you'll need to be prepared. The crowds are small – typically a couple of hundred through to a couple of thousand – and any atmosphere has to be self-generated in grounds that may be short on creature comforts. The standard of football is variable too. Even though what's known officially as 'Level 8' of the game, meaning the Ryman League Division 1, has its share of ex-pros, never-quite-made-its and young prospects, don't expect Arsenal-like wit and wizardry.

There are, however, a multitude of compensations. You will generally find camaraderie rather than antagonism among the opposing fans, and a warmth from clubs to whom your payment at the turnstile really matters. Merchandise too is rarely a rip-off. Games still kick off at the familiar time of 3pm on a Saturday afternoon and are not arbitrarily moved to suit TV schedules. You'll be up close to the action and, with none of the spectator health and safety restrictions imposed on the pro clubs' stadiums, you'll have the chance to stand rather than sit if you prefer. If you hang around afterwards, you can also probably share a pint with the big number nine you've spent 90 minutes roundly abusing.

Here are ten great non-league destinations offering history, tradition, pride, passion and a determination not merely to survive, but to thrive. And, with admission costing £10 or less at every one, you might discover that after all these years you're ditching that Spurs scarf and cheering for Enfield FC instead.

Leyton FC
Nothing to do with Orient of that parish, but London's oldest senior football club. Founded

Dulwich Hamlet FC

Dulwich Hamlet FC

in 1868, playing in the Ryman League Division 1 North and perenially cash-strapped, you'll find the Lilywhites behind the 'E10 Club' on Lea Bridge Road.
8539 1780/www.leytonfc.co.uk.

Hampton & Richmond FC
'Steptoe & Son' scriptwriter Alan Simpson is club president and has a stand named after him at the tree-fringed Beveree Stadium in the heart of salubrious Hampton village. Former West Ham hero Alan Devonshire has led the club to the Blue Square Conference South, despite being saddled with one of the game's worst nicknames: the Beavers. Fans like to think of themselves as, ahem, the Beaver Patrol...
8941 2838/www.hamptonfc.net.

Clapton FC
Founder members of the Southern League along with Luton, Millwall, Reading and Southampton (Tottenham Hotspur's application was rejected), the Tons are five times winners of the FA Amateur Cup.

They became the first English team to play in Europe when they beat a Belgian XI in Antwerp way back in 1892 and, then in 1956, were the first amateur club to play under floodlights. Clapton are still based at the famous (well, slightly famous) Old Spotted Dog Ground in Forest Gate but times are hard and

they've slipped down to the modest Essex Senior League.
8472 0822/www.claptonfc.moonfruit.com.

Carshalton Athletic FC
Surrey's oldest club (founded in 1903) and now one of the county's most active in terms of community football development, the Robins are on a mission 'to become the most friendly football club in the league pyramid'. The team's not bad either and going well in the Premier Division of the Ryman League.
8642 8658/www.carshaltonathletic.co.uk.

Enfield Town FC
Until 1999, Enfield were one of England's top amateur clubs and close to gaining admission to the Football League. Then they sold their stadium and began a series of catastrophic groundshares, which alienated most fans and led (like the well-known example of AFC Wimbledon) to the formation of fan-owned Enfield Town FC.

The Towners share amicably with nearby Brimsdown Rovers and are making solid progress in Division 1 North of the Ryman League. The old Enfield club was liquidated in 2007 having rebuffed a suggestion by the Enfield Town chairman that if the two clubs pooled their resources and fan base they could 'take Enfield back to the top of non-league

football'. Enfield rejected the merger proposal and formed a new team of their own, competing in the Essex Senior League.
8804 5491/www.etfc.co.uk

Bromley FC

Record attendance at the Lilywhites' Hayes Lane ground is 10,798 for a game against Nigeria, who must have been very exotic opposition back in 1950.

Crowds are rather smaller these days for matches in the Blue Square Conference South (averaging around 400), but Bromley's technology is the envy of the non-league scene. The club are online pioneers in the world of London's non-league teams: they run a website carrying full video match highlights.
8460 5291/www.bromleyfootballclub.co.uk.

Dulwich Hamlet FC

Pink and navy striped shirts. The giants of the amateur game between the two World Wars. One of the great football addresses: Champion Hill Stadium, Dog Kennel Hill, SE22. What's not to like?

When the Hamlet are playing away (they're in the Ryman League Division 1 South), you can watch tenants Fisher Athletic tussling in the higher-grade Blue Square Conference South.
07816 076582/www.dulwichhamletfc.co.uk.

Hoddesdon Town FC

Inaugural winners of the FA Vase back in 1975, the Lilywhites (yet another club with the nickname) rather bizarrely play in the Spartan South Midlands League, despite being only 25 minutes from Liverpool Street.

They picked up last season's best programme and best pitch awards to compensate for the long away trips and have former Spurs legend Ossie Ardiles as club patron.
01992 463133/www.hoddesdontownfc.co.uk.

AFC Hornchurch

The Urchins emerged from the ruins of Hornchurch FC, who collapsed in 2004-05 when their backers went bankrupt. Grandiose plans to reach the Football League were abandoned and a roster of ex-pros on big wages proved unsustainable.

However, the reconstituted club have shown that they can be successful even with more cautious financial management. They are already in the Premier Division of the Ryman League and held Football League Division 1 rich kids Peterborough United to a single-goal margin in the 2008-09 FA Cup.
01708 220080/www.afchornchurch.com.

Corinthian-Casuals FC

This is the story of a club that has survived more than 125 years with its ideals intact.

The Corinthians were founded in 1882 (Casuals FC were established in 1878; the pair merged in 1939) as a reaction against the tide of professionalism sweeping through football in the late 19th century. They had no home ground and at first refused to enter anything as vulgar as the FA Cup. Training was outlawed and only challenge matches played. The team would refuse to take a penalty if awarded one, and would remove their goalkeeper if a spot kick was conceded, on the basis that the foul must have been serious enough to warrant a goal.

All this may sound somewhat sickly given today's style of play, but the players were genuinely talented. They inflicted Manchester United's record defeat, twice fielded the entire England side and scored 12 goals in a game against the Belgian national side.

The club spread the gospel of good sportsmanship as a globe-trotting equivalent of rugby union's Barbarians. A tour of Brazil in 1910 inspired the formation of the Corinthians Paulista club and, when they returned nearly 80 years later, the legendary international Socrates donned their kit for one game. Real Madrid adopted the Corinthians' strip in tribute and have played in white ever since.

Social change brought an end to the club's sporting superiority, though Corinthian-Casuals are battling on in Division 1 South of the Ryman League. Despite securing their first-ever home ground (King George's Field) in 1988, players are still picked off by wealthier teams.

Some things never change, though, like their spectacular chocolate and pink halved shirts. That and the first rule of the club: 'to promote fair play and sportsmanship, to play competitive football at the highest level possible whilst remaining strictly amateur and retaining the ideals of the Corinthian and the Casuals football clubs'. The greatest amateur football club ever? No contest.
8397 3368/www.corinthian-casuals.com.

86 Take up orienteering

A sport that's been likened to tackling *The Times* crossword while enjoying a jog, orienteering is the art of navigating a course in the shortest possible time set using a map and compass. The British Orienteering Federation (01629 734042, www.british orienteering.org.uk) has a list of clubs and courses and you can also buy a map of the permanent courses in London. It's a sociable sport, with regular club events (colour-coded to suit different skill levels) and an easy and family-friendly way to get some real exercise that feels just like messing about outdoors.

87 Tour the private garden at Spencer House

Designed by John Vardy, Spencer House was built between 1756 and 1766 for John Spencer, who became Earl Spencer the year before his house was completed. The building is one of the capital's finest examples of a Palladian mansion. The Spencers moved out just over a century ago and the lavishly restored property is now used chiefly as office space and for corporate entertaining. However, the spectacular garden – almost half an acre at the back of Green Park, stocked with plants and shurbs appropriate to the period – is open for limited hours in spring and summer; phone to check times.
Spencer House *27 St James's Place, SW1A 1NR (7499 8620/www.spencerhouse.co.uk). £9.*

88 Meditate at the London Buddhist Centre

Opened in 1978 in a building that was once a Victorian fire station, this is one of the largest urban Buddhist centres in Europe. The LBC (51 Roman Road, E2 0HU, 0845 458 4716, www.lbc.org.uk) offers lunchtime and evening drop-in meditation classes (£1-£7), creative writing and poetry events, retreats both on site and in the Suffolk countryside and works in the wider community through outreach projects.

89 See London by gaslight

Tired of the neon glare of the West End? Do you yearn for some ye olde city charm on your evening strolls? If so, then you'll find it, free of charge, in the parts of London still lit by gaslight. Some of the earliest street lighting in the city was established in the Royal Parks, where oil lamps were hung from the trees, but gas lighting soon followed, installed along Rotten Row in Hyde Park.

A green plaque at 100 Pall Mall commemorates Frederick Winsor, who put up London's first gas street lamps in Pall Mall in 1807 and became one of the pioneers of gas lighting in the UK and France. Born in 1763 in Brunswick, Germany, Winsor went to Paris in 1802 to investigate the 'thermo-lamp' that French engineer Phillipe Lebon had patented three years earlier. Over the next two decades, about 50,000 gas lights were installed across the city's streets.

Today, around 1,600 gas lights still illuminate up central London every night. Keep your eyes peeled and in many parts of town you'll see the tell-tale bars sticking out of lampposts – before the process became automated these used to support the lamplighter's ladder. Ignore the orange glare of the city's many sodium lamps – London's standard street light – and head for the capital's grander postcodes. Fine examples of ornate lights can be seen outside Buckingham Palace, along Queen's Walk in Green Park, in St James' Park and at St James' Palace, around the Palace of Westminster and Westminster Abbey, along the Mall, in Horse Guards Parade, and at Covent Garden. Several tiny and picturesque alleys off the Strand are also still lit by gas (Bull Inn Court, Lumley Court) and there's even a gaslight in Carting Lane that is run by sewage gas – though unfortunately on recent inspection it had been bashed into by a car. Heading east into the City, the Temple is famously still gaslit, as is Charterhouse Square and the Guildhall.

90 Drive dodgems on the South Bank

If you're put off by not only the queues but the prices for the London Eye, why not nip into its neighbour Namco Station (County Hall, Westminster Bridge Road, SE1 7PB, 7967 1067, www.namcostation.co.uk, free admission) and drive dodgems instead. Everything at this indoor entertainment centre is token operated, so you just pay as you go (£2 for the bumper cars; 1.4m height restriction applies). There are also 12 bowling lanes (£3 per person per game), US pool tables and 150 arcade games, simulators and dance machines (tokens cost 50p). Far better than being trapped in glass sphere for half an hour with people you've never met, Namco Station is open until midnight, and has a pub-priced bar.

91 See two-for-the-price-of-one at the Riverside Studios

Better known for dance and theatre events, Riverside Studios also screens intelligently selected film retrospectives and double bills (Terence Davies, Bette Davis, Harry Potter). Ticket prices (£7.50, £6.50 reductions) come in at less than the cost of a single bill at a West End cinema.
Riverside Studios *Crisp Road, W6 9RL (8237 1111/www.riversidestudios.co.uk).*

92 Visit the Charles Dickens Museum

After the success of The Pickwick Papers in 1836, Dickens left his cramped chambers in Holborn and moved up to Doughty Street for three years, at that time a private street sealed at each end with gates and porters; *Oliver Twist* and *A Christmas Carol* were written here. The building, the author's only surviving London residence, is crammed with memorabilia and artefacts, and in the basement visitors can watch a 25-minute film on Dickens's life in London. Admission £5, £4 reductions.
Charles Dickens Museum *48 Doughty Street, WC1N 2LX (7405 2127/www.dickensmuseum.com).*

93 See the stars of the future at the Royal Opera House

Every November the Linbury Studio at the Royal Opera House stages a season of 'Firsts', an experimental programme of diverse, contemporary performances that span dance, opera and other music genres, some of them specially commissioned for the space. There are usually three or four programmes spread over the month, with several acts in each show, plus more entertainment in the bar (previous years have seen the likes of jugglers, folk bands and magicians) before and after the performance. Every seat costs just £5 (thanks to the support of the Helen Hamlyn Trust) and quality is guaranteed, so you'll have to move fast to get a ticket (they usually go on sale at the end of September but it's worth checking the website nearer the time).
Royal Opera House *Bow Street, WC2E 9DD (7304 4000/www.roh.org.uk).*

Royal Opera House

A few of my favourite things

94-99

Scroobius Pip, musician

Subtone (93 Feet East, 150 Brick Lane, E1 6QL, 7247 3293, www.93feet east.co.uk) is a free bi-monthly music and spoken word event organised by a hat company called Red Shift Rebels. The gigs serve as advertising for the headwear and the headwear serves as advertising for the gigs, and the advertising industry doesn't get a penny – it's genius! The nights are a mix of poetry, dance music, bands... and I'll host one whenever I can.
I was a photographer by trade for a year or two, and when I was a student the Photographer's Gallery (relocated in 2008 to 16-18 Ramillies Street, W1F 7LW, 0845 262 1618, www.photonet.org.uk) was one of the only galleries I could afford to go to. They have everything from war photography to humorous portraits, and it's great just to stroll around.
Of course there are lots of vintage clothes and things on Brick Lane, but the best thing is playing carrom near the food stalls (at Sunday UpMarket, The Old Truman Brewery, E1 6QL). Carrom is a square wooden board with holes in each corner, and you dust it with a powder and slide discs across it. If you buy a coffee you can sit down and have a game at one of the spare boards, and there's always someone happy to teach you.
A lot of poetry gigs are in dingy pubs. PoeJazzi (Volupté, 9 Norwich Street, EC4A 1EJ, 7831 1622, www.volupte-lounge.com, £10) is downstairs in a burlesque cocktail bar with seating and waiter service; they have jazz acts too. It's run by a spoken word collective called Poem In Between People, and they'll only put on nights when they have acts they're really excited about, which means it's always a really high standard.
The Covent Garden Odeon (135 Shaftesbury Avenue, WC2H 8AH, 0871 22 44 007, www.odeon.co.uk, £6.50-10 before 5pm Mon-Fri) is a great cinema (although obviously you'll need to smuggle in your own food and drink, otherwise you're looking at more like £50...). When I'm not touring I go to the cinema during the day all the time, and I take as much influence from film as from music. Essex, where I'm from, just has your multiplexes and blockbusters. This place has a lot of world cinema and unusual stuff. I saw *City Of God* **and** *The Pianist* **here in one go, before they were on general release.**
I write on the move, so for anyone looking to fill time in London I'd recommend a travel card (www.tfl.gov.uk). The bus I've done most of my writing on is the N8 nightbus from Tottenham Court Road to Bethnal Green. I pop some music on and just take it all in. I'm writing a track about getting the last train home at the moment, so I'm doing a lot of research. People-watching is one of my favourite pastimes.

100

Watch international athletics for free at Crystal Palace

Crystal Palace's annual Grand Prix meeting gives several good reasons to head out to SE19. First, it tends to draw the niftiest movers in world athletics, from Jamaica's Usain Bolt to the UK's very own Christine Ohuruogu. Second, it takes place in late July or early August, meaning a better-than-average chance of sunshine. And third, the elevation of the surrounding park makes it possible to watch the action without a ticket. It goes without saying that you won't have a box or be in prime position with a full 400m panorama, but you'll be near enough to feel part of the event. And how often do you get to watch a pole vault world record attempt while walking the poodle and playing frisbee?
Crystal Palace Athletics Stadium *Crystal Palace Park, Ledrington Road, SE19 2BB (8778 0131/www.ukathletics.net).*

101-110

Pick a perfect place to picnic

There's no need to leave town to picnic in the fresh air, surrounded by trees and flowers. Concrete jungle it may be, but London is also one of the world's greenest capitals. We've rounded up ten of the city's most perfect spots from Tudor gardens to space-age parks.

Battersea Park

Once marshland and also a notorious duelling spot, the 200 acres of greenery that constitute Battersea Park (8871 7530, www.battersea park.org, free) are a far more salubrious place these days (and have recently been given an £11 million Lottery-funded boost). We recommend the calming Peace Pagoda.

Fulham Palace Gardens

If you fancy sipping a crisp Chablis on the shady lawn of a lovely formal garden, head to Fulham Palace's (7736 8140, www.fulham palace.org, free) tranquil Thames-side grounds by Bishops Park. The palace and its gardens, country retreat for centuries for the medieval bishops of London, are a well-kept local picnicking secret. Full of unusual plant species, the 12 acres offer plenty to explore as well as the lawns: there's woodland, an 18th-century walled garden full of herbs, an orchard and a wisteria-clad pergola.

Ham House Gardens

Ensconce yourself on the lawns of Ham House's garden (8940 1950, www.nationaltrust.org.uk, entrance to garden only £3.30). These glorious 17th-century grounds have both formal splendour in their lavender, box and yew parterres as well as a so-called wilderness of maze-like hornbeam.

Hampstead Heath

Hampstead Heath is, of course, full of great picnic spots – and stunning views – but we especially love the slope above Highgate Pond where you can hide out in the long grass and gaze across to the City and Canary Wharf.

Holland Park

With its charmingly secluded hideaways, Holland Park has loads of great private picnic spots. If you want to make more of a splash, though, there's the Japanese garden and the lawns just north of Holland House. Just make sure you don't leave food lying around for the curious resident peacocks.

Horniman Museum Gardens

There are many good reasons to visit the Horniman Museum (8699 1872, www.horniman. ac.uk, free), but the gardens, with their roses, woodland, stange exotic shrubs and wild flowers are as enchanting a reason as any. If you are planning a trip to the museum anyway, don't forget to pack a picnic.

Regent's Park

Regent's Park can get pretty busy if the weather's good and during the holidays, but for dreamy, summer perfection, head to its northern reaches and lay out your rug near the colourful blossoms and luscious scents in the Rose Garden (www.royalparks.org.uk, 7298 2000, free).

Springfield Park

Hackney's Springfield Park (www.hackney. gov.uk/cp-parks-springfield.htm) is a good spot for a picnic with a view: nibble cucumber sandwiches while looking out over the River Lee, with its narrow boat marina, and the Hackney Marshes beyond.

Thames Barrier Park

A masterpiece of contemporary landscape gardening, it's worth making the effort to get to the Thames Barrier Park (7476 3741, www.thamesbarrierpark.org.uk, free). Plonk yourself in the midst of 22 acres of lawns, trees and surreal yew and maygreen topiary and look out over the mighty silver shells of the Thames Barrier.

Waterlow Park

Try the lawns of Highgate's Waterlow Park (www.waterlowpark.org.uk, free) for more exhilarating views of London as well as three spring-fed ponds. Sweeping down the steep face of Highgate Hill, the scene is dotted with elegant, mature trees framing a fabulous view of the City's skyscrapers.

111 Hunt for Horatio Lord Nelson

At least we know where to start: Nelson stands three-times life size – but then he was only five and a half feet tall – 145 feet up in the centre of Trafalgar Square, so named after his final, fatal victory over Napoleon's fleet in 1805. Even so, the most popular military hero in British history didn't rise to this distinction until almost 40 years after his death, when his statue was finally placed on his column in 1843. He faces south-west, into the prevailing winds, and towards the fleet at Portsmouth. Visit the National Portrait Gallery for a fine view of the back of his tricorn hat from the eighth floor bar; alternatively, go and look at one or more of its ten portraits of him in the primary collection (they have at least 57 more in the archives), which is bound to be on display somewhere in the gallery.

From here, head towards Mayfair via Soho and 33A Dean Street (now Gino's barbershop) which, as Walker's Hotel, was where Nelson spent his last night in London before heading off for Trafalgar. He set up home at 5 Cavendish Square, with his new, and soon to be long-suffering wife Frances. Although they only lived here for four years, much was made of the fact that this address was to be used as a YMCA for US officers towards the end of the World War I.

After this, make your way to the Royal Arcade, at 28 Old Bond Street, once the first premises of Dollond & Aitchison, the firm from which Nelson bought a telescope after losing an eye attacking Corsica in 1793. He also lodged nearby in New Bond Street on his return from the Battle of Cape St Vincent in 1797. (In the same year, he lost his right arm at the Battle of Santa Cruz, off Tenerife.) The Goat Tavern, at 3 Stafford Street, was a favourite haunt he later used for shenanigans with his mistress Lady Hamilton.

Trade in Nelson memorabilia was huge after his death and a trail of his personal effects can be tracked down around town: the shoe buckles that he wore at Trafalgar are on the wax effigy in the Westminster Abbey Museum (20 Dean's Yard, SW1P 3PA, 7222 5152, www.westminster-abbey.org), as well as some of his clothes; his razor is in the Wellcome Museum of the History of Medicine at the Science Museum (Exhibition Road, SW7 2DD, 0870 870 4868, www.sciencemuseum.org.uk, free); and his solid gold, combined knife and fork, made for a left-hander and given to him by Countess Spencer, is in the Lloyd's Nelson collection exhibition. (You can see this on their trading floor during a tour of One Lime Street, EC3M 7HA, 7327 1000. Contact Martin Leach at tours@lloyds.com.)

The collection also includes Nelson's favourite breakfast plate, his collar for the Order of the Bath and Lady Hamilton's toothpick box. The jewel-encrusted sword, also designed for a left-hander, presented to him with the Freedom of the City in 1800, should be on display in the brand-new Capital City gallery at the Museum of London by 2010.

Nearby, you can find a fine statue of our hero, sculpted in 1810 by James Smith, in the Guildhall City Art Gallery, but then it's high time you made tracks to Greenwich, the official home of Horatio worship. The Nelson Gallery at the National Maritime Museum (Romney Road, SE10 9NF, 8858 4422, www.nmm.ac.uk, free) houses the clothes he was wearing at Trafalgar (see the musket-ball-hole in the shoulder) among other fantastic artefacts. Then there's the Coade stone Nelson Pediment above the King William Block of the Old Royal Naval College, inspired by the Elgin Marbles, and showing Neptune bringing the admiral's body to Britannia.

Real devotees should also visit Southside House (Woodhayes Road, SW19 4RJ, 8946 7643), which he enjoyed visiting with Emma Hamilton when she was living nearby at Merton Place. Also check out the Marine Society & Sea Cadets headquarters (202 Lambeth Road, SE1 7JW, 7654 7000, www.ms-sc.org), where liaison officer Roger Busby can show you one of Nelson's flags.

Finally, no hunt for Horatio would be complete without visiting his tomb in St Paul's Cathedral. His black marble sarcophagus was originally designed for Cardinal Wolsey, who had died over 200 years earlier.

112 *See Regent Street without the traffic*

One of London's busiest shopping streets, Regent Street is mercifully traffic free for a day every September to host the Regent Street Festival, part of Visit London's festival month. Each year the celebrations take on a different theme, but there's always free live music and other entertainments as well as food and drink – last year's fun included a mini Borough Market near the Piccadilly end and a Hamley's 'English country garden' for kids to let off steam in. If you're still more interested in retail therapy, it's a great day for a shopping trip too: – you'll be able to take advantage of various in-store entertainments, food and wine tastings and special promotions, as well as fashion shows and competitions.

Regent Street Association *(7038 3718/ www.regentstreetonline.com).*

113

Eat pie and mash at Manze's

You only need to glance briefly at the seedier burger joints around town to understand that cheap food often also means cheap decor. We know London's got loads of good value places to eat, but it's rare that you'll be spending less than a fiver on food in as lovely surroundings as those at Manze's on Tower Bridge Road. London's oldest pie and mash shop (eels – jellied and stewed – also available, of course) was established in 1902 by the present owner's grandfather, Michele Manze, of Ravello in southern Italy, and the same art nouveau-style green and cream tiles grace the walls as did back then. Those solid wooden benches also look like they've done decades' worth of sterling service propping up hungry folk.

M Manze's *87 Tower Bridge Road, SE1 4TW (7407 2985/www.manze.co.uk).*

114-118 *Tour the capital's breweries*

Mass produced lagers are not only a burden on your taste buds but on your wallet as well. By way of therapy, we recommend a tour of one of London's breweries to get you in the mood for cheaper and tastier ales. The Fuller's brewery in Chiswick (Chiswick Lane South, W4 2QB, 8996 2063, www.fullers.co.uk) is open for two-hour guided tours at £10 a pop; this includes a tasting session and should be booked in advance. If your interest lies more in the drinking than the watching, London boasts a handful of bars with their own microbreweries. Chief among them are Zero Degrees in Blackheath (29-31 Montpelier Vale, SE3 0TJ, 8852 5619, www.zerodegrees.co.uk) – phone for details of free tours of their microbrewery; Covent Garden's Bünker (41 Earlham Street, WC2H 9LD, 7240 0606, www.bunkerbar.com), with its three house draughts and a try-before-you-buy policy; West End stalwart Mash (19-21 Great Portland Street, W1W 8QB, 7637 5555, www.mashbarandrestaurant.co.uk); and the Greenwich Union (56 Royal Hill, SE10 8RT, 8692 6258, www.greenwichunion.co.uk), fine flagship of the Meantime Brewery.

119 *Visit Ernö Goldfinger's House*

James Bond author and Hampstead resident Ian Fleming was so enraged by this modernist creation on Willow Road that he used the name of its architect – Ernö Goldfinger – for one of his greatest villains. Built in 1939, 2 Willow Road was the architect's home until his death (Goldfinger had fled Hitler's Europe and, like many émigré artists and intellectuals of the time, settled in leafy Hampstead). The furniture was designed specially for the house and there is lots of clever living space and plenty of storage. And with Goldfinger's books and art collection still in place you'll feel as though the man has just stepped out for a stroll on the Heath, which is just across the road and perfect for a post-tour architectural discussion.
2 Willow Road *NW3 1TH (7435 6166/ www.nationaltrust.org.uk). £5.10.*

120 *Learn to belly dance*

Belly dancing, Egyptian dancing, Raqs Sharqi... call it what you will, this sensuous and exhilarating Middle Eastern dance performed to stirring Arab beats is also fabulous exercise. Sample a taste of the excitement at one of Reshma Rose's Saturday morning beginner's drop-in classes in Archway. Rose, who has performed at venues ranging from London's top Middle Eastern restaurants to the British Museum, teaches an earthy and powerful modern Egyptian style of belly dancing. To find lessons near you, check out www.london bellydance.com; many teachers offer taster sessions for beginners.
Reshma Rose *www.reshmarose.com. £6.*

121 *People-watch at the National Portrait Gallery...*

Possibly your best bet for celebrity spotting – on canvas and film – this is one of our favourite London galleries. The prestigious BP Portrait Award and the Taylor Wessing Photographic Portrait Prize are both annual highlights. The permanent collection is free, some exhibitions carry an entrance fee (never more than £10).
National Portrait Gallery *St Martin's Place, WC2H 0HE (recorded information 7312 2463/www.npg.org.uk).*

122 *...then animal-watch at the Natural History Museum*

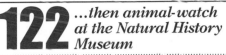

In January, the Natural History Museum hosts the annual Wildlife Photographer of the Year exhibition, which attracts submissions from all over the world. The winning shots, displayed for around six months, have interesting explanations of the conditions under which they were taken. Winner for 2008 was Snowstorm Leopard, an extraordinary snap of this elusive big cat taken against a starry sky, which took ten months to capture. Admission to the exhibition costs £7 (the museum is free).
Natural History Museum *Cromwell Road, SW7 5BD (7942 5000/www.nhm.ac.uk).*

123

See the world at the Greenwich and Docklands International Festival

Billed not unreasonably as 'London's most spectacular free festival', the Greenwich and Docklands International Festival (8305 1818, www.festival.org) throws up all the eccentricities of urban multiculturalism. A host of different venues – from the O2 and Cutty Sark Gardens to the Royal Observatory – have welcomed giant French caterpillars, tango demonstrations and a South Asian dance/football fusion. A four-day mid-June slot makes it a colourful portal into the summer.

124

Hear voices at the British Library Sound Archive

There are 3.5 million recordings in the British Library's Sound Archive, which is one of the most extensive facilities of its kind in the world and includes published and unpublished material dating back to the late 19th century. Founded in 1955, the collections are now divided into six main sections: classical music, featuring many rare and unpublished recordings; literature (including the voices of James Joyce, Antonin Artaud, Leo Tolstoy, William Burroughs, Kurt Schwitters and Sylvia Plath) and drama (which also holds video recordings); oral history including unpublished interviews with historic figures like Churchill as well as commercial recordings (there's an oral history of Tesco); wildlife sounds, including the work of the RSPB; and popular, international and traditional music (published and unpublished). It's also the main point of public access to archived BBC Radio broadcasts. The easiest way to get a flavour of the extraordinary scope of the collection is to visit a SoundServer in Humanities, Floor 2, or, if you have specific requests, make a listening appointment beforehand. The Sound Archive also accepts published and unpublished recordings from the public if they are suitable (in three of the basic categories – spoken word, music, wildlife). If you are interested, send recordings to the address below.

Sound Archive Information Service *British Library, Sound Archive, 96 Euston Road, NW1 2DB (7412 7676/www.bl.uk).*

125 Catch the BP Summer Big Screens

In an attempt to bring opera out of its elite closet, the Royal Opera House is continuing its annual tradition of screening its most popular work for free in Trafalgar Square and other locations around central London. Screenings happen on various dates between June and July. Check the website for details.
www.roh.org.uk

126 Get a handle on Handel

The baroque composer George Frederic Handel moved from Germany to Britain in 1710, aged just 25, having secured the position of *kappelmeister* to George, Elector of Hanover and soon to be King George I of England. He received an annual salary of £200 and by 1723 had established himself comfortably in his London home, where he lived for 36 years until his death in 1759. The house, in Mayfair, is now a museum and provides a good opportunity to get under the skin of the great man.

Following a meticulous restoration project, the interior has been lovingly restored and includes some beautiful replica instruments. The best way to get the feel for it is at the recitals of baroque music that take place every Thursday and regularly at the weekends (£9, reductions £7.50). The programme of events will increase in 2009 to celebrate the 250th anniversary of the master's death.
Handel House Museum *25 Brook Street, W1K 4HB (7495 1685/www.handelhouse.org).*

127 Hear leather on willow at Walker Ground

Back in cricket's heyday, crowds of up to 10,000 would flock to watch United All England XI play titanic matches at Walker Ground. Established in 1855 by the seven cricket-mad Walker brothers who lived locally and who went on to found Marylebone Cricket Club (MCC) and Lord's, Walker Ground is one of the capital's oldest and perhaps most idyllic cricket fields. Today the it's home of Southgate Cricket Club, and located as it is by pretty Southgate Green, surrounded by tall oaks with the spire of Christ Church rising above the treetops, you can squint and imagine that you're deep in the English countryside. Post match, head for Ye Old Cherry Tree on the Green for refreshments. The MCC play regularly at the ground, check the website for match schedules.
Southgate CC *Walker Ground, Waterfall Road N14 7JZ (8886 8381/www.southgate. play-cricket.com).*

128 *Go bargain hunting in Bermondsey*

Up until 1995, Bermondsey Market enjoyed marché ouvert status thanks to a medieval loophole law, which handily made it legal to buy and sell goods of dodgy provenance during the hours of darkness. Now, with the rise of eBay, changing fashions in antiques and the redevelopment of Bermondsey Square, the market stallholders have to work harder to earn a crust – and so do punters looking for a bargain. But Bermondsey is still a market traders' market, where antiques change hands between traders from all over the country, and there are still some great deals to be had. If you're up at dawn have a root around in the 'everything £1' boxes, which are full of pre-loved, worn out and eminently curious vintage knick-knackery.

Bermondsey Antiques Market
Bermondsey Square, SE1 3UN.

129 Have a cup of rosie with a cabbie

If you look carefully you'll find a few curious little green huts scattered across the city. Like stray (if rather posh) garden sheds, these are Cabman's Shelters – London institutions that date back to the 1870s when the Earl of Shaftesbury and his philanthropist chums set up a charity to provide cabbies with 'wholesome refreshments at moderate prices'. Of the 61 original shelters, only a dozen remain (among them those at Chelsea Embankment, Hanover Square, Russell Square, Temple Place, opposite the Victoria & Albert Museum). You'll wonder how they can possibly accommodate a working kitchen plus up to ten cab drivers. Pop by for a chat and eyebrow-raising tales of recent celebrity fares. If you ask nicely you may be served a cup of Rosie Lee (tea), for the absolutely princely sum of 50p.

130

Lively up your Sundays

If it's Sunday evening and you've already got the Monday morning blues, head for lovely local gastropub Paradise by Way of Kensal Green, plonk yourself on the faux gilt French furniture for one of Club Skaaville's twice-monthly Lively Up Sunday sessions. A sizzling finale to any weekend; Club Skaaville traditionally hosts a staggering array of Africa-influenced rhythms from ska, afrobeat and jazz to blue beat, calypso, rocksteady and back again. Top Caribbean and African musicians often perform – like the legendary singer and composer Dorothy Masuka (who penned many Miriam Makeba hits) and South African jazz pianist Mervyn Africa. Lively Up Sundays start at 7pm and cost Club Skaaville members £3 (non-members £5).
Paradise by Way of Kensal Green
19 Kilburn Lane, W10 4AE (8969 0098/
www.theparadise.co.uk/www.clubskaaville.co.uk.

131 Visit London's loveliest public lavatory

Featuring heavily in Joe Orton biopic *Prick up your Ears*, the palatial grade II-listed public loos next to the bus terminus at South End Green, NW3, were the recent benefactor of a £50,000 renovation courtesy of the National Lottery. Built in 1897 by the London and North Western Railway, it's now a positive pleasure to visit such an historical temple of convenience, all vaulted ceilings and cream and green Doulton tiles. If you don't think it's worth trekking across town just to visit a loo, it's also conveniently located for Hampstead Heath.

132 Get shown the money at the Bank of England Museum

Attached to the Bank of England itself, this museum is housed in a replica of the original 18th-century bank's interior designed by Sir John Soane. As part of the exhibition you can test the weight of a real-life gold bar (28lbs) and check out the complete set of NatWest piggy banks, circa 1983. Rumour has it that there's gold in the porky fellows and ceramics collectors are falling over themselves to snap them up. You can also discover how *Wind in the Willows* creator Kenneth Grahame foiled an armed bank robber in a new, permanent display on the author who worked here for 30 years and was Secretary of the Bank from 1898 to 1908.
Bank of England Museum *Bartholomew Lane, EC2R 8AH (7601 5545/ www.bankofengland.co.uk). Free.*

133 Tour the BBC

For your £9.50 (£8.50 concessions) you get an award-winning visit to the TV studios and BBC News, and, intriguingly, 'a play in the interactive studio'. Plus, in the two hours or so that you're in White City's giant television centre there's always the potential added bonus of bumping into your favourite Beeb star in the hallowed broadcasting corridors.
www.bbc.co.uk/tours.

Crunch clubbing

The gloomy economic future signals good times ahead for London's clubbers, argues Kate Hutchinson.

Perverse as it may seem, for nightlife fans the credit crunch suggests some thrilling times ahead. While the economic climate is ominous, credit crises have often proved a catalyst for radical change in clubland. Look at 1930s New York with its now iconic speakeasy culture and furious jazz sessions. At the same time Berlin saw the birth of bohemian and sexually ambiguous cabaret – another trend currently back in favour in London. Disco rose up from the New York underground and celebrated black and gay liberation during the Vietnam war, and in the UK raving took off in the wake of the Black Monday financial crisis, a disaster which tarred Thatcher's Britain.

You only have to step outside in Shoreditch to witness the effects that rave culture has had: neon fever once again dresses East London's streets, with people and parties everywhere embracing rave's futuristic beats and culture with DIY fashion and a carefree attitude (*see p228* for tips on how to do out-there club couture on the cheap). And what's more, most of the nights catering for this breed of club lover are as good value as the charity shop garb that adorns their clientele.

But clubbing on the cheap has not always been the norm; traditionally, partying in London meant carrying wads of cash to get you past the velvet rope. But the age of superclubs with extortionate cover charges is drawing to a close. Furthermore, even if they wanted to party in bigger venues, with the demise of legendary clubs like the Cross, Canvas, the Key, Turnmills, Astoria and the End in the past year or so, Londoners are now being forced to look for alternative and cheaper places to dance. Finally, with travel costing almost as much as getting in, people are looking for nights out that are closer to home. For that reason we've split up our selection of top venues by area.

East

East London has become a well-established but still vibrant after-dark playground for art school types, up-and-coming musicians, artists and armies of media monkeys, and it's also the new frontier for London's alternative gay scene. Competition for crowds is fierce and so it's easy to find an inexpensive nightspot.

Shoreditch is an obvious starting point. Head first to the Old Blue Last (7739 7033,

Lock Tavern

www.theoldbluelast.com) where the indie rock and electro music and shabby-chic interior encapsulates Shoreditch's trendy, youthful style. It's owned by *Vice* magazine so expect an above average quota of so-over-it hipsters. On the plus side there are good live bands and DJs until late most nights. Raucous, rammed to the rafters night Dollop (third Friday of the month, free entry, www.myspace.com/dolloplondon) and prog-punk-metal noisenik Skill Wizard (second Saturday of the month, free entry, www.myspace.com/skillwizard) are especially zippy club forces, but rock up on any night and you're bound to stumble across organised chaos of some kind.

Similar wayward antics can be found down the Kingsland Road. Between Herbal (7613 4462, www.herbaluk.com), still going strong with cut-price drum 'n' bass and dubstep on most nights, and ever-popular watering hole DreamBagsJaguarShoes (7729 5830, www.jaguarshoes.com), you'll find tipsy locals stumbling out of Catch (7729 6097, www.myspace.com/thecatchbar). This two-floor venue is on the edgy side thanks to its diverse clientele of fashionistas and reprobates, who come for relatively cheap drinks, bubbling atmosphere, and music courtesy of vodka-lubed electro-disco shindig Meat Raffle (fourth Saturday of the month, www.meatraffle.co.uk, free) and multicoloured mess-fest Girlcore (last Thursday of the month, www.myspace.com/girlcorerules, free). Plus, look out for the new T Bar – the palace of freebie techno and electro – opening in March 2009 in a new nearby location.

Debauched polysexuals rejoice – for the new Ghetto (7287 3726) and Trash Palace (7734 0522, www.trashpalace.co.uk) are now together under one roof on Old Street. Favourite nights include girl-oriented Mis-Shapes (Thursdays, £1-£4) and pop-playing Wig Out (Saturdays, £5-£8) as well as newbies Kill Your Pets (Fridays, £3-£5), with its new DJ tag team including Warboy, Buster Bennett and Hanna Hanra, and Meat Whiplash (Tuesdays, free-£2), which promises to keep it punky and pumping on the dancefloor.

But the forward thinking gender-bending crowds are moving from Shoreditch deeper into Hackney. The antics of post-neo-futurist crew Nuke Them All are a hit at strip bar Images (first Saturday of the month, www.myspace.com /nuke_them_all, £7-£5), where you should expect a downright dirty party – with jungle, grime, hardcore, fidget and electro bass.

> ## 'Camden, although slightly stagnating in a swamp of trilby-toting Hawley Arms hangabouts, still has a few diamonds up its sleeve.'

Bardens Boudoir (7249 9557, www.bardens boudoir.co.uk) in Dalston attracts gypsy punk and Balkan beat lovers for nights like Gypsy Hotel (third Saturday of the month, £6.66-£9.99, www.myspace.com/gypsyhotel) and Le Vagabond Boogaloo Club (second Friday of the month, £7, www.myspace.com/vagabond boogaloo). Other magnets include the youth club-styled Visions Video Bar (588 Kingsland Road, 7275 7520), home to underground gay disco night Disco Bloodbath (www.myspace. com/discobloodbathdisco) and bi-monthly bassline house club Wifey (£5).

The party has also moved out into Bethnal Green. Brand new pub-club the Star of Bethnal Green (7729 0167, www.starofbethnal green.com) caters for the more discerning pub-raver with its quality mix of disco treats for under a fiver, like disco nights SOUP (every Friday, free) and ESP (second Saturday of the month, free-£5) and DJ Hannah Holland's wonderfully named techno-dubstep-electro-bass explosion Bastard Batty Bass (first Thursday of the month, free-£5).

North

Trendy boozers have filled the void left by the demise of clubs like the Cross and the Key with pub-price drinks and low entry fees. The Westbury in Kilburn (7625 7500, www.westburybar.com) and the Old Queen's Head in Islington (7354 9993, www.theold queenshead.com) are such places. Steve Blonde who owns both, used to book FabricLive on Fridays, so expect top-quality DJs on a crystalline soundsystem – for a fraction of the cost. Our favourite night is Tape the Top 40 with Barry Peters (third Thursday of the month at the Westbury), a hilarious delve through your guilty pop pleasures.

Camden, although slightly stagnating in a swamp of trilby-toting Hawley Arms hangabouts, still has a few diamonds up its sleeve. Namely the Lock Tavern (7482 7163, www.lock-tavern.co.uk), which despite its diminutive size, attracts star DJs to its decks to crank out killer electro while you scoff your roasts. Bloggers Delight's free all-dayers on the last Sunday of every month are the perfect dose of jiggly indie-electro, slices of techno and big basslines. Over towards King's Cross you'll find a sliver of truely unadulterated hedonism at the multi-room extravaganza EGG (7609 8364, www.egglondon.net). They're slowly but surely attracting Hackney's fluoro-wearing scenesters in their droves for signature club night Always Fridays, which boasts internationally acclaimed DJs for the Ed Banger generation – from Justice to Edu K (£12 tops but it's £5 before 11pm).

West and South

For clubbers, West London starts and ends with the Notting Hill Arts Club (7460 4459, www.nottinghillartsclub.com). Its brilliant programming features endless multimedia dance parties, from hip hop to tropical electronica. Seb Chew and Leo Greenslade's Thursday nighter YoYo is a must: its DJs mash together some of the best R&B, '80s boogie, hip hop, ragga and Bmore beats around live sets from tipped-for-the-top acts. You could say it plays world music but at Radioclit's tropical electro bash Secousse (first Friday of the month, free before 8pm, then £5) – where you'll hear the freshest Brazilian *baile funk* to African *coupé décalé* to Argentinian digital *cumbia* – there's not a bongo in sight. Alan McGee's famed indie shindig Death Disco is now free entry every Wednesday (*see p212*).

Down south, the increasingly gentrified Brixton and New Cross are nightlife meccas.

Try the Dogstar (7733 7515, www.anticltd.com), a gold-corniced DJ bar that has always had its finger on the pulse: we recommend Audiosushi every Saturday with its bleeping catherine wheel of electro, house, dubstep, drum 'n' bass, funk, reggae and hip hop block party – all for a maximum £5. And if you want to dance mid-week, free night Latin Quarter on Thursdays is your best bet for tropical house, hip hop, chill out and funk. Elsewhere in Brixton, Plan B (7733 0926, www.plan-brixton.co.uk) hones in on quality hip hop every Friday (£5, £3 before 11pm); also worthwhile is the monthly beatboxing-meets-breakdancing-meets-MC medley: Throwdown (second Thursday of the month, £4-£5). Dub heads queue around the block for legendary bi-monthly rumble DMZ at Mass (www.mass-club.com, www.dmzuk. com, www.myspace.com/dmzuk), with its consistently stellar DJs and ribcage-rattling basslines. Southside Bar (8671 0286, www.the southsidebar.co.uk) is packed most nights for its range of nights – expect anything from Salsa to breaks to deep house, all with low door tax. Brixton stalwart Jamm (7274 5537, www.brixtonjamm.org) is still going strong hosting live bands and guest DJs (often of the former Brit pop star variety).

In Kennington, South London Pacific (7820 9189, www.southlondonpacific.com) keeps on giving with its carnivalesque weekend parties for those who like their parties funky, rare vintage and boogie-styled, but it's still only £5.

Lastly, New Cross's hot venue, the Amersham Arms (8469 1499, www.amersham-arms.co.uk), has been bursting with gig goers and disco deviants. Students from nearby Goldsmiths populate the stools, yes, but it's also a stomping ground for south London's many filmmakers, label owners and musicians. No Pain In Pop, both a riotous clubbing affair and a quality rock label, are monthly regulars (second Saturday of the month, £5) and nomadic dubstep, fidget and ghetto bass lovin' promoters Deadly Rhythm have been known to stop by from time to time.

Central and West End

The central scene has, well, shrivelled thanks to strict licensing laws and property developments. But for the ultimate in budget discos the Roxy (7255 1098, www.theroxy. co.uk) and indie night After School at the Quad (7955 7136) are both musts. The former has a well-loved stable of twisted indie, pop, rock 'n' roll and electro parties to suit all tastes and levels of drunkenness, but those are best sampled on weekdays – from Monday's Rehab (£1-£5) to Thursday's Teenage Kicks (£3-£5).

The Social (7636 4992, www.thesocial.com) has been a firm party staple for years and still packs a (free) punch with the new filthy electro and retro pop Your Mum's House (second Thursday of the month) recreating an unruly house party vibe with bands and a fresh crowd. Meanwhile Sean Rowley's ever-popular Guilty Pleasures downsizes to become Pop Head every fourth Thursday.

'At Secousse you'll hear Brazilian baile funk, African coupé décalé and Argentinian digital cumbia – and there's not a bongo in sight.'

Want style for your moolah in the centre of town? Scenesters revel in dressing up boxes and kitsch performance fun at Punk's (0871 223 1242, www.myspace.com/punksoho) weekly Smash & Grab (Thursday, £5-£8). Run by indie DJ linchpins Queens of Noize, it's been a massive hit with the fashion kids and even Kate Moss has deigned to shimmy on its dancefloor. Or if you're feeling more samba than supermodel, Brazilian restaurant-bar-club Guanabara (7242 8600, www.guanabara.co.uk) vibrates to Forró, Bossa Nova and other Brazilian beats, and even offers free dance classes five nights a week (see p250).

One of the last West End clubbing stalwarts without a £20 entry ticket price is Bar Rumba (7287 6933, www.barrumbadisco.co.uk). Saturdays have become home to the Metro's '60s-styled indie night Blow Up (and they've kept the retro purse-friendly prices, too), and, 15 years on, revered bi-monthly Thursday drum 'n' bass excursion Movement will still only set you back £8.

159

Keep up with the cutting edge at the Free Range Graduate Art Fair

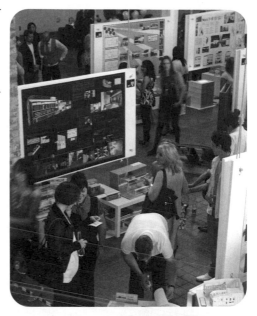

The annual Free Range Graduate Art and Design Summer Show has become a serious event in the art world's calendar since its first show eight years ago. Displaying the work of over 3,000 graduate students from some of the UK's leading art colleges, and held each year over 11 acres in Brick Lane's enormous Old Truman Brewery, it's also one of the world's largest art fairs. You'd be hard pressed to buy anything for under a tenner, admittedly, but admission to the vast display of artworks covering a multitude of different media is free and a perfect way to spot the YBAs of the future. The exhibition runs between May and July each year.
www.free-range.org.uk.

160-167

Examine the city's sick past in London's medical museums

Considering London's past record of poverty-ridden slums, overcrowding and successive immigrant influxes, it's no wonder that the city is also blessed with a rich medical history. There are more than 20 locations listed by the London Museums of Health and Medicine website (www.medicalmuseums.org): wherever you turn the work of early pharmacists, surgeons, anaesthetists, nurses and hospitals is being dissected and displayed.

Kick off your consultation at the atmospheric attic home of the Old Operating Theatre Museum and Herb Garret (9a St Thomas Street, SE1 9RY (7188 2679, www.thegarret.org.uk, £5.45),

tucked behind London Bridge station. Climb the steep spiral staircase to the top of the baroque church of St Thomas's and stumble through the beautifully ramshackle apothecary store to a pre-antiseptic surgical theatre where students once crammed in to watch amputations, gallstone removals and trepanning operations. You can still feel the grooves in the original wooden operating table where unwashed saws once hacked through nervous patients.

For a more clinical approach, head for the Hunterian Museum at the Royal College of Surgeons (35-43 Lincoln's Inn Fields, WC2A

Old Operating Theatre and Herb Garret

3PE, 7869 6560, www.rcseng.ac.uk/museums, free). Packed with swish, display cases of gruesome specimens and scary surgical instruments, the 400-year-old collection also includes distorted skeletons, before and after photographs of early plastic surgery and video presentations of modern operations. You can even peek at Charles Babbage's brain and Winston Churchill's dentures.

More interested in non-surgical interventions? Pop into the foyer of the Lambeth-based Royal Pharmaceutical Society of Great Britain (1 Lambeth High Street, SE1 7JN, 7572 2210, www.rpsgb.org/museum, free). The tools of the trade on display include pill presses and brand name medicines from the 1700s, lurid green 'poison' bottles and jars for leeches.

While you're here, it makes sense to pop into the nearby Florence Nightingale Museum (2 Lambeth Palace Road, SE1 7EW, 7620 0374, £5.80). You'll get a chronological lowdown of the remarkable nurse and campaigner's life along with some interesting mementos, including her stuffed pet owl, Athena.

If your appetite for gore hasn't been sated, there's plenty more: see the laboratory where Alexander Fleming discovered penicillin at St Mary's Hospital (Praed Street, W2 1NY, 7886 6528, www.imperial.nhs.uk/aboutus/museumsandarchives/index.htm, £2 adults £1 reductions); pay homage to Joseph 'elephant man' Merrick at the Royal London Hospital (Whitechapel, E1 1BB, 7377 7608, free but donations welcome); follow the stories of 27,000 hospitalised 'exposed and deserted children' at the Foundling Museum (40 Brunswick Square, WC1N 1AZ, 7841 3600, www.foundling museum.org.uk, £5); or try the museum of Bart's Hospital (West Smithfield, EC1A 7BE, 7601 8152, www.bartsandthelondon.org.uk/aboutus/museums_and_archives.asp, free), founded in 1123 as part of St Bartholomew's priory, where, as well viewing as the surgical wares, you can learn about William Harvey, a physician at the hospital who discovered the circulation of blood in the 15th century. Beware: these collections are almost guaranteed to bring on a nasty case of hypochondria.

168 Kayak the Regent's Canal

Despite the proximity of the roaring corridors of City Road and nearby Upper Street, the first thing that strikes you out on Islington Basin is the placid silence. Fully paid-up members of the Regent's Canoe Club (16-34 Graham Street, N1 8JX, www.regentscanoeclub.co.uk) meet two evenings a week, but there are also two-hour introductory nights on the second Monday of each month. After a change of clothes – you'll get wet – it's off for a few warming jars in the nearby Prince of Wales.

169-176

Drink in a pub with a real fire

The height of civilisation and all yours for the price of a pint. We recommend the following:

Anglesea Arms *35 Wingate Road, W6 0UR (8749 1291).*
Crooked Billet *14-15 Crooked Billet, SW19 4RQ (8946 4942).*
Earl Spencer *260-262 Merton Road, SW18 5JL (8870 9244/www.theearlspencer.co.uk).*
Fire Stables *27-29 Church Road, SW19 5DQ (8946 3197).*
Golden Heart *110 Commercial Street, E1 6LZ (7247 2158).*
Grand Union *45 Woodfield Road, W9 3BA (7286 1886).*
Holly Bush *22 Holly Mount, NW3 6SG (7435 2892/www.hollybushpub.com).*
Three Kings of Clerkenwell *7 Clerkenwell Close, EC1R 0DY (7253 0483).*

177 Search for the original Chinatown

Stepping off the DLR at Westferry, where once hundreds of ships' masts towered over fortified docks, there's nothing left on Limehouse Causeway to suggest the maze of alleyways, Chinese cafés and grocers that clustered here from the 1880s to the 1930s. Nothing to suggest the exotic hubbub of real docklands, the whiff of opium smoked openly, the excitement of the *puck-apu* numbers racket or the gambling den at Ah Tack's Lodging House – all conjured up by the fiction of Conan-Doyle and Sax 'Fu Manchu' Rohmer. Even Dorian Gray dropped by E14 for his opium.

Well – almost nothing. A tin dragon sculpture at the end of Mandarin Street hints at what used to be, as does Ming Street, now lined with '60s blocks instead of the Confucian temple and local Tong HQ – all of which were part of the slums that were razed in 1934.

Among the ships chandlers and mastmakers, the Merchant Navy Officers' Club and Dock Constables' houses – traces of real docklands, all recycled as flats – Amoy Place was once the epicentre of those 'kind of Limehouse Chinese Laundry Blues'. The old wharves (and new 'gated communities') of riverside Narrow Street were once Fu Manchu's lair – 'the river was his highway, his line of communication along which he moved his mysterious forces' – now the street houses a Gordon Ramsay pub, the Narrow. The decline in the docks, from the 1930s onwards, meant the dwindling of the Chinese population of the area.

At Commercial Road is the striking British & Foreign Sailors' Hostel (or 'Sailor's Palace'), one window ablaze with the telltale pictograms of the Chinese Association of Tower Hamlets. Opposite, the Star of the East pub, with its original gaslights outside, is a hulking Victorian Gothic take on a Chinese temple. At the end of Canton Street lies the Chinese Sunday School & Chun Yee Society with an old people's drop-in centre in the basement. At last, here are people with actual memories of London's original Chinatown.

178 Pitch and putt near Richmond Park

Just adjacent to the one-time regal hunting grounds of Richmond Park sit the more modern delights of Palewell Pitch & Putt Golf Course. A gentler and cheaper alternative to the capital's 18-hole options, it's more about honing your skills and enjoying a quick round than thrashing 3-woods and clomping off down the fairway. It boasts pretty surrounds too – the nine holes are spread either side of babbling Beverley Brook – and the greens are well maintained. Coaching sessions are also offered. In short, it's the kind of place you can have a swing without worrying about disdainful eyes.
Palewell Park Pitch & Putt Golf Course
Palewell Park, Richmond-upon-Thames, SW14 8RE (8876 3357/www.pitchandputtgolf.net/palewell.htm). £4.20 for 9 holes, clubs £1 a pair, balls £1.

179 Test Albert Bridge

'All troops must break step when marching over this bridge', says the sign on the end of Albert Bridge, but you could always plan a meet up with a battalion of friends and see what happens if you don't.

180-187

Tuck into something sweet at the capital's best ice-cream parlours

Fortnum & Mason

David Collins-designed and delightfully dinky, Fortnum's Parlour celebrates the sweet with a coffee-and-cream colour scheme and a menu that takes ice-cream and Middle European pastries seriously. It's not cheap, but it is a treat and the postcard-perfect views over Piccadilly make it a lovely spot for meeting friends. Ice-cream sodas, milkshakes and smoothies are £4-£5, a flight of three ice-creams £6, Austrian strudel served with whipped cream or vanilla ice-cream £4. The coffees may seem expensive at £3.50 but each comes with a mini ice-cream cone on the side.

181 Piccadilly, W1A 1ER (7734 8040/ www.fortnumandmason.com).

Gelateria Danieli

This tiny shop was a hit from the day of opening thanks to its superb own-made ice-cream. Now with branches in Kingston (Bentall's) and Battersea (Queenstown Road), Gelateria Danieli offers a daily-changing selection of flavours drawn from over 100 recipes. Chocolate sorbet is the *specialità della casa*, one of several gorgeous dairy-free ices; if health is a concern you'll also find options based on yogurt. There's virtually no room to stand, let alone sit, so take your selection down to Richmond Green to enjoy. Prices start at £1.95 for a single scoop.

16 Brewers Lane, Richmond, Surrey TW9 1HH (8439 9807/www.gelateriadanieli.com).

Gelateria Valerie

An offshoot of popular chain Pâtisserie Valerie, this eye-popping glass and metal structure strikes a fashionable pose on the King's Road and is, like all the ice-creams, sorbets and yogurt ices that are made on site, authentically Italian. Eat-in prices start at £3.80 for two scoops of your choice from around 20 flavours;

one scoop in a cone to takeaway is £1.50. Just like the *gelaterie* of Rome you'll find ice-cream incarnations of popular confectionery and desserts: After Eight, Ferrero Rocher, tiramisu, and crème brûlée – plus nut and fruit flavours. Sundaes (£5.75-£6.50) are all named after famous artists and laden with whipped cream, though there is a diet option based on vanilla and wild berry yogurt ice-cream.

Duke of York Square, King's Road, SW3 4LY (7730 7978/www.patisserie-valerie.co.uk).

Gelato Mio

Pesca, pompelmo, limone – the Italian labels reflect the heritage of this modish parlour and café in the centre of Holland Park's ritzy parade of shops, though specials may include the likes of green tea ice-cream. Prices start at £2 for one scoop; 500ml take-home packs are a tenner. Alternative refreshment comes in the form of *frappes* (Italian milkshakes) and *cremolata* (a Sicilian drink made with ice, seasonal fruit and soda). You'll also find breakfast pastries and Illy coffee.

138 Holland Park Avenue, W11 4UE (7727 4117/www.gelatomio.co.uk).

Marine Ices

Chalk Farm's iconic parlour has been on this site since 1931 but the ice-cream (or rather sorbet) production began back in Gaetano Mansi's original Euston grocery business – because he didn't like to waste fruit. The family hails from Italy's Amalfi Coast so expect classic Italian favourites such as *gianduia, marsala* and *stracciatella*. Eat inside and a single scoop costs £1.90; coppe from £3.40 (one scoop with pear and hot chocolate sauce). You can have a full meal here too – Italian, of course – pasta main courses start at £7.65.

8 Haverstock Hill, NW3 2BL (7482 9003/www.marineices.co.uk).

Morelli's Gelato

Everybody orders chocolate, but it's worth exploring the rest of master *gelatiere* Gino Soldan's ice-creams at this bustling stall in the heart of Harrods food hall. Honey and rosemary is just one of the beautifully balanced combinations that you'd be more likely to find in a haute cuisine restaurant. Gino is particularly proud of the boozy adults-only ice-cream cocktails such as mango mojito. Dieters and those with dairy allergies are also well catered for. A single scoop to takeaway costs £2.40. Hey, it's Harrods.
Food Hall, Harrods, 87-135 Brompton Road, SW1X 7XL (7730 1234/www.harrods.com).

Oddono's

Outclassing many rivals, Oddono's gelato is not just made on the premises, but made from scratch. By using their own recipes rather than the ready-made mixes common in some cheaper establishments these are some of the best and freshest ice-creams around. The hazelnut, coffee and chocolate (made from a unique Ecuadorian cocoa variety), and the mandarin sorbet, are highly recommended but the range changes frequently – Oddono's has developed over 130 flavours since opening in 2004. Prices start at £2 for a single scoop cone or cup.
14 Bute Street, SW7 3EX (7052 0732/www.oddonos.co.uk).

Scoop

Were it not for the queues snaking out of the door on sunny Friday lunchtimes it would be easy to miss this authentic Italian *gelateria* discreetly tucked away in Covent Garden – but to those in the know a shopping trip in the area is incomplete without a tub or waffle cone of its artisan-made ices. The place is wonderfully picky when it comes to the ingredients they use – which include Piedmontese hazelnuts, Sicilian pistachios and Tuscan pine kernels – flavours that are readily discernible in the ice-creams. Health fiends need not compromise, though – the low-fat and sugar-free ices made from rice are utterly delicious too. Prices start at £2.30 for a small cone or cup and rise to £4.30 (but look out for winter discounts).
40 Shorts Gardens, WC2H 9AB (7240 7086/www.scoopgelato.com).

Scoop

www.treesforcities.org

Trees for Cities
Charity registration number 1032154

Travelling creates so
many lasting memories.

Make your trip mean
something for years to
come - not just for you
but for the environment
and for people living in
deprived urban areas.

Anyone can offset their
flights, but when your
plant trees with Trees for
Cities, you'll help create
a green space for an
urban community that
really needs it.

Leave
Your
Mark
Create a green future for cities.

188 *Have a cheap and cheerful day in Sloane city*

Much to the chagrin of the local businesses, Shepherd's Bush-based shopping behemoth the Westfield has poached many of Chelsea's weekend customers. The upside of this, though, is that Saturdays in Sloane land are now a much less hectic proposition.

Start at the lively food market where over 100 speciality food producers sell a mix of hot and cold treats outside upscale food store Partridges (2-5 Duke of York Square, SW3 4LY, 7730 0651, www.partridges.co.uk). This being west London, it's the acme of polite civility and nearly all the stalls offer generous samples – artisan breads (dipped in flavoured olive oil), rare cheeses, decorated cupcakes and spiced meats are usually all there for the tasting. Be sure to head to the Patchwork (0845 123 5010, www.patchwork-pate.co.uk) stall where you can taste a liberal splatter of rustic Cointreau and orange chicken liver pâté against the backdrop of playful tunes from the Dixie Ticklers, a street jazz band who are a King's Road fixture.

Next stop is the much-hyped Saatchi Gallery (Duke of York's HQ, King's Road, SW3 4SQ, www.saatchi-gallery.co.uk) which, despite its free admission, isn't quite the oversubscribed scrum of the likes of Tates Modern and Britain. The inaugural show here in October 2008 featured a giant dog turd encrusted with toy soldiers and a donkey mechanically humping a skyscraper, so it's probably safe to expect some tabloid-provoking sculpture and painting.

Ultra-affluent residents in this area see to it that the local charity shops are well stocked with near mint condition designer garb. Join the bargain hunters a short walk up King's Road on the left at Shawfield Street, where you'll see a well-hidden boutique-style Oxfam (123a Shawfield St, SW3 4PL). Further up still, on Old Church Street, sits a well-organised British Red Cross (67 Old Church Street, SW3 5BS, www.redcross.org.uk) packed with Ralph Lauren, Marc Jacobs and some vintage Gucci and Chanel. Within eyeshot is the Stockpot (273 King's Road, SW3 5EN, 7823 3175), the Chelsea outpost of Soho's much-loved cut-price bistro where a main course and a half bottle of red won't cost you more than a tenner.

Top the day off with a play at the Royal Court Theatre (Sloane Square, London SW1W 8AS, 7565 5000, www.royalcourttheatre.com), where day standing tickets to all shows cost ten pence. Arrive early, and there are comfortable leather sofas and free broadsheets in the downstairs bar.

Saatchi Gallery

189

Get to know your folk...

The somewhat ascetic surroundings of Cecil Sharp House, the home of the English Folk Dance and Song Society (2 Regent's Park Road, NW1 7AY, 7485 2206, www.efdss.org), play host to a variety of folk events. Check online for details of barn dances, ceilidhs and folk-dance classes, banjo and accordion lessons and gigs from a variety of traditional British musicians.

190-197

...then explore London's other folk venues

No longer relegated to back-room nights huddled round the fire, folk gigs – from lively, monthly events to intimate one-off happenings – are popping up all over town. Firstly, there's the antifolk circuit, a loose collective of like-minded songwriters, rebels and general mischief-makers convening regularly at the Blang nights at the 12 Bar Club (26 Denmark Street, WC2H 8NL, 7240 2120, www.12bar club.com), a venue which also hosts old-school folk shows. The Green Note in Camden (106 Parkway, NW1 7AN, 7485 9899, www.greennote.co.uk) is lively and books its fair share of traditional artists, along with blues musicians and singer-songwriters.

The Magpie's nest (www.themagpies nest.co.uk) is the best of the new breed of folk clubs, putting on up-and-comers as well as revered old hands. In addition to their mid-monthly Wednesday night gigs at Islington's Old Queen's Head (44 Essex Road, London, N1 8LN, 7354 9993), they throw one-off bashes at bigger venues such as Cargo.

There's further folky fare at London's weekly folk clubs, which are dotted around the capital and scattered through the week. Among the best are the often irreverent Islington Folk Club, held on Thursdays (except in the summer) at 8pm at the Horseshoe in Clerkenwell (24 Clerkenwell Close, EC1R 0AG, 7253 6068, www.islington folkclub.co.uk) and the Cellar Upstairs, every Saturday at 8.15pm at Euston's Exmouth Arms (1 Starcross Street, NW1 2HR, 7281 7700, www.cellarupstairs.org.uk) – the last word in woolly jumper-wearing folk purism and showcasing traditional British, Irish and US artists. Less beardy is the eclectic, more-or-less monthly The Goose Is Out (www.thegooseis out.com) in Dulwich.

Finally, Walthamstow Folk Club, every Sunday at 7.30pm at the Plough Inn (173 Wood Street, E17 3NU, 07931 142 400, www.walthamstowfolk.co.uk). Line-ups are engaging and the crowd is down-to-earth, making this is one of London's most approachable folk clubs for newbies.

198 Prove that you're too cool for pool

The smoke-filled halls may have gone, but snooker still boasts a deliciously louche image despite (or perhaps because of?) the immense skill required to play the game. While almost anyone can sink a few balls on a pub pool table and imagine they're a real hustler, the greater dimensions of snooker's green baize and the requirement to pot in a specified order pose a far stiffer challenge. Unlike many venues which still live down to their back-street reputation, Acton Snooker Club, with a triangle of red balls forming its logo above the main entrance, is a plush place. There are 13 tables, all kept in exemplary condition.

Acton Snooker Club *Old Oak Common Lane, W3 7DJ (8743 8284/www.londonsnooker.co.uk). £10 annual membership.*

199 Glimpse a secret Mayfair castle

Hidden away among the swank hotels and mansions of Mayfair are the elusive turrets of Berkeley Castle, built in the 1930s by artist Frederick Etchells. Inside, the mock-medieval hunting lodge reflects the leading Modernist's curious passion for fixtures and fittings recycled from earlier, tumbledown castles; but the best we can do is catch a glimpse of the Gothic front door – through an electric portcullis, up a small alley on Mount Row between Berkeley Square and Grosvenor Square.

200 Take in tea and typography on the Strand

The Twinings shop on the Strand (No.216, WC2R 1AP, 7353 3511) is London's oldest shop still to be found in its original location. The golden lion over the doorway dates from 1787 and refers to the sign outside the original Tom's Coffee House of 1706 (before street numbers had been devised). The twin mandarins in the sign refer to tea's original importation exclusively from China, and 'Twinings' is the world's oldest logo still in continuous use.

201

Visit the waxworks at Westminster Abbey Museum...

Never mind Madame Tussauds, Westminster Abbey will cost you more than a tenner to see; at least, that is, if you haven't been invited to a coronation or you're not there to worship the Lord. Entirely free of charge, however, is the Abbey Museum, which occupies one of the oldest parts of the building – the 11th-century vaulted undercroft of St Peter on the east side of the cloisters – and it contains a series of extraordinary wooden and wax effigies. The wooden ones are the earliest known likenesses of English medieval monarchs: Edward III's was used at his funeral in 1377; and Henry VII's death mask is exceptionally lifelike. The waxworks are more modern, dating from the late 17th century, and include Charles II, William III and Queen Anne, as well as Frances Stuart, the Restoration model for Britannia, dressed in her Coronation robes and even accompanied by her pet parrot (one of the earliest stuffed birds extant in the UK).
Westminster Abbey *20 Dean's Yard, SW1P 1PA (7222 5152/www.westminster-abbey.org).*

202

...then have a rest in College Garden

After you've looked around the museum, visit the cloisters and wonderful College Garden surrounded on one side by 14th-century walls and with a great view of the Victoria Tower of the Palace of Westminster's Victoria Tower. The grounds of Westminster Abbey were once used by the monks for growing both medicinal herbs and vegetables and, extraordinarily, have been under continuous cultivation for over 900 years.

Westminster Abbey

College Garden

203

Sing your heart out at Hot Breath Karaoke

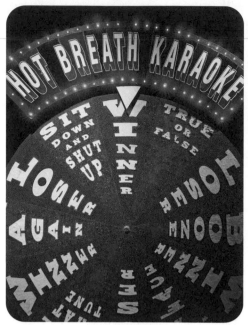

Karaoke is officially a cool pastime these days. Every Tuesday the Shoreditch masses flock to the *Wheel of Fortune*-style party that is Hot Breath Karaoke, where wannabes can choose from a whopping 7,000 classic tracks. There are bargain-bin prizes for all who are brave, or misguided, enough to enter and the whole evening is based on throwing your inhibitions to the wind. There's even a membership scheme for regulars; start flexing those vocal chords now.

Hot Breath Karaoke *The Legion, 348 Old Street, EC1V 9NQ (7729 4441/www.myspace.com/ hotbreathkaraoke). Weekly Tuesdays, £8.*

204-214

Go to a film festival

London's film festival scene is buzzing. Since the advent of the capital's film development agency Film London in 2003 with its remit of bringing new audiences to film, its lottery funding has fuelled a film fest explosion. There are dozens of them showcasing every nation, minority, niche or genre you can think of.

Try an indiefest like Raindance (7287 3833, www.raindance.co.uk, September and October) or trendy Portobello Film Festival (8960 0996, www.portobellofilmfestival.com, July and August). Want to see women filmmakers? Then check out the highly rated Birds Eye View (7704 9435, www.birds-eye-view.co.uk, March). Black filmmakers from across the globe are featured at BFM International Film Festival (8531 9199, www.bfmmedia.com, October), while Human Rights Watch International Film Festival (7713 2773, www.hrw.org/iff, March) aims to put a human face on threats to individual freedom and dignity.

Thrusting young festivals screening the output of up-and-coming regions such as eastern Europe and Latin America have left the traditionally dominant film-producing countries of western Europe far behind on the festival scene. The Institut Français has Mosaiques (7073 1350, www.institut-francais.org.uk, May), a celebration of cultural diversity. Among the best from eastern Europe is Kinoteka (7440 0241, www.kinoteka.org.uk, April and May) showcasing Polish films, and there are two Latin American film festivals. Discovering Latin America (7358 3817, www.discoveringlatin america.com, November) offers films, docs and shorts that rarely get distribution, while the Latin American Film Festival screens commercial features (07530 752 384, www.latinamericanfilmfestival.com, November).

Closer to home are the East End Film Festival (7364 7917, www.eastendfilmfestival.com, April), exploring cinema's potential to cross boundaries, and the Rushes Soho Short Film Festival (7851 6207, www.sohoshorts.com) – no entry is over ten minutes and much of the festival is screened via the net in coffee shops and wine bars around Soho.

215 Celebrate Mr Punch's 'birthday'

Every year on 10 May you can catch Punch and Judy 'Professors' from all over the country celebrating the moment in 1662 when Samuel Pepys first recorded having seen an Italian Pulcinella (Punch's esteemed ancestor) puppet show on his way back home from the pub.
Covent Garden Puppet Festival *St Paul's Church Gardens, Bedford Street WC2 (7375 0441). Free.*

216 Acquire contemporary art at the Free Art Fair

Founded by anti-Saatchi provocateur Jasper Joffe, this maverick art exhibition is a counter-punch to the Damien Hirst-style hype of the Zoo and (ticket-only) Frieze art fairs, which are also held in October and are sited nearby. The main difference being that all the work here, which has included pieces by Gavin Turk and Stella Vine in the past, debunks the commercialised thwack of a Sotheby's hammer and is given away for free. Be prepared for a queue, though – perhaps unsurprisingly hopefuls have been known to camp out days in advance for the chance to take home some of the big-ticket works on offer. The value of 2008's big give-away totalled over £100,000.
www.freeartfair.com.

217 Frighten the life out of yourself at the London Bridge Experience

Hidden away in the vaults of London Bridge, this part educational museum, part CGI-assisted gore fest neatly sidesteps the glib animatronic kitsch of the nearby London Dungeon. It starts with an intriguing history lesson of the crossing's 2,000-year past, then it's underground for a ghost train-style journey through the bridge's haunting catacombs where disembowelled zombies and severed heads on sticks await. It's properly frightening and it's only a tenner if you go after 5pm.
London Bridge Experience
2-4 Tooley Street, SE1 2SY (08000 434 666/ www.thelondonbridgeexperience.com).

1000 songs, films and books to change your life

1000 **Films** to change your life

1000 **Songs** to change your life

1000 **Books** to change your life

1000 Films to change your life

THE MOVIES THAT MOVE US, BY

Monica Bellucci / Nick Broomfield / Jonathan Demme / Atom Egoyan
Holly Hunter / Terry Jones / Takeshi Kitano / Ken Loach / Michael Mann
Samantha Morton / Christopher Nolan / Roman Polanski
Isabella Rossellini / Steven Soderbergh
and many more

**TIME OUT GUIDES
WRITTEN BY
LOCAL EXPERTS**
visit timeout.com/shop

218

Discover the ultimate power source at the Royal Institution

Even the most ecologically sound power stations need generators and transformers to transport electricity from source to user and you can see the first incarnations of Michael Faraday's world-changing inventions and the lab where they were built in the basement of the 200-year old Royal Institution. Formerly the Faraday Museum, there's now also a quirky video guide that enlivens other geeky contraptions and shows how other bright RI sparks (14 of whom were Nobel prize winners) discovered ten chemical elements, explained why the sky is blue and engineered the safety lamp that revolutionised miners' working lives. Check out Faraday's digitised notebook and the singing periodic table wall before recharging your batteries at the swanky Time and Space cocktail bar.

Royal Institution of Great Britain *21 Albemarle Street, W1S 4BS (7409 2992/www.rigb.org). Free.*

219

Be a philosopher at Café Philo

If the level of discourse at the watercooler is getting you down, you can always spend your Saturday mornings exercising the little grey cells by debating the philosophical question *du jour* at the Institut Français' Café Philo. The informal gathering is open to all – and, as was the case in ancient Athens, philosophy degrees are definitely not required. Just roll up at the Institut's classy art deco premises in South Kensington at 10.15am for a prompt 10.30am kick-off. The discussion (which alternates between French and English each week – check which one it is before you go) bounces back and forth between the participants until about noon. Haven't got much to say? No problem. Just sit back and listen – there will be plenty who do.

Institut Français *17 Queensberry Place, SW7 2DT (7073 1350/www.institut-francais.org.uk). Contact Christian Michel (cmichel@cmichel.com) to book a place. £2.*

220

Sink (into a steam room) or swim at Ironmonger Row Baths

Originally a public wash house, Ironmonger Row Baths are still providing a Turkish bath (with steam room, various hot rooms, a plunge pool and marble slabs for massages) for less than a tenner if you go in the mornings (sessions are mixed on some days – check the website for details). As well as all the steam, there's also a 30-metre swimming pool open to the public (£3.70 per session).

Ironmonger Row Baths *Ironmonger Row, EC1V 3QF (7253 4011/www.aquaterra.org/ironmonger-row-baths).*

No Non Swimmers Beyond This Point

Ironmonger Row Baths

Deal or No Deal?

Jenni Muir does the maths and finds that some of London's traditionally pricey farmers' markets are good for a bargain after all.

It's 4.30pm on a damp Saturday afternoon at Borough Market, the capital's favourite foodie destination. Trading is scheduled to halt in half an hour, but most visitors are oblivious to this detail as they huddle around stalls picking at samples, line up for hot food and take photos.

Over in the Green Market, where the more itinerant traders set out their wares, a male voice tries to rise above the din: '50 per cent off pâtés.' There's not much on his stall and it's set up at the market's edge where there's no cover from the drizzling skies. He continues his cry, '50 per cent off pâtés,' but while the occasional head turns towards him, most feet don't.

Maybe pâtés aren't in fashion. In any case, there's not much sign of other traders following his lead – until there's a ruckus by one of the bakery stalls where they have brought out some fresh trays and a female voice broadcasts the siren song, 'Two for one on brownies'.

Given these fine specimens are the bakery's most popular product, and (rather controversially, admittedly) priced at £2 each most of the time, two for the price of one is indeed a bargain. Still, it's a while before they start to move; after all, the only time you don't want brownies is when you've spent half a day grazing on all manner of rich foods, cakes, coffees and hot chocolate at a fine food market.

A rival stall realises they, too, are overstocked and offer the same two-for-one discount on loaves of bread. 'It's cheap at half the price', as the singing street traders from *Oliver!* so memorably reminded us, but two-for-one is not the same as half price. Regardless of the cost, if you decided to take up the offer you would be buying two (or four, or six) loaves of bread. What are you going to do with them – open a branch of Pret a Manger? Even a good quality white loaf will be stale in a couple of days, so unless you have space for the second one in the freezer, most of it could wind up in the bin, not only a waste of money, but a waste of food.

All the way from the other side of the market, male and female voices chant a well-practiced duet: 'Any bowl a pound, one pound any bowl.' Deal or no deal? Let's take a look. The stall has several mixing bowls lined up with various combinations of veg – baking potatoes, onions, carrots, cauliflowers and so on, plus the occasional bell pepper (unseasonal, pale in colour and not particularly fresh). It has none of the lush speciality produce that gets chefs so excited on the other stalls; there's no Soil Association logo to indicate the veg is organic, or a sign explaining what local farm they are from. In fact, the stall looks like one you might encounter outside a tube station. Don't be

cold Smoke
Jenison wrap

cured in sweet pick
brine then smoked
over beech chippin
£3.00
served in a tortilla
wrap with mayo, Sa

confused by the exalted Borough location: there is nothing gourmet about this stall whatsoever. Still, a regular cauliflower alone would cost over £1 in a big name supermarket, and baking potatoes 15-25p each, so £1 for a selection of four or five veg *is* still a good deal.

Modern fine food markets and farmers' markets, on the other hand, have a reputation for being expensive. It's sometimes deserved – after all these places are meant to showcase the very best artisan produce to be found in the UK, and such foods understandably carry a premium – but it is also possible to do a weekly food shop at a gourmet market at prices that compare very favourably with the best products in supermarkets – if you know what to buy.

To recognise these bargains, simply start taking note of typical prices. Quality bacon and sausages at farmers' markets are usually a good deal. In supermarkets you can expect to pay £3-£4 for 200g of British free range or organic dry cured bacon: exactly the price bracket in which it's sold at various farmers' markets across the capital. At the time of writing, Northfield Farm, a popular Borough Market stall specialising in rare breed meats, sells sausages from £7.25-£7.50 a kilo, while Sainsbury's best sausages range from £6.48 per kilo for its Taste the Difference label, right up to a whopping £14.95 per kilo for Helen Browning's organic quick-cook sausages. Caveat emptor indeed.

When it comes to vegetables, you can confidently expect staple seasonal produce to be 20-35 per cent cheaper at a farmers' market than it is at the superstores. But be aware that wherever you choose to shop you need to beware the cost of trendy speciality veg (Tuscan black cabbage, say, or purple potatoes). It's worth keeping up to date with food fashions so that you know what *not* to buy. As foods become more desirable, retailers and traders find they can get away with charging more and tend to take the opportunity to do so. Lamb shanks and chicken thighs were once considered bargain buys, and pollock was a cheap alternative to cod, but in recent years the cost of all three has risen as their status as speciality food rises.

It also pays to be product-savvy when buying breads – don't splash out on fancy white loaves flavoured with olives, nuts and herbs that will disappear in one sitting when a simple half

of organic sourdough will cost less, last longer and prove more versatile. Similarly, traditional British territorial cheeses such as Wensleydale, Caerphilly and Cheshire can be a gourmet treat when made by a respected farmhouse producer, but tend to cost much less than many of the new British artisan varieties and imported continental cheeses. Why pay £30 a kilo for roquefort or some bizarre-smelling goat's cheese when you could be enjoying fine Colston Basset stilton, Keen's unpasteurised cheddar or Mrs Kirkham's Lancashire for £18 a kilo?

There will always be somewhere in London where you can find dirt-cheap, crappy food that may literally have fallen off the back of a lorry; the trick is to find quality food at bargain prices. Depending on the neighbourhood, street-side stalls can be an excellent source of fresh fruit, vegetables and herbs. Realise, however, that they rarely stock organic or local produce and, when it comes to favourites such as apples, are just as happy as the supermarkets to flog American, Chinese and New Zealand varieties at the height of the British season.

Old established street markets such as those on Ridley Road in Hackney, Portobello Road in Notting Hill, Chapel Market in Islington, Queen's Market in Newham, and Brixton and Walthamstow Markets are without doubt the best sources of imported fresh produce for ethnic cooking – plantains, yams, chillies, ginger and massive bunches of herbs. Check out their fish stalls too – top quality fresh fish and seafood always costs a lot but prices at these stalls tend to be keen and if you're looking for something inexpensive to eat that day, you could well catch a bargain.

The best advice is to experiment until you find the stalls you trust (becoming a regular, recognisable face does help) or, better still, choose one that lets you select your own produce. The tradition of bunging a dodgy piece or two from behind the stall into customers' bags does still exist on some high street markets, despite the fact that such habits helped drive customers away from market stalls in the first place. But now that Borough and the other farmers' markets have raised the bar for quality and reminded many supermarket-goers of the social pleasures of market shopping, there's no reason why we shouldn't look forward to the reinvigoration of food markets right across the capital.

222

Let someone else sing for your supper

A paean to Parma, Viva Verdi is an exciting new addition to the slightly sterile corporate environs of Canvey Street (behind Tate Modern). Inside the swanky goldfish bowl with its monochrome decor and red leather seats you'll find the more traditional refreshments usually on offer in the Emilia Romagna region of Italy. And, yes, there's also music courtesy of Parma boy-made-good Giuseppe Verdi. A genuinely great value-for-money experience, the knowledgeable staff are happy to talk you through the range of charcuterie and cheese platters (from £4.50) as well as the interesting list of wines on offer (from £3.45 a glass). Once a month the piped Verdi arias are replaced with the real deal – on our visit talented young soprano Demelza Stafford went down a storm with diners. Check the website for her next performance date.

Viva Verdi *6 Canvey Street, SE1 9AN (7928 6867/ www.vivaverdiwinebar.com).*

A few of my favourite things

223-229

Dominic Cooke, Artistic Director, Royal Court Theatre

A really good place to see quality fringe theatre is the Arcola in Dalston (27 Arcola Street, E8 2DJ, 7503 1646, www.arcola theatre.com). They have a great range of work, from revivals of classics to new plays, often by a diverse range of writers, but what defines it is the fact that the productions are always the work of emerging actors and directors. The space itself is also really interesting because it's a former factory. And it's right in the heart of London's Turkish community, so it's surrounded by really excellent and cheap Turkish restaurants.

On Mondays at the Royal Court (Sloane Square, SW1W 8AS, 7565 5000, www.royalcourttheatre.com) you can get £10 tickets for both the upstairs and downstairs theatres. We get some of the best actors and writers in Britain working here and the production values are very high, so it's very good value for money. Any night of the week you can also get in with a standing ticket for just 10p.

I'm quite big on open spaces so when I have the time I like going for walks. One of my favourites is along the north side of the Thames, from Hammersmith down to Chiswick. You pass some wonderful old buildings along the way, and the views over to Barnes are beautiful, because it's not as developed on that side of the river. The last bit, near Chiswick, has a great stretch of 18th century houses with front gardens going down to the water. It's a wonderful walk to do on a Sunday afternoon and you can follow this with a trip to one of the pubs by the river.

We're so lucky in London compared to cities like New York, because we have so many amazing parks here. Richmond Park (8948 3209, www.royalparks.org.uk /parks/richmond_park) is one of the more unusual ones, because it's wild and there are deer roaming free. You really feel like you are in the countryside, miles away from anywhere. It's especially good in May and June when the rhododendrons are out in the Isabella Plantations.

I'm quite greedy, and luckily West London is full of very diverse restaurants. There's a Syrian place called Abu Zaad (29 Uxbridge Road, W12 8LH, 8749 5107, www.abu zaad.co.uk), near Shepherd's Bush Market tube station where you can get a great value (easily under a tenner) meze meal with beautiful breads and houmous, which are all made in-house, and fantastic chicken shawarma sandwiches.

Another place in Shepherd's Bush that does really good but unpretentious food is Rajput (144 Goldhawk Road, W12 8HH, 8740 9036, www.rajputrestaurant.com). Unlike so many Indian restaurants where you get gloopy, over-coloured stuff, everything they do is fresh and homemade – and without using colourings. I like the chicken biryani and the lamb rogan josh, but the thing that's really special there is the bindi or cauliflower bhajis, you can really taste the vegetables in them.

If I've been running around London on the weekend, or been to see a matinee, I always drop in to Maison Bertaux (28 Greek Street, W1D 5DD, 7437 6007) in Soho for tea. It's a very French pâtisserie with a real sense of bohemian London meets Paris. They do beautiful homemade cakes and pastries, but the best thing about it is that, unlike other places, they don't chivvy you along, so you can sit there for hours having a pot of tea with a group of friends.

230-239
Spot some street art

What with councils' high pressure hoses and Banksy's work selling for hundreds of thousands of pounds, you may need to be quick off the mark to catch some of the best graffiti in town.

One Nation Under CCTV

An apocalyptic retort to Britain's imposing closed circuit TV culture, this is one of the clandestine street artist Banksy's largest and most visible works and can be seen from across Oxford Street and Soho Square. A red-hooded schoolboy paints a sinister, Orwellian message in large white font while a stencilled security guard looks on.
Newman Street, W1 (www.banksy.co.uk).

In Tesco We Trust

Painted on the wall of an Islington pharmacy in early 2008, this chilling visual satire depicts two young children seemingly pledging allegiance to a Tesco flag being hoisted by a third infant. Just meters away from an Islington outpost of the supermarket, attempts were made to conceal the branding of the

flag but it was restored by an unknown artist not thought be Banksy. It's one of a handful of his works protected by Perspex.
Essex Road, N1 (www.banksy.co.uk).

CCTV

London has been 'invaded' by the renegade tilers behind this global phenomenon several times since 1999 and there are countless examples of their colourful mosaics stuck high on walls across the capital. All depict pixelated retro space invaders in some form but one of the largest and boldest works is the black and yellow CCTV piece at the Liverpool Street end of Shoreditch High Street above the entrance into Fleur De Lis Street.
Shoreditch High Street, E1 (www.space-invaders.com).

Exciting/Scary

Responsible for the bright circus-style giant letters that colour the metal shutters of many east London shops, the hugely popular alphabet artist Eine's two boldest murals can be found on the exterior of Old Street's 333 club ('Exciting') and under the bridge outside Cargo on Rivington Street ('Scary').
Shoreditch, N1 (www.einesigns.co.uk).

New World Odor

One of the most influential and best-known street artists currently operating in the US, urban art nihilist Shepard Fairey was responsible for what went on to become one of the most iconic and enduring images of Barack Obama during his 2008 election campaign. His macabre 'Big Brother' work on Bateman Row in Shoreditch has all but gone but this mix of collage and stencil is his best surviving and most poignant London piece.

Truman Brewery, E1 (www.obeygiant.com).

Portobello Banksy

As close to a straight-up Banksy piece as you're likely to find, this one adorns the wall of a media production firm just off Portobello Road and was reportedly sold on ebay for over £200,000 in January 2008. A tweedy painter cuts a grandiose stance while finishing off the lettering of the artist's moniker. Currently covered in transparent acrylic, it awaits removal by the winning bidder at an estimated cost of £5,000.

Acklam Road, W10 (www.banksy.co.uk).

Moona Lisa

Versions of this cheeky stencil by the Bristol-based spray can clown Nick Walker appear all over Europe but its London incarnation can be found on the wall outside nightclub Cargo. A coy Mona Lisa lifts a heavy green dress to reveal a pert and less than enigmatic bottom.

Rivington Street, EC2 (www.apishangel.com).

Ron and Reg

One of the best examples of ubiquitous East End hitter T.wat's murals shows the Kray twin gangsters striding forward towards the viewer, their menacing stare blunted somewhat by the baby blue background and the Tesco carrier bags they hold. In a separate piece beside them Kate Moss brandishes a machete with the words 'Killer: The London Look' beneath it, also his work.

Hackney Road (Shoreditch end), E2.

Yellow flower

In one of the more playful pieces by the stencil-happy ironist Banksy, the double yellow lines of the street climb the pavement and up the walls of a building to form a large yellow flower while a seated artist looks on defiantly. Although mercilessly 'dogged' by other lesser-talented taggers it still rewards the schlep into Bethnal Green's warrens.

Pollard Street, E2 (www.banksy.co.uk).

Tamara Prt 2

PART2ISM, real name Keith Hopewell, has been assaulting London's asphalt since the early '80s. Viewable from Brick Lane, this impressive piece shows a gas mask-clad female nude on a nuclear yellow background. Also jostling for attention here is Mighty Monkey's colourful mural, which again references the capital's surveillance culture.

Bacon Street, E1 (www.myspace.com/part2ism).

240-257 Blow your tenner in the capital's best pub jukeboxes...

Unless otherwise stated, £1 will buy you five songs at the following pubs.

Approach Tavern
Jazz, blues and R&B faves at this updated Bethnal Green boozer, ideally located for a stroll in Victoria Park.
47 Approach Road, E2 9LY (8980 2321).

Boogaloo
A justly famous jukebox, spinning everything from Dusty Springfield to the Pogues; three tunes for a quid.
312 Archway Road, N6 5AT (8340 2928).

Bradley's Spanish Bar
London's best vinyl juke, loaded with Hendrix, Presley and the Dead Kennedys (£1 for three plays).
42-24 Hanway Street, W1T 1UT (7636 0359).

Crobar
£1 for three hard and heavy tracks from the likes of Lynyrd Skynyrd, Led Zep and a lot of Iron Maiden.
17 Manette Street, W1D 4AS (7439 0831).

Dublin Castle
The sweaty rear room venue hosts aspiring guitar bands; the juke in the pub out front is full of indie faves.
94 Parkway, NW1 7AN (7485 1773).

Endurance
Over 100 tunes to choose from, including the likes of Kings of Leon, Killers and the Stones.
90 Berwick Street, W1F 0QB (7437 2944).

Half Moon
From Johnny Cash to the Klaxons to unsigned acts who've played here.
93 Lower Richmond Road, SW15 1EU (8780 9383/www.halfmoon.co.uk).

Hobgoblin
Over 7,000 indie and glam rock tracks, in keeping with the student vibe (ten tracks £2).
272 New Cross Road, SE14 6AA (8692 3193).

Hope & Anchor
Both jukeboxes at this grizzled rock boozer are packed with punk/indie faves and always on full-whack. £1 buys three plays, but staff often give out free credits.
207 Upper Street, N1 1RL (7354 1312).

King Charles I
A quid buys four songs, covering all corners from reggae and country.
55-57 Northdown Street, N1 9BL (7837 7758).

Mucky Pup
Great name, great jukebox: marvelously mixed-up (Nick Drake, Jesus Lizard, Mastadon), and best of all, free.
39 Queen's Head Street, N1 8NQ (7226 2572).

Prince George
One of Hackney's finest jukes; ranging from Sinatra and Dolly Parton to the White Stripes.
40 Parkholme Road, E8 3AG (7254 6060).

Reliance
Rock, soul, funk, soul and blues from the 1970s to '90s.
336 Old Street, EC1V 9DR (7729 6888).

Royal Exchange
Traditional and modern Irish plus jazz and '60s-'90s favourites. Three songs for a nugget.
26 Sale Place, W2 1PU (7723 3781).

12 Bar Club
The jukebox in this wonderfully tatty Tin Pan Alley music venue/café/bar is free and classics-packed.
26 Denmark Street, WC2H 8NL (7240 2120).

Three Kings
A selection of 80 vinyl seven-inches that changes each week; at £1 for seven songs, it's a bargain.
7 Clerkenwell Close, EC1R 0DY (7253 0483).

The Social
New music from the Heavenly Social label plus regularly changing CDs (seven plays £1).
5 Little Portland Street, W1W 7JD (7636 4992).

Swimmer at the Grafton Arms
800 CD tracks that rotate every couple of months from Elbow to Ella Fitzgerald.
13 Eburne Road, N7 6AR (7281 4632).

258

...or go to a free gig in a record store

Instore gigs have become central to a band's marketing plan, so most of the retail giants regularly host free gigs, as do independents such as Rough Trade East (Old Truman Brewery, 91 Brick Lane, E1 6QL, 7392 7788, www.roughtrade.com), which has featured top-class bands and DJs from Beirut and Boys Noize to Crystal Castles and Of Montreal. Pure Groove (6-7 West Smithfield, EC1A 9JX, 7778 9278, www.puregroove.com) has also hosted the likes of Ladyhawke, Supergrass, Laura Marling and the Mystery Jets. Check the websites for details of performances. You may need to apply in advance for a wristband to gain entry if it's a popular band.

Get the local experience

Over 50 of the world's top destinations available.

259 *Learn Afro-Brazilian drumming*

Energetic carnival-style funkateers TRIBO are a London-based Afro-Brazilian samba-reggae outfit originally from Salvador who run a weekly two-hour workshop for anyone interested in their indigenous percussive arts. It involves learning how to beat a huge samba drum to a set rhythm – not as easy as it sounds, but the emphasis here is very much on finding your groove at your own pace. The classes are casual and welcome all ages and abilities, ultimately working towards students being able to perform in *blocos* (street parades) in London (including Notting Hill Carnival) and in Brazil. TRIBO beginners have even gone on to play with bands back in Salvador. The group are also a regular fixture at the capital's buzzing Latin American clubs such as Guanabara (Parker Street, WC2B 5PW, 7242 8600, www.guanabara.co.uk) if you're more interested in listening than playing. **TRIBO** *Studio 2, Portobello Fitness Centre, 3-5 Thorpe Close, W10 5XL (www.triboband.com/expo_movie.swf). £7 per person.*

£60

Roller disco
All over the capital rollergals and guys are squeezing into lycra leggings, donning fluoro leg warmers and hitting the rink at the Renaissance Rooms (0844 736 5375, www.renaissancerooms. co.uk). Start the weekend early at Thursday's session, which is less crowded and cheaper (£10, or £7.50 if you have your own skates).

261 Spend Sunday with the French

For some guaranteed Gallic flair, pop along at 2pm on a Sunday to the Ciné Lumière's screenings of classy French flicks (tickets £7-£9). Launched by Catherine Deneuve in 1998, this recently refurbished, plush cinema puts on a variety of excellent film seasons (including Turkish and Spanish movies) but its Sunday slot is always a French classic from the likes of François Truffaut, Jean Renoir and Jean-Luc Godard. There are also screenings in the library; tickets for documentaries are £4.

Ciné Lumière *Institut Francais, 17 Queensberry Place, SW7 2DT (7073 1350/www.institut-francais.org.uk).*

262

Work out at a green gym

Are you keen to improve your fitness but not a fan of indoor exercise? Organised by the British Trust for Conservation Volunteers (01302 388883, www.btcv.org.uk), Green Gym may be just what you're after. A fresh-air alternative to sweaty aerobics classes and soul destroying treadmills, Green Gym groups undertake a variety of tasks to enhance the local environment, such as clearing undergrowth, building an outdoor seat or reinstating a pathway. Research has shown that you can burn almost a third more calories in an hour doing some Green Gym activities than in a step aerobics class. If you fancy giving it a go there are currently three Green Gym groups in London (Camden, Lewisham and Newham) – or you could start one yourself. The website has full details.

263 Sail from Tate to Tate

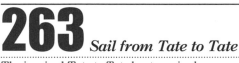

The inspired Tate to Tate boat service leaves from the striking Marks and Barfield Millbank Pier (Tate Britain) to Bankside Pier (Tate Modern) every 20 minutes during the day (0870 7815049, www.thamesclippers.com).

264-270 Be late

Over a few weeks in October, the Mayor's office runs the annual Lates Festival focussing on a trend that was already happening in many of London's museums. Lates offers a coordinated month of late-night openings and associated 'happenings' – DJs, performances, the all-important cash bar – which are designed to draw culture-phobic 25- to 35-year-olds into institutions such as the Barbican, National Portrait Gallery, V&A and British Museum.

Outside October, a number of attractions have continued the habit, staging regular evening events: Whitechapel Art Gallery and a large number of other East End galleries open late for *Time Out First Thursdays* (www.first thursdays.co.uk): the Hayward Gallery is open until 9pm on Fridays; on the first Friday of each month Tate Britain opens its doors until 10pm for the always intriguing 'Late at Tate' which entitles you to half-price entry to any current exhibition and a range of other themed events; Tate Modern offers Saturday Live, an all-day events programme featuring music, film, performance, discussion and art running late into the evening. Less arty but more atmospheric are the candlelit evening openings of Dennis Severs' House (*see 234*) and Sir John Soane's Museum (*see p26*)

Lates Festival *7983 4000/www.lates.org.*

271

Observe a Rake's Progress

William Hogarth was an archetypal Londoner but even he needed to escape the teeming streets of the city from which he drew so much inspiration – which is why you'll find his country retreat in Chiswick. Here you can see his great series of satirical engravings including *A Rake's Progress* and *Marriage à-la-mode*. Afterwards, make a pilgrimage to his tomb in the graveyard of nearby St Nicholas Church (Church Street, W4 2PH).

Hogarth's House *Hogarth Lane, Great West Road, W4 2QN (8994 6757). Free.*

272-274

Search for bats in London's woods and wetlands

Once London's bats have crawled out of hibernation in late spring, you'll have a number of opportunities to observe these fascinating and endangered mammals close up in the city's wilder locations. Whichever sunset foray you choose (see www.londonbats.org.uk for a list of locations, further information on other walks and bat groups around London), you'll learn about the country's 16 species before heading out to look for them (armed with ultrasonic bat detectors) as they leave their roosts. The detectors translate the echo location signals emitted by bats into sound audible to the human ear, and once you've tuned in you're almost guaranteed a sighting of Britain's smallest bat, the pocket-sized pipistrelle, as it swoops in on its nightly dinner of around 3,000 midges.

Popular bat walks in London take place at lovely Highgate Woods, which were granted to Londoners as an open space by the Lord Mayor in 1886. Here you can bat spot among the oaks and hornbeams of one of the city's most atmospheric parks.

At the London Wetland Centre in Barnes (which has 10 confirmed species) there are 30-minute introductory presentations before groups of around 10 head out with guides and their bat detectors into the 100-odd acres of the award-winning Site of Special Scientific Interest. There's also chance to spot Britain's biggest bat, the noctule, which can reach speeds of around 30mph (contrary to popular belief, they don't dive-bomb you). Or if you don't want to go down to the woods, the London Wildlife Trust (7261 0447, www.wild london.org.uk) offers occasional urban alternatives at the Horniman Museum and in Dulwich Park.

Bat walks usually take place at twilight in the summer months and walk dates tend to be sporadic; ring ahead to check times and to book (sessions are often heavily oversubscribed). Even in summer you may have to do a lot of standing around so dress warmly and take a torch. All start times vary with sunset.

Highgate Woods *Muswell Hill Road, N10 3JN (8444 6129/www.cityoflondon.gov.uk/openspaces). Bat watches June-Sept (at least once a month). Free.*
Sydenham Hill Woods *junction of Lordship Lane and Dulwich Common, SE23 (7261 0447/ www.wildlondon.org.uk). Bat walks May-Sept (at least once a month). £4, children free.*
WWT London Wetland Centre *Queen Elizabeth's Walk, SW13 9WT (8409 4400/www.wwt.org.uk). Big Batty Walks May, July-Sept (at least three a month). £10.*

275 *Go up the creek in Deptford*

Once an important industrial tributary of the Thames, for centuries Deptford Creek, with its huge, twice daily 7m tidal surge – like an inhalation and exhalation – was an inherent part of Deptford's identity. Even the name Deptford means Deep Ford; a place where people could cross the creek's stony bottom at low tide. But as dockyards, slaughterhouses, tanneries, granaries and tidal mills moved elsewhere in the last century and the river's importance slowly diminished, the tributary sank into neglect and stagnation, gradually becoming a repository for shopping trolleys and other human detritus. That is until 2002, when the Creekside Centre charity decided to clean things up and bring the creek's fragile but unique ecosystem to people's attention.

That's why we're now flailing around in an attempt to don thigh high waders. It's a chilly Sunday morning in December and although perhaps not the most immediately enticing weekend activity, we're struggling to contain our excitement at the prospect of wading through the exposed mud of 'London's Grand Canyon'. Our infectiously enthusiastic guide is Nick Bertrand, local conservationist and Deptford Creek hero and it's into a seemingly new dimension that he's about to lead us. Eventually, our group of around ten waddle off, armed with walking poles ('they're your third leg'), leaving behind the centre's wild grounds full of trolley sculptures and artworks assembled from assorted reclaimed creekside materials.

Down on the creek bed, the raucous world of the City, with its buildings hanging high above us, silhouetted darkly by the sun, does indeed seem almost threatening – or perhaps it's just that the river bed quickly becomes more of a comforting, if muddy, cocoon the further we tramp along its course. Over our two-hour tour Nick shows us a stretch not more than about a mile in length, but even on this wintery day there's enough wildlife to see – from kingfishers and herons to chinese mitten crabs, and other squiggly shrimp-like creatures, as well as delicate wild plants. In summer, the place is teeming with butterflies, dragonflies, flounder – the creek is an important breeding ground – prawns, crabs, around 120 species of wildflower, as well as a lot more birds, including cormorants and sometimes even the rare black redstart. You're so low down here that it's easy to get sucked (literally in one case) into the opaque and mysterious world of viscous silt. We poke about like wannabe Swallows and Amazons, delighted not only by a caught mitten crab and the wriggling contents of our white 'pond dipping trays' but also by unidentifiable metal chunks that have perhaps fallen off one of the boats moored (and in some cases still inhabited) in the creek.

But it's worth looking up as well as down. There's a unique perspective to be had from the riverbed – just imagining what would happen to London if those towering flood defence walls were breached makes you dizzy for starters. And those looming constructions even higher above you? Well, Nick's no fan of architects – don't get him started on Norman Foster's £127 million Lewisham College redevelopment plans – but there's no denying the ingenuity of Joseph Bazalgette's pumping station; the simple, solid and pragmatic beauty of Mumford's Flour Mill; the graceful sweep of the DLR bridge or the shimmering chutzpah of Herzog and de Meuron's Laban dance centre with its pink, green and blue polycarbonate panels. But there's also a problem here too: Deptford has been slated as one of London's key areas for residential housing development and in the Deptford Creek area alone – about 25 hectares in all – a staggering 3,400 new homes are expected to be built in the next five years. All of which of course means that the creek and its inhabitants – human and animal – are under threat. Go and see it for yourself before the developers have their wicked way with it.

Creekside Centre *14 Creekside SE8 4SA (8692 9922/www.creeksidecentre.org.uk). Low tide walk £8.50.*

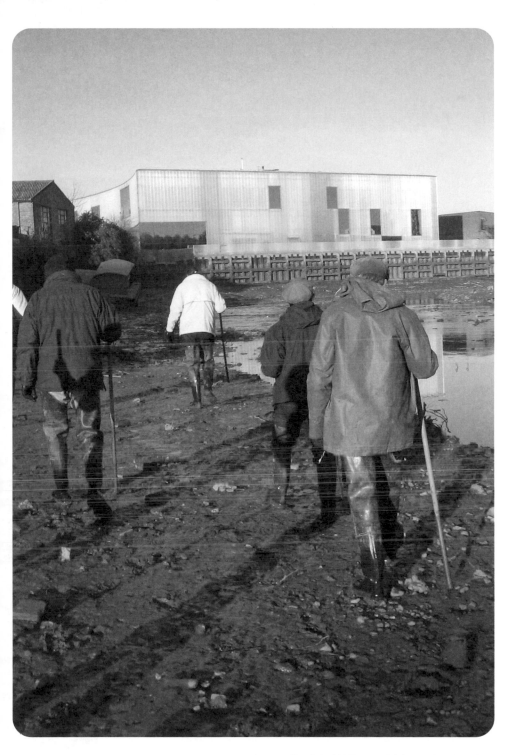

Make the most of London life

276

Swing by Viva Cake

Tea dances are all the rage among the boho squad. There's an array of 'ballroom and biscuit' affairs to choose from but nowhere does it better than Viva Cake, who throw regular shindigs in Shoreditch. Hosted by three rock 'n' roll-loving '50s nostalgics – otherwise known as the Viva Cake Bitches – this is one seriously swinging soirée. As the evening progresses, the tea sets, a beauty bar, knitting circle and some brightly coloured cakes make way for jive classes and rockabilly bands. Who needs the modern world when you can have this much fun for a fiver?
www.myspace.com/vivacakebitches.

277

Catch blooms all year round

Kew Gardens may cost more than a tenner, but horticultural die-hards on a budget can take solace from the fact that the Isabella Plantation, tucked away in the south west corner of Richmond Park is completely free. An enchanting ornamental woodland garden, dotted with clearings, ponds and streams, it was established in the 1950s and today there's always something in bloom – or at least colourful – among the collection of exotic plants and trees. It's also a good place to see birds: resident species include redpoll, bullfinch, woodpecker, sparrowhawk and tawny owl.
www.royalparks.org.uk.

Isabella Plantation

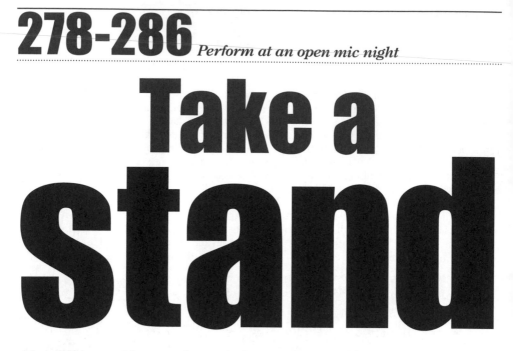

Take a stand

Alan Rutter guides you through the dos and don'ts of stage performance.

'My hands were shaking so much that I couldn't hold the piece of paper I was reading from. I had to take the microphone off its stand, put the paper on the floor, and then kneel down to do my poem. I was that nervous.'

Niall O'Sullivan is describing the first time he ever performed a poem live to an audience, at an open mic night at the Poetry Café in Covent Garden, back in 1997. Given the traumatic nature of that experience, you'd be forgiven for assuming that he promptly vowed never to put himself through it again – but he's now a successful poet, reading across Europe, and he's taken over as compere at the night that caused him so much pain: Poetry Unplugged.

O'Sullivan is just one of a number of big names who have braved the microphone at Unplugged, which has been running for 12 years. Established poets such as Tim Wells (editor of the *Rising* series of poetry magazines) and Tim Turnbull (winner of the inaugural Edinburgh Book Festival Slam) both came through Poetry Unplugged, Scroobius Pip (*see p43*) was a regular before he hit the

big time with Dan Le Sac, and troubled troubadour Pete Doherty has performed there several times.

'We're completely democratic,' explains O'Sullivan. 'Anybody can turn up and put their name down between six and seven o'clock, and everybody gets five minutes to perform. There's no vetting of material, and no restrictions on content or style. I occasionally get established performers asking if they can do a featured slot, but I tell them that they'll have to put their name down like everyone else.'

The inclusive nature of the night ensures a mixed bill of performers. 'We get everyone – old women on the 'poem about my cat' circuit, hip-hop MCs who are looking to do something a bit more lyrical, ranters… the whole gamut. Usually around half the audience are there to perform as well.'

There are no shortcuts to getting over the nerves. 'Some people are slick from the word go – they've got it all scripted out, and they read it from memory. Other people need the words in front of them, and some do get the jitters.

Green Note

The best thing to do is just to throw yourself into it – the crowd will always be welcoming. It is worth checking you're comfortable with the five minute time-limit, and maybe building in a minute for margin of error.'

And leave any high-minded preconceptions about poetry at the door. 'Some people come along expecting it to be an elitist thing – that we'll be a bunch of grammar-Nazis, or that it will be highbrow, precious or cliquey. It's not like that at all – and as compere, if I see things going in that direction, I'll try to step in.'

However, there *are* a couple of points of etiquette worth bearing in mind. 'If you bring an entourage of mates to watch you, remember to be mindful of the other performers. And it's considered bad form to "read and run" – do your slot and then leave without listening to everyone else. The only thing I'll really say no to, though, is somebody turning up with an acoustic guitar. I don't want the night to drift into a showcase for singer-songwriters.'

Fortunately that category of peformer is well-catered for elsewhere, however. There are

a plethora of acoustic music open mics across London – although, given that they're not exactly cash-cows for the organisers, they do tend to appear and disappear quite rapidly. You'll find them in small spaces – typically a room above a pub – and they tend to fill the quieter gaps in a venue's weekly schedule, often Sunday, Monday and Tuesday nights.

The Green Note is a cosy vegetarian café-bar in Camden Town. It has hosted an open mic on Sunday afternoons since September 2007, and the music ranges across folk, blues, roots, world, jazz, country and bluegrass. 'We get a variety of acts,' says Siobhan Watts who runs it along with performing in her band the More Story Fours. 'But I think we get an unsually high quality for an open mic. We get quite a few regularly gigging musicians – Stephen Cracknell, who plays with the Accidental, is down quite often. But we also get at least one first-time performer each week.'

There are between 12 and 25 acts at the Green Note each Sunday, with a pre-booked featured artist slot at 3pm (donations are

CellarDoor

encouraged), and open mic virgins are definitely welcome. 'I set it up to try and bring together a community of people. It's a really welcoming atmosphere. Some people get really nervous and might stumble over their song, but the audience will give them encouragement and egg them on.'

There are other acoustic open mics with a similarly welcoming vibe. Down in south London, the Half Moon Pub in Herne Hill is a stalwart for acoustic acts – as well as the odd spoken word performer. Up north, Monkey Chews in Chalk Farm has open mic nights on Tuesday evenings. They're run by Joel Armsden and eARmusic, who specialize in promoting up-and-coming performers – the eARmusic website (www.earmusic.com) is an excellent place to get up-to-date information on open mics across London. Over in Finsbury Park there's an open mic at the retro T-Bird – a hugely eclectic session where anyone from rappers to singing harpists are welcome,

provided they have a positive attitude and a willingness to try and gee the crowd up.

Some sessions cater for more than singer-songwriters. The open mic session at Soho's 12 Bar Club happens every Sunday (unless the venue is booked for a private party), and is run by nearby Enterprise Studios. 'A lot of the bands that play the open mic rehearse at the studios, so we've got a fairly good idea of what standard the acts are,' says Lee Jones at the Enterprise. 'But there's no actual vetting of talent. We'll generally have five bands who book their spot in advance and play 25 minutes each, plus as many singer-songwriters as we get on the night.'

If you're going to play an open mic, it's definitely worth checking out the facilities in advance – and one advantage of venues such as the 12 Bar Club and other central open mic venue Spice of Life on Shaftesbury Avenue is the fact that they provide a fair amount of equipment. 'We've got a full back line, including mics, high-watt amps and a drum kit,' says Jones. 'Which means all you need to bring are your instruments and yourselves.'

These kind of events are also a good place to meet like-minded performers and possibly even share costs and any profits. 'Most of the acts are doing it for the experience, and they might get together with some other performers to do a gig together. It also means there's less risk of having death metal and jazz on the same bill and if any band brings more than 21 people with them then they can get a percentage of the takings of the door.'

If you're keen to play with other performers, but haven't got a band, you could always head for a jam session instead. The Ain't Nothin But the Blues Bar on Kingly Street in Soho runs a jam night on Mondays until 1am. The standard is high and slots are popular – to get a definite chance of being involved, get your name down before 8.30pm or 9pm at the latest. Or if you want to sing but you're entirely incapable of playing a musical instrument you can take part in Rockaoke at the Roundhouse in Chalk

Farm on Monday and Wednesday nights – pick a song, and sing live with the backing of one of the bands who play regularly at the venue. To keep the evening from tumbling into a Spinal Tap-esque shambles, you'll need to register in advance (with your choice of song), and it will be much appreciated if you at least learn the lyrics before you turn up. Another more serious option to Karaoke comes in the form of Trash Tuesday nights at the tiny cabaret basement CellarDoor. If you're a solo vocalist you can head along to Champagne Charlie's session for cabaret, musical theatre and jazz singers – all you have to do is take your sheet music and plenty of support.

Whatever flavour of performance you're into, open mics offer a unique opportunity for beginners to get over the hurdle of playing in front of an audience. 'For some people it's the first time they've ever played in front of another person, which can be really scary,' says Watts at the Green Note. 'My biggest advice is just to relax. Remember: even top performers were in that position once upon a time.'

Open mic nights
Ain't Nothin' But The Blues Bar
Venue: 20 Kingly Street, W1B 5PZ (7287 0514/www.aintnothinbut.co.uk). 9.30pm-1am Mon. Entry free. Contact: www.myspace.com/mondaybluesjam.

Trash Tuesday
Venue: CellarDoor, Zero Aldwych, WC2R 0HT (7240 8848/ www.cellardoor.biz). 9pm-1am every Tuesday. Entry Free. Contact: open@cellardoor.biz.

eARmusic Open Mic
Venue: Monkey Chews, 2 Queens Crescent, NW5 4EP (7482 4981/ www.monkeychews.com). 8-11pm Tue. Sign-up from 7.30pm. Book ahead to guarantee a performer's slot. Entry free. Contact: 07732 396468, www.earmusic.co.uk.

Green Note
Venue: 106 Parkway, NW1 7AN (7485 9899/ www.greennote.co.uk). 1-4.30pm Sun. Entry free. Contact: www.myspace.com/greennoteopenmic.

Half Moon Open Mic
Venue: 10 Half Moon Lane, SE24 9HU (7274 2733/www.halfmoonpub.co.uk). 8pm-midnight Tue. Sign-up from 7.30pm.

Entry free. Contact: www.myspace.com/needleandthreaddotorg.

Poetry Unplugged
Venue: Poetry Café, 22 Betterton St, Covent Garden, WC2H 9BX (7420 9887/ www.poetrysoc.com). 7.30-11pm Tue. Sign-up 6-7pm. Entry free. Contact: 7420 9887.

Rockaoke
Venue: The Roadhouse, 35 The Piazza, Covent Garden, WC2E 8BE (7240 6001/ www.roadhouse.co.uk). 5.30pm-3am Mon. Booking ahead essential if you want to perform. Entry free before 10pm, £5 after. Contact: 7240 6001.

Spice of Life
Venue: 6 Moor Street, W1D 5NA (7437 7013/www.spiceoflifesoho.com). 7-11pm Mon. Sign-up from 6.30pm. Entry free. Contact: 07903 871 358.

T-Bird
Venue: 132 Blackstock Road, N4 2DX (7503 6202). 6-11pm Thur. Entry free. Contact: 07903 871 358.

12 Bar Club
Venue: Denmark Street, WC2H 8NL (7240 2622/www.12barclub.com). 6-8pm Sun. Sign-up from 5pm. Entry free. Contact: Enterprise Studios 7379 1166.

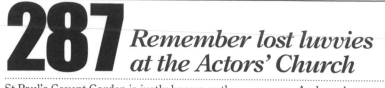

287 Remember lost luvvies at the Actors' Church

St Paul's Covent Garden is justly known as the Actors' Church. Thespians commemorated on its walls range from those lost in obscurity – step forward Percy Press, one-time Punch and Judy man – to those destined for immortality – that'd be Charlie Chaplin, then. Perhaps most charming are the numerous sublunary figures. William Henry Pratt, for example, better known as Boris Karloff, and universally famous as the real flesh behind unforgettable monsters – Frankenstein, being one of them. Take a bow too, Hattie Jacques, archetypal matron in the interminable series of Carry On films. The Jacques memorial is so plain you wonder if the inscriber felt that any embellishment would seem an impertinence in the face of such a big comic persona. And surely no more romantic tribute is paid anywhere in the city than that to Vivien Leigh. Her plaque is simply inscribed with words from Shakespeare's Antony and Cleopatra: 'Now boast thee, death, in thy possession lies a lass unparallel'd.' When we visit, however, our first homage is always paid to the memory of the mysterious 'Pantopuck the Puppetman', one AR Philpott, a master puppeteer whose work included films such as *The Dark Crystal*, *Labyrinth* and *Star Wars*. We choose to imagine his spirit wooing the excellently named Hollywood actress Edna Best, remembered not far away as 'The Constant Nymph'.

St Paul's Church *Bedford Street, WC2E 9ED (7836 5221/www.actorschurch.org). Free.*

288 Go old-school...

Ragged schools, providing tuition, food and clothing for destitute children, were an early experiment in public education, and this one was London's largest; Dr Barnardo taught here in Mile End. Kids love the mocked-up classroom, where formal lessons – complete with slates – are staged. There's also an Edwardian kitchen, displays on local history and industry, and popular holiday activities.
Ragged School Museum
46-50 Copperfield Road, E3 4RR (8980 6405/ www.raggedschoolmuseum.org.uk). Free.

289 ...or 'Suffer the children' at the Foundling Museum

England's first hospital for abandoned children, was established by Thomas Coram in 1739 and was home to 27,000 children until its closure in 1953. The museum tells the story of these children (the exhibit of humble tokens left by the mothers who had to give up their babies is especially poignant) and the adults who campaigned for them, such as Thomas Gainsborough, William Hogarth and George Frederic Handel. Hogarth's support and gifts of paintings enabled the hospital to establish itself as Britain's first public art gallery and a selection of Handel's manuscripts are displayed on the top floor.
Foundling Museum *40 Brunswick Square, WC1N 1AZ (7841 3600/www.foundlingmuseum.org.uk). £5, £4 concessions.*

290
Get a Wren's-eye-view of St Paul's

Over the 33 years that it took to transform an optimistic architectural plan into St Paul's Cathedral, Sir Christopher Wren resided over the river on Bankside at Cardinal Cap Alley in order to give him the best possible perspective on his work. It's a view you can take in yourself from the ceramic plaque that now marks the spot.

291-295
Take a whistle-stop tour of Roman London

It's now 21 years since Museum of London archaeologists discovered the epicentre of Londinium, and six years since the 2,000 year old Roman amphitheatre was opened to the public underneath the Guildhall Yard. Admission into the savage realm of slaves, gladiators and wild animals is via the Guildhall Gallery (Guildhall Yard, EC2Y 5HN, 7332 3700, £2.50, free on Fridays). It's an amazing chance to step back into the city's bloody past which even trumps the previous chart-topping subterranean Roman thrill – admiring the pavement and villa remains in the undercroft of St Bride's Church (Fleet Street, EC4Y 8AU, 7427 0133, free), hidden treasures which had been lost before bombs struck during the Blitz.

The fortifications of London Wall were constructed and continually developed between 200 and 410AD, when the Romans upped and left for home. Its six gates are still easy to find in the *A-to-Z*, with the best surviving stretches at Tower Hill (along with a statue of Emperor Trajan) and on the Barbican Estate, where one of the regular lookout towers, or bastions, survives next to the church of St Giles-without-Cripplegate.

Nearby, the grounds of the Museum of London (150 London Wall, EC2Y 5HN, 7001 9844, www.museumoflondon.org.uk) boast a 13th-century tower built on top of London Wall and a Roman fort gate beneath pavement level (unfortunately only rarely open for public viewing). Inside, the museum houses a cool 47,000 Roman objects uncovered by building work over the centuries, including the wonderful marble sculptures of gods from the Temple of Mithras (Minerva, Venus combing her hair, the Egyptian god Serapis, and, of course, the bull-fighting Mithras himself) as well as ceramics, coins, metalwork, mosaics – and leather bikinis. Discovered in 1954, the foundations of the Temple of Mithras – the soldier's temple, later rededicated to wine god Bacchus – are set to be removed during 2009 from Temple Court, Queen Victoria Street, EC4, to their original location on Walbrook, EC4.

Discover the city from your back pocket

Essential for your weekend break, 25 top cities available.

POCKET SIZED
from £6.99

296-299

Find yourself a cure for... anything!

Focus your intelligence with the warmth of the lin zhi mushroom (ganoderma). Try mo yao resin (myrrh) to activate blood circulation. Ju hua (chrysanthemum) flowers dispel wind-heat, and are a common treatment for flu symptoms, and you can eliminate 'food stagnation and bloating' with the sweet, pungent seeds of the lai fu (radish) plant. Alternatively, ventilate your lungs with the roots and rhizomes of the aster plant or supplement your yang and give your kidneys a boost with the stripped bark of the hardy du zhong rubber tree (eucommia). London has hundreds of Traditional Chinese Medicine (TCM) practitioners: from those promising to 'Help You With Acne, Hair Loss, Gynecology! Losing Weight In One Months!' to more authoritative sounding places.

At the beautifully presented, traditional clinic Hong Yuen (22 Rupert Street, W1D 6DG, 7439 2408) they are 'very low key', according to its owner. 'No advertising. No propaganda.' What better recommendation than a centre that allows results to generate custom via word of mouth?

The Institute of Chinese Medicine (44-46 Chandos Place, WC2N 4HS, 7836 5220, www.instituteofchinesemedicine.org) is one of several rival institutes that have attempted to form an affiliation of practitioners, it commands respect as a supplier of herbs to many of London's other practices, and runs its own highly rated treatment centres.

Benny May of the Acumedic Centre (101-105 Camden High Street, NW1 7JN, 7388 5783, www.acumedic.com) is something of a leader in the traditional Chinese medicine community. He started out writing technical books and as a supplier to other practices, but is long established at this treatment centre.

SEN (59 South Molton Street, W1K 5SN, 7629 2243, www.senhealth.com) has an accent on east-west fusion and accessibility. Look past the beautiful Sen brand packaging for consultations on chronic illness, herbal and acupuncture treatments and massage and acupressure full-body healing.

300 *Muck out at Spitalfields City Farm*

Given the smells and the sounds – it's all quack-quack, oink-oink, bah-bah round here – emanating from Spitalfield City Farm, you'd be surprised to learn that you're less than a mile from the Square Mile. Set up in 1978 on a disused railway goods depot just off Brick Lane, the farm has been a favourite with local Tower Hamlets families ever since. Kids and parents come down for workshops on healthy eating, sustainability and animal welfare, as well as to learn where milk and eggs come from. For 8-13 year olds there's an after-school club on Thursdays and a Young Farmers Club on Saturdays, as well as courses during the holidays (all are free; ring to book). Unsurprisingly though, the main attraction is meeting the animals – typical city farm friendly beasts, made cocky from the vast amount of attention showered on them from visiting children. Favourites include donkeys, that can be ridden in spring and summer (£1), strokeable mice and rabbits, Itchy the pig, who has been taught to sit on command and Tilly, a cheeky – and chunky – Shetland Pony. Check the website for details of their volunteer programme if you fancy mucking in – or out? **Spitalfields City Farm** *Buxton Street, E1 5HJ (7247 8762/www.spitalfieldscityfarm.org).*

301-309

...then check out the others

Deen City Farm *off Windsor Avenue, SW19 2RR (8543 5300/www.deencityfarm.co.uk).*
Freightliners City Farm *Paradise Park, Sheringham Road, N7 8PF (7609 0467/www.freightlinersfarm.org.uk).*
Hackney City Farm *1A Goldsmiths Row, E2 8QA (7729 6381/www.hackneycityfarm.co.uk).*
Kentish Town City Farm *1 Cressfield Close, off Grafton Road, NW5 4BN (7916 5421/ www.ktcityfarm.org.uk).*
Mudchute City Farm *Pier Street, E14 3HP (7515 5901/www.mudchute.org).*
Newham City Farm *Stansfeld Road, E16 3RD (7474 4960/www.newham.gov.uk/services/cityfarm).*
Stepping Stones Farm *Stepney Way, junction with Stepney High Street, E1 3DG (7790 8204/ www.steppingstonesfarm.org.uk).*
Surrey Docks Farm *Rotherhithe Street, SE16 5EY (7231 1010/www.surreydocksfarm.org).*
Vauxhall City Farm *165 Tyers Street, SE11 5HS (7582 4204/www.vauxhallcityfarm.info).*

310-319 *Have cocktails*

It's hard to find exquisite cocktails when you're on a budget, so here are a few top watering holes where your tipple will set you back less than a tenner.

Annex 3

Annex 3 is a camp extravaganza. Be prepared to be dazzled by starburst chandeliers, rococo mirrors, gaudy floral wallpaper and fairy lights on glass-topped tables. The cocktails are similarly flamboyant: the Octopussy (pink vodka, pear cognac and champagne mixed with juices of passion fruit, pear and lemon, £9); Wasabi Kiss (vodka, coconut rum mixed with wasabi, basil and kiwi, £8); Love Letter (raspberry vodka mixed with elderflower cordial, cranberry and grape juice, £8); and Lounge Lover (fig liqueur, prosecco, sweet vanilla and lemon oil, £8).

6 Little Portland Street, W1W 7JE (7631 0700/ www.annex3.co.uk).

Café Kick

As you might have guessed, football is the name of the game at this Clerkenwell hotspot. Table football is the main draw – you can reserve one of the three table football tables – and soccer paraphernalia adorns the walls. The feel is retro meets Lisbon, and tapas, sandwiches and charcuterie can be washed down with great Kick cocktails – mojitos, caipirinhas, martinis and margaritas (£6.95).

43 Exmouth Market, EC1R 4QL (7837 8077/www.cafekick.co.uk).

Crazy Bear

This low-lit, Lilliputian basement bar has won design awards for its slick aesthetic (warm brick walls, cowhide stools, red leather armchairs). But it's the cocktails that have really put the place on the map. They are mixed to perfection, and exotic, from the White Orchid (champagne with cucumber, pink grapefruit, elderflower cordial and ginger, £9.50) to the fragrant Thai Kiri (Mount Gay Eclipse rum with plums, blueberries, lemongrass and lime, £9). However, a degree of sobriety is required to face the disorientating loos (the doors are hidden in the walls and everything is mirrored).

26-28 Whitfield Street, W1T 2RG (7631 0088/ www.crazybeargroup.co.uk).

Christopher's Martini Bar

Americana is all the rage in London right now and Christopher's, with its super-sized list of martinis and old-school cocktails, fittingly bills itself as the American Bar (although it's not to be confused with the famous Savoy watering hole). The retro medley includes a sloe gin martini (£8.50), side car (£8), mint julep (£7.50) and a classic martini (£8). The maroon-striped booths, globe lights and swivel bar chairs add to the Big Apple feel.

18 Wellington Street, WC2E 7DD (7240 4222/ www.christophersgrill.com).

Dollar

Another Yankee Doodle Dandee, Dollar is also cashing in on the trend. Outside, the gaudy red neon sign says 'Grills & Martinis' – inside, the vibe is more *Sex and the City*. The signature cocktail is the Porn Star martini (£8) – Cariel vanilla vodka and passion fruit. The gingerbread old-fashioned (£7.50) is another fun twist on an American classic.
2 Exmouth Market, EC1R 4PX (7278 0077/ www.dollargrills.com).

Floridita

Named after the famous Hemingway haunt in Havana, this glitzy bar has a suitably Cuban cocktail list: most concoctions (priced around £8) blend Havana Club Anejo Blanco expertly shaken with fresh mint, fresh lime, sugars and various dashes by a vivacious barman. The Hemingway Special also contains fresh grapefruit and Maraschino; the Presidente sweet Vermouth and orange Curaçao; and the Chicago Flip – one of 14 *nuevo cubano* choices – vintage port shaken with egg yolk.
100 Wardour Street W1F 0TN (7314 4000/www.floriditalondon.com).

Hawksmoor

Hawksmoor isn't much to look at – a plain interior of beige, brick and wood, with no dedicated seating beyond a few barstools. But said stools are ringside seats for the celebrated bar staff – London's cocktail intellectuals. They know their stuff, and the menu makes for entertaining reading too: it gives a history of the classics, such as juleps and 'aromatic cocktails'. Its Gin and Pine (conceived in 1862) is served in a chilled glass; Scoffy Law (1924; whisky, Noilly Prat, pomegranate and lemon) is a refreshing drink that originated during Prohibition and is named after the brave souls who defied the booze ban .
157 Commercial Street, E1 6BJ (7247 7392/ www.thehawksmoor.com).

Lobby Bar

Housed in a swanky Edwardian bank building, the Lobby Bar at One Aldwych hotel is a thing of quiet elegance, with high ceilings, arched windows and avant-garde art (a sculpture of a bemused rower takes centre stage). The cocktail list is extensive and although most top the £10 threshold (£10.25), you can get a classic martini – gin, vermouth and a chunky, booze-soaked

Annex 3

olive – for £9.95. In such glossy surroundings and with service like this, it seems like a steal.
One Aldwych, WC2B 4RH (7300 1070/www.onealdwych.com).

1 Lombard Street

Another converted bank in the heart of the City, this swanky Michelin-starred restaurant boasts a bright and suitably posh glass-domed circular bar, but a round of cocktails won't leave you in the red. And there are a couple of financially themed libations: the bank hall (Cognac, kahlua, fresh raspberry and cream, £7), the Ftse 100 (Absolut, triple sec, lemon juice, fresh apple and raspberry, £7.50) and the Dow Jones (espresso, grappa, vanilla and Grand Marnier, £7).
1 Lombard Street, EC3V 9AA (7929 6611/www.1lombardstreet.com).

Shochu Lounge

Part *Shogun*, part 21st century cosmopolitan chic, Shochu Lounge is the basement bar of Roka, the contemporary Japanese restaurant. It's named after a Japanese vodka-like spirit made from rice, barley and buckwheat, which forms the basis for its divine cocktails. The Noshino martini (shochu with cucumber, £8.30) and Lemongrass Shochu (£8.30) are exotic finds, while the Plum Plum (plum shochu, plum vodka) is a sweet treat and the Hei sour (jasmine shochu, lemon, almond syrup and ylang ylang) is fragrance in a glass.
Basement, 37 Charlotte Street, W1T 1RR (7580 9666/www.shochulounge.com).

Get paddling...

Thames Dragons (www.thamesdragons.com) train crews to row in lung-bursting races, usually over 500 metres and occasionally longer distances such as this 22-mile annual Great River Race marathon. The first training sessions are free, although there are membership subscriptions if you then decide to join the club.

321-323
...or let others take the strain

Hang on a minute: glass of Pimms in hand? Balmy spring weather? Total absence of aching limbs? Maybe watching Oxbridge types grunt their way through the Boat Race is more your cup of tea? If so, join 250,000 fellow revellers along the riverbank for the next installment of the 150-year-old Boat Race (www.theboat race.org, late March or early April). See the two 'eights' power past from viewpoints at the start (Putney Bridge, Putney Embankment or Bishops Park), by the bridges at Hammersmith or Barnes, or at the finish (Dukes Meadows and Chiswick Bridge), perhaps taking advantage of big screens (usually in Bishops Park and Furnival Gardens) to watch the rest of the race.

If watching two crews of burly ringers isn't to your taste, the Doggett Coat & Badge Race (www.watermenshall.org/history/doggett.htm) is much more sparsely supported, but far more historic. Contested since 1715 by young Watermen (once a Thames-borne equivalent of the modern-day cabby), the race is rowed each July in traditional 'gigs' over four miles and five furlongs (nearly 7.5km) from London Bridge to Chelsea.

Or you could try the Great River Race (8398 6900, www.greatriverrace.co.uk). Every September, 300 traditional rowed boats from all over the world – and a variety of historical epochs – race a frightening 22 miles between Richmond's Ham House and Island Gardens. Hungerford Bridge, the Millennium Bridge and Tower Bridge are all good viewpoints.

324 See a performance at the Scoop

The Scoop at More London (www.more london.com/scoop.html), to use its full name, is a sunken open-air amphitheatre seating 800 people on the South Bank (in front of City Hall) that runs a programme of free films, concerts, plays and other events from May to October each year; one evening each Christmas it's also a magical setting for carols and storytelling.

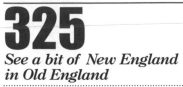

325
See a bit of New England in Old England

The Grosvenor Chapel on South Audley Street is widely known as the American Church in Mayfair. Virtually unaltered since its construction in 1731, with its Tuscan portico, square tower and steeple it now looks as though it could have been airlifted in from New England: that's how popular the look subsequently became in the States. The secluded gardens between the chapel and the Roman Catholic Church of the Immaculate Conception on Farm Street is full of benches dedicated to Americans, and became a favourite dead-letter drop during the Cold War. It has been suggested that Richard Caring, the new owner of Harry's Bar next door, along with an impressive number of other exclusive London clubs and restaurants, has expressed an interest in buying the chapel – so catch it before you need to get on the guest list.

Grosvenor Chapel *24 South Audley Street, W1K 2PA (7499 1684/www.grosvenorchapel.org.uk).*

326
Go to the Proms

True to its original democratic principles, you can still attend Promenade concerts for a fiver. Of the 70-odd performances held at the Royal Albert Hall during the Proms season (www.bbc.co.uk/proms, from mid July to early September), most offer same-day cheap tickets – up to 1,400 standing tickets are released 30 minutes before each performance. You have a choice of standing (or sitting on the floor) in the Arena pit in the middle or standing in the gallery running round the top of the hall. Queues form early and snake around the block for the popular shows, but for many you will rarely have to wait more than half an hour to see world-class classical music performances. Forget the slightly frightening bombast of the Last Night (you're unlikely to get a tickets under a tenner for this anyway) – there's so much more worth queuing for.

327 *Make Michelin starred meals at the Kitchen*

Unlike most Michelin-starred kitchens, mistakes at this Parsons Green-based concept deli-cum-casual cookery school are not punished by shouty, self-esteem sapping tirades from ego-pumped celebrity chefs. Instead, you can sip a glass of wine at your own private work station while you assemble a meal from well sourced, partially prepared fresh ingredients with the help of experienced culinary heavyweight Thierry Laborde – and you don't even have to do the washing up afterwards. You'll leave laden with sealed meals that can be cooked in minutes and served to unsuspecting dinner guests. Perfect for gastro rookies and time-starved full-timers.

The Kitchen *275 New Kings Road, SW6 4RD (7736 8067/www.visitthekitchen.com). Dishes start at £4.95 (one serving), £9 (for two).*

328

Go bargain hunting, or seal the deal, at the Wills-Moody Rock and Roll Jumble Sale...

Hugely popular with in-the-know students, this well-established indie gem happens on the third Sunday of the month (1-8pm) in the fittingly eccentric environs of St Aloysius Social Club on the Euston Road. Either pitch up and sell your own casts-offs or priceless retro gems or spend the day rummaging around for second hand offerings such as Britpop-era band tees, rare vinyl, vintage comics and hand-made jewellery. Of course, this being a rock 'n' roll jumble sale, there's also a dirt cheap bar and racy but not too intrusive – it is a Sunday, after all – rock tunes on the stereo. *www.willsmoody.com.*

The Kitchen

329-333
...or rock out on Denmark Street

Perhaps only Abbey Road is more significant to the story of London's rich rock and roll heritage than this tiny West End thoroughfare that connects Charing Cross Road with St Giles High Street. It's thought there are over 10,000 instruments for sale at the seven leading stores here, and you can usually try before you buy. Regent Sounds (4 Denmark Street, WC2H 8LP, 7379 6111), now specialising in Fender electrics, was once a recording studio where the Rolling Stones recorded their first album; head to Rhodes Music (21 Denmark Street, WC2H 8NJ, 7836 4656) for Gibsons; Tin Pan Alley Drum Company (21 Denmark Street, WC2H 8NJ, 7240 7307) is the percussion ace; and Hank's Guitar Shop (24 Denmark Street, WC2H 8NJ, 7379 1139) should fulfil all your acoustic needs.

Alternatively, if you're suffering from stage fright, just check out the museum-like shop windows with their displays of curious vintage and collector pieces, or visit during the Tin Pan Alley Festival (usually in July; www.tinpan alleyfestival.co.uk), when the street closes to make way for a (free) indie street party with music from emerging and established rock bands.

334
Find the word on the street in Notting Hill

Paved with gold? Pah! How coarse! West London's streets are paved with something infinitely more profound (and probably more useful in these black economic times) – poetry. Thanks to a local artist and life-long resident Maria Vlotides, Notting Hill now boasts seven specially designed manhole covers. Each is engraved with a lyrical ditty from other local writers including Margaret Drabble (who describes the Coronet Cinema as a place of 'diamonds, dreams and tears'), PD James, Sebastian Faulks and John Heath-Stubbs. All are based near Notting Hill Gate; start at Daunt Books (112-114 Holland Park Avenue, W11 4UA) and stroll around to see if you can find the rest.

335
Watch hockey for free

Unlike the premier division games of most other team sports, professional hockey is usually free to watch – though you might be quietly nudged into buying a programme for £1. Games are played at weekends: check out the likes of the Hampstead & Westminster, Old Loughtonians and Surbiton. For details of who to see and where to see them, check the website. *www.englandhockey.co.uk.*

336-345
Search for beautiful trees

London still has hundreds of magnificent trees despite disease and redevelopment. Here are our top ten: for detailed information on how to get to them, see www.treesforcities.org.

Ash (*Fraxinus excelsior*) in Old St Pancras Churchyard, King's Cross, NW1.

Fig (*Ficus carica*) in Amwell Street, EC1. Free food.

Holm oak (*Quercus ilex*) Fulham Palace Gardens, SW6. A 500-year-old evergreen oak.

Huntingdon elm (*Ulmus x hollandica*) on Marylebone High Street, W1. The last elm surviving in Westminster.

Hybrid strawberry tree (*Arbutus x andrachnoides*) in Battersea Park, SW11.

Indian bean tree (*Catalpa bignonioides*) in the yard outside St James's Church, Piccadilly, SW1.

London plane (*Platanus x hispanica*) in Berkeley Square, W1. The quintessential street tree.

Queen Elizabeth's oak (*Quercus robur*) in Greenwich Park, SE10. The remains of this ancient oak, where Henry VIII wooed Anne Boleyn and young Bess played, are fenced off and marked by a plaque. A new sapling has been planted in its place.

Royal oak (*Quercus robur*) in Richmond Park, TW10. This tree is 700-800 years' old.

Yew (*Taxus baccata*) in St Andrew's Church, Totteridge, N20. Over 500 years old.

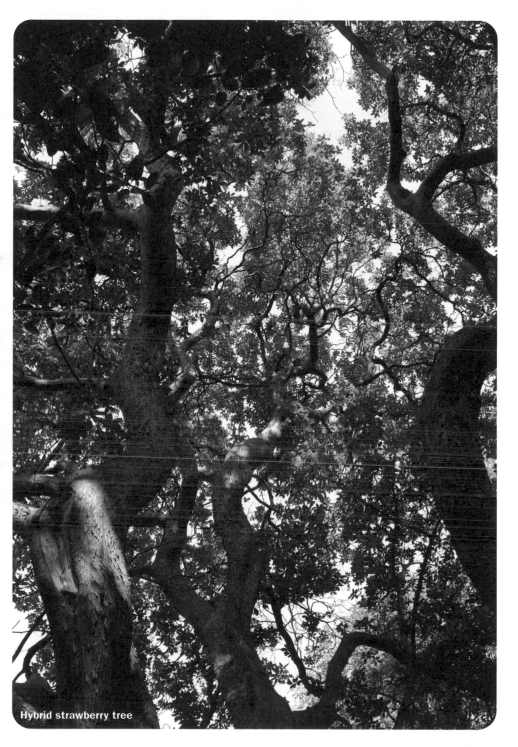

Hybrid strawberry tree

Going underground

Hankering for the glamorous – and grimy – world of latter-day espionage, Time Out's agent Robin Saikia goes undercover.

If you stand outside Tate Britain on Millbank and look across the Thames, you can't miss Vauxhall Cross, the striking headquarters of MI6, the British secret service. But for all the moody green cladding and bullet-proof glass, and despite its guest appearances in a couple of recent Bond films, this is a resolutely practical and functional building. As such, it may be something of a disappointment for the espionage fan in search of mystery, deception, eccentricity, romance and sleaze.

However, these attributes are all to be found in greater or lesser degrees in former secret service headquarters: 54 Broadway, SW1, with its brass plaque proclaiming 'Minimax Fire Extinguisher Company'; 21 Queen Anne's Gate, SW1, lair of Captain Sir Mansfield Smith-Cumming, the first 'C', with his swordstick, wooden leg, false moustaches and phoney German accent; Bush House, WC2, HQ of Claude Dansey, 'Uncle Claude' or 'Colonel Z' to his few friends and many enemies; originator of 'Z Organisation', an alternative MI6 of his own devising; Curzon Street House, W1, the quarters (it was rumoured) of hundreds of specially trained carrier pigeons – and home to the

'Registry', an ever-expanding filing system including the details of over two million people, hidden behind windows so encrusted with grime that they could doubtless have resisted a massive explosion.

Those were the days – and if Vauxhall Cross has any glamour at all it is surely a corporate, ostentatious glamour, not remotely redolent of the covert blackmail, silk stockings and cyanide of yesteryear. For mementoes of those, one has to go north of the Thames: Dolphin Square in Pimlico, SW1, an eminently respectable development of some 1,250 flats built in the mid 1930s, delivers a good measure of intrigue, sleaze and secret service history. There are 13 blocks in the square, each named after a naval hero – Drake House, Collingwood House, Hood House and so on. There is an agreeable bar, a good restaurant and pleasant gardens. Former residents include Princess Anne, Harold Wilson, William Hague and Peter Finch as well as a steady stream of more or less blameless judges, politicians, writers and journalists. But there were dark horses too. Call girl Christine Keeler (a sub-tenant of Dolphin Square) caused a national scandal

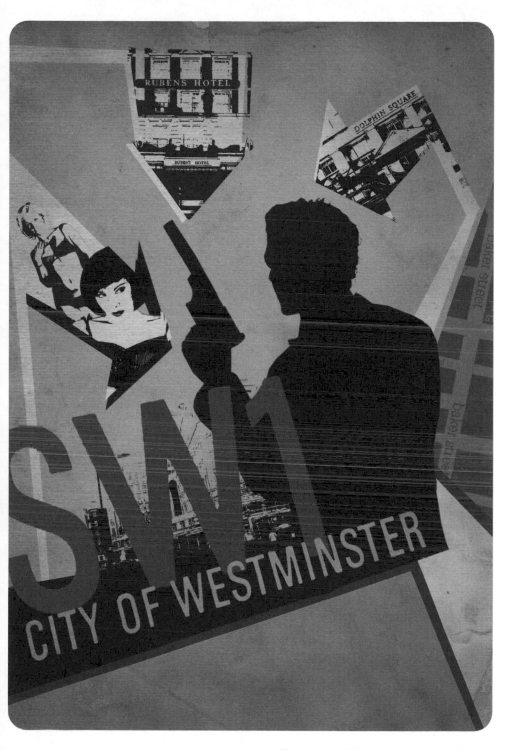

when it was revealed in 1961 that she had had affairs with both the Conservative politician John Profumo, Secretary of State for War, and Yevgeny Ivanov, a Soviet naval officer.

But despite the nation's outrage, these were trifling indiscretions in comparison with the antics of John Vassall, resident of Hood House in the late 1950s. Vassall, a naval attaché in the British Embassy in Moscow, was lured to a homosexual party organised by the KGB and photographed in what he later conceded was 'a complicated array of sexual activities with a number of different men'. The KGB blackmailed him into working for them, though many claimed that Vassall, poorly paid and yearning for the high life, needed little coercion. He subsequently sold secret documents to the Russians, smuggling them out of the Admiralty in a copy of *The Times*, squandering the proceeds on expensive suits from Savile Row, rare antiques and exotic holidays. The Square's respectable spy – an important figure in the history of British espionage – was Maxwell Knight, who, from 1925, ran Section B5(b) of MI5 from his flat in Hood House. The purpose of B5(b) – 'Knight's Black Agents' to those in the know – was to infiltrate subversive groups, which under Knight's leadership it did with some success. (Knight also pursued a successful career as 'Uncle Max', broadcasting nature programmes for children for the BBC.)

A well-run hotel is the perfect spot to strike a Faustian bargain, and hotels will probably always be popular meeting places for secret agents. Brown's Hotel (Albemarle Street, W1S 4BP) was an occasional and very elegant secret service rendezvous, notably for the interrogation by Peter Wright of the scientist Alastair Watson, suspected in the 1960s of passing technical information to the Soviets. As Roy Berkeley observes in his excellent book *A Spy's London* '…the Soviets took their people to the basement of the Lubyanka, while the British took their people to Brown's'.

Wladislaw Sikorski, the Polish Prime Minister and Commander-in-Chief of Polish forces in World War II, set up his headquarters at the Rubens Hotel (39 Buckingham Palace Road, London, SW1W 0PS) in 1940. From here the Polish Resistance operated an extensive spy network until Sikorski's death in 1943.

The Mount Royal Hotel (now the Thistle Marble Arch, Bryanston Street, W1H 7EH),

was a meeting place for Russian double agent Oleg Penkovsky and agents from MI6 and the CIA. Penkovsky passed on invaluable secrets to his new colleagues in British and US intelligence, detailing the extent of the Soviet nuclear arsenal. In 1962, as a result of a tip-off from the British agent George Blake, he was arrested by the KGB. It is said that he was tied to a board with piano wire before being fed feet first into the oven of Moscow Crematorium.

The former Ebury Court Hotel (now Tophams Hotel, 28 Ebury Street, SW1W 0LU) was a known meeting place for the secret service and the Special Operations Executive (SOE) during World War II and it is still an agreeable place to meet for a quiet drink. Its unassuming wartime manageress, Yvonne Rudellat, was recruited into SOE and subsequently became a heroine of the French Resistance, successfully running a network in France. She was eventually captured by the Germans and died in a concentration camp.

St Ermin's Hotel (2 Caxton Street, SW1H 0QW) was another wartime outpost. Here, potential recruits were routinely interviewed in the subdued glamour of the restaurant, successful candidates (among them Noël Coward) being spirited up to the fifth and sixth floors which in those days had been completely requisitioned by MI6. It was here that Kim Philby was interviewed and recruited into the secret service by Guy Burgess – a deal they sealed with a weekend of heavy drinking prior to an early start in Section D (for 'Destruction' – stirring up active resistance to the enemy) in the summer of 1940.

MI9, the World War II escape and 'exfiltration' department, set up shop on the second floor of the old Great Central Hotel (now the Landmark Hotel, 222 Marylebone Road, NW1 6JQ), having outgrown its former ad hoc HQ in room 424 of the Metropole Hotel (no longer in existence) in Northumberland Avenue. An underrated and too little known wing of the secret service, MI9's principal task was to help allied servicemen stranded or imprisoned in enemy territory to escape or find their way back home. Footsoldiers such as Airey Neave masterminded the repatriation of troops and agents after disasters such as Operation Market Garden at Arnhem, while resourceful agents like the theatrical conjuror Jasper Maskelyne and the former pilot

Christopher Clayton Hutton developed a series of useful gadgets and devices – tools concealed in cricket bats, maps in gramophone records, compasses in buttons and so forth.

These survival innovations are not to be confused with the rather more sinister devices developed at 35 Portland Place, W1, by SOE: exploding rats, exploding pencils, exploding animal droppings, collapsible crossbows, suicide pills, a .22 calibre cigarette gun, garrottes and a tear gas fountain pen. (Gadgets of this sort are the stock in trade of spies of all allegiances. Later, during the Cold War, the KGB developed the 'kiss of death', a lipstick tube containing a 4.5mm single-shot pistol that was used by both female agents and by the notorious KGB 'ravens', gay men on entrapment missions.)

Throughout World War II, SOE progressively requisitioned whole blocks in Baker Street, so much so that members would refer to themselves and the section simply as 'Baker Street'. No. 64 became the operational HQ in October 1940. No. 83, Norgeby House, had a plaque proclaiming it as the 'Inter-Services Research Bureau', but in reality the whole of 'F Section' ('F' for France) was run here by Colonel Maurice Buckmaster. F Section was split into cells, some large, some consisting of a single agent or a small team. Their codenames and personnel are resonant to this day: 'Wrestler', run by Pearl Witherington, the 'best shot in the service'; 'Salesman', with Violette Szabo, nicknamed 'la p'tite Anglaise'; 'Physician', a larger team that included Yvonne Rudellat, formerly of the Ebury Court Hotel and the beautiful Indian agent Noor Inayat Khan, the first female radio operator sent to France by SOE.

Agents needed a wide range of skills to survive in the field, everything from lockpicking to noiseless assassination, and these were taught at Michael House, 82 Baker Street. The second-floor flat in Orchard Court, Portman Square, with its famous black onyx and marble bathroom, was a briefing and debriefing station for SOE recruits. Officers would check that agents looked and behaved in a suitably 'Gallic' fashion before despatching them on a tour of duty with the French Resistance. Chiltern Court was HQ to the Scandinavian section of SOE, while 221

Baker Street housed the clothing and disguise section, where tailors would work round the clock making 'authentic' continental clothing for agents.

'The KGB developed a 'kiss of death' lipstick containing a 4.5mm single shot pistol that was used by agents on entrapment missions.'

Buckingham Palace may seem an odd landmark to include – but it is there, after all, that art historian Anthony Blunt continued to fulfil his duties as Surveyor of the King's (and subsequently the Queen's) Pictures, long after he had confessed in 1964 to Arthur Martin of MI5 that he was a Soviet agent. Blunt was a member of the 'Cambridge Spy Ring' – a group working for the Russians that had met at Cambridge University and included fellow KGB agents Guy Burgess, Donald Maclean and Kim Philby. Blunt was spared exposure and imprisonment in exchange for a full confession. Until his retirement as its director in 1974, Blunt also had the run of the Courtauld Institute of Art, then housed at 20 Portman Square. It was only in 1979, after the publication of Andrew Boyle's book *Climate of Treason*, that he was finally publicly disgraced (though he was never prosecuted). Named as a traitor by Margaret Thatcher in 1979, Blunt was stripped of his knighthood and, memorably, booed out of a cinema in Notting Hill Gate. Ever the cosmopolitan scholar-boulevardier, and seemingly unfazed by these very English setbacks, he quietly set about completing a definitive book on the Italian painter Pietro da Cortona without so much as a twang of piano wire to trouble him.

362 Get into korfball

Korfball, a mix between netball and basketball, was invented in 1901 in Holland. Which is perhaps surprising given the '90s-fad-sounding name and the impressively progressive basic premise: fat, thin, tall, short, male or female; the only thing that matters is your ability to cooperate with your team mates. Twelve teams – each comprised of four men and four women – compete in London's regional league, all of whom welcome beginners; see the website for more information.

www.londonkorfball.co.uk

363 Be careful you don't get nicked in Trafalgar Square

The smallest police station in London is to be found hidden away in a lamp pillar in the south-east corner of Trafalgar Square. If you didn't know, you might take it for an ice-cream kiosk; but, no, it's really a one-man, auxiliary police station.

364 Watch nature among brutalist concrete

Ducks? Check. Reeds? Check. You're at the London Wetland Centre, right? Wrong, wrong, wrong. The Barbican Centre (Silk Street, EC2Y 8DS, 7638 8891, www.barbican.org.uk) is known by those who loathe it as a concrete monstrosity, but city-lovers know to linger by its lake and ponds, the water and waterfowl all the more delightful for the unlikely setting. Take a coffee to one of the outdoor tables and gaze out over the main lake, taking in the fountains, the waterfall (at the eastern end), St Giles's church (Milton's last resting place, directly opposite the café) and, yes, nature: waterlilies in summer, mallards, moorhens and their offspring in spring, even the occasional heron. You can pop out here during the interval – it's just as lovely at night – and there are more landscaped water gardens if you arrive at the Barbican on the Highwalkway from Barbican station. Even more transporting is the steamy Conservatory (open noon-4pm Sun, unless there's a private event), a lush jungle of tropical plants and carp ponds. You won't believe you're still in the centre of town.

Barbican Centre

365-371
Take the capital's best fashion advice for free – if you dare

Kate Riordan tells frugal fashionistas where to style it out in the world of personal shopping.

Canny fashionistas in the capital know that there's a wealth of sartorial advice on offer for free if you only ask – or, rather, if you book a personal shopping appointment. In fact, practically every big department store worth their salt has their own service. Let's be clear about the rules, though. While most of the services are complimentary, there is clearly an unspoken understanding that you're going to be spending some money. Of course you could take the advice and ideas and run, but be prepared for a little awkwardness. For example, Liberty's (Great Marlborough Street, W1, 7573 9944, www.liberty.co.uk) 'Style Service' is complimentary in itself – and includes advice on homeware and accessories as well as fashion – but the assumed minimum spend is £1,200, an ever so slightly alarming figure for the budget-conscious shopper.

Selfridges (400 Oxford Street, W1, 7318 3536, www.selfridges.co.uk) boasts a very classy service, where specialist personal shopping consultants wait on you hand and foot. Their suite of private rooms has the hushed atmosphere of a five-star boutique hotel, with deep carpets, tactile fabrics in cream and caramel and enormous, flattering mirrors. The emphasis is on contemporary fashion and the experts will dip into Selfridges' designer 'Superbrands' to find your perfect look. Even if you go in not intending to spend any money (there's no minimum spend), you might find your perspective altered when you've slipped on a Balenciaga pencil skirt and seen your silhouette transformed in a way that the high street never can (as this reviewer did).

Naturally, Harrods (87-135 Brompton Road, SW1, 7893 8000, www.harrods. com), the world-famous department store that once procured a baby elephant (for Ronald Reagan, no less), has a well-established personal shopping service. Though Harrods no longer holds any royal warrants, the personal shopping service alludes to past royal connections with its name, 'By Appointment'. Once again,

they're aiming high with prospective customers, citing 'private jets, fine jewellery and complicated watches' as some of the items they can help you choose between. Situated on the first and lower ground floors, there are two dedicated and separate departments for women and men. Mininum spend is a frightening £2,500.

Harvey Nichols (109-125 Knightsbridge, SW1X, 7259 6638, www.harveynichols. com) have long been in on the personal shopping act, but relaunched with a new and comprehensive service towards the end of 2008. The entirely refurbished suite has been turned into a luxurious oasis of pale leather sofas and sleek fittings. The expert fashion advice on offer is not just geared towards Sloaney balls and bashes; they'll also kit you out with the perfect work wardrobe. Advice also extends to fabulous party food and drink, and inspiration for the perfect gift and there's no obligation to buy.

Back on the high street, it's also possible to get savvy advice for free on clothes that won't cost the earth. Debenhams (334-348 Oxford Street, W1C, 084 4501 6161, www.debenhams.com) and Marks and Spencer (458 Oxford Street, W1N 0AP, 7935 7954, www.marksandspencer.com) both offer personal shopping at their Oxford Street flagship stores. Debenhams' personal shoppers make a point of discussing budgets before they do a trolley dash on your behalf. The specialist field here is weddings, but even if you're just after a new party dress and the right accessories to go with it, they're happy to help. Just sit back with a magazine and a coffee and let them do the leg-work.

Topshop (36-38 Great Castle Street, W1, 0844 848 7487, www.topshop.com) also offers the 'Style Advisor' service. There is no obligation to buy and you can kick back while the 'fashion industry trained' shoppers run around, or join a supervised sweep of the shop if you prefer. If you do splash out, you'll get your goodies gift-wrapped for free and you can jump the queue. Book early, mind – the slots go fast.

A few of my favourite things

372-378

Leslie Grantham, actor

One of my favourite places in London is the Horniman Museum (100 London Road, SE23 3PQ, 8699 1872, www.horniman.ac.uk). Horniman was a tea merchant who collected all sorts of amazing objects on his travels, from huge totem poles from America to silks from China and sundials from around the world. The museum is only 15 minutes from the centre of London and it's free.

I've filmed a lot around the Docklands area and have become quite interested in its history. The Museum of London Docklands (West India Quay, E14 4AL, 7001 9844, www.museumindocklands. org.uk) tells you the whole story of the place from Roman times; it's also great to just stroll around the docks and see how all the various warehouses have been converted.

At St Mary Overie Dock in Southwark you can go and see a replica of Sir Francis Drake's ship, the *Golden Hinde* (Cathedral Street, SE1 9DE, 7403 0123, www.golden hinde.org). They have recreated what life was like on board a ship in his day, which is fascinating. It's the sort of thing they taught us about back when I was at school, and it's great to go and see it come to life. For £7 you get a guided tour and you can even hire the place out for parties.

I think one of the best things to do in London is go for a walk down the Thames from Docklands to Twickenham. You can stop off on the way for a drink and a bite to eat in one of the riverside pubs, and then when you get there, visit the Twickenham Museum (25 The Embankment, TW1 3DU, 8408 0070, www.twickenham-museum.org.uk). It covers the history of the local area of Twickenham, Hampton and Teddington, but it also has a lot about the history of the river itself.

You won't see many Wombles on Wimbledon Common (SW19 5NR, 8788 7655, www.wpcc.org.uk), but it's a great place to go to watch the world go by. There's a lovely tea shop on the edge of the common called the Windmill (Windmill Road, SW19 5NQ, 8788 2910, www.windmilltearooms.com) where you can park up and have a coffee or something to eat and watch people riding past on their horses.

Lots of kids I know love going to Leicester Square when there's a big movie premiere on to do some star spotting. Loads of films have their premieres there, from the Bond films to Harry Potter. You can get a cup of hot chocolate from one of the cafés nearby and stand by the barriers as all the luvvies go in, and the earlier you get there, the closer you can get.

Whenever I used to go on TV shows like *Noel's House Party* I'd always see the same people in the audience and that's because they'd be on a BBC mailing list. You can contact the BBC and ask for tickets to be in the audience for your favourite show (0370 901 1227, www.bbc.co.uk/tickets, free). Going inside a TV studio and actually seeing how programmes are made is fascinating.

379

Take the long view in Richmond Park

You can put this 'thing to do' on the back burner if you like; the view is not likely to change any time soon because it is protected by law. That means nothing can be built that obstructs the ten-mile sightline from the top of King Henry VIII's mound in Richmond Park (the Tudor monarch used to hunt in these parts) all the way to St Paul's Cathedral in the City to the east. After you've taken in the vista make your way to the Isabella Plantation (*see p97*).
Richmond Park, *TW10 (8948 3209/ www.royalparks.org.uk/parks/richmond.*

Richmond Park

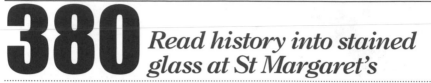

380 *Read history into stained glass at St Margaret's*

The parish church of the House of Commons since 1614, St Margaret's is well worth a visit for its stained glass windows alone. As old in foundation as Westminster Abbey, the building now dates largely from the 16th century. Highlights include the east window, which is 15th-century Flemish and was paid for by Catherine of Aragon. It depicts the Crucifixion scene, flanked by St George and St Catherine of Alexandria. Underneath is the sickly Prince Arthur, elder brother of Henry VIII and Catherine of Aragon's first betrothed. The west window is by the eminent Victorian Arts and Crafts window makers Clayton and Bell, and shows Sir Walter Raleigh (in the middle), who was executed only a few yards away, in Old Palace Yard. The south aisle windows are by John Piper and were added in 1966.

St Margaret's *20 Dean's Yard, Westminster Abbey, SW1P 3PA (7222 5152/www.westminster-abbey.org).*

381-384
Go for a walk in a wood

Epping Forest
The big one. Nearly 6,000 acres of woodland, interspersed with heaths, lakes and rides. The wood formed after the last Ice Age and is mainly oak, beech and hornbeam. Watch out for the massive branches of previously pollarded trees, left to grow since the passing of the Epping Forest Act in 1878. A good starting point for walks is the area around Queen Elizabeth's Hunting Lodge, which is now a museum.
Queen Elizabeth's Hunting Lodge, Ranger's Road, E4 7QH.

Highgate Wood/Queen's Wood
Highgate and, on the other side of Muswell Hill Road, Queen's Woods are remnants of the ancient forest of Middlesex, which once covered most of north London and the county of Middlesex. The smaller Queen's Wood has the more diverse ecology with its predominant oak and hornbeam canopy and strangely named 'wild service tree' – a marker for the age of the woodland. Highgate Wood also has a café, a playground and playing fields.
Muswell Hill Road, N10.

Holland Park
Although Holland Park is one of London's grand formal parks, there is a surprisingly extensive wood in its northern half. Set off down one of the shaded paths and within a minute the sounds of the city will become muffled and then all but disappear.
Abbotsbury Road, W11.

Shooters Hill Woodlands
Oxleas, Jack and Shepherdleas woods – remnants of the post-glaciation wildwood that once stretched over the whole country – cover Shooters Hill with a mixture of oak, sweet chestnut and hazel, plus the tell-tale maple-like leaves of the 'wild service tree'. The rare palmate newt lives in ponds in the woods.
Shooters Hill, SE9.

385
See the future, now
In mid September each year design junkies descend on the London Design Festival (www.londondesignfestival.com), which showcases the best of the capital's creative designers, artists and fashion makers. Held at various locations across town, the fun usually centres on Brick Lane's Truman Brewery, and the programme features a couple of hundred commercial and cultural events.

386
Get into the Tower for free – but don't be late
The ticket price puts a normal visit to the Tower of London beyond the scope of this book, but – if you're organised – you can see something the hordes of paying tourists won't be able to see… and without paying a penny. Dating back seven centuries, the Ceremony of the Keys happens at exactly 9.53pm each evening, when the Yeoman Warders begin the process of locking the Tower's entrances. They have failed to do so on the dot only once since the Ceremony began, when shockwaves from nearby Blitz bombs tumbled the party to the ground, causing a delay of several minutes. (The Yeoman Warders were sufficiently ashamed of this failure to write an apology to King George VI.)

The ticketed public assembles at the West Gate at 9pm, through which they enter the outer wall and follow the ceremony around each gate. When it's all over at about 10pm the Last Post sounds. This little piece of repeated history is understandably popular, of course, so you'll need to apply for tickets (offering two possible dates) at least two months in advance. For full details, see www.hrp.org.uk/toweroflondon/whatson/ceremonyofthekeys.aspx. Tower Hamlets residents are, however, unusually blessed: they can get into the Tower of London for just £1, without applying in advance for anything. And they get to see the Crown Jewels and inside all the various towers. Just take proof of residence with you when you go to the ticket office.

387-394

Savour the capital's finest kebabs...

London may be beset with dodgy doner houses, but it is also blessed with some of the finest kebabs this side of Istanbul. Here are some of our favourites.

Abu Zaad

This Syrian restaurant in Shepherd's Bush has reasonably priced Damascene food ranging from meat-heavy kebabs to vegetarian-friendly mezze and, being Syrian, the odd spicy kebab and lots of oven-baking in yoghurt. Try the kebab bil tahina – a traditional dish of spicy lamb topped with yoghurt and rich tahina.
29 Uxbridge Road, W12 8LH (8749 5107/ www.abuzaad.co.uk).

Kebab Kid

This little takeaway is a cut above the rest, with no greasy doners of fatty minced lamb, just proper shawarmas (chicken or lamb) of prime cuts of meat (from Smithfield Market), or shish kebabs cooked on skewers to order. We also like the crunchy shredded salad, and the (optional) smear of own-made taramasalata. A medium shawarma costs £5.20.
90 New Kings Road, SW6 4LU (7731 0427).

Mangal 1 Ocakbasi

Come to the original branch of Turkish Mangal in Dalston for heaps of prime meat at low prices – and its BYO policy. There's no printed menu; you choose skewers of meat from the glass display counter and they're grilled in front of you. Shish (marinated lamb chunks), beyti (spicy minced lamb) and pirzola (lamb chops) are all exemplary and served in generous portions with a huge mound of salad and warm leavened bread (from £8).
10 Arcola Street, E8 2DJ (7275 8981/ www.mangal1.com).

Patogh

This tight-packed Iranian café off Edgware Road offers wonderful flatbreads with minced lamb or chicken wrapped around skewers,

then chargrilled (from £6). Most mains are served on grim metal plates, but somehow it all adds to the authentic experience. The salads include whole fresh fronds of mint and tarragon, which really make the flavours sing.
8 Crawford Place, W1H 5NE (7262 4015).

Pomegranate

This Greek grill, bar and restaurant on Upper Street serves simple no-frills souvlakia (grilled meat on skewers). Choose from lamb, chicken or pork (from £6.20) and it will come to you fresh from the chargrill on a bed of red onion and topped with a flurry of wild rocket. Supplement this with fresh-tasting taramasalata or tsatsiki and delightfully chewy pitta.
139 Upper Street, N1 1QP (7704 1002).

Ranoush Juice

The original branch of this Lebanese café chain is a great pitstop for either an easy lunch or post-partying sustenance. The Lebanese mezze of houmous, chicken livers, sujuk sausages and so forth are all excellent, but the pièces de résistance are the two formidable shawarmas (chicken and lamb) rotating at the front of the shop. Juicy slices are deftly shorn off by the staff and scooped into the waiting arrangement of bread (£3.50).
43 Edgware Road, W2 2JR (7723 5929).

Sitaaray

This Bollywood-themed restaurant is camper than a Rajasthani caravan, yet its cooking is surprisingly sophisticated. We particularly like mint-marinated, chargrilled tiny lamb chops and the unusual variation on shaami kebabs studded with sweetcorn but tasting

Ranoush Juice

of fenugreek. Vegetarians are also well catered for, even if kebabs are the star attraction. *167 Drury Lane, WC2B 5PG (7269 6422/ www.sitaaray.com.*

Tayyabs

This Pakistani canteen in Whitechapel has consistently been popular: there's almost always a queue. Among the starters are chicken or mutton tikkas, lamb chops, seekh kebabs and shami kebabs – all of which are seriously low-priced (starting at £1) and beautifully cooked. *83-89 Fieldgate Street, E1 1JU (7247 9543/ www.tayyabs.co.uk).*

395 *...or go for the band instead*

The kebabs may not be up to much, but that's not really the point at after-hours party palace Marathon Kebab. Local stop-outs cram into this raucous backroom venue hosting everything from swing jazz bands to zombie Elvis impersonators.
Marathon Kebab *87 Chalk Farm Road, NW1 8AR (7485 3814).*

396 *See the Rose theatre*

Built in 1587, 12 years before the original Globe theatre, the Rose is the only Elizabethan playhouse that has been excavated on a large scale. Shakespeare probably worked here as an actor; he staged his early plays here and the venue also saw premieres of plays by Christopher Marlowe, Ben Jonson and Thomas Kyd. Fast forward to 1989 when the buried remnants of the pit and two stages were uncovered by builders. After a high profile campaign to save the space from redevelopment, excavation work began in earnest. Now you can visit the theatre as part of the Globe's tours (*see p266*) or get tickets (ticket prices are rarely more than a tenner) to one of the various low-key theatrical events held here.
Rose Theatre *21 New Globe Walk, SE1 9DT (7261 9565/www.rosetheatre.org.uk).*

397 *Remember the watergate scandal*

Between the bottom of Buckingham Street and Embankment Gardens stands a weathered stone gate – once the watergate belonging to the great 17th-century York House, which stood between here and the Strand. It isn't now immediately recognisable as a watergate that once led from a grand garden down to the Thames – primarily because it's fully 150 yards from the river, thanks to Joseph Bazalgette's 1864 construction of the Embankment.

Today, clues to York House's ownership still lie in the surrounding streets. George Street, Villiers Street, Duke Street (now gone) and the absurdly named Of Alley (now York Place, Formerly Of Alley) in the immediate vicinity of Buckingham Street, together serve to remind us of George Villiers, Duke of Buckingham. Sexy George swanned into London in 1614, and quickly became the court favourite of King James I, who referred to him as 'sweet child and wife': rumour and intrigue followed him for the rest of his life, but if nothing else it was a canny short-cut to having a whole corner of London named after you.

398 *Reflect on a crime of passion over a pint*

Today, the Magdala pub in Hampstead (2A South Hill Park, NW3 2SB, 7435 2503) is a sedate spot with huge leaded and stained-glass windows and is also home to the monthly Alpine comedy club. However, back in 1955, this is where Ruth Ellis, the last woman to be hanged in Britain, shot estranged lover David Blakely on Easter Day, and two weathered bullet holes on the outside front wall (plus framed press cuttings) mark the event. While supping a pint of Canterbury Jack or Greene King IPA you can eavesdrop on the various walking/murder tour guides' commentaries and reflect on Ellis's admission that 'it is obvious when I shot him I intended to kill him'.

399 *Learn to scuba dive*

If you fancy exploring life beneath the surface you can book a two-hour 'Discover scuba' session with London Scuba for just £10. It's a relaxed, informative 'try dive' format sanctioned by the world-leading training organisation PADI (Professional Association of Diving Instructors). Each two-hour workshop, held in a swimming pool, begins with some basic theory and a safety run-through before you take the plunge and decide whether the sport is for you. It also serves as a valuable foundation if you then want to progress to full scuba certification.
London Scuba *(01342 837711/ www.londonscuba.com).*

400 *Eat a Krispy Kreme... in Harrods*

Famously the shop where you can buy (almost) anything, it's still hard to believe that there's a Krispy Kreme outlet at this swanky London department store. Indulge in a guilty pleasure and sink your teeth into the warm doughy goodness (when the queue's long, staff have even been known to offer free samples).

401 *Learn Brazilian dance at Guanabara*

Salsa is a bit '90s and tango's a little too technical – if you want to learn to dance Latin-style go Brazilian. One of the capital's best Brazilian bars Guanabara (Parker Street, W2CB 9PW, www.guanabara.co.uk) runs free dance classes five nights a week; try samba, forró and even Brazilian ballroom dancing, gafieira. Classes take place before the place fills up with regulars, which means that when the lesson ends you can practice your moves on the dancefloor with those who really know their stuff. Alternatively, hit the bar for a caipirinha.

402

In Peckham's Bellenden
Road, street bollards are
designed by Anthony
Gormley, pavements and bus
stops by Zandra Rhodes and
local artist Tom Phillips
created the curlicue lamp
posts and wall mosaics. Restored Georgian and Victorian terraces,
upmarket bistros, boutique fashion and book stores all add to the
burgeoning café culture.

403-404
Drink sherry

That's everything from the light tangy Puerto Fino through to intense fruity PX sherries such as the 1975 Don Pedro Ximenez Gran Reserva. If you can't stretch to the top-notch four-course Saturday sherry lunch at Moro (34-36 Exmouth Market, EC1R 4QE, 7833 8336, www.moro.co.uk), then sip an old favourite such as Tio Pepe Fino (£3.50/glass) at the bar and snack on the excellent tapas dishes instead. The bright, stylish surroundings at Fino (33 Charlotte Street, W1T 1RR, 7813 8010) are another fine spot to sample a list of around 20 sherries; most start at £5.50 a glass.

405
Get crafty at Origin

At Origin, the annual London Craft Fair held in Somerset House (www.craftscouncil.org.uk/origin, £8), you'll find plenty of inspiration to get creative yourself, even if the works on display are unlikely to cost less than a tenner. Expect to see top quality ceramics, glass, textiles and jewellery whose creators are on hand to tell you all about the work. As well as the stalls (150 on each day), there's a lively programme of talks, discussions, handling sessions and makers' demonstrations. There are also family workshops where you can make your own precious objects.

406
Watch out for Appearing Rooms

Danish artist Jeppe Hein's water sculpture *Appearing Rooms* has proved so popular (especially with children) that it's set to return to the South Bank for the summer. The rows of fountains, in grid formation, are liable to squirt unpredictably – trapping you in one of the square 'rooms', unless, of course, you're up for a soaking. Find it in front of the Royal Festival Hall.
Southbank Centre, Belvedere Road, SE1 8XX (0871 663 2501/www.southbankcentre.co.uk)

407
Board Hammerton's ferry

This tiny boat, taking just 12 foot passengers (and the odd bicycle), operates daily from Marble Hill House to Ham House (and vice versa) from mid-February to the end of October. It's the sole survivor of the numerous ferries that plied this stretch of the river for hundreds of years. Times have changed: the boat has an electric motor these days, and the fare – a penny when it was started in 1908 by one Walter Hammerton – is now £1 for adults, 50p for children (but there's no extra charge for bikes).

408
Don't touch anything in the Islington Museum

In the newly opened Islington Museum you'll find a bust of communist leader Lenin (who published his radical Iskra at nearby 37a Clerkenwell Green). Originally gracing the Russian Embassy, it was later moved to Finsbury Town Hall but, following repeated vandalism, it's found a safer, and perhaps more appreciative, audience here. Once you've finished doffing your cap to Lenin, check out the museum's curiously ironic relic: the books from Islington's libraries that were famously defaced by playwright Joe Orton and his lover Kenneth Halliwell. What a difference a few decades make: back in 1962, the pair were jailed for six months for their ill-advised doodling.
Islington Museum *245 St John Street EC1V 4NB (7527 3235/www.islington.gov.uk/Leisure/ArtsAnd Entertainment/Museums/IslingtonMuseum). Free.*

409
Experience the heavy hand of the law

Members of the public can watch British justice in action at the Central Criminal Court (open 10am-4pm), so long as they leave any bags, cameras, dictaphones, mobile phones or food at home (there are no storage facilities provided at the court). The front door details forthcoming trials.
Central Criminal Court *Old Bailey, EC4M 7EH (7248 3277/www.hmcourts-service.gov.uk). Free.*

A few of my favourite things

410-415

*Johnny Vaughan,
radio presenter,
95.8 Capital FM*

In my opinion, nothing beats a good, simple British boozer. The Beehive in Clapham Junction (197 St John's Hill, SW11 1TH, 7207 1267) is like an English themed pub from the '70s and it's just brilliant – juke box, fruit machine, nice landlord, no food served and children not welcome. Fantastic. The clientele tend to be one man and his dog, or blokes doing the *Evening Standard* crossword. If you show up there with a mate it's like you're being flash. It's where I slope off to read a paper if I'm on my own.

A trip to Lollipop (201 St John's Hill, SW11 1TH, 7585 1588) is another nice bit of nostalgia-lite. It's a really old-school sweet shop, with all your Merry Maids, Cola Cubes and Tom Thumb Drops. None of this jelly babies in plastic – everything's packed in white and red striped paper bags. They might not be penny sweets anymore but it's still cheap. Every adult who goes in there starts reminiscing about Bulls Eyes or some other obscure childhood sweet, and you get people arguing about important subjects like Opal Fruits becoming Starburst.

Whenever the Carters Steam Fair (01628 822 221, www.carterssteamfair.co.uk) is in town we always visit that. It's basically how a funfair should be, with merry-go-rounds, carousels, old-fashioned dodgems, stalls – and because it's run by real enthusiasts everything is so well looked after and beautiful. You walk around and sort of imagine World War II soldiers going there for a last night out before going back to war. It's class.

I'd advise anyone who hasn't done it to take the Woolwich Ferry (8921 5965, www.greenwich.gov.uk/Greenwich/Travel). It's just a car ferry which crosses the Thames, but it's free and the river is quite wide at that point so it makes for a nice little cruise. Often you can pay quite a lot to go on river boat tours and they take so long and are so boring but this one just does the job.

I've been going to Maroush (21 Edgware Road, W2 2JE, 7723 0773, www.maroush.com) for years. Two of you can eat for under £20 and the food is delicious. They do a chicken or lamb shawarma with garlic sauce and huge chillies which comes rolled up really tight in pitta bread – and we all know the power of pitta to make anything taste good. And their mixed fruit cocktail is all you'll need to sort you out if you have a hangover.

If you're going to museums or galleries you've got to avoid places where it's all about the gift shop, otherwise you just end up blowing your budget even if it's free entry. I think the Imperial War Museum (Lambeth Road, SE1 6HZ, 7416 5000, www.iwm.org.uk) is great. It's really good for kids to see things like tanks close up, which they've previously only played with in miniature. And they have the Victoria Cross room which is so moving – when we think we're going through bad times it provides a reminder of the people who faced something a bit bigger than our own struggles.

416 *Make the world more beautiful...*

In late 2004 gardening radical and Elephant & Castle resident Richard Reynolds set up his own underground movement, inviting others to join him 'to fight the filth in public spaces with forks and flowers'. The idea is to overhaul neglected areas of greenery. You can check out which digs are planned – and suggest your own on the website, www.guerilla gardening.org. In May 2008, for example, guerrilla gardeners planted sunflowers beside Westminster Bridge Road, while December saw the Christmas tree in the four-year-old St George's Circus guerrilla garden gain a home-made silver-foil star. Awww!

417 ...or take a short cut and visit a garden that is already beautiful

During Open Squares weekend (held in the middle of June, see www.opensquares.org) wrought iron gates are swung back and city oases, usually hidden behind high laurel hedges, are opened to the public. There are around 200 gardens and squares to choose from and they come in all shapes, colours and sizes: there are the impressively grand set pieces – Belgrave Square, SW1, is an enormous four-acre garden with an enviable collection of statuary, and a tennis court – and there are the hidden City jewels such as the Salters' Garden (Salters' Hall, 4 Fore Street, EC2Y 5DE, pictured), redesigned as a knot garden by David Hicks in 1995 to mark the 600th anniversary of the Worshipful Company of Salters. That impressive pedigree is in evidence in the old medieval city wall which forms the garden's southern boundary.

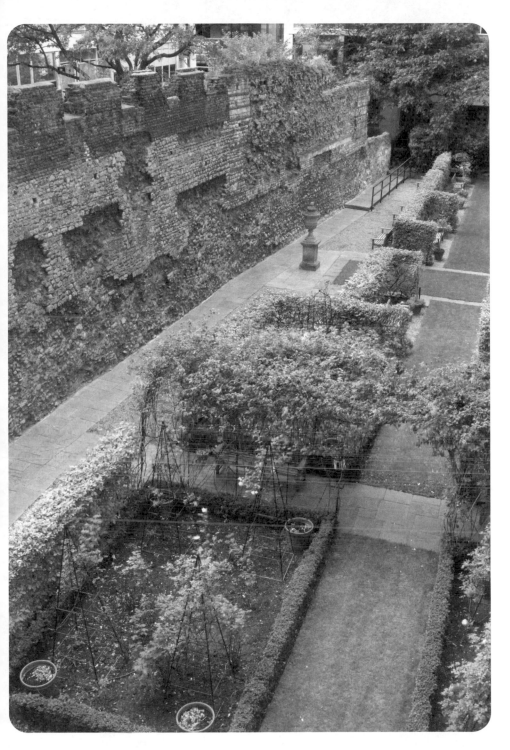

Take it to the bridges

Wealth, death and a lot of bad language, Charlie Godfrey-Faussett talks us through traversing the Thames.

It was thanks to Hadrian that Londinium, with its timber bridge over the river, was able to consolidate its prestige a century after being sacked and burned by Boudicca. And without London's bridges it's quite possible that we'd still be waiting for a waterman to ferry us across to the other side of the river in his boat – though we probably wouldn't have to wait very long. In Elizabethan times, when there was still only one bridge in London, there were some 40,000 watermen working the river (to put that in perspective, there are around 20,000 licensed black cabs in the city today). A famously feisty and foul-mouthed bunch (a law was once passed attempting to moderate their backchat), when more bridges were proposed in the 17th century, it was the watermen (along with the City of London) who successfully opposed the idea. Let's give thanks, then, that you can now walk across the Thames free of charge, keeping your feet dry and your thoughts clean, on no less than nine different bridges in the two miles or so between the Tower of London and the Houses of Parliament.

A pleasant stroll through Tower Gardens leads round the medieval walls of the Tower of London and up some steps on to Tower Bridge Approach. And what an approach it is: this preposterous neo-Gothic construction, the first bridge ever built downstream of London Bridge, has become even more iconic than the fortress it was supposed to complement. And what's more, it actually works. With its lifting 'bascules' and pedestrian skywalks, it looks more like the entrance to an elfin wonderland than a bridge. But perhaps the real reason it's so popular is that it has buildings on it – harking back to Old London Bridge, which was packed with houses – and you can hire the Bridge Master's Dining Room in the south abutment for a day, or an evening, of private dining.

Thanks to one of those feats of continuity that the City of London does so well, the Bridge House Estates, founded in 1097 by King William Rufus for levying taxes for the repair of London's only bridge, are still paying for the upkeep of the five City bridges today. They

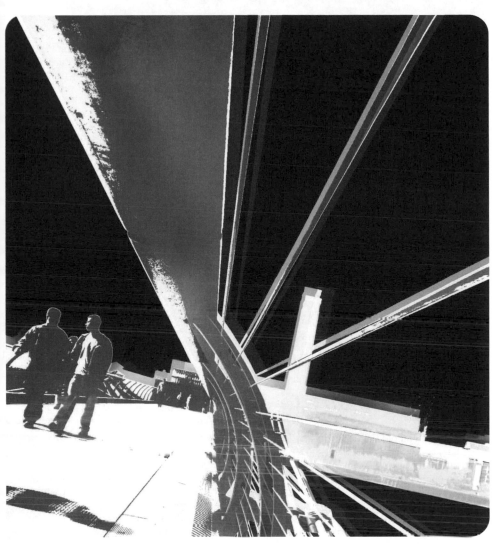

grew considerably in importance during the Middle Ages, after the new stone bridge became the City's lifeline, and were given a Royal Charter in 1282. They now manage some £700 million worth of assets and, as the City Bridge Trust, also give £15 million to charitable causes in London each year. They also paid for Tower Bridge, which opened with much pomp and ceremony in 1894.

At the south end of the bridge, head down the steps and turn right on to the riverside Queen's Walk. It passes the glass kidney of City Hall, the gleaming office blocks of MoreLondon and

HMS Belfast – which is moored at the end of Battle Bridge Lane, apparently named after the supposed site of Boudicca's final rout by the Romans. Further along, a plaque on the embankment wall marks the site of Old London Bridge, its first stone laid in 1176. It was replaced in 1831 by a new one designed by the indefatigable Scottish engineer John Rennie (who also built the first Waterloo and Southwark bridges). His London Bridge was famously sold to McCulloch Oil in 1968 and rebuilt in Lake Havasu City, Arizona. The new London Bridge, finished in 1973, with its three arches, is hardly a beauty but it's still well worth crossing for the view of Tower Bridge downstream – and for the beeline it makes into the City, towards the imposing offices of the Guardian Royal Exchange Assurance Group (1921). On the left, Cannon Street station's brick towers, and its iron railway bridge were constructed in 1865 and are early works of John Wolfe Barry, who later saw Tower Bridge through to completion (he was the son of Sir Charles Barry, who designed the Houses of Parliament).

'There were some 40,000 watermen working the river – to put that in perspective, there are around 20,000 licensed black cabs in the city today.'

At the north end of London Bridge, by the Egyptian art deco Adelaide House, take the steps down to the riverside on the right. Carrying on upstream from here, great views of Southwark cathedral open up across the river from Watermen's Walk (a name loaded with cruel irony, given that they would surely have preferred you to take a ride in their boats). On the north side of the river, Watermark Place, with its swish wooden gantries and euro-chic dining options, is set to open in the place of Mondial House, the stylish 1970s bomb-proof telephone exchange that once stood here. Expect fine views over the water to Pickford's Wharf, Winchester Wharf, the old Thameside Inn, and the replica of Sir Francis Drake's world-circling little *Golden Hinde* in its dock.

Just before you pass under Cannon Street station, note the plaque unveiled in 2005 'to celebrate 60 years of peace between the peoples of Britain and Germany, and to commemorate 600 years during which some 400 Hanseatic merchants inhabited peacefully in the City of London from the 13th to 19th centuries, in the German self-governing enclave on this site known as the Steelyard.' Steelyard Passage, running under the bridge and lit by dinky blue lights dotted on the ground, leads to a refreshing stopover in the shape of the Banker on Cousin Lane. Its funny little outdoor deck, right on the river, looks across to the more famous (and busy) Anchor on Bankside, but this one gets all the sun in the afternoon. Fortify yourself before continuing along Walbrook Wharf past Cory Environmental's Transfer Station, where the City of London's garbage is containerised before being floated out of town on big barges to the Mucking Marshes (thankfully a remarkably odourless operation these days).

The approach to Southwark Bridge is up Fruiterer's Passage (check out the Fruiterers' crest on the wall showing Adam and Eve in the garden, proving what a serious matter fruit and veg can be). Southwark Bridge, built between 1913 and 1921, and designed by Sir Ernest George, mentor to Edwin Lutyens, has a beautiful old gold, eau-de-nil and cream colour scheme and lovely lamps that are especially atmospheric when there's a mist hanging over the river at night. Crossing south over the bridge – apparently aligned with the older Blackfriars Bridge upstream to minimise tidal turbulence – you're confronted by the spinnaker façade of Riverside House, home of media regulator Ofcom. Heading right along Bankside at the end of the bridge, you pass the reconstructed Globe Theatre, its thatched roof now authentically mossy.

However, St Paul's Cathedral and Tate Modern are the big events here – and the Millennium Bridge connects the two. Also in the care of the Bridge House Estates, the first new pedestrian bridge over the river for a century is a shining wonder to walk across. Famously wobbly on first opening, the cunning design of its flattened out suspension cables means that there are great views to the left and right and it's a memorable approach straight across towards the great dome of St Paul's.

Don't get distracted by the cathedral though: you've got more bridges to cross. From the north end of the Millennium Bridge drop hard left onto riverside Paul's Walk. Outside the entrance to the City of London school is a Polar

Sundial, the time indicated by the shadow of its oxhead gnomon (a gnomon is a sundial's 'needle', in this case positioned in the centre of the sundial and vaguely ressembling an oxhead). Paul's Walk continues along the river past flower-filled tubs, wooden pergolas and benches backed up against the brick wall of the Blackfriars Bridge Underpass. Pass beneath Blackfriars Railway Bridge (another of John Wolfe Barry's works, with Henri Brunel, son of Isambard, opened in 1886) which stands next to the shadow of its former self – the massive supports of the London, Dover and Chatham railway bridge of 1862 jutting purposelessly out of the water.

The original Blackfriars Bridge was put up in 1769 (then only the third in London) and the watermen were duly compensated. It was then replaced by 1869 and opened by Queen Victoria, at that time so unpopular she was hissed by the crowd at the opening ceremony (a statue of her stands at the northern end of the bridge, notwithstanding). Dickens described the bridge as 'one of the handsomest in London … the general outline is bold and the ensemble rich, if perhaps a trifle gaudy, especially when the gilding, of which there is an unusual proportion, has been freshly renewed.' In honour of this being the river's tidal turning point – the point at which fresh and saline water meet   you'll notice that the bridge's piers are decorated with stone seagulls and seabirds on the downstream, seaward side, and kingfishers, herons and other freshwater birds on the upstream side. It also has a surprisingly low Venetian gothic balustrade: could it be coincidence that it was from this bridge that the Italian banker Roberto Calvi, known as the Pope's banker, was found hanging in 1982?

At the other end of the bridge avert your eyes from the ugly Sea Containers House before passing the successful OXO Tower Wharf redevelopment into the attractive, tree-lined and laid-back approach to Waterloo Bridge. Before long, however, the great blocks of the National Theatre announce a different, concrete world – sterner and more practical perhaps but certainly, in the case of the bridge at least, more beautiful. Not only are the views from the thing itself inspiring – wedged as it is on a sharp bend in the river – but with it the architect, Sir Giles Gilbert Scott, surely produced

his finest work. Bearing its name proudly on its side, like a ship, its five leaping spans, supported by massive concrete box girders, manage to appear wonderfully light. It was completed during World War II, in 1942, and much of the construction work was carried out by women. It is the people's bridge.

> ## 'Waterloo Bridge, bearing its name proudly on its side like a ship, was completed during World War II.'

After a break at the terrace café in Somerset House on the northern side, Victoria Embankment Gardens are well worth strolling through on the way to your penultimate bridge. The footbridges on either side of Hungerford Bridge were opened in 2003, making them the newest bridges on the river. Take the left-hand Golden Jubilee footbridge to see the City; take the right hand one to see Westminster.

Now you're in the busiest and most popular bit of the South Bank, home to the London Eye and County Hall, but you can avoid the crowds (nearly) by going through the tunnel beneath the Coade stone South Bank lion then taking the southern pavement of Westminster Bridge towards the Houses of Parliament. The first bridge on this site was constructed in 1750, after overcoming the usual long held objections from the watermen and the City. Wordsworth immortalised it with his reflections from it on the city at dawn but this one replaced Wordsworth's in 1862. It was designed by Thomas Page with input from Sir Charles Barry, architect of the Houses of Parliament, and possibly the reason why it complements them so neatly. Follow the bridge to its west end on the north bank and you'll find a striking statue of Boudicca. If she – or the watermen – had had their way, there might never have been any London bridges at all.

427-430

Hear church choirs

There are many glorious church choirs in London and all of them can be heard for little more than the cost of a bus fare or whatever donation you feel inclined to leave in the plate. The choirs of Westminster Abbey (www.westminster-abbey.org), St Paul's Cathedral (www.stpauls.co.uk), Westminster Cathedral (www.westminstercathedral.org.uk) and the Brompton Oratory (www.brompton oratory.com) are all well known (visit their websites for details), but there are also several less prominent churches that offer a great opportunity for musical uplift.

One such is the Parish Church of St George (Hanover Square, W1S 1FX, 7629 0874, www.stgeorgeshanoversquare.org), an elegant Queen Anne church. There is animated carving on the reredos from the workshop of Grinling Gibbons and the 16th-century Flemish glass in the east window has a uniquely smoky beauty. Famous for high society weddings, St George's was the venue of choice for Eliza's upwardly mobile dustman father, Alfred Doolittle, in *My Fair Lady*. The choir sings every Sunday morning at the Parish Eucharist and at Choral Evensong once a month.

At the end of one of North London's most lovely residential streets, Church Row, you'll find a grand church and graveyard, dating back to 986. The Parish Church of St John-at-Hampstead (Church Row, NW3 6UU, 7794 5808, www.hampsteadparishchurch.org.uk) has a strong musical heritage originally created by its great organist and choirmaster, the late Martindale Sidwell. That heritage is upheld by the present director of music, Lee Ward, and generously supported by the urbane and enthusiastic Hampstead congregation. There is a sung Parish Eucharist and Choral Evensong every Sunday (4.30pm in winter, 6pm in summer, check website for details).

St Mary's Church (Bourne Street, SW1W 8JJ, 7730 2423, www.stmarythevirgin.org.uk) is an offbeat haven in the heart of Belgravia. The church is Anglo-Catholic, and you are therefore just as likely to hear a polyphonic *Salve Regina* by Juan de Aranda as you are Anglican music by the likes of Stanford and Parry sung by the 'invisible' choir on high in the west end gallery.

The Parish Church of St Mary the Virgin (Elsworthy Road, NW3 3DJ, 7722 3238, www.smvph.org.uk) near Swiss Cottage offers a sung Eucharist every Sunday morning and Evensong once a month. St Mary's figures prominently in the Anglican choral tradition and its vicar in Edwardian times, Percy Dearmer, collaborated with Ralph Vaughan Williams on the New English Hymnal. Dearmer was as much renowned for his sense of sartorial style as he was for his interest in music, favouring a cassock, gown and velvet cap during day-to-day parish rounds. 'To hell with the Pope!' shouted a rude little boy on seeing Dearmer in this outfit. 'Are you aware,' replied Dearmer, 'that this is the precise costume in which Latimer went to the stake?'

431

Hide away at Greenwich Peninsula Ecology Park

At the Greenwich Peninsula Ecology Park you can delight in being in a way-out wet place bouncing with life and beauty – just a stone's throw from the O2 centre. If it's astonishing enough that a park like this should exist here, given the area's industrial history, it's even more amazing that the animals living here are not put off by the encroaching city. But then the park was always intended as an urban project, providing a new wetland habitat and enabling scientists to find out more about urban ecology. Abundant wildlife – frogs, toads, newts, beetles, brightly coloured dragonflies and damselflies, butterflies and wild flowers – throngs the inner and outer lakes. You can go on evening bat walks (*see p93*) and there are also specially designed hides from which you can check out the various resident and visiting bird species in more detail. Check the website for more details of the different monthly and seasonal events.

Greenwich Peninsula Ecology Park
The Ecology Park Gatehouse, Thames Path, John Harrison Way, SE10 0QZ (8293 1904/www.urbanecology.org.uk).

432

Spend a Sunday morning on Columbia Road

One of London's most visually appealing markets, Columbia Road overflows with bucketfuls of flowers on a Sunday morning – and rings with the patter of chirpy Essex barrowboys. An early start is recommended (the market opens at 8am) so get breakfast when you arrive. Starting from the Haggerston Park end of the street, turn right when you reach Ezra Street, next to the Royal Oak gastropub (73 Columbia Road, 7729 2220, www.royaloaklondon.com). Here the delightful little square is a great place to eat delicious treats and listen to the buskers. Grab coffee and a bagel at ivy-covered, farmhouse-kitchen-style Jones Dairy Café (23 Ezra Street, 7739 5372, www.jonesdairy.co.uk), or stock up on artisanal cheeses and fresh bread in the café's provisions store. A mooch around the Courtyard, also on Ezra Street, will provide drooling opportunities with the restored furniture of B Southgate (4 The Courtyard, 07905 960792) and the art in Columbia Road Gallery (7 The Courtyard,

07812 196257). Back on Columbia Road itself, when you've had your fill of flower traders, check out the attractive shops that run either side of the street. This end is best for gawping at art, with Elphick's (no.160, 7033 7891), Nelly Duff (no.156, www.nellyduff.com) and Start Space (no.150, 7729 0522). Fun shops include friendly accessories boutique L'Orangerie (no.162, 8983 7873) – chunky bead necklaces, straw sun-visors and fat glass rings are among the cheaper items – old-fashioned sweetshop Suck & Chew (no.130, 8983 3504) and retro kitchenware shop Treacle (nos.110-112, 7729 5657), where you could invest in a cupcake. Columbia Road institution Milagros (no.61, 7613 0876, 07931 705 202, www.milagros.co.uk) offers Mexican curiosities and trinkets, including single tiles for 70p, while Supernice (no.106, 7613 3890) sells Thomas Paul melamine plates and trays that start from £6. Ready for lunch? The Fleapit café at no.49 serves delicious vegetarian food and organic juices.

Forget those cheap and nasty bars at supermarket checkout counters: spend £10 on chocolate from the capital's finest chocolatiers.

Demarquette Fine Chocolates

Despite a French-Chinese background, savvy chocolatier Marc Demarquette hasn't let the trend towards British produce pass him by, adding Surrey blackcurrant, Kentish pear and Yorkshire rhubarb, among other fruits, to his range of exquisitely made chocolates. Still, it's his infusion combinations (Tunisian Bharat; Nile cumin; Japanese cherry blossom) that distinguish this premium-priced operation. Connoisseurs of single origin bars should look out for the chocolates made from 'wild cocoa' grown in the Bolivian Amazon.
285 Fulham Road, SW10 9PZ (7351 5467/ www.demarquette.com).

L'Artisan du Chocolat

L'Artisan du Chocolat, London's most experimental chocolate shop, is a good bet for spectacular ganaches, truffles, mints and candied fruits. Irish-born proprietor Gerard Coleman makes all of his trademark tobacco 'couture chocolate' (smoky, silky and intense) by hand. He has also created many other delicious innovations, among them the best-selling liquid salt caramels.
89 Lower Sloane Street, SW1W 8DA (7824 8365/ www.artisanduchocolat.com).

Maison du Chocolat

Robert Linxe's Parisian choc palace is a browser's paradise: spacious and slick, with giant glass windows, the store sells seasonal individual cakes – perhaps a chocolate, mango and ginger Maiko in summer, or a Rigoletto caramel mousse-filled cake for winter.
45-46 Piccadilly, W1J 0DS (7287 8500/ www.lamaisonduchocolat.com).

Melt

Watch the chocolates being made in the pristine white open kitchen at the rear of this pretty Notting Hill boutique. Melt's bars are all made by hand and come in inspired flavours such as milk chocolate with raspberry and black pepper, or sesame. Love bars (silky milk chocolate with creamy filling) have a secret pocket in the pack for your own private message. The takeaway hot chocolate is dark and delicious.
54 Ledbury Road, W11 2AA (7727 5030/ www.meltchocolates.com).

Montezuma's Chocolates

In contrast to the precious attitude of some of their competitors, Montezuma's has a lighthearted attitude towards chocolate, and their variety of giant chocolate buttons, animal shapes and dipped fruits make quirky, colourful presents. Much of the range is organic and Fairtrade and they also offer a service where you can create your own one kilo bar.
51 Brushfield Street, E1 6AA (7539 9208/ www.montezumas.co.uk).

Paul A Young Fine Chocolates

A gorgeous boutique with almost everything – chocolates, cakes, ice-cream – made in the downstairs kitchen and finished in front of customers. Young is a pâtissier as well as chocolatier and has an astute chef's palate for combining flavours. In summer, try Pimm's cocktail truffles featuring cucumber, strawberry and mint flavours, and white chocolate blondies made with raspberries and blueberries.
33 Camden Passage, N1 8EA (7424 5750/ www.payoung.net).

Prestat

Another British business that has long since proved itself alongside the chocolate masters of Brussels, Prestat's 'Appointment to the Queen' status is echoed in glorious packaging – pretty boxes in regal purples and ruby reds, embellished with gold crowns and elegant script. The store's strongest product is its plump, round, velvety truffles.
14 Princes Arcade, SW1Y 6DS (7629 4838/ www.prestat.co.uk).

William Curley

Rococo

Chantal Cody's Rococo has a fondness for unusual flavours (cardamom, chilli pepper or orange and geranium bars, say), but combines this with some nostalgic ones: English rose and violet creams, plus fresh cream truffles, for example. It has also been a pioneer in the UK when it comes to ethical practices. Try the Grenada 71% bar, made on the same estate the cocoa is grown on.
321 King's Road, SW3 5EP (7352 5857/ www.rococochocolates.com).

Theobroma Cacao

Phil Neal hand-makes the chocolates spread over the counter and adjacent dresser of this cosy Chiswick shop. There are large truffles, fruit-flavoured whips in chocolate cups and good marzipan options but our favourites are the cocoa-dusted chocolate 'sticks', rich enough to serve as dessert in themselves. Look for the discreetly boxed Erotique range including 'decolletage', stilettos and gold-tipped phalluses.
43 Turnham Green Terrace, W4 1RG (8996 0431/ www.theobroma-cacao.co.uk).

William Curley

This charming pâtisserie is the brainchild of husband and wife duo William and Suzue Curley. The couple opened their shop in Richmond a number of years ago to rave reviews. It sells an exquisite range of cakes and chocolates including a tropical *entremet*, orange and praline cake and sea-salt caramel chocolate.
10 Paved Court, Richmond TW9 1LZ (8332 3002/ www.williamcurley.co.uk).

443 Relive the jet set days at Croydon Airport Museum

If the words 'terminal building' invariably summon 'terminal boredom' to mind, you'll find an antidote in the free visitors' centre at Croydon Airport. Defunct since 1959, this vestige of empire relives the early days of aviation: a time when getting airborne and staying there was no mean feat, when air traffic control was a thing of the future (1921), and when the expression 'jet set' was invented to imply impossibly glamorous luxury. The beautifully crafted art deco terminal building was constructed on two World War I airfields, and this was the main commercial airport for London until Heathrow opened in 1953. In its heyday the great aviators all came here – Charles Lindbergh touched down in 1927 shortly after his solo trans-Atlantic flight,

and Amy Johnson flew from Croydon to Australia – and, incredibly, back again.

All the surprising romance of Croydon's lost past is celebrated at the visitors' centre in the old control tower, where the world's first air traffic control system has been recreated with original equipment. You can see Amy Johnson's flight bag and even dress up as a passenger from the 1930s. There's a De Havilland Tiger Moth in the preserved booking hall and a Heron outside the door. All it lacks is Hercule Poirot, en route to solve a high-class murder in Paris. Never let it be said that romance is dead in Croydon.

Croydon Airport Visitors' Centre *Airport House, Purley Way, Croydon CRO 0XZ (8669 1196/www.imperial-airways.com).*

444-448 *Pedal...*

The odd argument with drivers aside, the capital can be a great place to cycle through – and it's free! We especially like the following routes.

...through the City at night

This five-mile jaunt is best left for the weekends when the hordes of suited workers have gone home and the place is shrouded by an eerie calm. It's the ideal time to drink in the stagily magnificent architecture – from Richard Rogers's ultra modern Lloyd's building to the Acropolis-like Royal Exchange – especially at night, when it's all aglow and the lack of traffic allows you to pause in front of buildings without dismounting. Start at Bishopsgate, continue on to Leadenhall Street, St Mary Axe, Cornhill, Threadneedle Street, Poultry and Cheapside, before ending at St Paul's.

...to the shops

Head to Holborn, Farringdon and Islington for a spot of window shopping and bargain browsing. Start at Bayley Street and take in Russell Square and Guilford Street, before heading up Calthorpe Street into Farringdon, Rosebery Avenue, Upper Street and Camden Passage. Highlights, in order of appearance, include the lovely Russell Square Gardens, Lambs Conduit Street with its idiosyncratic independent outlets including Persephone Books and Symphonic Records – and Exmouth Market with its eccentric clothes shops. After zipping past Sadler's Wells you'll reach Camden Passage near Angel, a cobbled lane with everything from high-end jeweller's to heavily laden junk shops.

...around the south-east

This is a workout for serious cyclists that meanders through 13 miles of gorgeous river views and renovated docks. The route takes in two quirky river crossings as well as great maritime institutions, dockside industries and plenty of parkland. Begin at Greenwich and head to village-like Charlton and Woolwich, where you'll cross the river by ferry. Then it's on to car-free Canary Wharf and Island Gardens where you can get the lift down to the Greenwich foot tunnel (you have to dismount here) and head back south under the river to the station and where you started. Unless, of course, you're tempted to do the whole thing again.

...by Battersea

This pleasant 12-mile waft along the Thames to Kew starts at Westminster Pier (you can return by ferry). Take the road behind the Houses of Parliament and continue along to Millbank, past Tate Britain and Vauxhall Bridge; soon Battersea Power Station pops up on the other side. Further on, just before Battersea Bridge, there's a little colony of houseboats on the river. (The path is privately owned for some stretches here so you may have to dismount.) The ferry back to Westminster leaves from Kew Pier and takes about an hour and a half (7930 2062, www.wpsa.co.uk). If it's busy, you might not be able to take your bike, but you can always catch the train from Kew Bridge Station to Waterloo.

...from east to west

This 9-mile schlep starts with the trendy grit of London Fields in Hackney, before heading north west towards Islington, where at Canonbury Park, you may be shocked to discover that some Londoners have gardens the size of your street. Next, it's over Upper Street through leafy Barnsbury and down to Camden, pristine Regent's Park and on to the grand streets surrounding St John's Wood. After Lord's cricket ground head downhill to Maida Vale before scooting round swish Sutherland Avenue and along the foliage-shaded canal to Portobello Road. Where it's time for a sit-down and a cup of tea.

449 Get into the Inns of Court

Meandering in a broad zig-zag from Holborn down through Chancery Lane to Blackfriars and the Embankment, the Inns of Court are the four self-contained precincts where barristers traditionally train and practise – an oasis of academic calm in the middle of the city. Like hushed and venerable Oxbridge campuses with their Grade I-listed medieval chapels, Tudor-style libraries, quads and lawns dominated by majestic plane trees, it's no wonder so few Londoners realise that they are open to the public.

The Inns – Lincoln's Inn, Gray's Inn, Inner Temple, Middle Temple – trace their history back to the 14th century, when the old manor house belonging to Sir Reginald de Grey, Chief Justice of Chester, was converted into a 'hostelry' for law students fleeing the disarray of King Edward's court (hence Inns). They then spread to incorporate land owned by the medieval Christian military order of the Knights Templar (hence Temples). While the Inns no longer accommodate students, judges are still entitled to stay overnight in advantageously apportioned apartments, though they rarely do in practice (it's 'a security nightmare', according to those in the know).

In true Dickensian style, the first thing you'll notice when you visit are the off-putting signs announcing the removal of anyone 'constituting a nuisance'. (The best of these is at the entrance to Staple Inn, just by Chancery Lane station, which expressly forbids the presence of 'old clothesmen' and 'rude children'.) Anyone bold enough to venture further, however, will find paved courtyards dominated by tinkling fountains and impressive swards such as Gray's Inn Gardens or the rolling fields of Lincoln's Inn.

As well as being well and truly pickled in history, the Inns of Court are unsurprisingly no strangers to celluloid either: the huge Tudor Hall dominating Lincoln's Inn (a 19th-century facsimile of the 15th-century original) was one of the settings for *Bleak House*, the latest period drama (after *Wilde*, *Pride & Prejudice*, and also, of course, *Harry Potter and the Order of the Phoenix*) to use the Inns as a backdrop for Ye Olde London. In fact the place is so popular with location finders that the road around Lincoln's Inn Fields can often be blocked up with camera crews. When it isn't, however, we urge you to stop on one of the generously sized benches and watch the gas lamps being lit as dusk falls (*see p41*). Squint just enough to blur out the modern appurtenances – the Audis in the parking slots, the synthetic colours of the cyclist's lycra – and you can imagine yourself in a palimpsest of the modern, frenetic city that lies outside the gates; a London that's more tranquil, more civilised and, somehow, more mysterious.

If you want to visit the redoubtable Halls, with their august stained glass and old-buffer wood panelling (and, in the case of Middle Temple Hall, genuine minstrels' gallery), you'll need to be organised (or riding on a barrister's coat-tails). You must group-book ahead, and even then you're strictly forbidden to disturb the Inns' most sacred ritual: dining. But the Inns also have their own places of worship – and these are generally open to the public (11am to noon and 1pm to 4pm, outside of special services). The Inner Temple Church is built on the site of a 12th-century Knights Templar church and graveyard. Here you'll come across effigies of crusty old knights, as well as Nicola Hicks' sculpture of a pair of knights on a scrawny horse which sits on a plinth in the adjacent square. If you turn up on Fridays you can catch the current 'Master' of the church, Robin Griffith-Jones, lecturing weekly to tourists on the inadequacies of Dan Brown's da Vinci 'research'.

Conspiracy theories and Dickensian locations aside, however, there's plenty to keep you occupied here. The Inns have a singular ambience; and a simple stroll along the cobbled lanes – through archways and into secret gardens – is reward enough for most, especially on a crisp sunny day.

450 *Start skateboarding*

Although skateboarding in the some parts of the city may incur a fine if you get caught, it's fair to say that the capital's skateboarders have never had it so good as far as legitimate or semi-legitimate skate spots are concerned. Up north there are the streety bowls in the southern corner of Finsbury Park, N4, and Cantelowes skatepark (www.cantelowesskatepark.co.uk) halfway up Camden Road, NW1. There are unconfirmed whispers about a new concrete skatepark in Clissold Park, Stoke Newington N16. In west London you'll find the oddly named skatepark siblings Meanwhile One (a series of interconnecting concrete bowls next to the Regent's Canal at Westbourne Park tube) and Meanwhile Two (a small, smooth, covered concrete street course with a 1970s freestyle ramp under the Westway at Royal Oak tube). There's also the large covered Bay66 skatepark near Ladborke Grove (Bay 65-66 Acklam Road, W10 5YU, 8969 4669, www.baysixty6.com).

Just behind the Brixton academy in south London is the expansive and recently resurfaced Stockwell skatepark (Stockwell Park Road, SW9, www.stockwellskatepark.com), while out east there's the tight concrete Mudchute skatepark, near Mudchute DLR (the corner of Westbury Road and Spindrift Avenue). More central is the imaginatively designed White's Grounds concrete skatepark underneath the railway arches off Tooley Street, SE5, next to Tower Bridge. More centrally, Shoreditch's skaters have two grindblocks in Shoreditch Park, N1.

But no discussion of skateboarding in the city would be complete without mention of the hallowed blocks, banks and steps of the South Bank, SE1, which, after a campaign to preserve its status as UK skating's spiritual home, is as busy as ever.

For the latest places to skate, the Slam City Skates shop (16 Neal's Yard, WC2H 9DP, 7240 0928, www.slamcity.com) has a tourist-friendly map of London skateparks. Ask nicely and they'll also give you the lowdown on up and coming spots.

Stockwell skatepark

451-460
Go in search of heroes and kings

Tick off some of London's quirkiest and most fascinating statues, starting at Trinity Church Square in SE1. Here stands a weather-worn full-length statue, probably dating from the 14th century, usually identified as King Alfred. The only statue of the great English hero in London, it was moved here from medieval Westminster Hall in 1824.

The oldest outdoor sculpture in London must surely be the 3,600-year-old carving of Egyptian warrior goddess Sekhmet which has guarded the door of Sotheby's Art Auctioneers (34-35 New Bond Street, W1) since the firm's move here in 1917. The black basalt bust was the subject of 'Sotheboy' Bruce Chatwin's first published piece of work, in 1966.

In Victoria Embankment Gardens, WC2, you'll find a memorial to composer Arthur Sullivan (the tuneful half of Gilbert and Sullivan). This bust was carved by the Welsh sculptor William Goscombe Johnand depicts a scantily draped embodiment of Music fainting on Sullivan's pedestal, having apparently just let slip the score of the *Yeoman of the Guard* from her hand.

Hyde Park is home to a huge bronze statue of Greek hero Achilles wielding his short sword and buckler behind the Duke of Wellington's former home Apsley House (149 Piccadilly, W1J 7NT, 7499 5676, www.english-heritage.org.uk). Made from captured French cannons and paid for by 'the women of England' in gratitude to the Duke, it was erected in 1822 – the first nude public statue in Britain. The fig leaf added later to protect the Greek hero's modesty has been removed twice – most recently in 1961.

Best viewed from the top deck of a bus, John Bunyan looks down from a niche above the door of Baptist House, Covent Garden (6 Southampton Row, WC1). The full-length statue of the great non-conformist preacher is underscored by the first lines from his most famous work, *Pilgrim's Progress*: 'As I walked through the wilderness of this world, I lighted upon a certain place, where was a den, and I laid me down in that

place to sleep, and as I slept I dreamed a dream.'
It's hard to imagine that happening on
Southampton Row today.

A bust of Virginia Woolf, apparently a copy
of the only one ever taken from life, was erected
in Tavistock Square. It was unveiled in June
2004 by 'the last member of the Bloomsbury
Group', Anne Olivier Popham Bell, wife of
Quentin Bell, Virginia's nephew. Anne was a
member of the Monuments, Fine Arts and
Archives section (MFAA) during World War II.
The 'Monuments Men', as they were known, a
group of 345 people from 13 different countries,
are credited with locating and eventually
returning some five million artworks looted
by the Nazis. The gardens also contain a
cherry tree planted in 1967 to commemorate
the victims of Hiroshima – and a beautifully
contemplative statue of Mahatma Gandhi.

Mary, Queen of Scots surveys Fleet Street
from the first floor of a building now called
Mary Queen of Scots House (143-144 Fleet
Street, EC4). The statue was erected in the
1880s by the MP for Caithness, Sir John George
Tollemache Sinclair. Sir John released various
recordings on Columbia, Gramophone and
Odeon in 1906, including his recitation of the
'Adieu of Mary, Queen of Scots', an English
translation of the French poem by the
revolutionary Napoleonic poet Béranger.

Shakespeare can be found leaning out of
the first floor window of a corner pub on
Carnaby Street, W1, casting a quizzical (if
poorly modelled) eye on the swinging street
scene below. Ashen-faced, looking like a clown,
and wearing blue-striped pyjamas and a ruff, he
appears to be staying in the Shakespeare's Head
pub behind Liberty, which was once owned by
the Shakespeare brothers, supposedly distant
relatives of the playwright. The figure has been
in place since just before World War I and lost
a hand to a bomb in World War II.

Sir Winston Churchill and Franklin D
Roosevelt are relaxing in conversation on a
park bench on New Bond Street, W1. The
bronze, entitled *Allies*, was modelled by
Lawrence Holofcener and was unveiled by
Princess Margaret in 1995, to commemorate
a half century of peace. The sculpture shows
little evidence of Roosevelt's famous distrust,
bordering on dislike, of Churchill, though he
did once concede to the drunken PM that 'it
is fun being in the same decade as you.'

461 *Ponder the mystery of Pages Walk tank...*

Take a left off the Old Kent Road in south
London on to Mandela Way, just after the
Tower Bridge Road roundabout, and you are
quickly confronted with an enormous 32-ton
Russian T-34 tank that someone has seen fit
to park in a garden at the end of Pages Walk.
Rumour has it that a doting father bought
this Soviet relic for his seven-year-old son's
birthday. The years may have passed but the
gift never palled and is still there for all to see
(one year it was painted pink, now it's back
to black and white camoflage). Apparently
the council once tried to have it removed but
failed because the overgrown land it sits on
also belongs to the tank's owner. He may not
have forgiven them: according to local legend, its
gun points towards Southwark Council's offices.

462 *...or head along to the Imperial War Museum*

Housed in the old lunatic asylum known as
Bedlam (the Bethlehem Royal Hospital) just
down the road from Pages Walk in Lambeth is
another more impressive collection of military
hardware. Focussing on the history of conflict
from World War I to the present day, the
Imperial War Museum has a vast tank, antique
guns, aircraft and artillery parked in its main
entrance hall – and a gratifying wealth of
information about them inside.
Imperial War Museum *Lambeth Road, SE1 6HZ
(7416 5320/www.iwm.org.uk). Free.*

463 *Try pole dancing*

Pole dancing is arguably more sport than
sleaze these days. You can try for yourself
for free at the London Academy of Pole
Dancing taster lessons. So, will we see it in
2012? They used to scoff at synchronised
swimming, you know...
London Academy of Poledancing *(8520
1985/www.laphq.co.uk). Classes are held at
the Waldorf Hilton Hotel, WC2B 4DD.*

464

A fully functioning bell production workshop, the Whitechapel Bell Foundry (7247 2599, www.whitechapel bellfoundry.co.uk, £8) began operations in 1420 and was responsible for one of the definitive sounds of London: Big Ben. The immensely popular tours (on alternate Saturdays) offer a detailed explanation of the entire process: how the loam or wet sand moulds are made, how the metal is heated and poured, and how the finished bells are tuned, polished and fitted.

A few of my favourite things

465-470

Patrick Wolf, musician

I like learning about medieval London – the London of before the Fire – and the Clink Prison (1 Clink Street, SE1 9DG, 7402 0900, www.clink.co.uk, £5) is such a beautiful, interesting museum. It's located in the city's oldest jail, and it tells the history of punishment and policing... violinists would be put in the stocks for playing in the street because the authorities thought fiddling was the devil's music. And you can try on a chastity belt here as well!

I'm going to sound like a right crustie here, but a great food tip is to go around Borough Market (SE1 1TL, 7407 1002, www.boroughmarket.org.uk) and eat all the samples. You can have your whole lunch there for free. They see me coming every week, 'Oh god, it's him again!' The hot Polish sausage is the best.

Just across from Spitalfirlds market, you can listen to the choir rehearse every Sunday afternoon at Christ Church Spitalfields (Commercial Street, E1 6LY, www.spitalfieldsvenue.org, 7377 6793). You get to hear all the songs they are going to perform in the next week's concerts for free, and you can just relax and listen. **Another great place to hear free classical music is from the buskers in Covent Garden. A lot of the people playing there are from professional orchestras, because orchestras really don't pay very well, so you can hear world-class musicians as you wander around. I used to busk there every week when I was 17.** When I feel depressed, instead of going to counselling, I go to the National Portrait Gallery (St Martin's Place, WC2H 0HE, 7306 0055, www.npg.org.uk). I think that you can really find your own identity within portraits of other people. For me, it's like a biography museum. My favourite is a portrait of a woman called Lady Ottoline Morrell, a wartime aristocrat. She started off very rich and then descended into madness. There was a story that she used to keep flies in the net of her hat because she thought that they were her friends. In Augustus John's portrait of her, her head's held high with her big hat on, and you can sort of feel the flies. **I grew up around Northcote Road in Wandsworth and there are about 11 charity shops in one stretch – the kind where nothing has been priced and there's just a pile of old clothes that you have to rummage through. That's how I used to dress myself when I was 11 and wanted to look like Jarvis Cocker. My best buy was a Burberry trench coat for £2, but I'd buy all my synths down there too.**

471

Go camping

Camping in London? Well, yes – in the 10,000 rolling acres of countryside that is the Lee Valley Regional Park, and which stretches all the way south from Hertfordshire, through Essex and down to the Thames, taking in a number of attractions along the way – from Gunpowder Park on the outskirts of Waltham Abbey, through the Waterworks Nature Reserve in Leyton and the Walthamstow Marshes, to the Bow Creek Ecology Park. You could also try thwacking your irons at the WaterWorks Golf Course – a mere £6.85 for an 18-hole, par three course located in the nature reserve.

The Lee Valley Camping & Caravan Park has all the basics – heated showers, on-site shop and a playground for children – and it's a bargain for London accommodation: adults pay an £8.60 minimum charge, under-16s pay £3.10. Open all year round.

Lee Valley Camping & Caravan Park
Lee Valley Leisure Complex, Meridian Way, N9 0AR (8803 6900/www.leevalleypark.org.uk).

472

Head for Belgravia

With its grand white houses, secluded gardens and elegant squares, Belgravia is another world – and a fantastically rich one at that. You'd need a small fortune to own even a kitchenette in these rarified surroundings but going for a walk is free – though it may cost you your soul in envy. Start outside the Thomas Cubitt pub (44 Elizabeth Street, SW1W 9PA, 7730 6060) dedicated to the memory of the master builder who constructed most of this district in the 1820s. Cubitt was supposedly the first to introduce tea breaks for labourers, so celebrate his humanity with a pint, before heading north-west along the street to Eaton Square, one of London's most expensive addresses. Notable residents have included Neville Chamberlain at no.37, Sean Connery at no.6 and Vivien Leigh at no.54. But to really get a sense of how the other half lives, head for no.100, London residence of Gerald Grosvenor, 6th Duke of Westminster and owner of the freehold on most of the square and surrounding district. The area is named after him too – given that he's Viscount Belgrave, as well as a Duke.

From this elegant abode, it's a short stumble up Belgrave Place to fabulous Belgrave Square, one of London's grandest Victorian squares. As well as a sprinkling of swish embassies (the German, Turkish, Portuguese and Norwegian among them) there are statues of great explorers (Christopher Columbus, Prince Henry the Navigator), the Liberator of South America (Simón Bolívar) and the 1st Marquess of Westminster, who was grandfather of the first Duke of Westinster and another key figure in the development of this area.

Make your final salute to the follies of the rich in the south corner of the square. This mansion – known in the early 20th century as Downshire House – was the London home of Lord James Pirrie. It was here that, one evening in July 1907, the managing director of the White Star Line came to dinner and planned the production of three new ships, the largest in the world. One of them was, of course, the *Titanic*.

473 *Celebrate midsummer the way the French do*

On a midsummer's day (21st June), music – classical, jazz, hip hop – reverberates from street corners right across France. London's version of Fête de la Musique may not have the geographical scope of its forebear, but it's certainly got depth. Since its launch by the Institut Français, Exhibition Road Music Day (www.exhibitionroadmusicday.org) has drawn in most of the heavyweight local cultural institutions (the Goethe-Institut, Imperial College, the Natural History Museum, the Royal College of Music, the Serpentine Gallery, the Ismaili Centre, the Victoria & Albert Museum) and now occupies Hyde Park, using a sound stage opposite the Royal Albert Hall. The 2008 festival – a collaboration with the London Architecture Festival – saw Exhibition Road closed to traffic. Expect anything from experimental electronica to Sufi chants on this day of midsummer musical madness.

474-483

De- (and re-)clutter your house at a car boot sale

There's no question that car boot sales are more fun than the depersonalised world of eBay – yes, you lose the thrill of swooping in with a last-second winning bid, but you gain ridiculous sales patter, the opportunity to off-load your unwanted junk, bargains aplenty and the chance to just potter around laughing at the tat. Here are our suggestions for the best places to find cut-price loot. Note that the entry fee is listed for buyers; the cost for sellers varies, but you can expect to pay between £10 and £15 for a pitch.

Battersea

The Battersea Tech College transforms itself into a lively trading hub each Sunday. It attracts a mix of house-clearance vultures as well as well-heeled local residents having a de-junk.

Battersea Park School, 401 Battersea Park Road (entrance in Dagnall Street), SW11 5AP (07941 383 588). Open 1.30-5pm Sun. Entry 30p.

Cuffley

Well over 100 pitches sell a varied selection of secondhand and antique items every Sunday in this north London suburb.

Just north of Potters Bar, at the junction of Cattlegate Road and Northaw Road, Cuffley, EN6 (01707 873 360). Open Apr-Sept from 7am Sun, bank holiday Mons. Entry 50p.

Epsom

This site outside Espom, half and hour from Waterloo by train to Ewell West station, is the daddy of bank holiday car boot sales. Expect a great mix of new and secondhand gear from its 700 pitches.

Hook Road Arena, at the junction of Hook Road and Chessington Road, Epsom, Surrey KT19 8QG (01372 724 568). Open from 7.30am bank holiday Mons, except the late spring bank holiday. Entry 50p (£1 before 8am); children free.

Hatfield

There are loads of bargains to be found at this impressive sale. It's strictly secondhand, which means no men in white vests selling bog roll.

Birchwood Leisure Centre, Longmead, Hatfield, Herts AL10 0AN (01992 468 619/ www.countrysidepromotions.com). Open Apr-Oct from noon Sun. Entry free.

Holloway

This small sale on the Holloway Road is well worth a rummage. It attracts a mix of sellers – from regulars peddling DVDs, electrical goods and fake perfume to local homeowners looking to profit from a one-off clearout.

Opposite Odeon Cinema, Holloway Road, N7 6LJ (01992 717 198). Open from 8am Sat; from 10am Sun. Entry free.

Kilburn

Kilburn's big car boot sale has a wide variety of new and secondhand stock from sellers from all over north and west London.

St Augustine's Church of England Primary School, Kilburn Park Road, NW6 5SN (8440 0170). Open from 8am Sat. Entry 50p (£3 before 11am).

North Weald/Harlow

New and secondhand gear is sold from over 150 pitches at this popular Essex sale.

Bluemans Field, on the A414 to North Weald,

near Talbot Roundabout, Essex (01992 468 619/ www.countrysidepromotions.com). Open May-Sept from 10.30am Sat. Entry £3 (£2 from 11am; free after noon).

Orpington

The stock at this well-established sale is high in both quantity and quality thanks in part to the affluent location. You'll find mainly secondhand goods at the 75 pitches.

Hewitts Farm, Court Road, Orpington, Kent BR6 7QL (01959 532 003). Open from 9am Sun. Entry free.

Wimbledon Stadium

This is a big, spread-out boot sale with a good mix of sellers peddling all manner of unexpected secondhand goods. It's especially good for bargains on furniture and crockery.

Wimbledon Stadium, Plough Lane, SW17 0BL (01932 355 538). Open from 7am Sat, bank holiday Mons. Entry £1 (£2 before 8.30am).

Wood Green

The 65 pitches at this small and focused boot sale sell an interesting mix of new and secondhand.

New River Sports Centre, White Hart Lane, N22 5QW (01992 468 619). Open from 6am Fri. Entry free.

'Crash course

After gatecrashing her way around the capital, Serena Kutchinsky imparts some useful advice.

The best things in life may be free, but that doesn't necessarily make them easy. You don't always have to work hard to unlock London's freebie potential, but if your lust for the party lifestyle is bigger than your bank balance (and assuming you don't have celebrity parents and you're not an *X Factor* finalist) you will need to become an expert in the art of the blag. So what does it take to live it up for free in London? Apart from a degree of shamelessness, nerves of steel and some forward planning, of course. Having devised a gruelling 'crashing schedule with a friend – complete with multiple costume changes and myriad props – we put my blagging skills to the test over the course of a long weekend.

After a few frantic phone calls and a decent bout of research, we were ready to hit the party scene. Any good gatecrasher knows that the weekend starts on Thursday night, and we decided to kick things off on a cultural high note, venturing into the heart of the East End art scene for an evening of gallery hopping, high-brow mingling and, more to the point, gratis boozing. Our first port of call was Bethnal Green's Vyner Street, scene of multiple exhibition openings on the first Thursday of each month.

Dressed in my best art-school threads (blaggers, take note: heels are a no-no on cobbled East End streets) and with a sizeable bag slung over my shoulder (useful for stockpiling free beers), I approached the Vilma Gold gallery (7729 9888, www.vilmagold.com). Imperceptible, apart from the hipster crowd smirting (that's smoking and flirting) outside, Vilma Gold is the epitome of warehouse chic: concrete floors, video art illuminating blank white walls and two large buckets brimming with ice and beer. Bingo!

Aware of the need to look like we belonged – and to gain crucial information on which gallery to visit next – we engaged two young dandies in conversation. We'd done some research on the featured artists and, after wowing them with our art speak, were ready to move on to Fred (8981 2987, www.fred-london.com), an enticingly hard-to-find gallery at the back of what looks like a car park. As well as some outlandish, cartoon-style

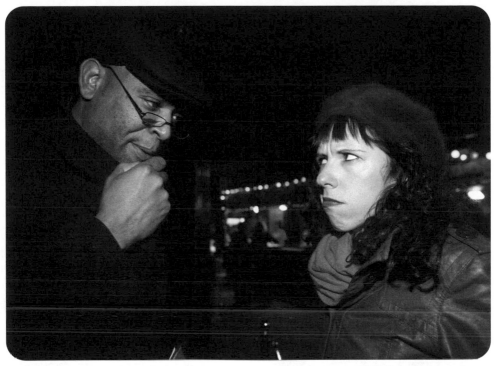

drawings, we were happy to find not just wine but interesting looking cocktails on offer. After a few more drinks with my new best friends ('key players on the curator scene', they assured us), it was time to tackle the after-party. Given that artists generally have limited (if any) funds, this usually consists of piling into the nearest pub – in this case the Victory, also on Vyner Street. But by midnight I'd exhausted my stash of smuggled beer and was ready to depart, happy in the knowledge of a mission accomplished: I'd had a great evening, met new people, not spent a penny – and even learnt a bit about art.

Several hours and a few Nurofen later, we were just about ready for Friday night's challenge. The plan was to blag our way into a sell-out gig posing as makers of a forthcoming documentary about the nation's hottest new bands. Sticking to the plot, we'd chosen the hyped Foals gig at the Brixton Academy (211 Stockwell Road, SW9 9SL, 7771 3000, www.o2academybrixton.co.uk), a hip band whose distinctive dance-punk was making serious waves. (If you're a novice blagger, it's wise to pick a mid-range band for your first attempt; security is more relaxed and success will give you the confidence you need to move on to bigger and better blags.)

After a hectic afternoon spent convincing the promoter to let us film, we rocked up at the venue a few hours before doors opened dressed in regulation leather jackets, jeans, trainers and sunglasses. Thankfully a huge camera is not a necessity these days: lots of filming is done on tiny digital models. We headed straight for the stage door, located the band's manager and moments later – after proudly clipping our 'Access All Areas' passes to our jackets – we were in.

Backstage is not exactly glamorous at the Academy, but it was still heaving with groupies and assorted hangers-on. The band even popped open a bottle of pre-gig bubbly. Invites to the after-party at nearby Plan B (418 Brixton Road, SW9 7AY, 0870 116 5421, www.plan-brixton.co.uk) were handed out and we headed off to do some more 'filming' in the pit at the front of the stage, basking in the warm glow of a successfully handled gatecrash.

Saturday night was always going to be the big one. We started early with a free makeover courtesy of Selfridges (0800 123 400, www.selfridges.co.uk). A bit of advance research was required to work out which counters have waiting lists and which ones expect you to buy products afterwards. Playing it safe, we went for Bobbi Brown, where there was plenty of availability and lots of products for under a tenner. Despite looking slightly like a cross between the Pussycat Dolls and Blondie, we were nevertheless impressed with the results. Our first evening stop was a lively Thai buffet in Soho where both of us were regulars. We'd rung up and booked a table for a few mates, stressing the fact it was an important occasion (my 25th birthday, of course). As soon as we walked in, the manager swooped on us letting the whole place know it was my birthday. Several free shots of a strong Thai whisky followed, plus a rather embarrassing rendition of 'Happy Birthday' from the entire restaurant. Feeling in danger of whisky overload, we quickly paid our super-cheap bill and headed off into the Soho night.

Our next stop was meant to be swanky members' bar, 5 Cavendish Square (0870 780 8164, www.no5ltd.com), into which mere mortals are allowed for free on Saturdays before 11pm. However, here we got derailed. First there was the hen party in a pink limo, who caught sight of my massive birthday badge and insisted we climb in for a glass of bubbly. And then, hooked on the idea of the improvised challenge, we decided that 'crashing our way into Candy Bar, at that point Soho's most famous lesbian bar, was a good plan. Apparently, a few famous 'drag kings' were hosting a club night and there were some celebrities inside. Unable to believe our luck, we pulled out the record bag we'd been carting around. I walked confidently up to the butch bouncer and informed her I was there to play a fill-in DJ set.

Everything was going swimmingly until the manager appeared. 'So,' she said, peering down at me, 'you're here to play with DJ Wicked?' 'That's right,' I said, playing it cool. 'He asked me to help out at the last minute.' Her look of irritation turned to one of total outrage as she slowly repeated my words, 'He did, did he? What kind of bar do you think this is? DJ Wicked is a woman.' Red-faced and stuttering, clutching the record bag to my chest for protection, I knew the game was up and we legged it.

Reaching the climax of our blagathon, our final destination was hip club night Secretsundaze (www.secretsundaze.net), a mecca for East End trendies, music bods and fashionistas. Bundling into the back of a cab, we engaged in a hasty costume change. Pulling on burlesque-style black bob wigs, futuristic techno clothing and a few carefully placed tattoos, we were ready to roll. The plan was simple: I would impersonate world-famous DJ Miss Kittin (I've been told I look a bit like her anyway) and a mate would pose as my assistant. We would pull up at the club, strut out of the cab with hefty-looking record bags, introduce ourselves and walk straight into the club. Give or take the odd accent slip from me, we played our respective parts to perfection. Not only did it work, but I even had to give the bouncer my autograph. Safely inside, we ditched the wigs, checked the now empty bags into the cloakroom and danced the night away.

Free fun is there for the taking in London – you just have to know where to look and what to say when you get there. We might not have managed to score any goodie bags, but we'd had a few seriously fun-packed nights: we'd partied everywhere from art galleries to cool clubs, paid for very little and lived dangerously on our blagging wits.

'Give or take the odd accent slip from me, we played our parts to perfection – I even had to give the bouncer my autograph.'

485 Go down to the docks for the river view on London history

Nowhere in the capital gives you a better sense of the importance of the Thames to the evolution of London than this museum. Set in a 200-year-old warehouse (itself a Grade I-listed survivor of the city's extensive trading history), this isn't a place that ducks the big subjects: witness the thought-provoking 'London, Sugar and Slavery', examining the city's involvement in the transatlantic slave trade, and the hard-hitting 'Docklands at War' section. Over several storeys, models, videos, artefacts and reconstructions tell the story of the river from Roman times through to the commercial redevelopment of the docks in the 1980s and 1990s. The impressive exhibits include a full-scale, walk-through mock-up of a working quay and of a 'Sailortown' back alley. The £5 entry fee, which unusually allows readmission at any time for a full year, leaves exactly enough change from your tenner for you to arrive by boat – see www.thamesclippers.co.uk for details of sailing times to Canary Wharf.

Museum of London Docklands *No.1 Warehouse, West India Quay, Hertsmere Road, E14 4AL (0870 444 3851/www.museumindocklands.org.uk).*

486-488
Split your sides without breaking the bank

London is a superb place to see live comedy – even when you want enough money left over from £10 to buy yourself a drink. In the big, roundhouse setting of Banana Cabaret (the Bedford, 77 Bedford Hill, SW12 9HD, 8673 8904, www.bananacabaret.co.uk), prices come down to a brilliant £3 every Tuesday. This is the night for new acts: you might even spot the next Harry Hill, Eddie Izzard or Marcus Brigstock, all of whom have played at this popular club.

Purpose-built Shoreditch venue the Comedy Café (66-68 Rivington Street, EC2A 3AY, 7739 5706, www.comedycafe.co.uk) has free open mic nights on Wednesday each week. You'll also be able to afford the £8 entry for a Thursday night, although your drink would have to be either a half or a £1.20 cuppa. On the other hand, you get three or four stand-ups of the calibre of Dan Antopolski and Friday Night Project regular Rob Rouse.

Finally, Downstairs at the King's Head (2 Crouch End Hill, N8 8AA, 8340 1028, www.downstairsatthekingshead.com) was a club was started by Pete Grahame in 1981, when the alternative comedy scene was just beginning. It remains a favourite with big-name comedians for trying out new material, but has always showcased new talent too: the long-running Thursday 'try-out night' (£4) – where up to 16 new acts take the mic each week – kick-started the careers of Mark Lamarr and Eddie Izzard. Even a Saturday night here only sets you back £9; Tuesdays and Sundays are even cheaper.

489-495

Hound Holmes and Watson through the London streets

It's got to be one of London's most agreeable cheap thrills, emerging from the Baker Street Tube only to bump into a certain long-striding, meerschaum-sucking, deerstalker-sporting figure drumming up business for his detective agency… his gentleman's lodgings… OK, the eponymous museum at 'The World's Most Famous Address' (221b Baker Street, NW1 6XE, 7935 8866, www.sherlock-holmes.co.uk, £6). The whole point about Sir Arthur Conan Doyle's appropriation of 221b Baker Street was that the address didn't exist at that time, but never mind, the study here is now a loving recreation and a splendid photo-op for fans of Victoriana: the bedrooms are scattered with appropriate personal effects, make-believe papers and other paraphernalia, while waxwork tableaux depict scenes from the stories.

Near Baker Street, 2 Devonshire Place (the site of Conan Doyle's medical practice) and 9 Queen Anne Street (where Dr Watson roomed) are essential destinations for fans, and, if you can find a Hansom cab and a foggy night, it's still possible to recreate the route of Holmes and the murderous Moriarty – from *The Memoirs of Sherlock Holmes*: 'As I passed the corner which leads from Bentinck Street on to the Welbeck Street crossing, a two-horse van furiously driven whizzed round and was on me like a flash. I sprang for the footpath and saved myself by the fraction of a second… I kept to the pavement after that, Watson, but as I walked down Vere Street a brick came down from the roof of one of the houses and was shattered to fragments at my feet…'.

Further south, a walk along the Strand can take in 12 Burleigh Street, once the offices of the *Strand Magazine* and where many of the stories were first published. Then there's the site of the original Scotland Yard and the Sherlock Holmes pub (10-11 Northumberland Street, WC2N 5DA, 7930 2644) – formerly the Northumberland Hotel, which appears in *The Hound of the Baskervilles*. Upstairs, a waxwork Holmes awaits, but the main attraction is another replica of Holmes and Watson's sitting room and study.

Spot the fake houses

Strolling past the grand stuccoed terraces in Bayswater's Leinster Gardens, you might notice the windows of nos.23 and 24 look a little strange. That's because they're trompe l'oeil works of plaster and paint. Walk round the back, to Porchester Terrace, and you can see the great iron struts that support the film-set façade of these fake houses – and you might catch a District Line tube thundering through the 'garden' below.

497 Brush up on anarcho-syndicalism

Hidden down Angel Alley, just off Whitechapel High Street by the art gallery, you'll find the headquarters of Freedom Press and Bookshop, England's oldest anarchist publishers. Pass the mural of prominent anarcho rabble-rousers and head up the stairs into a cosy den of books and pamphlets that cover history without government, sex without rules and struggle without end. They also sell cool posters and T shirts.

Freedom Press & Bookshop *Angel Alley, 84b Whitechapel High Street, E1 7QX (7247 9249/www.freedompress.org.uk).*

498

Shoot a few hoops

London 2012 is giving a real boost to basketball in the capital, with more players getting involved at all levels, and the National Basketball Association now making regular trips across the Atlantic from the States to showcase the sport's biggest names. If you want to play competitively yourself, www.basketballinlondon.co.uk is a useful resource and has details of the London Metropolitan League.

499

Jump on board the Deptford Project

Housed in converted 1960s South East Trains rolling stock, the Deptford Project is not your typical eaterie and the menu is considerably better than you'd find on most trains. Inside, a brightly painted table spans the length of the carriage, and cheery decking out front adds to the laid-back, arty vibe. The café is part of a regeneration plan for the area that includes a creative industries market and various art galleries and pop-up installations – the website details future plans. The food on offer here is unpretentious and comforting, ranging from muffins and free-range eggs (laid by the Project's own chickens) for breakfast to light lunchtime salads and satisfyingly spiced curries. A bright spark in a newly rejuvenated neighbourhood.

Deptford Project *121-123 Deptford High Street, SE8 4NS (07525 351 656/ www.thedeptfordproject.com).*

500

See the birthplace of a very special relationship

Scientist, diplomat, philosopher, inventor and Founding Father of the United States, Benjamin Franklin lived behind the doors of this grand, Grade I-listed Craven Street house between 1757 and 1775. As much of his time here was spent brokering peace between Britain and America on the eve of the American Revolution, it is considered to be the site of London's first *de facto* US embassy; the birthplace, then, of our enduring transatlantic love-in. It is also Franklin's only home to have survived. The 45-minute tours give a strong sense of the scale of the man's myriad achievements, as well as the times in which he lived.
Benjamin Franklin House *36 Craven Street, WC2N 5NF (7839 2006/www.benjamin franklinhouse.org).*

501

Look round the stationery museum (but choose carefully if you want to take something home)

Smythson's is an ancient London shop that doubles as a museum. In it, you'll find upmarket items such as original Smythson diaries dating from 1902, old engraved die stamps, stationery used by a Maharajah, condolence books opened for John F Kennedy and Princess Grace of Monaco, old Christmas cards and wartime telegrams. The Queen is a fan of Smythson writing paper, but if you feel inclined to buy something be warned that this is a no-price-tag kind of place: costing a cool £9, one of the gilt pencils is probably your best bet.
Smythson *40 New Bond Street, W1S 2DE (7629 8558/www.smythson.co.uk).*

502 *Join London's Rath Yatra*

Spiritual bliss is the promise of this spectacular annual Carnival of Chariots (www.ratha yatra.co.uk), a day-long parade organised by the capital's supernal street noiseniks the International Society for Krishna Consciousness. In celebration of the Hindu god Krishna's return to his home, three brightly decorated wooden chariots bearing waving, toga-clad Hindu deities ('who come out of the temple to freely distribute their loving glances to anyone and everyone') are carried by hand (quite a feat in itself) by the chanting faithful from Hyde Park to Trafalgar Square. Here, among the street performers and stalls selling crafts and books, a free vegetarian *prasadam* (a gracious gift) is available to all.

503 *Get naked – and rich*

If you're an exhibitionist, the tendency will pay off at the Bare Facts workshop, designed for aspiring life models. You won't make Jordan-scale money (the fee is £12.50 an hour), but there are worse things you could do with your time… You'll be assessed for basic aptitude and blush factor, and – if you are deemed to be up to scratch (most are) – you can join as a life model, then watch the cash roll in. You get to test your inhibitions on Wednesday evenings at the life-drawing classes held at the Islington Arts Factory (2 Parkhurst Road, N7 0SF, 7607 0561, www.islingtonartsfactory.org.uk); should you wish to draw rather than doff your pants, classes cost £10 a session.

504 *Take in the views from Severndroog*

Hidden away high in Oxleas Wood in Eltham is the 18th-century folly, Severndroog Castle (www.severndroogcastle.org.uk). It's derelict and usually closed to the public, but you can visit during Open House weekend (*see p21*). From the top, on a clear day, there are views out over seven counties.

505-514

Eat more for less

Cyrus Shahrad, editor of Time Out's Cheap Eats guide, spills the beans on his super-cheap favourites.

Assa

The food at Korean restaurant Assa is as authentic as it is delicious. A set lunch of *bibimbap* (£4.50) comprises a hot bowl of rice with assorted vegetables, an unexpected helping of minced beef and a raw egg yolk, the flavours melding deliciously as the contents cook in the container. A range of hotpots cater to couples sharing – try the rich chilli kick of the bubbling broth of beef and *kimchee* (fermented, seasoned vegetables).

53 St Giles High Street, WC2H 8LH (7240 8256).

Canela

Baozi Inn

The decor – Beijing, circa 1952 – favours kitsch over culture, but the street snacks served here are 100 per cent authentic. The eponymous *baozi* (steamed bread filled with pork or vegetables) are typical of northern China and can be accompanied by a bowl of slightly sweet millet porridge to make up an inexpensive meal (£1.20). Otherwise, try spicy *dan dan* noodles (£4.50), handmade on the premises daily.
25 Newport Court, WC2H 7JS (7287 6877).

Benito's Hat

London's Tex-Mex eateries are currently ten a peso, but this one, its bright lime walls overlooking sturdy wooden tables, serves some of the best burritos in town – a snip at just £5. A hearty meal in themselves, the soft, floury tortillas come loaded with slow-cooked pork (or chicken or beef), fiery salsa brava, refried or black beans and avocado leaves.
56 Goodge Street, W1T 4NB (7637 3732/ www.benitos-hat.co.uk).

Bonnington Café

This vegetarian restaurant is community-run and uncommonly friendly. Local cooks take turns at the helm each night, so the cuisine – and therefore the standard – varies wildly. The prices, however, are consistent, and low: £10 for three courses. Mains might include penne panna, packed with porcini mushrooms or comforting tomato nut roast, accompanied by a dressed bean salad. Help yourself to crockery and cutlery, and note that Thursday is vegan night.
11 Vauxhall Grove, SW8 1TD (no phone/ www.bonningtoncafe.co.uk).

Canela

The menu at this café-bar just off Seven Dials ranges from Brazilian favourites – chewy cheese bread (£1.50) and rich, filling *feijoada* (meat and black bean stew served with rice and manioc flour, £5.90) – to Portuguese staples like *bacalhau* (salt cod, £6.50) and creamy *pasteis de nata* (custard tarts, £1.80). There are also other good, not quite so exotic, offerings – lasagne or cheesecake, say. Don't ignore the drinks: refreshing caipirinhas, mojitos and Brazilian *açaí* fruit juice.
33 Earlham Street, WC2H 9LS (7240 6926/ www.canelacafe.com).

Hummus Bros

The formula at this Soho canteen-style café/ takeaway is to serve creamy, flavoursome houmous as a base for a selection of toppings, which you scoop up with warm, fluffy pitta bread (£4-£7.70). Choose from fresh-tasting, zingy guacamole, stewed mushrooms, slow-cooked beef and fava beans, and round it all off with a brownie, baklava or *malabi* (a milk-based dessert with date honey) if you still have enough room.
88 Wardour Street, W1F OTH (7734 1311/www.hbros.co.uk).

Little Bay

The menu at this funky modern European restaurant takes in burgers, duck breast, plenty of fish and, in the vegetarian dishes, a lot of goat's cheese. The chips, fried in goose fat, are terrific. Starters are all £2.25 at lunch or £3.25 in the evening; mains range from £6.45 to £8.45.
171 Farringdon Road, EC1R 3AL (7278 1234/ www.little-bay.co.uk).

Ooze

Here risotto is the USP, though there are alternatives: tiger prawns with garlic, chilli and *trebbiano* (a type of grape) to start, say, or pasta of the day. Risottos, both hearty (ribeye with sweet onions, rocket and montepulciano), and light (with clams or chilli and garlic), come in two sizes – the larger one starting at £8.50.
62 Goodge Street, W1T 4NE (7436 9441/ www.ooze.biz).

Rasa Express

This Keralan curry house is legendary among local office workers. A chicken biryani, say – comes with chapati, a chickpea curry, a mild mung bean curry, a dry lentil side and a sweet rice pudding – for £3.50 or £4.
5 Rathbone Street, W1T 1NQ (7637 0222/www.rasarestaurants.com).

World Food Café

In the hippy headquarters that is Neal's Yard World Food Café's food is stomach-filling stuff: root vegetable and chickpea masala with a mound of brown rice, for example, or a Turkish meze plate with aubergines, tabouleh and pitta bread costing £7.95. Closed in the evenings.
1st floor, 14 Neal's Yard, WC2H 9DP (7379 0298).

515-519

Play games in the pub

The Shipwrights Arms (88 Tooley Street, SE1 2TF, 7378 1486) really pushes the boat out with its free Wednesday board games night, run from about 6pm to 11.30pm by the Swiggers Games Club. As well as the usual Monopoly-type offerings, you'll have the opportunity to play the likes of Civilization, Diplomacy, Escape from Colditz, Family Business, History of the World, Settlers of Catan, Antike, Caylus, Louis XIV, Power Grid, Puerto Rico, Shadows over Camelot and Zepter Von Zavandor. If you'd rather stick to the classics, though, there are loads of pubs that can oblige. We particularly like the Three Kings of Clerkenwell (7 Clerkenwell Close, EC1R 0DY, 7253 0483), the Big Chill House (257-259 Pentonville Road, N1 9NL, 7427 2540, www.bigchill.net) and the Flower Pot (128 Wood Street, E17 3HX, 8520 3600), which all have chess, draughts and dominos. The Westbourne (101 Westbourne Villas, W2 5ED, 7221 1332) ups the ante with backgammon, Cluedo, Monopoly and a card version of Deal or No Deal.

520

Remember the Royal Opera House

Go to the opera – or ballet – for a tenner? Certainly. First off, you can attend the Royal Opera House's excellent weekly series of free lunchtime concerts. Starting at 1pm and always held on the premises (either in the splendidly baroque Crush Room or the Linbury Studio (*see also p42*), the music ranges from Debussy to Wagner. You must collect your tickets from the box office by 12.40pm, but a limited number can be reserved online a few days in advance. Check the website for the current programme.

Also gratis is the annual Ignite festival (www.roh.org.uk/deloitteignite), which began auspiciously in 2008 with a madcap array of art installations, dance performances, concerts and film screening events spread throughout the opera house. Whatever the programme in the coming years, the opportunity to wander freely about various grand rooms and the outdoor terrace is priceless, even if they are obliged to search your bag as you enter.

You will have to pay for the traditional tea dances, held on monthly Friday afternoons since 2001 in the airy Paul Hamlyn Hall, but your £10 ticket buys you the opportunity to waltz and cha-cha-cha to the exemplary Royal Opera House Dance Band. No tuition is given (unless one of the friendly dancers takes pity on you), but you do get free tea and biscuits. Be sure to book ahead; for forthcoming dates, see the website.

And, perhaps most surprising of all, you can get into a proper, 24-carat opera for less than £10. Honest. Restricted-view seats start from £7, and while you might be perched rather uncomfortably in the gods, you can console yourself with the thought that some fellow auditors will have paid as much as £195 to see the same glorious show. Tee hee.

Royal Opera House *Bow Street, WC2E 9DD (7304 4000/www.roh.org.uk).*

521

Watch the Great Gorilla Run

This annual charity fundraising event gets runners dressed up as gorillas to pound the pavements in an effort to raise awareness and money for the endangered gorillas of Rwanda. The 7km circular route begins and ends (amusingly) at Mincing Lane, passing Tate Modern and Tower Bridge, and the 'run' is all about having fun, not who's fastest. Participants are encouraged to customise their outfits, so you'll see anything from power-pramming mums with their little monkeys dressed in furry suits to hirsuite blondes in bikinis – even the route marshals are in fancy dress. If you wanted to take part, the registration fee would be £75 (including a complimentary gorilla suit and fundraising support), but you can always watch for free and donate a voluntary £10 to the cause. For more details, see www.greatgorillas.org/london.

522 *Get bowled over*

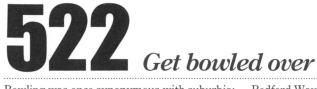

Bowling was once synonymous with suburbia: alleys were situated in bland retail parks, the decor comprised blaring arcade machines and sticky floors, and sustenance peaked at the level of chicken nuggets and fluorescent blue 'raspberry' slushies that surely came from no earthly fruit. Even then, the bowling always seemed to take a back seat to birthday parties and boy-girl groups of randy teenagers. No longer. 'Boutique bowling alleys' – darker, less sticky, with bars serving cocktails and no kids – are flourishing in the US. And now, in the wake of Britain's current cultural obsession with retro Americana, Londoners can score strikes in properly cool venues: Bloomsbury Bowling Lanes (basement of Tavistock Hotel, Bedford Way, WC1H 9EH, 7183 1979 www.bloomsburybowling.com) and the burgeoning All Star Lanes minichain (www.allstarlanes.co.uk), with locations in Bloomsbury (Victoria House, Bloomsbury Place, WC1B 4DA, 7025 2676), Bayswater (Whiteleys, W2 4YQ, 7313 8363) and Brick Lane (Old Truman Brewery, 87 Brick Lane, E1 6QR, 7422 8370). All Star is the pricier option (£8.50 a game at peak times), but each of the venues comes with a swanky diner and cocktail bar. Bloomsbury Bowling Lanes has a scruffier bar and diner, but it's better value at £7.50 per game during peak time (even cheaper during the day from Monday to Wednesday), and the worn booths lend the place a certain old-school cred.

Bloomsbury Bowling Lanes

523-539

Take a Sunday City architecture stroll...

Traffic-light Sundays are perfect for architectural rambles in the City. Construction has gone into overdrive in recent years and there are interesting buildings popping up all over the place. Here's a jaunt round some of the less obvious new buildings (and a few of the older ones), all of them only a short distance from St Paul's Cathedral.

Start at one of the City's most striking new structures: the very pointed City of London Information Centre beside St Paul's (2007, Make Architects) then head down towards the Millennium Bridge approach. At 101 Queen Victoria Street, you'll find Sheppard Robson's elegant, light-filled Salvation Army HQ (2005), with its 'floating' ground floor supported by splayed white-painted legs. Next, go east up Queen Victoria Street and cross over to the dark brick Renaissance-style palazzo of Bracken House (1959, Albert Richardson), sitting on its red sandstone plinth at nos.110-112. Turn left beside it to see the Michael Hopkins 1992 revamp that gutted the building. Outrageous vandalism or fabulous update? You decide, but while you are here, take a look at the old Cannon Street frontage with its wonderful Zodiac clock.

Cross Cannon Street and look back at the flirty concrete arcades of no. 30 (1973-77, Whinney, Son & Austen Hall) – very 1970s, but also suddenly looking very now. Turn north up narrow Bow Lane and then right along Watling Street to the corner of Queen Street. You're now at Peter Foggo's HSBC Building, with its bluish-green chemically created patina and external window grilles. From here, go north up Queen Street, turn left on to Cheapside, right on to Wood Street and then right again at Gresham Street. Kohn, Pedersen, Fox's 20 Gresham Street (2008) is on your right, as is Norman Foster's wavy-fronted 10 Gresham Street (2003). On the left, the cantilevered 'hand-stitched' frontage of Nicholas Grimshaw's 25 Gresham Street extends over the trees of an old churchyard.

Heading west on Gresham Street, turn right up Noble Street. Take another right on to Oat Lane and straight through the light-grabbing scoop of Norman Foster's 100 Wood Street (2000) to one of the City's most fascinating assemblages of architectural heavy-hitters. Plonked in the middle of the road is the surviving tower of Wren's St Alban's church – one of two bombed-out Wren churches in the City that are now private residences – and on the east side of Wood Street is McMorran & Whitby's police station (1966), a compelling pale-stone riff on a Renaissance palazzo (compare with Bracken House). Beside Foster's building is Richard Rogers' 88 Wood Street (2000), while across the road is the back of Eric Parry's coolly elegant 5 Aldermanbury Square (2007) with its silvery external steel frame and classical entasis tapering towards the roof. The street ends with the very 1980s, postmodern bombast of Terry Farrell's Alban Gate at 125 London Wall.

Cut through Parry's building to see its Aldermanbury Square frontage, then return by continuing along the side of 88 Wood Street, allowing you to see the full extent of Rogers' airy masterpiece, sheathed in glittering Saint-Gobain glass. Now you get a splendid view of yet another Foster building: curvy, deco-ish 1 London Wall (2003). Turn left down Noble Street again and along Foster Lane, ending at Michael Aukett's 150 Cheapside (2008) and Jean Nouvel's huge 1 New Change project (2010).

540

...then see the Lloyd's building lit up at night

Time your day tour of the city's buildings carefully so that you're heading east along Cornhill to 1 Lime Street just as the lights are coming on. The Lloyd's of London building is still the city's best-known example of high-tech architecture, its commercial and industrial aesthetics combined by Richard Rogers to create what is arguably one of the most significant British buildings produced since World War II. Mocked on completion, the 'inside out' building still manages to outclass much of the more recent, much vaunted competition. You can usually see the inside of the building during Open House weekend (*see p21*), but get there early and expect to queue.
Lloyd's of London *1 Lime Street, EC3M 7HA (7327 6586/www.lloyds.com).*

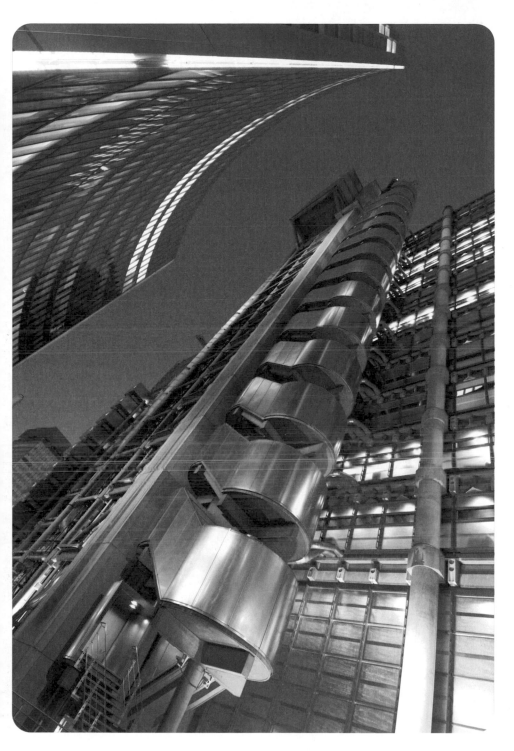

541

Play bike polo
The rules are simple: in teams of three, put the ball in your opponents' net with a wooden mallet while mounted on a bike. The first to five goals wins. Mallets and balls are provided so you need only bring a bike. See www.london bikepolo.wordpress.com for details.

542 Experience peace and reconciliation at St Ethelburga's

A place for people of all faiths and none, St Ethelburga's Centre for Reconciliation and Peace is a tiny spiritual oasis in the heart of the City. Step through an unassuming medieval door on Bishopsgate and you'll find yourself in an interfaith prayer tent before you enter the building proper. A church dedicated to St Ethelburga stood here for nearly 800 years before it was destroyed by an IRA bomb in 1993. Rebuilt as a centre for reconciliation and peace – it is no longer a parish church – it hosts lectures and discussion evenings on conflict and faith, as well as concerts ranging from flamenco to Afro-Caribbean music, and nights of African storytelling. One recent session brought together dissidents and secret police from South Africa; another looked at violence and the sacred in film. And if it's old-fashioned spirituality you're after (or simply a break from urban life), there are several free weekly meditation sessions, including one every Friday lunchtime.

St Ethelburga's Centre for Reconciliation and Peace 78 Bishopsgate, EC2N 4AG (7496 1610/www.stethelburgas.org).

543 Don't get Court!

Marlborough Street Magistrates Court, opposite the northern end of Carnaby Street, was once infamous for cases involving unfortunate notables such as Oscar Wilde, Christine Keeler and the *International Times* obscenity defendants. It was drugs offences that saw the Rolling Stones, Johnny Rotten and Lionel Bart kept here under lock and key, while John Lennon was pulled up for exhibiting a little too much of Yoko Ono in his sketches on show at the London Art Gallery. Now, at the Courthouse Hotel, you can enjoy Thai fusion nosh in number one court, and a drink in the cells – complete with hard bunk, 'ice-bucket' lav and warden's peephole in the lead door.

Courthouse Hotel 19-21 Great Marlborough Street, W1F 7HL (7297 5555/www.courthouse-hotel.com).

544 Hear classics in the City's halls

The City of London Festival (7796 4949, www.colf.org) is a well-established favourite, both for music fans and those intrigued by the Square Mile's many historic buildings. A huge range of concerts take place from late June to early July each year, in some of the finest churches and halls in the Square Mile. While concerts in the grander venues (among them St Paul's Cathedral) are likely to be ticketed, many of those held in the atmospheric City churches and livery halls are absolutely free. The programme is mostly traditional classical music, but there are also more unusual offerings from the worlds of jazz, dance, visual art, literature and theatre.

545 Visit the address Richard Rogers must wish he could have

One Hyde Park – the name of Rogers Stirk Harbour & Partners' superprime, exquisitely located block of duplex flats – is pretty impressive, but how much do you think the architect would have paid to get his hands on No.1 London instead? You and those Russian oligarch flat owners have equal rights to visit the latter: stump up £5.40 and step right in. Right on Hyde Park Corner, Apsley House was called No.1 London back when Kensington was still a village, since it was the first building you reached on the way into the city. For more than three decades it was the Duke of Wellington's residence (a Goya portrait of the Iron Duke is among the treasures on display) and parts of the building – strictly out of bounds to the public – are occupied by his descendants to this day.

Apsley House 149 Piccadilly, W1J 7NT (7499 5676/www.english-heritage.org.uk).

546 *Get slammed, the literary way*

You think you know all about book readings? The silences, the shuffling feet and smothered coughs, the pitiful bribe of precisely two wineboxes – one lukewarm white and one ice-cold red. Well, you've clearly never been to Book Slam (www.bookslam.com). This is a monthly musical-literary club night for which you're best advised to book tickets well in advance. Still organised by co-founder Patrick Neate – now with Elliot Jack and Angela Robertson of funky Scottish publishers Canongate – it is most often to be found at Ladbroke Grove's 12 Acklam Road. Tickets are only £6 in advance (£8 on the door), for which meagre sum you might get lucky and see authors like Irvine Welsh, Zadie Smith or Jonathan Safran Focr, supported by musicians such as Kate Nash or Soweto Kinch.

Book Slam

547 *Get near to the neolothic*

Ask most East Enders if it is possible to walk the ramparts of an iron age hill fort in their manor, and they'd most likely suggest you were having a proper larf. Head out to Epping Forest on the further reaches of the Central Line, though, and you'll find two of them – the huge wooded circles of Ambresbury Banks and Loughton Camp. A natural spring rises in the former, and both can be cut off by their broad moats in rainy weather. An awesome discovery, half an hour from Oxford Street. Visit www.eppingforestdc.gov.uk for details of how to get to them.

548 *Add a string to your bow at the Royal Academy of Music*

At the RAM's free museum, you can inspect hundreds of different musical instruments, including over 200 violins and a number of pianos dating back to the early 19th century, as well as see regular temporary exhibitions.
Royal Academy of Music *Marylebone Road, NW1 5HT (7873 7373/www.ram.ac.uk/ facilitiesandcollections).*

549-554

Lesley Lewis, owner of the French House

I asked my granddaughter what she would like to do in London if she could do anything and she said, 'Feed the ducks'. So I took her to St James's Park and it was wonderful. Then we watched the changing of the guard at Buckingham Palace and walked down the Mall.

The French House have a cricket team and every summer we go and watch them play on Parliament Hill, on Hampstead Heath, NW3.

Annie, one of the barmaids here, suggested walking along the river path from Hammersmith and having a beer outside the Dove (19 Upper Mall, W6 9TA, 8748 5405) then continuing on to Richmond Park.

Danny, another barmaid, recommends a comedy night called Old Rope at the Phoenix Bar on Cavendish Square (37 Cavendish Square, W1G 0PP, 7493 8003, www.phoenixcavendish square.co.uk). It's only a fiver to get in and you get to see top-notch comedians trying out their new material. If the new stuff doesn't work and they have to resort to using tried and tested gags then they have to hold on to an old rope as punishment.

You can sometimes watch the dress rehearsals at English National Opera (London Coliseum, St Martin's Lane, WC2N 4ES, 0871 911 0200, www.eno.org) but you have to grab tickets because they disappear quickly. **The Soho Festival (www.thesoho society.org.uk), held every July, is wonderfully old fashioned. It takes place in the gardens of St Anne's Square off Wardour Street and it's like a village fête for the Soho community; so you'll find everything from drag acts to Chinese food to live bands.**

555

Admire an original Crapper

You can see the founder Methodist John Wesley's nightcap, preaching gown and personal experimental electric-shock machine in his austere home, but if you head downstairs (to the right) you'll see some of the finest public toilets in London, built in 1899 by Sir Thomas Crapper. Some parts are now replica, but the cisterns are original.

John Wesley's House & Museum of Methodism *Wesley's Chapel, 49 City Road, EC1Y 1AU (7253 2262/www.wesleyschapel.org.uk).*

556

Look up at Gresham's grasshopper

Spend less time staring at the pavement and look up! You'll be endlessly rewarded. We're particularly fond of the stone relief grasshopper at the top corner of the Royal Exchange, EC3. It's the family symbol of Thomas Gresham, pioneering Tudor financier, sometime arms smuggler and founder of the original version of this building. Another grasshopper makes the Exchange's weathervane, and a third hangs from a wall on nearby Lombard Street.

557

Drink vodka in a Polish bar

More often than not bars in the West End merely nod towards a theme, but Bar Polski (1 Little Turnstile Street, WC1V 7DX, 7831 9679) is the real deal. Polish sausages, bigos, pierogis and Polish sweetmeats are available all day, but by the evening all anyone's seriously interested in are the vodkas. Divided into 'dry and interesting', 'clean and clear', 'kosher' and 'nice and sweet' (try the Lancut rose petal) – they're here by the vatload. Most cost around £2.50 a shot.

558 Visit Dulwich Picture Gallery

Sir John Soane's neo-classical, purpose-built art gallery (the first of its kind) has been described as the most beautiful art gallery in the world, but its contents are worth a look too: you'll find work by Rubens, Van Dyck, Rembrandt, Gainsborough, Hogarth, Raphael, Canaletto and Reynolds, among others. It's also worth timing a visit around the series of musical evenings held in the galleries (check website for a list of events). It's a fiver's worth of admission very well spent.

Dulwich Picture Gallery *Gallery Road, SE21 7AD (8693 5254/www.dulwichpicturegallery.org.uk).*

559 Take time out at the Clockmakers' Museum

Overseen by the Worshipful Clockmakers' Company, this one-room museum houses the oldest collection of clocks, watches and sundials in existence. Among the hundreds of ticking and chiming horological pieces dating back to the 16th century is an early 19th-century gas-powered clock, and the watch Sir Edmund Hillary carried with him to the top of Everest in 1953, as well as some stunning timepieces by British modern craftsmen. Admission is free.

Clockmakers' Museum *Guildhall Library, EC2V 7HH (7332 1868/www.clockmakers.org).*

Dulwich Picture Gallery

Carry on cabaret

From supper clubs to stripping, Simone Baird explores a scene where creativity matters more than cash.

London nightlife fads come and go with breathtaking speed, but the current cabaret and burlesque revival is proving no mere flash in the pan. The past decade has been dominated by all things vintage – whether that be second-hand clothing, Lindy Hop dancing, decadent 1920s club nights or just lashings of red lipstick. But while burlesque dominated the early variety shows, the past year or so has seen an increasing number of exceptionally talented cabaret performers step up to show off. Whereas, previously, a dubious drag queen or a tired rendition of a Weimar Berlin classic – performed in fishnets and a black bowler hat, yawn – was about as good as you'd get, today London's full of cracking cabaret nights – and breathtaking performers.

And burlesque? Well, is there anyone in London who hasn't seen a pair of nipple tassels twirl? With every other London girl, and now quite a few boys, dabbling in the retro art of comedic striptease, it's a long way from the glamorous, underground scene it was back when the Whoopee Club threw parties in 2000 – but it's still popular across the capital.

Supper clubs, usually held at gorgeous venues such as Volupté (9 Norwich Street, EC4A 1EJ, 7831 1622, www.volupte-lounge. com) offer dinner and a show for a glamourous, grown-up crowd. They are great for special nights out, but, amazingly, shows on weekday evenings are often just a tenner, or less. Admittedly the 'supper' bit will cost you a lot more but at Volupté, at least, this is optional.

Swanky supper clubs aside, London's cabaret and burlesque scene has always been famous for its creativity above all else – which is good news for bargain hunters. It's less about spangle and swank, and more about discovering cracking new performers with a wide range of occasionally eye-watering skills. The chairs might be a bit shabby and the glasses your wine comes in may not match, but you'll go home thinking you've discovered a side to London – and, hell, the human body – you hadn't seen before.

Volupté

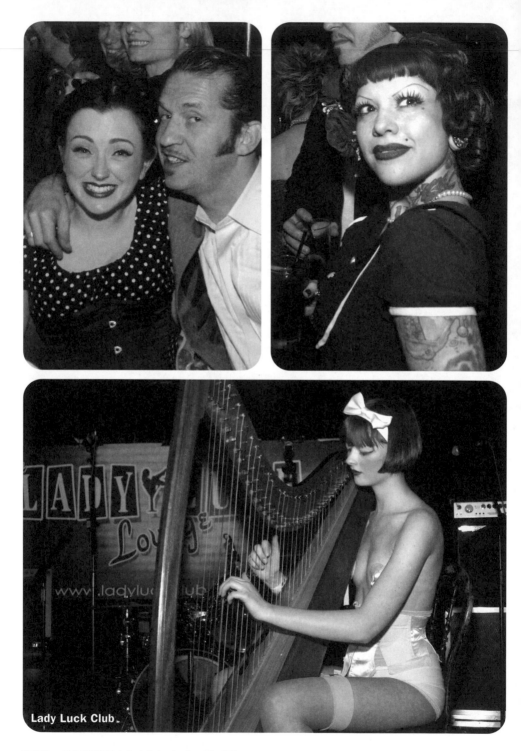

Lady Luck Club

'Absolutely,' agrees Mike Slocombe, promoter of free Brixton cabaret, music and arty happening Offline (at Jamm, Brixton Road, SW9 6LH, 7274 5537, www.urban75.org/offline). 'There are tons of interesting things going on in London for next to nothing. With a bit of effort you can end up with a social diary as hectic as Peaches Geldof's, except you won't be surrounded by idiots and be paying a fortune for booze.'

It's a scene in which creativity trumps cash every time. Down at the long-running Lady Luck (Platinum Bar, 23-25 Paul Street, EC2A 4JU, 7638 4601, www.ladyluckclub.co.uk) – DJ El Niño's famous vintage grind and burlesque night held in a three-floored strip club – the hep cats and doll-faces are not the ones in achingly expensive couture suits and Bond Street frocks. Everyone's actually looking at those who have spent time rather money putting their outfits together, finding stylish second-hand originals rather than looking like they're off to a Prohibition era-themed fancy dress party. It doesn't cost much to learn to dance, either, and your ability to charleston without kicking your dance partner in the shins will be much appreciated. Get down before 11pm and it's a tenner to get in.

At many places, it's also surprisingly easy to get in for free. Just like Steve Strange's legendary Blitz club of the early 1980s, it's all about making a highly creative effort. Nowadays, the door whores may be less draconian, but if you want to sail through without paying a penny, make sure you observe the usually themed dress code. For example, dress up for Dusty Limits' neo-Weimar cabaret spectacular at the Royal Vauxhall Tavern (372 Kennington Lane, SE11 5HY, 7820 1222, www.theroyalvauxhalltavern.co.uk) and you'll not only get in for free, but you'll receive complimentary cocktails for your effort. Of course, it's as likely to be a psychedelic mix of strange blue liquors as something more palatable, but it all helps to make whichever 'silent film' Mr Limits has chosen to start the proceedings with, more intelligible. (Picking surreal old films and then narrating over the top may be an odd way to start one's cabaret party, but it seems to work a treat every time.)

Avoid Friday and Saturday nights: midweek is when the really cool stuff happens. And more importantly for our purposes, it's much, much cheaper then.

UnderConstruction is Bistrotheque's (23-27 Wadeston Street, E2 9DR, 8983 7900, www.bistrotheque.com) showcase series of cabaret nights. Here you can catch upcoming and established acts such as Jonny Woo, Scottee and Dicke Beau trying out works-in-progress. The tables are tiny and the chairs crammed in side by side, but this small cabaret room packs a mighty punch. It costs a fiver and features some of the most forward-thinking performers you'll see this side of New York. If you want to know who next year's alternative performance superstars are going to be, this is where you'll see them.

'Avoid the rip-off clubs and soulless groovy style bars in the West End and save yourself a pocketful of cash by supporting local venues instead,' suggests Slocombe. 'Get involved! If your neighbourhood pub is struggling, why not see if you can put on a music night there yourself and feature the kind of stuff that'll get the locals rocking? If you go along to a free music night, help support the venture by spending as much dosh as you can at the bar and rewarding the acts with warm applause for their efforts.

'I doubt if we could persuade any venues to let us put on our club nights for free in the West End, and we prefer Brixton anyway. We love the fact we get such friendly, mixed crowds, with boozed up freeloaders, young hipsters, grizzled old punks, poets, rockers and 70-year-old Jamaicans getting down on the dance floor. What's more they're prepared to listen to the sometimes oddball acts we put on, and are always generous with their applause. It's a great crowd to DJ to as well because we can get away with murder!'

Finally, burlesque trailblazers Oh My God I Miss You (7739 2727, www.ohmygodimiss you.com) are behind several of the East End's most eye-popping parties. The brainchild of two artists, a carpenter and a DJ respectively, these nights are renowned for their stunning sets, cracking cabaret line-ups and flamboyant fancy dress themes. You can choose between the speakeasy-style shakedown 'Grind A Go Go', the bawdy 'Birthday Party' that's just for grown-ups or the circus-tastic 'Get In The Ring'. All events take place at Bethnal Green Working Men's Club (42-44 Pollard Row, E2 6NB, 77397170, www.workersplay time.net) and cost just £8.

567
Get digging

Annie Dare digs for victory with some of the capital's community gardening projects.

The third meeting of the Transition Town's (TT, www.transitiontowns.org) Belsize Park branch has something of the Women's Institute about it. Twenty-two of us sit in a circle in a dimly lit room in a local library; there's a marked preponderance of ladies in cardies and practical heels, and we're knitting a (somewhat symbolic) scarf together. And then there's the baking: side-tables groan with home-made fare. Yet the ambition here is somewhat loftier than the staging of a village fête.

TT's goal is to inspire local communities to prepare for the end of the 'Oil Age' and at its heart is 'local resilience' – in other words community cohesion and sustainable environmental practice, particularly with regard to food and energy use (hence tonight's hand-fired hurricane lamps, to spare the National Grid a few gigawatts). It may sound like a radical fringe but there are now 130 Transition Towns worldwide and three in London: Brixton, Kingston and Belsize Park.

Although there is some hand wringing about the urgent need to change Londoners' shopping habits and convince us all to eat and waste less – at which point those who lived through rationing 'tsk' approvingly – by and large the group seems optimistic and avoids being overly earnest. There's home-grown hooch to wash down the homemade cakes and jams and a local gent waxes wonderfully lyrical about the history of fruit trees. Nor is it all knit-one, pearl-one in the Transition movement: the Brixton branch's festive shindig was at Brixton's Dogstar bar.

Tonight's main aim is to establish a local food-growing strategy, so we're scoping out possible plots that we can take over within the borough: housing association plots, school yards, derelict gardens, and even cemeteries are the prime contenders – and World War II survivors suggest we arm-twist the Corporation of London into allowing us to turn Hampstead Heath back into vegetable plots, as happened during the 1940s' 'Dig for Victory' campaign.

Over the past few years, growing your own reached a tipping point, and actually became cool. Cool – and cheap. In a classic case of necessity being the mother of invention, as the true gravity of the recession dawned last year, London Mayor Boris Johnson and his food advisor Rosie Boycott launched Capital Growth, a scheme that will match-make 2,012 London plots with willing metropolitan gardeners so that the city can be a pin up for sustainability by the time of the Olympic Games in 2012.

It looks likely that the food-growing phenomenon will continue to expand at grassroots level too. Lucie Stephens, head of co-production at the left-wing think-tank the New Economics Foundation (NEF), sees the Transition Town movement and community food cultivation schemes across London as symptoms of a larger trend: that of local communities making positive, non-financial based interventions to prevent social breakdown. She cites Rushey Green in Catford, where a local doctor's surgery began prescribing voluntary work and community involvement to patients suffering from poor mental health largely caused by isolation.

Whatever their reasons for getting involved, it seems that Londoners are queuing up to get dirt under their fingernails. Dozens turn up for bimonthly conservation digs set up by the British Trust for Conservation Volunteers (www2.btcv.org.uk), Britain's largest practical conservation charity. At 10am on a Saturday morning I join a knot of wellied workers outside Alexandra Palace. We push wheelbarrows and lug drinking water canisters and thermoses towards a pond, and are then introduced to our tools: scythes, rakes and loppers, with which we'll prune back shrubs, clear vegetation and bring briar-strewn ditches under control. This is just one of scores of schemes BTCV runs across London, including the 15 Green Gyms in London (*see p92*), which rebranded gardening as a sport every bit as legitimate as pilates or ab crunching. There's no membership fee and you can't help feeling that brandishing shears in a park, dog walkers and joggers beaming at you as you work, certainly beats a session on the running machine.

Flash mob

Have you ever stumbled across a mass pillowfight outside Tate Modern or a rabble dancing like maniacs in the middle of a railway station? Welcome to the surreal world of the flash mob. First staged in 2003 in New York, when 100 people gathered, for no apparent reason, around an expensive rug at Macy's department store, flash mobs are bizarre spectacles that involve a crowd of strangers assembling briefly in a public space and performing some strange ritual (the second ever flash mob comprised 200 people suddenly bursting into applause for 15 seconds in the lobby of the Hyatt hotel). They may seem like a relic of the early Noughties, but London's mobs continue, coming up with new and intriguing spins on the format. Public pillowfights became particularly popular for a while and then waterfights were all the rage. For the next weird happening, visit the website.
www.geocities.com/londonmobs.

569

Get the blues at Brooks Blues Bar

An authentic version of the blues can be had at the Telegraph pub (Putney Heath, SW15 3TU, 8788 2011, www.brooksblues bar.co.uk, tickets from £10). Every Friday night Brooks Blues Bar (the name is a hangover from a previous venue) provides the only event in London dedicated to pure acoustic country blues from the 1920s, '30s and '40s – with some later Chicago blues and rhythm 'n' blues also thrown in every now and then. This is vintage stuff and you'll find a roster of musicians. The intimate venue (50 people maximum) gets lively, so book a table in advance. Doors open at 8pm and the music starts around 8.30pm.

570-579

Investigate ten of London's lesser-known squares

Bonnington Square, SW8

Incorporating a 'Pleasure Garden' designed by local residents, this bohemian pocket of Vauxhall is a community hub, complete with a vegetarian restaurant operating a chef-rotation system and hosting weekly vegan nights. An inexplicable wooden rowing boat suspended above the entrance welcomes visitors into what is an overgrown jungle of a square.

Cabot Square, E14

Although Canada Square, with Ron Arad's impressive Big Blue sculpture as its centrepiece, has its advocates, we're more taken with neighbouring Cabot Square. Located to the west of Canary Wharf tower, it has a broad, calm fountain, as well as views over the docks on either side. Wander south to see the beautifully manicured Japanese-style garden by the Jubilee Line exit from Canary Wharf station.

Cleaver Square, SE11

Just off Kennington Park Road, this quiet residential square was beautifully restored using Lottery money. It's a peaceful place for a game of pétanque (*see p29*) or to sup a beer.

Cloudesley Square, N1

Holy Trinity Church, which sits in the middle of this square, was built by Charles Barry in 1828 and is said to be an imitation of King's College Chapel in Cambridge. The diminutive square (built in 1826) was the earliest of the Barnsbury squares, all of which boast late Georgian and early Victorian architecture.

Edwardes Square, W8

Built by Louis Changeur in the early 19th century, this superb garden square in Kensington features a Greek Revival-style gardener's lodge, a rose pergola and a croquet lawn. It's normally closed to the public, so visit on the annual Open Squares Weekend (*see p134*).

Fitzroy Square, W1

Designed by Robert Adam in 1793, Fitzroy Square was built in two stages: the first, from 1793 to 1798, saw the construction of the east side (a unified Portland stone palazzo of individual houses); the second produced the stucco-fronted north and west sides. Former residents include George Bernard Shaw, Virginia Woolf and Lord Salisbury.

Gordon Square, WC1

A verdant alternative to the neighbouring Russell and Bloomsbury Squares, this quiet space is frequented by students from the surrounding colleges intent on loafing and exerting themselves with some light Frisbee action. One of Virginia Woolf's residences (the blue plaque is to be found at Fitzroy Square nearby), Gordon Square was the epicentre of the Bloomsbury Group's literary activities.

Hanover Square, W1

Dominated by the art deco presence of Vogue House, this shady spot behind Oxford Street unites fashionistas, shoppers and workmen looking for an impromptu lunchtime picnic spot. St George's, an 18th-century church to the south of the square, was once the most fashionable place in town to exchange your vows: George Eliot and Teddy Roosevelt were both married here.

Hoxton Square, N1

The square that spawned a thousand haircuts. Since the 1990s, this nocturnal green has been well known for its fashionable bars, clubs and, at the White Cube and now Yvon Lambert galleries, contemporary art. But the area's rambuctiousness was already being felt several centuries earlier: in 1598 playwright Ben Jonson killed actor Gabriel Spencer in a duel here, narrowly escaping a public hanging.

Lincoln's Inn Fields, WC2

This 17th-century square, laid out by Inigo Jones, is now a favourite spot for lunching lawyers from the Inns of Court. As well as the lawns, there are trees and tennis courts, in an area that's almost big enough to be considered a park. Sir John Soane's Museum (*see p26*) and the Royal College of Surgeons (*see p62*) face off across the greenery.

Fitzroy Square

580-583
Revisit Clerkenwell's radical roots

Now a trendily gentrified enclave for London's creative industries, Clerkenwell has travelled far from its time as a hotbed of radicalism. But much survives from the area's revolutionary heyday and you can still trace the footsteps of its radicals, rebels and reformers.

From the 18th century the skilled artisans who lived and worked in the area met to discuss politics and far-reaching ideas of social justice in the coffee houses and inns around Clerkenwell Green, giving rise to the term 'Clerkenwell Radical'. The green became the focal point for demonstrations and mass meetings – like that welcoming the Tolpuddle Martyrs (agricultural labourers transported to Australia for forming a trade union) on their return to Britain in 1836, after being pardoned.

Under the beady eye of the Old Court House on the green stands the Marx Memorial Library. It once housed a coffee house where radical organisations such as Karl Marx's International Working Men's Association met, and William Morris and Eleanor Marx addressed crowds from the building. In 1902-03 Lenin edited his revolutionary journal *Iskra* (The Spark) here in an office that is still preserved. One of Lenin's favourite watering-holes was the nearby Crown Tavern and an apocryphal story lingers that he met Stalin there for a quiet pint in 1903.

The struggles of Irish Nationalism came to London in 1867 at the House of Detention on Clerkenwell Close when a huge explosion – an attempt to free two jailed members of the Irish Republican Brotherhood (or Fenians) – killed six and injured 40, marking the diminution of working class support for the Irish cause.

By the 1930s the area, with its Communist councillors and radical health programme, was known as the People's Republic of Finsbury. You can see a legacy of this in one of London's finest Modernist buildings, the Finsbury Health Centre on Pine Street, designed by Berthold Lubetkin.

584
Badger a beadle in the Burlington Arcade

Recently treated to a multi-million pound renovation, the Regency-era Burlington Arcade (www.burlington-arcade.co.uk) off Piccadilly is England's longest covered shopping street, Britain's first ever shopping arcade – and the precursor of many similar oases of cashmere, jewellery and other classy craftsmanship throughout Europe. Upscale window shopping is the order of the day here – that, and sneaking a peek at the top-hatted beadles, aka Georgian security guards.

585 Applaud a real Choc Star

Run from a converted ice-cream van by owner Petra Barran, the Choc Star (www.chocstar.co.uk) mobile chocolate service has recently been travelling the length and breadth of our sweet-toothed nation selling cakes, cookies, ice-cream, milkshakes and other chocolate goodies. When it's next back in London (check the website for details), you can expect the likes of Malteser muffins, millionaires' shortbread, chocolate brownies, Mexican chocolate ice-cream, a 'triple-chocolate malted bliss' milkshake (topped with a Valrhona-dipped cherry and worthy of its name) and espresso-style Venezuelan choc shots, flavoured with vanilla, chilli and cinnamon.

586 Subscribe to Time Out magazine for 33p!

Of course we like to think that you always get a good deal when you buy a copy of *Time Out* magazine, but for this book we've come up with a special offer: we'll send you nine issues for just £2.99 (that's an impressively inexpensive 33p each). Call 0800 068 0050 and quote tenner09 or subscribe online at www.timeout.com/subscriptions.

587 Take a peek into Hell

If you catch a double decker bus on St James's, you can take a peek into Hell, the first-floor gaming room of aristocratic club White's (37-38 St James's Street, SW1) – where gauntlets were once thrown down for dawn duels and vast fortunes have been won and lost.

588 Check out the Mighty Wurlitzer

This Brentford-based collection of melodic curios provides a fascinating history of pre-electronic musical gadgetry and houses one of the largest collections of automatic instruments in the world. Exhibits include ghostly self-playing pianolas, tiny Swiss musical boxes and the museum's grand centrepiece: the majestic 'Mighty Wurlitzer' that emerges from the orchestra pit of the 230-seat concert hall much as it once did in a 1930s picture house. Check the website for upcoming concerts.
Musical Museum *399 High Street, Brentford, TW8 0DU (8560 8108/www.musicalmuseum.co.uk).*

589 Explore Lesnes Abbey

The ruins of Lesnes Abbey are an unexpected find in suburban south-east London, overshadowed as it is by tower blocks and beside a busy main road. The Abbey was founded in 1178 by Richard de Luci, a supporter of Henry II, in penance for the murder of Archbishop Thomas à Becket in 1170. A small Augustian foundation, after passing through various private hands, in the 17th century it was bequeathed to Christ's Hospital, which sold it in 1930 to the London County Council. Nowadays the Abbey's scant ruins are surrounded by attractive gardens, featuring a 17th-century mulberry tree, as well as the surprisingly extensive Lesnes Abbey Wood. Particularly delightful in spring, when the daffs and bluebells are in bloom, it's worth a visit at any time of year for its even more ancient fossil bed – it's not unusual to unearth 50-million-year-old shark's teeth and rare seashells from the Eocene period.
Lesnes Abbey *Abbey Road, Belvedere, Kent (8303 7777/www.bexley.gov.uk/ service/parks/lesnesabbey.html).*

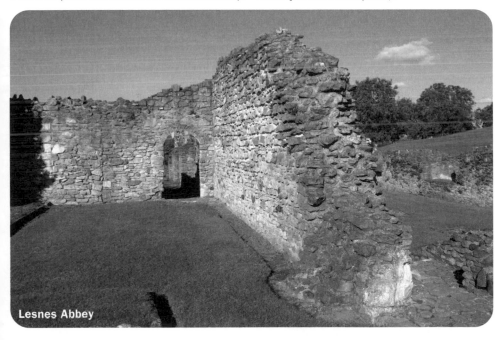

Lesnes Abbey

590

Revisit iconic scenes from London movies

Starting out with a classic establishing shot, Lewis Gilbert's *Alfie* takes some beating for an iconic opening scene. The Tower of London is, of course, still a tourist attraction, and the Thameside stretch overlooking the moat and ramparts is still a focus for buskers, artists, tat-floggers and thousands of happy snappers – if not quite Michael Caine's tourist photo scam. David Lynch's *The Elephant Man* also used real London buildings to brilliant effect: squint up into the overhead gantreys on a grey winter's day and it's almost possible to see Butler's Wharf on Shad Thames as the grim Dickensian world through which John Hurt shuffles. Likewise the façade of John Merrick's sanctuary, the Royal London Hospital on Whitechapel Road. Another 'slice of life' location well worth a visit is *Quadrophenia*'s pie and mash shop at the Goldhawk Road end of Shepherd's Bush Market, where mod Jimmy (Phil Daniels) meets greaser Kevin (Ray Winstone).

There's no more iconic or atmospheric a London film than Antonioni's *Blow Up*, and the unique Maryon Park in Charlton is virtually unchanged since 1966, when the Italian director happened across the strange landscape of Cox's Mount and immediately moved the focus of his swinging London film away from the West End.

Another south London location associated with surreal ultra-violence is the Thamesmead South estate, site of the slo-mo slicing 'tolchock' action between Alex and his three 'droogs' in Stanley Kubrick's *A Clockwork Orange*. Binsey Walk is the path in question, running at the side of the concrete Southmere Lake. Even 38 years on, the walkways and tower blocks of the Planner's Dream have a faintly futuristic – and grim – feel about them. Finally, no round-up of London film violence would be complete without a mention of *The Long Good Friday*. Sadly, there's no chance of visiting the Lion and Unicorn pub, because it was built temporarily on the Wapping riverfront just along from the Town of Ramsgate pub (*see p247*). But the interior of St Patrick's Church on nearby Greenbank was used when gangster Bob Hoskins took his old mum to church and the churchyard of St George in the East was where his Rolls-Royce got blown up. (Interestingly, the derelict location of the future Canary Wharf is visible when Hoskins takes to the Thames to view his proposed marina development.)

Grounds for a grand, all-encompassing conspiracy theory may be found in the fact that the Great Hall of Freemasons Hall, WC2 (*see p21*), was used as a ringer for the Kremlin in *From Russia With Love*. And there's yet more dastardly intrigue to be had at the Salisbury pub in the heart of Theatreland on St Martin's Lane. It wouldn't be giving too much away to say that in the landmark 1961 gay thriller *Victim*, Dirk Bogarde is blackmailed over his sexuality – or that the true, scene-stealing star of the film is the pub itself, all glancing mirrors and art nouveau table lamps.

And finally to music. American documentary-maker DA Pennebaker ushered in a whole new era with the groundbreaking sequence he filmed for the opening of *Don't Look Back*, in which Bob Dylan flicks though cue cards scrawled with the lyrics of *Subterranean Homesick Blues*. It was a '60s high, ultra-cool and oft-copied and these first shots of the coming video age were filmed, in 1965, in an alleyway called Savoy Steps, behind the hotel on the Strand.

It took Nic Roeg and Donald Cammell to signal the end of the '60s dream in *Performance*, in which Mick Jagger got to frolic with naked, drugged-up chicks, perform the cracking non-Stones tune *Memo To Turner* and swap personalities with psychotic hoodlum James Fox. It all happened (or was it just a bad trip?) behind the classical portico of 25 Powis Square, off the Portobello Road in Notting Hill.

591
Make tracks

Even people with a natural aversion to anoraks might find themselves unwittingly impressed at the London Festival of Railway Modelling (01778 391123, www.warnersgroup. co.uk/exhibitions/london). Every March this show at Alexandra Palace exhibits 40 miniature layouts, all products of frightening degrees of obsessive perfectionism. One can only marvel at the skills involved, from wiring up a 40-foot layout to creating a working steam engine one eighth the size of the original from brass sheets.

592
Horse around with avant-gardists...

Since 1993 a former Horse Hospital (Horse Hospital Colonnade, WC1N 1HX, 7833 3644, www.thehorsehospital.com) near Bloomsbury's Brunswick Square has been staging esoteric arts events that range from rare film screenings to gigs, from left-field theatre to séances and strange pagan celebrations. Lots of the events are free (among them the regular Raindance Film Club), and few – if any – cost more than a tenner. Check the website for details.

593
...or hang out at the Design Museum

For a former banana warehouse, the Design Museum has come a long way – most of it upwards. Conran and Partners' conversion was described by one architecture critic in 1989 as 'cool and logical, a counterblast to the feverish and feeble sub-vernacular styling which is almost de rigueur in Docklands'. Well quite – our thoughts exactly. Even the toilets are classy, thanks to Australian design star Marc Newson. And it's hardly necessary to look round the exhibits to enjoy the place: have a coffee in the café and look out over the river and Tower Bridge.

Design Museum *28 Shad Thames, SE1 2YD (7403 6933/www.designmuseum.org).*

Design Museum

594 Call in at Dover Street Market

Comme des Garçon's designer Rei Kawakubo's retail space combines the edgy energy of London's indoor markets – concrete floors, tills housed in corrugated-iron shacks, Portaloo dressing rooms – with a beautifully curated array of rarefied labels. True, it isn't the first place we'd direct the cash-strapped shopper to – you'll not walk out with any change from a tenner if you're hunting for clothes and even a bar of Comme des Garçon soap will set you back £14. But that doesn't mean you can't look. And what a space it is to look at: the theatrically designed displays give some of the capital's art galleries a run for their money and make for great browsing. If you really must buy something, nip into the Labour and Wait concession on the fourth floor for an ostrich feather duster (£10) or visit the Rose Bakery for a sit-down and one of its renowned carrot cakes (£4).

Dover Street Market *17-18 Dover Street, W1S 4LT (7518 0680/www.doverstreetmarket.com).*

595 Boost your brain power at a free public lecture

British Academy

Organising public lectures for over a century, the British Academy persuades serious intellectuals (of the likes of Jonathan Bate and Stuart Hall) to impart their wisdom. The series of endowed talks includes the annual Shakespeare Lecture on or around the Bard's birthday on 23 April. If titles such as 'Moral Panics: Then and Now' or 'From Shells and Gold to Plastic and Silicon: a theory of the evolution of money' tickle your fancy, these mostly ticketless talks usually start at 5.30pm.
10 Carlton House Terrace, SW1Y 5AH (7969 5246/www.britac.ac.uk).

Dana Centre

This state-of-the-art centre – affiliated to the Science Museum – encourages adults to take part in innovative evening debates about contemporary science, technology and culture. Topics might include 'An Experiment in Kissing' or 'DNA Testing: Science or Swindle?', covered in always entertaining and often interactive ways: regulars Punk Science explain themselves as using 'comedy, music, live experiments and rigged voting to explain real science to innocent bystanders'. Events are free – and very popular; always pre-book.
165 Queen's Gate, SW7 5HD (7942 4040/www.danacentre.org.uk).

Gresham College

Gresham College was set up 400 years ago precisely to provide free lectures. There are eight permanent lecturers in disciplines ranging from Geometry and Commerce to (brilliantly) Physic and Rhetoric, who talk about anything from 'The Search for Other Worlds' to 'Are Normal People Sane?'. Up to half a dozen lectures are held a week during termtime, mostly in the 90-seat Barnard's Inn Hall in Holborn; more popular lectures are sometimes forced to move elsewhere and may be ticketed.
Barnard's Inn Hall, EC1N 2HH (7831 0575/www.gresham.ac.uk).

National Gallery

The National Gallery runs several series of well-respected and informative free talks. These include lunchtime lectures (1pm Tue-Sat) on subjects such as 'Distant Lands, Uncharted Waters' (how can you paint an imaginary landscape?), as well as ten-minute talks (4pm Fri), lectures on the selected 'Painting of the Month' (perhaps Bronzino's *An Allegory with Venus and Cupid* or Degas's *Ballet Dancers*), and 25-minute 'After-work talks' that focus on a single painting each Wednesday (6pm).
Trafalgar Square, WC2N 5DN (7747 2885/www.nationalgallery.org.uk).

Royal Institution of Great Britain

The hugely popular, flagship Christmas Lectures series is for paying punters only, but the superbly refurbished Royal Institution, established in 1799 to spread scientific knowledge among the masses, also runs a lively programme of free events. Regular monthly features include 'Café scientifique', which begins with a brief presentation from an RI scientist before the floor is opened for drinking and debate, and the book club, 'Fiction Lab', for which Dr Jennifer Rohn (founder of Lablit.com) leads discussions of great fiction with a scientific bent. Evening lectures generally cost £8 (£4-£6 reductions).
21 Albemarle Street, W1S 4BS (7409 2992/www.rigb.org).

Royal Society of Arts

In the business of promoting public thought for two centuries, the RSA runs free lectures on a wide variety of subjects. Their 'Themes' strand has hosted speakers of the stature of Kofi Annan, Al Gore and Richard Rogers, while Thursdays offer a lunch hour top-up of arts or politics, perhaps 'Living with a Black Dog' (on depression) or 'The Element' (on how to fulfil your creative potential). See website for details.
8 John Adam Street, WC2N 6EZ (7930 5115/www.rsa.org.uk).

University College London (UCL)

Ingest your sandwich and get some intellectual nutrition at the same time by attending one of UCL's 40-minute lunchtime lectures, intended to offer an insight into research carried out at the university. Lectures start at 1.15pm (days vary) and subjects range from the intriguing 'The Man who Invented the Concept of Pi' to the abstruse 'The Reception of Homer in Byzantium' via the plain scary 'Physiology on Top of the World: Xtreme Everest'.
Darwin Lecture Theatre, Gower Street, WC1E 6BT (7679 9719/www.ucl.ac.uk).

596

Enjoy the view
Could this be the best view in London? Next to the Royal Observatory, the panorama from the summit of Greenwich Park is as splendid as anything you might see in the night sky. The genteel foreground, like something out of a period drama, makes a great contrast with the razzle dazzle of the Canary Wharf skyline.

597-605

Poke your nose into the City's livery halls

The City of London's 108 livery companies are the remnants of once-powerful guilds, or unions, for trades which mostly no longer exist. Many date back to medieval times, but were mainly formally established in the 16th century. Today, most of us would be hard pushed to describe exactly what a chandler does, never mind a fletcher or cordwainer; the relevance of a longbow maker and barber-surgeon is now, at best, symbolic, while the attraction of a decent currier is sadly illusory.

However, several of the worshipful companies still have a regulatory role and do a lot of fundraising for charity, pulling on their ruffles and big-buckled shoes for the Lord Mayor's Show. They also own a lot of property in the City. Most importantly, from our perspective, 33 of them have their own historic headquarters, or livery hall, secreted in some City backwater. It's fun to track them down – to spot and photograph their telltale ancient signs and coats of arms.

In terms of gazing at a secretive company's HQ façade, there are no greater thrills to be had than at the Cutlers' Hall (Warwick Lane, EC4M 7BR, www.cutlerslondon.co.uk) which boasts a magnificent 3D terracotta frieze of cutlers going about their work. It's groovier than it sounds. Ditto gazing through the outrageous ornamental gates of the Tallow Chandlers Hall (4 Dowgate Hill, EC4R 2SH, 7248 4726,www.tallowchandlers.org) into the haunted courtyard with its large Indian Bean tree.

Most livery halls are closed shops, though a surprising number are available to hire for functions, and some are occasionally open to visitors (call to check specific details of opening times). Top of the curiosities is at the Thames side 18th-century Fishmongers' Hall (London Bridge, EC4R 9EL, 7626 3531, www.fishhall. co.uk, tours for parties £5 each), where, amid a jumble of precious loot, you'll find the preserved 12-inch dagger used by fishmonger-Mayor William Walworth to stab Wat Tyler in the back and end the Peasants' Revolt of 1381. There's even a lifesize wooden statue of the murderous Walworth, dagger in hand.

Meanwhile, the treasures at Butchers' Hall (87 Bartholomew Close EC1, 7600 4106, www. butchershall.com) include a key cupboard from Newgate Prison; Vintners' Hall (Upper Thames Street, EC4V 3BG, 7236 1863, www.vintners hall.co.uk) boasts the Swan Banner (they own the swans on the Thames – it's a long story), archaeological finds and a collection of bottles; and Mercers' Hall (Ironmonger Lane, EC2V 8HE, 7726 4991, www.mercers.co.uk) a wonderful and expansive art collection, effectively lost to the world. Conversely, the Clockmakers' Company Museum is handily housed in the Guildhall Library (Aldermanbury, off Gresham Street, EC2V 7HH, 7332 1868, www.cityoflondon. gov.uk) – free admission, and true superstar timepieces. The Renaissance-style Goldsmiths' Hall (Foster Lane, EC2V 6BN, 7332 1456, www.thegoldsmiths.co.uk) is probably the most open to outsiders' prying eyes, and stages regular free art exhibitions to promote both the history and modern-day work of jewellers, gold and silversmiths.

Open House weekend (www.openhouse. org.uk) in September always features several livery companies. In addition, every June/July, the City of London Festival (www.colf.org) uses some halls for events, while at this time others open up their doors for architectural tours (and general nosying). In previous years the secret courtyards, ballrooms, roof gardens and treasures of the Butchers', Drapers', Leathersellers', Painter-Stainers', and Watermen & Lightermens' Halls (to name but a few) have all been opened up to the public.

606 Bag a vintage bargain

Brick Lane's vintage finds are hardly a secret anymore and as a result prices have rocketed, but that doesn't mean there are no bargains to be had. After window shopping your way along the Bethnal Green Road end of the street and gazing at 1920s dresses priced at well over £200, try the Shop (1 & 3 Cheshire Street, E2 6ED, 7739 5631). Here you can buy all manner of period wear (shawls, evening gloves) for a fraction of the price.

607-609

Wander, float or cycle along Regent's Canal

Opened in 1820 to provide a transport link between east and west London, Regent's Canal developed as a scenic public foot- and cycle path in 1968. The route's industrial trappings have been transformed into a delightful green corridor over the four decades since. Any stretch of the canal is worth a stroll (bear in mind that you can't follow it between Angel and King's Cross), but the most popular patch is from Camden Lock west to Little Venice, passing Regent's Park and London Zoo. Narrowboat cruises also travel along the water in summer and on winter weekends. They depart from Camden Lock and cost around £6.50 for a single fare, £8.50 return (Jason's Canal Boat Trip, 7286 3428; Jenny Wren, 7485 4433, www.walkers quay.com; London Waterbus Company, 7482 2660, www.londonwaterbus.com).

610
Watch glassblowers at work

In the fiery workshop at Peter Layton's London Glassblowing studio you can watch, mesmerized, as master craftsmen patiently and painstakingly create beauty out of molten silica molecules. Every object produced is unique and free blown and all are signed by their creators (there's currently a team of five working at the studio). This means, of course, that they don't come cheap (around £100 for a small perfume bottle and up to several thousand pounds for larger pieces) but the demonstrations themselves are completely free to watch – just drop in during working hours (but not between 1pm and 2pm). A word of warning: although there's no pressure to buy, the showroom next door is likely to prove a dangerous temptation. **London Glassblowing** *7 The Leather Market, Weston Street, SE1 3ER (7403 2800/ www.londonglassblowing.co.uk).*

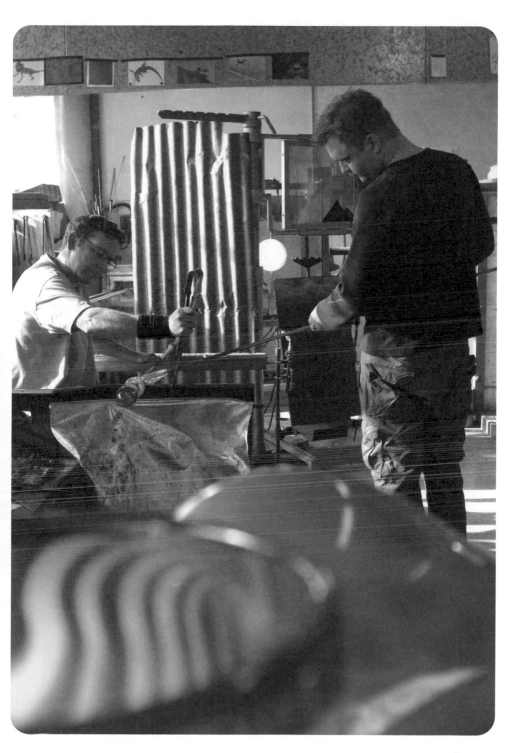

Brought to books

You'll only have a penny left to spend out of your ten pounds if you bought this book. So, by way of recompense, Charlie Godfrey-Faussett suggests some places where you can borrow it, along with many others, for free.

Who could disagree with Stephen Fry when he put public libraries firmly in his 'Room Lovely' on TV show *Room 101*? All that knowledge, all that power, the shelf stacks packed with promising titles, each one quite possibly a key to wisdom, information or inspiration. All effectively ordered, categorised and indexed, quietly awaiting enquiry. And all for free. Though most libraries now offer internet access (usually also free) and various other local services, their essence remains that thrill of discovery and the firing of imagination going on gratis under one communal roof. (And when it comes to roofing, libraries often do it much better than many other municipal buildings.)

Few cities contain such a fabulous array of libraries as London: there's the mother of them all, the British Library at St Pancras; the more than 300 local authority lending and reference libraries spread across the capital; and then there are the delights of the city's individual,

specialist, independent and academic libraries – the Marx Memorial, the Women's, the Lindley, the Weiner and many others. All in all, if you haven't found what you're looking for in a London library, you probably haven't been looking for long enough.

The British Library (96 Euston Road, NW1 2DB, 0870 444 1500, www.bl.uk) is one of the most extensive research resources anywhere on the planet. One of four copyright libraries in the country (the others being the National Libraries of Scotland and Wales, the Bodleian in Oxford, and Cambridge University Library) established by the Copyright Act of 1911, it receives a copy of everything published in the UK, as well as much more besides. Currently it requires about eight miles of extra shelf space each year for its growing collection of some 14 million books. It's free to join, but you need to have a professional reason to gain access to the reference-only reading rooms. All other visitors are more

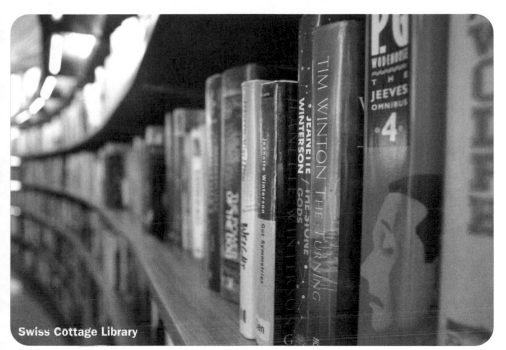

Swiss Cottage Library

than welcome at the great red-brick building at St Pancras, however. Much derided when it opened after years of expensive delays in 1997, it is in fact a superb light filled space inside and special exhibitions (which usually cost less than ten pounds admission) draw on the library's remarkable holdings: in 2009, for example, it celebrates the 500th anniversary of Henry VIII's accession to the throne by displaying a collection of books, letters and manuscripts actually read or annotated by the king himself. Another gallery contains a permanent free exhibition of some of the library's most precious treasures and displays, the likes of the Magna Carta, Shakespeare's First Folio, a Gutenberg Bible and Leonardo's notebooks – some extraordinary stuff, in other words.

Then there's the fantastic procession of public libraries in London. Many are the legacy of the Victorian drive to encourage self-help in the illiterate masses, but they've come a very long way since then. The City of London maintains several, but three are particularly noteworthy. Their flagship is the Guildhall Library (Aldermanbury, EC2V 7HH, 7332 1868, www.cityoflondon.gov.uk/guildhalllibrary), founded in the early 15th century by Dick Whittington and given its modern form in

1824 as a reference library on 'all matters relating to the City, the Borough of Southwark and the County of Middlesex'. As such, its collections on the history and topography of the capital are exceptional, including maps dating back to the 16th century and some 26,000 images of the City, viewable in its Print Room. This is also the place to see Lloyd's of London's historic marine collection of manuscripts relating to shipping; the wine and food libraries collected by André Simon, Elizabeth David and the Institute of the Masters of Wine, among others; and special collections devoted to Samuel Pepys, John Wilkes and Charles Lamb. The City Business Library (1 Brewers' Hall Garden, off Aldermanbury Square, EC2V 5BX, 7332 1812, www.cityoflondon.gov.uk/citybusinesslibrary) provides one of the most accessible and comprehensive practical sources of current business information in the UK. And the Barbican Music Library (Barbican Centre, EC2Y 8DS, 7638 0672, www.cityoflondon.gov.uk/barbicanlibrary) holds a huge number of recordings of all types of music (eight listening booths are provided) including the unique Music Preserved collection of recent live performances of classical music as well as musical scores and books about music and musicians for both lending and reference.

The City of Westminster's libraries are also pretty special. Bang in the middle of the West End, the Charing Cross Library (4-6 Charing Cross Road, WC2H 0HF, 7641 1300, www.westminster.gov.uk/libraries) is a public lending library that also serves Chinatown. It holds one of the largest collections of books in Chinese for loan in the country, has four Chinese-speaking staff, and stages a variety of China-related events. Nearby, just off Leicester Square, the Westminster Reference Library (35 St Martin's Street, WC2H 7HP, 7641 1300, www.westminster.gov.uk/libraries) is particularly strong in art and design and the performing arts. At the Westminster Archives Centre (10 St Ann's Street, SW1P 2DE, 7641 5180. www.westminster.gov.uk/libraries/archives), you can access www.ancestry.co.uk for free (for censuses from 1851 to 1901), as well as see illustrations dating back to the 16th century and search parish registers of baptisms, marriages and deaths.

Want to find out more about any given house, street, footpath or park in the mighty borough of Camden? Holborn Library (32-38 Theobalds Road, WC1X 8PA, 7974 6345, www.camden.gov.uk/holbornlibrary), with its wonderfully helpful local studies centre, is the place to come.

Staff will happily produce maps and resources relevant to your enquiry and point you in the direction of a variety of exhaustive card indexes.

Also in Camden, Swiss Cottage Library (88 Avenue Road, NW3 3HA, 7974 6522, www.camden.gov.uk) is worth a visit for its architecture alone. Designed by Sir Basil Spence, it's a superb modernist structure, looks a little like an enormous Rolodex, and was opened in 1964. It has a particularly strong psychology and philosophy collection.

Other public libraries around London have also pushed architectural boundaries: Peckham Library (122 Peckham Hill Street, SE15 5JR, 7525 2000, www.southwark.gov.uk) led the way with its colourful reading pods and glass walls. Opened in 2000, and designed by Will Alsop to undermine stuffy assumptions about libraries, it has become the busiest in Southwark. Tower Hamlets (www.towerhamlets.gov.uk) have gone a step further, ditching the word library altogether, with their Idea Stores: Whitechapel Idea Store (321 Whitechapel Road, E1 1BU, 7364 1742, www.ideastore.co.uk), opened in 2005. Designed by conceptual architect David Adjaye, it has glass walls and rubber studded floors, and as well as books it boasts 'learning spaces' (and classrooms), a crèche, dance studio, complementary therapy room, café, baby changing room and wheelchair accessible

Swiss Cottage Library

toilets. Further east, 2008 saw the opening of the Barking Learning Centre (2 Town Square, Barking, IG11 7NB, 8215 3028, www.barking-dagenham.gov.uk/blc), another award-winning new build.

If other local authority libraries have struggled to become less, how shall we say, pedestrian, no such problem faces London's extraordinary collection of specialist and independent libraries. We've only space to highlight a handful here, but more information on these and a huge number of others can be found at www.londonlibraries.org. Sadly, the most venerable of them all, the London Library (14 St James's Square, SW1Y 4LG, 7930 7705, www.londonlibrary.co.uk) costs around £400 per annum to join, though it is possible to book an introductory tour of the splendid old reading rooms.

If the muse takes you, then the Poetry Library (Level 5, Royal Festival Hall, SE1 8XX, 7921 0943, www.poetrylibrary.org.uk) could help harness your inspiration. Funded by the Arts Council, it's the major library of modern and contemporary poetry in the UK, and now holds some 100,000 books for loan and reference. Its sister in the visual arts is the National Art Library (Victoria & Albert Museum, Cromwell Road, SW7 2RL, 7942 2000, www.vam.ac.uk/nal). A reference library only, though with very well-appointed reading rooms, it's also the museum's curatorial department for the art, craft and design of the book. It holds fantastic documentary material on the fine and decorative arts of many different countries and periods. Simply register as a reader on your first visit if you want to explore the collections.

Anyone interested in the art and design of books will benefit from a visit to the St Bride Printing Library (St Bride's Passage, Salisbury Square, EC4Y 8EE, 7353 4660, www.st bride.org), which has 'something for everyone in the world of graphics'. Exhibits include everything from typefaces to artefacts illustrating the history of printing, along with thousands of books and magazines.

If you're more concerned with cultivating your garden, then the Lindley Library (80 Vincent Square, SW1P 2PE, 7821 3050, www.rhs.org.uk), the main library of the Royal Horticultural Society, is the place for you. It contains 22,000 botanical drawings,

and some 50,000 books on gardening. Take along two forms of identification to register.

Meanwhile, all matters medical are comprehensively covered at the Wellcome Library (183 Euston Road, NW1 2BE, 7611 8722, http://library.wellcome.ac.uk), the UK's most important resource on the history of medicine, in all its grisly detail. Recently acquired are the pioneering notes of the great forensic pathologist Bernard Spilsbury.

For the more politically inclined, the Wiener Library (4 Devonshire Street, W1W 5BH, 7636 7247, www.wienerlibrary.co.uk) is part of the Institute of Contemporary History and bills itself as 'the world's oldest holocaust memorial institution'. Founded in 1933 by Alfred Wiener in order to record the persecution of Jews in Nazi Germany, since 1956 the collections have been housed in Devonshire Street, where all are welcome to search the shelves for modern European history and current affairs. Also founded in 1933, partly in response to Nazi book-burning, was the Marx Memorial Library (37a Clerkenwell Green, EC1R 0DU, 7253 1485, www.marx-memorial-library, open for guided tours Mon-Thur, 1-2pm only, or by appointment) dedicated to the history of socialism and the science of Marxism. It was in this building that Lenin's *Iskra* magazine was printed before World War I.

Another hotbed of radicalism and free-thinking is the Bishopsgate Library (230 Bishopsgate, EC2M 4QH, 7392 9270, www.bishopsgate.org.uk) which holds famous collections on London, labour, free thought and co-operation and was founded in 1895 as part of the Bishopsgate Institute for the education of the working man. It's a reference library, restored in the 1990s to its original appearance, with research materials for local and family historians, as well as more general reference books and current national and local newspapers.

Not far away is the Women's Library (London Metropolitan University, 25 Old Castle Street, E1 7NT, 7320 2222, www.londonmet.ac.uk/thewomenslibrary) which contains the most extensive collection of works specifically relating to women's history in the UK. As well as the reading room there is a lively exhibition and events programme. Access here is free and open to everyone – just what libraries should be all about.

633

Celebrate the Thames

Without its river, London quite literally wouldn't exist, so it seems only right that there should be a proper celebration of the mighty Thames. The annual festival, nominally run by the Mayor's office, takes place over the middle weekend of September and populates the area between Westminster Bridge and Tower Bridge with an assortment of movies, food stalls, sculptures, the odd bar and an eclectic musical line up. 2008's event featured dubstep DJs and a thousand-voice adult choir. Sail on the water, dance in the streets and take a moment to reflect on the river that brought London to the world, and the world to London.
Mayor's Thames Festival *99 Upper Ground, South Bank, SE1 9PP (7928 8998/ www.thamesfestival.org). Free.*

634

Stick it to the whelks at Tubby Isaacs's seafood stall

What price a genuine taste of Cockney London? A couple of quid when it's Tubby Isaacs' whelks we're talking about. Standing outside the Aldgate Exchange pub on the corner of Goulston Street and Middlesex Street, E1, a few yards from the hustle and bustle of Petticoat Lane Market, Tubby Isaacs seafood stall has been trading since 1910. Currently owned by Paul – friendly-faced grandson of Tubby himself – the seafood is top quality (eels, whelks, cockles, crabs… they've got the lot). The whelks are served in a polystyrene cup: flavour them with a slosh of vinegar, chilli vinegar if you're feeling adventurous, and some salt and pepper, then dive in with your toothpick. How do they taste? Like the sea, of course. A cheap, charming sliver of London's seafood heritage, the stall is usually open on all market trading days (that means normally every day except Saturday).

635 *Take in a Midnight Matinee at Tristan Bates Theatre*

For your next up-all-Saturday-night escapade, ditch the club scene and dive into the world of cutting-edge drama at one of Tristan Bates Theatre's Midnight Matinees. The sellout performances on the third Saturday of the month were established as an incubator for experiments in theatre, and the venue gives actors, writers and directors a space to test challenging ideas and new theatre companies an opportunity to strut their stuff. Ticket prices are kept low and the bar buzzes post-show as performers mix with the audience of locals and luvvies. TBT's also perfectly positioned for checking out that other forum of experimental theatre – the night bus home.
Tristan Bates Theatre *1A Tower Street, WC2H 9NP (7240 6283/www.tristanbatestheatre.co.uk).*

636 *Kick off with the girls…*

Women's football has really taken off over the past decade and there are now dozens of local teams looking for players. If you are interested, either contact the London County Football Association (11 Hurlingham Business Stadium, Sulivan Road, SW6 3DU, 0870 774 3010, www.londonfa.com) or visit the Football Association website (www.thefa.com/Womens/GettingInvolved) to find a club that's convenient for you.

637 *…or watch the professionals play*

At a fiver a ticket to watch games in the FA Women's Premier League, it's cheaper than even non-league men's football (*see p36*), and yet professional women footballers are now playing at a seriously high (dare we say better?) standard. Most of London's pro clubs also have a women's team: Arsenal are far and away the best, but Chelsea and Fulham also have Premier League sides. *Time Out* magazine's weekly listings and www.timeout.com have details of key fixtures.

638 *Help reach a Critical Mass*

Part political movement, part breezy bike ride, Critical Mass (www.criticalmasslondon.org.uk) is a global cycling organisation that aims to reclaim the roads for pedal pushers. The website has links to cycling activism around the world as well as details of events in London – suffice to say the vibe is fairly anti motorised vehicle. The ride through the centre of town meets at 6pm on the last Friday of every month under Waterloo Bridge on the South Bank – if you want to take part just turn up with a bike.

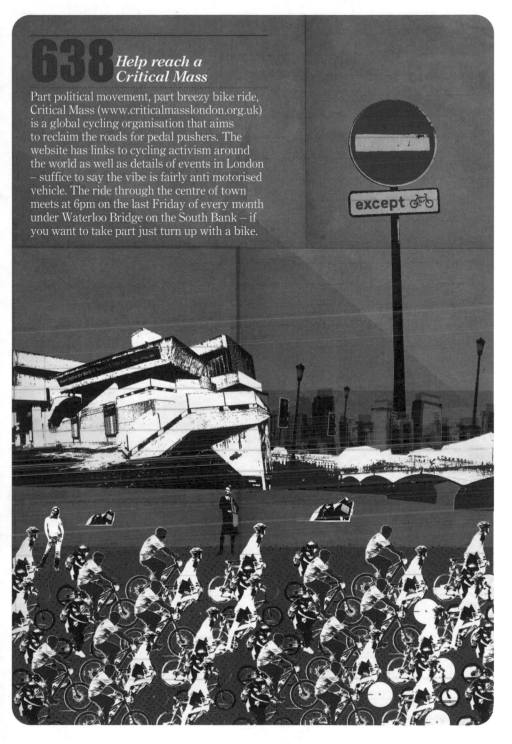

639-648 *Hear great bands live for less*

Live music for less than a tenner? Bella Todd tours the town in search of the capital's best pub back rooms.

Amersham Arms

A roomy yet homely pub, the Amersham is something of a beacon for music fans navigating the unfriendly straits of New Cross Road. Its 300 capacity room plays host to everything from big name DJs to folk festivals and ukulele jams, but it's probably best loved (especially by the students from the nearby Goldsmiths College) for pulling in well known electro pop acts such as Ladyhawke and Hot Chip. Ska Burlesque, their most imaginative monthly night, continues to make a success out of the unlikely combination of 2-Tone grooves and un-trussed flesh.
388 New Cross Road, SE14 6TY (8469 1499/ www.amersham-arms.co.uk). Free-£10.

Bedford

Gigs at this tardis-like Balham pub take place in the sizeable 'globe theatre', a round space ringed by a balcony and furnished with waited-on tables, where punters are quietly requested to switch off their mobile phones. The music policy is fairly middle of the road but there's an emphasis on breaking new talent – James Morrison and KT Tunstall both played here on the way up. There's live music five nights a week, including the excellent monthly Sunday afternoon event 'More Tea Vicar', where the hungover can have hand massages, eat cupcakes and buy vintage clothes while listening to acoustic acts. Pete Townshend once played an impromptu gig here, too. If you want a seat, book ahead.
77 Bedford Hill, SW12 9HD (8682 8940/ www.thebedford.co.uk). Free.

Betsey Trotwood

Set over three floors with a gig venue in the cellar and an acoustic room upstairs, this cosy Victorian pub hosts superior monthly alt-country and bluegrass nights (the latter in the form of an unplugged hoedown) and is a favourite with antifolk heroes over from the States. It's also recently become home to promising new modern folk club the Lantern Society, which commandeers the upstairs room for their candlelit harmonies.
56 Farringdon Road, EC1R 3BL (7253 4285/ www.thebetsey.com). Free-£6.

Dublin Castle

Indie heaven in the stickiest, sweatiest sense, this Irish pub (or, more importantly, it's back room) is slap bang in the heart of Camden Town and has seen more bands pass through its doors than its clientele have skipped hot dinners. Once Madness's second home, it's now the best place to go if your aim is to catch as many up and coming acts as possible (there are at least four bands a night) regardless of whether they're playing metal, psych-pop or techno-reggae. The day the Dublin Castle turns itself into a gastropub is the day the Rolling Stones take to their rocking chairs.
94 Parkway, NW1 7AN (7485 1773/ www.bugbearbookings.com). £4.50-£6.

Gladstone Arms

More like someone's candlelit front room than a venue, 'the Glad' in Southwark is often packed but always relaxed, with the chance to enjoy rootsy acoustic music (perhaps over a Pieminister pie and a game of chess) nearly every Thursday, Friday and Saturday. It's home to the mighty Moon Music Orchestra, who include the landlord among their number and play their groovy, mandolin and banjo-assisted psych-folk here once a month. Ramshackle blues man Adam Beattie also has a residency, while the Shortwave Set and Findlay Brown have tested new material here. A proper little charmer.
64 Lant Street, SE1 1QN (7407 3962). Free.

Haggerston

Formerly known as Uncle Sam's – and with a retro neon sign outside to prove it – this post-pub, pre-club venue, with its late licence, Hackney postcode, low-level lighting and leather sofas, somehow manages to straddle the divide between pretentious edginess and genuine good fun. Journey into Dalston for DJs and alt-ish bands on Saturdays and Sundays, but the jewel in its crown is Uncle Sam's Jazz and Blues, a weekly late night Sunday session, led by Alan Weekes's modern jazz quartet, where even the bar staff may take to the mic for the odd Billie Holiday classic.

438 Kingsland Road, E8 4AA (7923 3206). Free.

Half Moon Putney

Well, where do we start? KD Lang made her UK debut here; Kate Bush played her first ever show here; Elvis Costello had a residency, Nick Cave played a surprise gig, and the well-kept Wall of Fame pays testimony to shows by everyone from the Rolling Stones and U2 to, er, Gay Dad. The Half Moon has been putting on bands since the 1920s, and seems to have a special pull on performers. There are concerts every night of the week, the Monday night acoustic sessions have been going since the '60s, and these days you can order Lebanese food with your music every night but Monday.

93 Lower Richmond Road, SW15 1EU (8780 9383/www.halfmoon.co.uk). £2.50-£10.

Amersham Arms

Betsey Trotwood

Macbeth

To tabloid readers it's the pub where Amy Winehouse's hubby landed himself in jail. To the rest of us it's an intimate hipster Hoxton boozer where electronica, folk and leftfield indie acts play amid renaissance-style paintings and some very attractive tiling. It's also one of the only places where, thanks to the groundbreaking monthly 'Non-Classical' nights organised by Gabriel Prokofiev (grandson of the Russian composer), you can see string quartets perform opposite grime stars. Bjork's been spotted at the latter, while regular shows such as Raison D'Etre's open mics draw an arty crowd.

70 Hoxton Street, N1 6LP (7739 5095). Free-£6.

Old Blue Last

At times unbearably trendy (even more so since NME voted it 'the coolest pub in the world'), but this shabby-looking Hoxton watering hole is highly adept at generating a buzz. The Old Blue Last is famed for secret performances by the likes of Amy Winehouse and the Arctic Monkeys, but it also runs a pretty hip live music ship the rest of the time too (five nights a week). There are no frills here, and often barely room to shake your hips, but when you're enjoying early gigs by the likes of Kate Nash, Dan Le Sac vs Scroobius Pip and Santogold, who cares?

38 Great Eastern Street, EC2A 3ES (7739 7033/ www.theoldbluelast.com). Free-£6.

Slaughtered Lamb

Upstairs it's a trendy drinking post for the local office workers; down in the basement, a cavern like space packed with mismatched sofas, it's a top spot for leftfield acoustica and folky electronica thanks to promoters 'Electroacoustic Club', who ensure consistency by holding casual court from Monday to Wednesday. Lau played here shortly after winning Best Group at the BBC Radio 2 Folk Awards 2008, and it's also home to a great monthly, musician-hosted pub music quiz.

34-35 Great Sutton Street, EC1V 0DX (7253 1516/www.theslaughteredlambpub.com). £5-£10.

649 *Laugh, gaffaw, chuckle... ...but don't snigger*

Believe it or not, there are two groups in the capital dedicated entirely to the process of learning how to laugh. It's all about laughing for no reason (jokes are forbidden) – and tapping into your natural joy and inner playful child. Laughing also reduces stress hormones, boosts natural endorphins, strengthens the immune system and tones the stomach muscles, apparently. The Laughter Workout (07789 954972, www.laughingmatters.co.uk) is held twice a month from May to August in Lincoln's Inn Fields and costs £8 for an hour (the winter sessions are at indoor venues and therefore cost more than £10). At the London Laughter Community, held at the appropriately named Academy of Dreams (Quantum House, Churchway, NW1 1LT, 07904 334222, www.shinetime.co.uk, £9) chucklers lie on the floor and do laughter meditation. 'It's all about feeling happy because you laugh, and not laughing because you feel happy,' says Leela Bunce, who leads the sessions and tries to foster a sense of community through chortling. 'In these tough times, it's more important than ever to laugh. It doesn't take our problems away, but it makes them lighter.'

A few of my favourite things

650-655

Victoria Thornton, Director, Open House

Leighton House (12 Holland Park Road, W14 8LZ, 7602 3316, www.rbkc.gov.uk/leightonhousemuseum, which will open again after refurbishment at the end of 2009) just off Kensington High Street, is beautiful. It was the 19th-century home of Frederic, Lord Leighton, who was the president of the Royal Academy, and it's designed like an Italianate villa. The interiors are very richly coloured and there are Arab-style tiled fountains in the hallways which people always fall into. **Another amazing building is the house of the late architect Sir John Soane (13 Lincoln's Inn Fields, WC2A 3BP, 7405 2107, www.soane.org). It's preserved exactly as it was in the 1800s with all his paintings and sculptures. It's usually free to get in, and on the first Tuesday of each month they do an atmospheric candlelit evening tour.** St Martin-in-the-Fields church in Trafalgar Square (WC2N 4JJ, 7766 1100, www.stmartin-in-the-fields.org) has recently been renovated. It's got a lovely café in the crypt and a little exhibition space which has given the building a new lease of life. The church itself is also fantastic. It hosts a lot of really good concerts and the lunchtime ones are free.

What's nice about London is that you don't have to get very high up to get an amazing view. Since the Royal Festival Hall has been renovated it's a great place to go for a drink and from the café on the second floor (Riverside Terrace Café, Royal Festival Hall, Southbank Centre, Belvedere Road, SE1 8XX, www.southbankcentre.co.uk) you can enjoy a view of the north side of the river with all its grand buildings. I love going to Kenwood House for tea (Brew House, Kenwood, Hampstead Lane, NW3 7JR, 8341 5384, www.companyof cooks.com). The café is in the gardens of the grand old house and you can sit and have a pot of tea and fantastic cakes before a wander up Parliament Hill for an incredible view over London. On a good day you can actually see the skyline on the other side of the city right down to the South Downs. **On our office day out this year we went to Finsbury Circus for a picnic. This little park in the middle of the City has a bowling green and you can play bowls for £3.50 an hour (book ahead by calling 07768 536 874). It's wonderful to be able to play such a slow, genteel game amid all the noise and bustle of the City.** Open House (www.openhouse.org.uk) is a fantastic way to get to know the city – not just from the outside but from the inside. On the third weekend of September we open up 700 buildings to the public, from beautiful private houses to venues like the National Theatre and institutions that the public can't normally access. One of the most incredible is the Foreign Office in Whitehall. It has a wonderfully ornate interior and there's a lovely courtyard area in the middle with a glass ceiling. The great thing about it is that you can wander round at your own leisure, rather than being forced through on a tour.

656 *Respect your elders at the Age Exchange*

The Age Exchange centre in Blackheath (11 Blackheath Village, SE3 9LA, 8318 9105, www.age-exchange.org.uk) offers the senior citizens of south-east London a chance to meet, greet and wax nostalgic about the old days. There's also a museum here decked out like a 1930s shop that showcases products of yesteryear: a wind-up gramophone, vintage records, retro clobber and wartime paraphernalia (from gas masks to ration books). It features regular exhibitions (an end of war tea party, a recreation of London's docks) and invites schoolchildren to learn about the past. A nostalgia kick goes well with a nice cup of tea, served in the café. Admission is free for casual visitors, but there is a charge for groups.

657

Wrap up warm and watch the Peter Pan Cup

Every Christmas morning in the frosty waters of Hyde Park's pond you can see members of the Serpentine Swimming Club (www.serpentineswimmingclub.com) thrashing it out for the Peter Pan Cup Christmas Morning Handicap Swim. The club requires participants to endure several months of winter training to help their bodies acclimatise, as water temperatures rarely exceed 4°C. Every swimmer must be a club member and have competed in a series of competitions… and, last but not least, they must be sporting a Santa hat. Kicking off at 9am on 25 December on the south bank of the lake, it's great fun to watch from dry land in nice snug clothes.

658

Attend the olde Strawberrie Fayre in Ely Place

This hidden little place – or Place – is the site of St Etheldreda's Church (14 Ely Place, EC1N 6RY, 7405 1061, www.stetheldreda.com), commended in Shakespeare's *Richard III* for its garden's fine fruit ('My Lord of Ely, when I was last in Holborn, I saw good strawberries in your garden there: I do beseech you send for some of them.'). In recognition of this, an annual Strawberrie Fayre is staged in late June (check the website for the exact date). There's plenty of traditional fun, games and strawberries, with all proceeds going to charity.

659

Sit on a ferryman's perch

Bankside was once London's Pleasure Quarter, where gaming, drinking and womanising could take place out of sight and mind on the far side of the river. On the corner of Bear Gardens (named for its bear pit), there's an ancient waterman's seat let into the modern wall, where boatmen once drummed up trade with their nudge-and-wink cry of 'Oars! Oars!'.

660

Swap stuff

Call them what you like: swapping, swishing, or ditching 'n' switching events, where you exchange your clobber for someone else's – no cash required – are an excellent way to save money, the environment (it's recycling, see) and prevent wardrobe ennui. Of course it's also a great way to meet total strangers.

Of course the cheapest way to go about it is to hold your own clothes swapping party. Like the 21st century's answer to the Tupperware bash, you invite all your friends round, asking them to bring a bottle and the clothes they no longer want – then hope that someone else's cast-off is your own sartorial holy grail. And the rules are simple enough too: everyone brings a few items they're willing to relinquish and they can take home as much as they like. Reserving the best stuff before kick-off is frowned upon and, of course, remember your manners – all-out brawling is not in the spirit of swishing.

At the other end of the spectrum are organised club nights such as Favela Chic's Swap-a-Rama Razzmatazz (91-93 Great Eastern Street, EC2, 7613 4228, www.favelachic.com, free entry before 9pm). Here, it's more about fun than bagging a designer treasure: every time the klaxon sounds, get swapping with your neighbour on the dancefloor. It's not surprising that most of these nights take place in the East End, where many of their clientele are already appropriately attired in cheapo charity shop garb. Swapaholics @ Juno Bar (134-135 Shoreditch High Street, E1, 7729 2660, www.junoshoreditch.co.uk) is another regular swapping party night, costing a mere fiver to get in. See www.swishing.org for other upcoming events, and register at www.visa swap.com to find out when the pop-up shop run by Traid (www.traid.org.uk) and the credit card company is next due in town.

More shy and retiring sorts can get swapping online: try websites such as www.swapitshop.com, www.iswap.co.uk, www.swapshop.co.uk and www.swapx changeislington.org.

661 *Buy your lunch from an award-winning author*

A deliciously bucolic remnant of Old Spitalfields Market, upscale corner deli Verde & Co forms the ground floor of author Jeanette Winterson's restored Georgian home. Artfully presented – think linen-lined baskets of organic seasonal vegetables out front – and with an emphasis on Italian produce (to avoid competing with next door Brit specialist A Gold), the fruit and veg on sale here is carefully selected by ex-St John chef Harvey Cabaniss. He clearly takes pride in his artisanal lunchtime sandwich menu: try the chorizo, gorgonzola and sweet chilli, the suckling pig and balsamic onion or check the daily specials board.

Verde & Co *40 Brushfield Street, E1 (7247 1924/www.verde-and-company-ltd.co.uk).*

662

Have an epiphany in Neasden
A miraculous vision in marble,
the Shri Swaminarayan Mandir
(8965 2651, www.mandir.org)
is the biggest Hindu Temple
outside India. Fascinating
architecturally and cross-
culturally, the Mandir is open
to people of all faiths and none.

663

Visit the home of baseball

Baseball (unlike basketball) is a game of evolution rather than invention, and it may come as a surprise to learn that much of that evolving took place in Surrey rather than across the pond. Local records show that the game was played near Guildford in the 1750s, and there's even a reference in Jane Austen's *Northanger Abbey*. More than 250 years later, that tradition continues. The Croydon Pirates are one of the leading clubs in Britain's thriving baseball scene, competing in the National Premier League from their home at Roundshaw Playing Fields. The Pirates also host the London Tournament every July, with 16 top teams enjoying a weekend of pitching, pinch hits and put-outs. All games are free to watch and the season runs from April to September.
Croydon Pirates *www.croydonpirates.co.uk.*

664 Get your hands dirty in a 17th-century knot garden

Next door to Lambeth Palace, the old parish church of St Mary-at-Lambeth and its churchyard is home to the Garden Museum (formerly the Museum of Garden History), which exhibits the works of various green fingered luminaries in its beautifully refurbished galleries. Outside, a lovely churchyard garden laid out in a formal 17th-century knot garden design was the last resting place of the John Tradescants (father and son), gardeners to Charles I. If you are itching to share some of your horticultural knowledge or would like to learn more about the historic plant species growing here why not volunteer your services to help tend the garden (it is run entirely by volunteers). Visit the website for more information and application details.
Garden Museum *Lambeth Palace Road, SE1 7LB (7401 8865/ www.gardenmuseum.org.uk). £6.*

665

Wake yourself up at New Covent Garden Market

Stir your stumps at the crack of dawn, or even earlier, and head for 'the largest fresh produce market in the UK'. New Covent Garden Market is open from Mon-Fri 3am-11am, Sat 4am-10am (most of the wholesale action is over by 8am), and claims to supply almost half of all the food that London likes to eat while it's out. Covering 53 acres, the market opened here in Vauxhall after moving from Covent Garden in 1974, and is about to be given a thorough makeover. Even if you're not buying (and there's plenty of opportunity to – whether you are thinking wholesale or not), your £4 entry fee guarantees a feel for the market's buzz and there are plenty of market caffs where you can breakfast alongside the traders. In a separate building, the flower market offers the most spectacular profusion of plants for sale under one roof in the country. As well as supplying florists and flower-stall holders, it does brisk business with funeral directors, wedding planners and browsing brides-to-be.
New Covent Garden Market *Nine Elms Lane, SW8 5NX (7720 2211/ www.newcoventgardenmarket.com).*

666

Catch a new band showcase at Notting Hill Arts Club

Long established as a hang-out for the too-cool-for-school brigade, the Notting Hill Arts Club runs a selection of club nights through the week. And while Oasis 'discoverer' Alan McGee's Wednesday night Death Disco has forged a hip reputation in recent times, its free Saturday afternoon band showcase has been an institution for the best part of a decade. Known as RoTa – and organised in conjunction with Rough Trade record shops – it runs from 4pm to 8pm, usually hosting three bands loosely filed under 'alternative'.
Notting Hill Arts Club *21 Notting Hill Gate, W11 3JQ (7460 4459/www.nottinghillartsclub.com).*

667 *Play in a pub poker tournament*

'If after 20 minutes you can't spot the sucker at the table', goes the oldest adage in poker, 'then the sucker is you'. Fortunately, bets are minimal at this super friendly pub-based weekly meet-up of happy cardsharps – the most you can lose in one night is a fiver – so novices don't need to worry about losing big and having their hands cut off in a basement to the tune of *the Godfather*. The game is Texas Hold 'Em and each tournament sees up to 40 players of varying ability play on a five-pound 'freeze out' basis. This means that everyone begins with the same amount of chips and the game finishes when one player scoops the lot. Once you've 'busted out' you can't buy back in but part of the fun is the mind-reading high jinks and witty character jousting between the chatty regulars.
www.thebubblepokerleague.co.uk

668

Check out the boffins

A magnet for mad professors, wacky garden-shed types and yes, even the occasional serious entrepreneur and *Dragon's Den* wannabe, the British Invention Show brings offbeat creativity to Alexandra Palace for three-and-a-half days each October. The show was founded in 2000, and inventions on display have ranged from the practical – a solar- or wind-powered 'hospital in a box' that includes a defibrillator, monitors and even a medical tent – to, surprise, surprise, the downright bonkers – a wire headgear set designed to prevent wrinkles. A panel of judges give out annual awards for the best in show.

Alexandra Palace *Alexandra Palace Way, N22 7AY (01462 451111/www.britishinventionshow.com). £10.*

669

Explore Kings Place

In line with the recent regeneration of the King's Cross area, this major arts centre has recently opened to great fanfare and much critical acclaim. Incredibly, the airy modern building is home to the first new public concert hall to be built in central London since the Barbican Concert Hall opened in 1982. The building consists of a public open-plan ground-floor area with comfortable seating, a café and a restaurant while the two lower levels house a gallery and two concert halls, whose acoustics can be adjusted for music or speech. There are classical, choral and jazz concerts, with whole cycles dedicated to individual composers, as well as spoken word evenings and events for children. All art exhibitions are free, while lectures and music events can be attended for just £9.50 if booked in advance online. Elegant inside and out, this is a great addition not only to King's Cross, but to London as a whole.

Kings Place *90 York Way, N1 9AG (0844 264 0321/ www.kingsplace.co.uk).*

Kings Place

670-672
Get to know William Morris

Born in Walthamstow in 1856, Morris made it his mission to beautify the ends and means of mass production, most famously with his wallpaper designs inspired by natural forms, but more generally through a deep respect for craftsmanship and the dignity of labour.

In 1877, he rented a house on the lovely riverside path that runs from Hammersmith to Chiswick. He called it Kelmscott House (26 Upper Mall, 8741 3735, www.morrissociety.org, free) after his manor in Oxfordshire, and died here in 1896. Now home to the William Morris Society, founded in 1955, the basement and coach house, containing a library and a variety of Morris memorabilia, can be visited from 2-5pm on Thursdays and Saturdays.

Other key places in London associated with the pioneering socialist include the Red House (Red House Lane, Bexleyheath DA6 8JF, 8304 9878, £6.60), which Morris designed with architect Philip Webb and where he lived from 1860 for five years (before being forced to sell) and the wonderful William Morris Gallery (Lloyd Park, Forest Road, E17 4PP, 8527 3782, free) where he lived as a teenager and which now exhibits his famous designs in fabrics, glass, tiles, wallpaper and furniture as well as other works by other Arts and Crafts designers such as Arthur Heygate Mackmurdo and William de Morgan.

673
Ogle classic cars in South Kensington

In the mews off the Old Brompton Road lie three of the world's top classic car dealers: Hall & Bradfield, 8 Reece Mews (www.hallandbradfield.co.uk), Fiskens, 14 Queens Gate Place Mews (www.fiskens.com), Cars International, 6 Kendrick Place (www.racecar.com/cars international). Even if motors aren't really your thing, you'll be hard pressed not to drool over the Ferraris, Jaguars and Alfa Romeos, though your tenner won't be much use here.

674
Catch a film at the Exhibit Cinema

London has been at the forefront of a British cinema revolution and now boasts several exclusive and luxurious movie dens. One of the most favoured chocolates in the box is Balham's doo wop-style boutique picture house. The Exhibit offers the chance to see a mix of new-ish releases and art-house works on comfortable, chocolate-brown leather sofas for only a fiver. It's the perfect setting for a wallet-friendly date and the food here goes way beyond your local multiplex sludge: dine at the adjoining restaurant before a screening or take in a meze plate of continental meats and cheeses.

The Exhibit *12 Balham Station Road, SW12 9SG (8772 6556/www.theexhibit.co.uk).*

675
Get your jewellery valued at Hatton Garden

When the chips are *really* down, take the family loot to be valued at one of the sparkling stores of Hatton Garden, London's gem trading centre since the middle ages.

676
Go Dutch

Dutch bars aren't unusual these days, but what they don't have is the century-old history of De Hems. This ornate fronted hostelry was first a refuge for homesick Dutch sailors, then an overseas base for the wartime Dutch Resistance. Now a convivial two-floor pub with dark wood interior, the sturdy counters are lined with Grolsch Weizen, Oranjeboom and Kriek taps (£4/pint), with more unusual bottled beers such as Kwak, Vedett and Orval stored behind the bar. Traditional Dutch bar snacks such as *bitterballen* (deep-fried meat balls) cost from £3.95 a dish, or, if they don't appeal, it's conveniently located on the edge of Chinatown.

De Hems *11 Macclesfield Street, W1D 5BW (7437 2494).*

677-679 *Get your skates on*

Winter open-air ice skating has taken off in a big way and it's proved so hugely popular that many of the more established set piece backdrops (Somerset House, Natural History Museum) now charge over a tenner. Those listed here will cost £10 or less (at the time of writing) but you may be restricted to off-peak 'ice-time' only – check websites to find out details of session times.

Shepherds Bush Winter Village (www.shepherdsbushfestival.com) plays host to a 600 square metre ice rink along with a whole range of winter activities including a Ferris wheel, carousel and stalls serving up festive refreshments of the mulled wine and roasted chestnut variety. And at an off-peak price of £8 (£10 peak) it is the cheapest open air option in town.

The Royal Botanical Gardens at Kew (www.kewgardensicerink.com) have long been a pictureseque backdrop for annual icy thrills and spills (adult off-peak price £10, see website for details). Here you can glide (Bambi-like or not) to the classical music intended to sooth the nerves of beginners as they take to the ice. Be warned, though, Kew ice rink is popular, so advance booking is strongly advised if you want to beat the queues.

With the river only a few metres away and the fortress like walls looming right in front of you, the Tower of London (www.toweroflondonicerink.com) is an inspired place to try out your triple salcos and double toe loops. With an adult off-peak price of £10 this is the best deal you're going to get in central London.

680

Pay homage to the Tyburn martyrs

A neat and tranquil afternoon antidote to the toxic bustle of nearby Oxford Street, this peaceful convent is home to 25 cloistered nuns who watch over the relics of more than a hundred Roman Catholic martyrs who were executed here under the Reformation laws between 1535 and 1681.

In the chapel on the ground floor you'll find at least one sister mantaining contemplation before the cross while others are available at 10.30am, 3.30pm and 5.50pm daily for tours of the crypt below. The shrine, which contains some extraordinary wall mounted displays of various body parts of unfortunate Catholics dispatched here, is located near what was once the site of the infamous King's Gallows. Over 50,000 executions took place from 1196 to 1783 and most of the Catholics remembered here were hung from a triangular gallows that became known as the Tyburn Tree. The gallows became so infamous that 'to be taken to Tyburn' became a euphemism for execution. A replica of the Tyburn Tree can be seen in the convent's eerie crypt.

Tyburn Convent *8 Hyde Park Place, W2 2LJ (www.tyburnconvent.org.uk).*

681

Discover Eadweard Muybridge at Kingston Museum

Kingston Museum is worth anyone's pound – containing as it does a remarkably well-preserved Anglo-Saxon logboat – but for movie buffs it's an absolute must. The remarkable Eadweard Muybridge (1830-1903) was born in Kingston plain Edward James Muggeridge, but changed his name to Muygridge then to Eadweard Muybridge (taking the spelling of his Christian name from the name of Eadweard the Elder on Kingston's coronation stone).

He headed for America hoping to find a market for his topical photographs and soon made a name for himself with his landscapes of Yosemite, city-scapes of San Francisco and work with moving images (in 1872 he was asked to photograph the racehorse Occident belonging to a former governor of California, to prove that all four of the horse's feet left the ground at once when galloping – his experiments proved that they did).

Back at the museum in Kingston, there's a collection of his equipment and some of the prints that Muybridge bequeathed to the place on his death. You can see two of the revolving slotted drums or zoetropes that he experimented with – they show an ostrich running and a man jumping up and down, as well as a phenakistiscope, one of the world's earliest moving picture devices. Muybridge's second Zoopraxiscope, also on display here, was designed to project the movement and actions of various animals. The museum also holds one of only nine surviving copies of his 'Panorama of San Francisco', which is over 17 feet in length, and taken with a series of 13 cameras in 1878.

Kingston Museum *Wheatfield Way, Kingston upon Thames, KT1 2PS (8547 6460/www.kingston.gov.uk/museum). £1.*

682

Be a mystery shopper

Mystery Shopping is probably the closest you are likely to get to being a secret agent (well, a sort of consumer sleuth anyway). Posing as a real customer your mission, should you choose to accept it, is usually to check out customer service (sometimes in person, sometimes on the phone) and buy all manner of goodies incognito – some of which you may get to keep. With many big name clients out there determined to maintain their high levels of service, you can find yourself in some exciting places (free flights are not unheard of) – and any expenses spent while on a case are reimbursed (you may also earn a small fee for completing an evaluation form). Register online.
www.mystery-shoppers.co.uk.

Fringe benefits

Grant Gillespie uncovers the best theatre deals in town and discovers that we're spoilt for choice.

Battersea Arts Centre

One of the most common laments you'll hear from the would-be theatre going community relates to the expense of the tickets – if we had a pound for every time we'd heard a complaint along these lines we could afford the theatre every night of the week and dinner at the Ivy afterwards. But with more and more venues introducing 'pay-what-you-can nights' along with various other tempting deals to entice both the jaded and the cash-strapped back into theatres, things are looking up. What's equally encouraging is that the venues employing this non-elitist practice are generally also those that produce some of the most interesting and thought-provoking work in London. You won't come away humming a Lloyd Webber tune but you'll certainly have food for thought and enough money for food to boot (though not at the Ivy). OK, so you might not be seeing Kevin Spacey or Nicole Kidman gracing the stage but chances are you will be watching the next Kevin Spacey and hotly-tipped Nicole Kidman replacement.

Pay what you can

Pay-what-you-can means just that: you pay what you can afford and it's entirely at your discretion – some punters pay a pound, some pay full price, but a fiver or so is a good average. All of the theatres below offer this deal on certain nights – although you may need to be quick off the mark to take advantage. Keep your ear to the ground or, more usefully, your finger on the mouse.

The well established and respected Gate Theatre (7229 0706, www.gatetheatre.co.uk) in Notting Hill is the only London theatre venue exclusively dedicated to international writing. The great and the good either started off here or still work here, attracted by the diversity and quality of the company's output. It's an intimate but flexible space above the Prince Albert pub and seats about 70 people. 'Happy Mondays' here means pay-what-you-can tickets; these are available at the door on the night from 6.30pm on a first-come-first-served basis.

Tuesday night is pay-what-you-can night at the Battersea Arts Centre (7233 2223, www.bac.org.uk). Housed in a beautiful grade II building that was originally Battersea Town Hall, BAC's ambitious mission is to 'invent the future of theatre' and that means showing everything from huge site-specific pieces

that make use of the whole space (including the café, two theatres and the gallery) to intimate performances for just one audience member. 'Whether you want to pay £10 or just 50p we believe pay-what-you-can nights are a great way of introducing audiences to the best in theatre at BAC. It's a central strand of our commitment to knocking down barriers to attendance and has, over the last decade, introduced thousands of people to our work,' say David Jubb and David Micklem, the Joint Artistic Directors. Generally speaking, on pay-what-you-can nights at the BAC all tickets are pay-what-you-can tickets, and they are available from the moment the run goes on sale (there are occasional exceptions to this rule – check the website for details).

'Venues offering pay-what-you-can nights are often also those that produce some of the most interesting work in London.'

Arcola Theatre (7503 1646, www.arcola theatre.com) in a converted factory in Hackney, has been growing steadily in repute since it opened in 2000. The programming is varied, running from comedy through to the classics, and is staged by new and established practitioners alike. The larger studio space is vast and versatile, the smaller more cosy – but in a good way. Arcola is also well on the way to being the world's first carbon-neutral building and you can already enjoy a guilt-free drink or bite to eat in their eco-bar. The Arcola offer pay-what-you-can tickets on Tuesdays (40 tickets for Studio 1, 15 for Studio 2) which can be purchased from 7pm on the evening of the performance.

At the Riverside Studios (8237 1111, www.riversidestudios.co.uk) in Hammersmith the large warehouse space holds – among other

The theatre remit is all-encompassing, presenting a plethora of cutting edge productions, not only in theatre but also dance, comedy, and music; you can see some new names, some established, some home-grown and some flown in. 'Great entertainment is at its best when it surprises. But that means people need to be up for the risk of seeing a show that has no guarantees attached to it – no big names, no stars etc. That's the reason we offer cheaper tickets as often as we can – to instil a sense of discovery and adventure,' says Artistic Director, William Burdett-Coutts. Riverside has various pay-what-you-can nights and early bird tickets (*see below*) but you need to be fairly assiduous about checking the website for details of what the deal is and when because they change for each individual show.

Early bird tickets

Another way to get your cultural kicks on a limited budget is to look out for the early bird seats you'll find at the theatres below. Again, you need to be prepared to book promptly, but being quick off the mark will give you all the more time to look forward to the upcoming thrill. And bear in mind that seats are often easier to come by in the first week of the production before the reviews come out.

The Tricycle Theatre (7328 1000, www.tricycle.co.uk), says Artistic Director Nicolas Kent, remains 'committed to making theatre accessible to all of London's culturally diverse population regardless of income. Theatre is a two-way transaction, and the composition of the audience whether rich, poor, old, or young is a vital part of that experience'. The theatre, based in Kilburn, shows works by Irish, Afro-Caribbean, Jewish and Asian writers that invariably tackle political or topical issues, but don't expect overly worthy, mirth-free theatre – there are also plenty of laughs along the way. The building is spacious, with a gallery, cinema and café/bar, and the theatre space seats 225. Early bird tickets are available for £8 on certain dates for the first 80 tickets – keep a close eye on the website.

The Southwark Playhouse (7407 0234, www.southwarkplayhouse.co.uk) in the arches below London Bridge train station is an atmospheric Victorian vault of a place and houses a versatile 150-seat auditorium and a truly cavernous bar. The theatre, in the words of their Education Director Ellen Hughes, puts on 'inventive theatre for courageous audiences,' and offers seats for keen bookers at £8. They also have 'Secret' lunchtime shows, which are either experimental or at an early stage of production. These are a steal – for just £5 you get to see the show, sandwich and hot drink (presumably to stop any off-putting stomach rumbling mid-performance).

Lunchtime shows

There are a few other London fringe theatres that run regular lunchtime shows as well as the Southwark Playhouse. The Bridewell (7353 3331, www.stbridefoundation.org), a 136-seater theatre, in a converted Victorian swimming pool on Fleet Street, holds 'lunch-box' theatre, which costs just £5 a ticket and you can bring your own picnic. It showcases emerging talent and classic short plays, often comedies, by the likes of Oscar Wilde or Neil Simon, that last about 45 minutes. Tickets can be bought at the theatre office or on the day at the box office. Visiting companies set the ticket prices for the evening shows, and it is worth having a look on the website as some start from as little as £7.50.

Islington's King's Head Theatre (0844 412 2953, www.kingsheadtheatre.org) has regular

Tricycle Theatre

2953, www.kingsheadtheatre.org) has regular lunchtime shows, with ticket prices varying, but generally falling into the £7-£8 range. As Danielle Tarento, their Artistic Director, says: 'it's a great way to escape from the humdrum of your day – never more than an hour and you can be back at your desk before the boss starts getting cross!' The King's Head also hosts 'Showstopper!' on Monday nights for £10 (£8 concession) for that you get see a full-length comedy musical being improvised before your very eyes (it's based on suggestions from the audience, a fact possibly worth bearing in mind when choosing your companion for the evening). Also, you'd do well to check the website for events on a Sunday night; these are sometimes less than £10.

Other deals

The Royal Court (7565 5000, www.royalcourt theatre.com) on Sloane Square is Britain's leading national company dedicated to putting on new writing of the very highest quality. It was here in 1956 that John Osborne's *Look Back in Anger* was first performed, marking the beginning of a new wave of British theatre. The space is great, with a big restaurant and bar in the basement. They don't do pay-what-you-can, but they do have £10 Mondays in the downstairs space. Most seats are sold in advance but some are sold on the day, plus, if you are prepared to stand, there are eight tickets available every night for a paltry 10p. (Other theatres sell standing tickets 'in the slips' as well, but a lot of them don't advertise the fact, so it's worth asking at the box office.)

The National Theatre (South Bank, 7452 3000, www.nationaltheatre.org.uk) have their Travelex-sponsored tickets on sale for certain shows for a very reasonable £10, and if the performances are sold out you can buy standing tickets on the day for £5. At Shakespeare's Globe (21 New Globe Walk, 7902 1400, www.shakespeares-globe.org), you can feel like an Elizabethan peasant by parting with 5 British pounds to stand in the pit and be a groundling. The Donmar (41 Earlham Street, 0870 060 6624, www.donmarwarehouse.com) in Covent Garden offers 20 standing tickets a night at the back of the circle for £7.50 but only if the show is sold out (it generally is) while prices for the Almeida (Almeida Street, 7359 4404, www.almeida.co.uk) in Islington start at £6 though they are mainly restricted

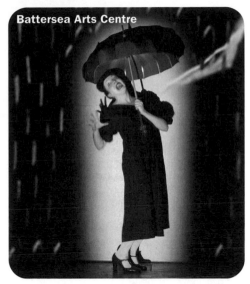

Battersea Arts Centre

view. In terms of the West End, you can try for Standby seats, go to the cut-price ticket boxes or, if you have good eyesight and don't mind heights, sit in the gods.

> *'Cheap seat deals are often easier to come by in the first week – before the reviews come out.'*

And finally, the Bush Theatre (8743 5050, www.bushtheatre.co.uk) has kindly offered Time Out readers the opportunity to pay just £9 for matinees and previews. To qualify, all you have to do is take along your copy of this book (one concession per copy). This award-winning theatre, above the Bush pub in Shepherd's Bush, has long been committed to showcasing promising new writing and boasts an impressive list of alumni including Stephen Poliakoff, Mike Leigh and Jim Broadbent.

And remember – it's always worth looking at the theatre section of *Time Out* magazine, not only for the latest reviews and listings, but also for two-for-one ticket offers and other regular deals.

698 Drink in the gardens at the Chumleigh café

In the otherwise slightly barren Burgess Park, the quaint Chumleigh almshouses (now used as conference facilities) and magnificent gardens come as a pleasant surprise. Capturing the spirit of five distinct gardening styles – Islamic, English, African/Caribbean, Mediterranean and Oriental – you'll find some unusual plant species here as well as two ponds, one for wildlife, the other a more formal, mosaiced Islamic-style affair. Another garden area north of the café is being landscaped by Groundwork London with a playground and walks. You can feast on some hearty snack fare (and roasts on Sunday) and Fairtrade drinks in the cheerful café (between the Mediterranean and Islamic Gardens) with its bright colours, samba music and peaceful outdoor seating.

Chumleigh Gardens *Burgess Park, SE5 0RJ (7525 2000).*

699 Birdwatch

Despite warnings of declining populations and lack of habitat, there's still a surprising amount of birdlife to appreciate in London – around 300 species of bird have been identified in the last few years and including large birds such as herons, cormorants, falcons and sparrowhawks. Even without a pair of binoculars (you'll have to pay more than a tenner for those) there's still a lot you can do to maximise your chances of getting some interesting sightings.

With the help of the RSPB's free guide to birds or a well-illustrated field guide you may soon be ticking off species (like tits, thrushes and finches) from your twitcher list before you've even left your back garden, but the best sites are obviously the places where there's a lot of vegetation. In the centre of town that means parks, where you can see some interesting species such as woodpeckers, redwings and fieldfares (in hard winters), goldcrests, wrens at different times of year as well as water birds like great crested grebes.

Further out, try wilder areas like Rainham Marshes, Brent's Welsh Harp Reservoir, Sydenham Hill Wood, the Lee River Valley, and – just 25 minutes from central London – the London Wetland Centre (www.wwt.org.uk), an international award-winning visitor attraction, considered the finest urban site in Europe for wildlife spotting. The Centre is home to some rare and beautiful birds including bitterns, redstarts, kingfishers, sky larks, red shanks and golden plovers.

If you want to learn more, you could always join a group – try the East London Birders Forum (www.elbf.co.uk), the London Natural History Society (www.lnhs.org.uk) or your local RSPB group (www.rspb.org.uk).

700-702 Play bar billiards

Providing an ideal, and not arduous, workout to accompany a pint, bar billiards involves sinking balls in holes of varying difficulty, without knocking down the skittles that protect the most high-scoring holes. A time limit is set on each game (eventually a bar drops inside the table preventing any more balls returning to be replayed), so unlike billiards and snooker even clueless novices know they won't be stuck at a game for hours. There are bar billards at Pembury Tavern (90 Amhurst Road, E8 1JH, 8986 8597), Selkirk (60 Selkirk Road, SW17 0ES, 8672 6235), and King Charles I (55-57 Northdown Street, N1 9BL, 7837 7758). Games cost £1.

703 Learn to free run

You know those montages you see of spring-heeled urban gymnasts running up lampposts, bounding over bollards and ping-ponging from wall to wall like hoodie-clad superheroes? They're free runners. And you know what? You can do it too. Founded in France and sharing much with the similarly acrobatic and equally dangerous practice of parkour (also sometimes known a *l'art de déplacement* or 'the act of displacement'), it has an official network, Urban Freeflow, which offers outdoor classes for small groups and individuals. The website has plenty of information on the UK free running scene.

www.urbanfreeflow.com.

704

Lunch at the French House

The French House in Dean Street is part of a dying Soho breed and still one of the best places to hole up for the afternoon with a bottle of Breton cider. As well as an impressive roll call of bohemian and ne'r-do-well patrons (Arthur Rimbaud, Francis Bacon and Dylan Thomas have all graced this intimate and charming bolt hole) the place also packed an impressive political punch. During World War II it was De Gaulle's Free French HQ in Britain. Today it's still crammed with the local boho set, enjoying long chats in a strictly phone-free environment. The lunchtime menu is short but sweet, listing soup (£4), haddock and chips or salt beef sandwiches (£7), perhaps accompanied by a beer (which, tradition dictates, they only serve in a half pint glass).

French House *49 Dean Street, W1D 5BG (7437 2477/www.frenchhousesoho.com).*

705

Listen to the experts at Stanfords

Stanfords Travel Bookshop in Covent Garden first opened for business in 1901, and even today its three floors of maps, guides and travelogues can conjure up an almost overpowering wanderlust. Its selection of maps and guidebooks make for pleasant browsing but the store also makes a fitting setting for the many lectures, presentations and book readings that it hosts, which feature some of the most established figures in the travel writing world. Michael Palin, Colin Thubron and William Dalrymple among other well-travelled luminaries have all spoken here and ticketed events, which usually include a glass of wine and few nibbles, take place most weeks. There's generally a Q&A session afterwards too.

Stanfords *12-14 Long Acre, WC2E 9LP (7836 1321/www.stanfords.co.uk). From £5.*

706

Keep TV (and radio) live

See TV and radio shows for free by offering your services as an audience member (and canned laughter substitute). A quick google search will reveal many companies offering free tickets but we recommend the following sites for the best shows: www.sroaudiences.com may be giving away tickets for *Alan Titchmarsh at Christmas* but they also have places for new comedies such as David Mitchell and Robert Webb's sitcom *Playing Shop*; and www.bbc.co.uk/tickets which offers a huge variety of entertainment from *Strictly Come Dancing* to the surreal world of Radio 4 comedy.

707

Become a theatre critic at the Old Vic Young Reviewers Club

All theatre critics had to start somewhere and now the Old Vic is offering the opportunity to a lucky few 13-19-year-olds. Participants are given free tickets to all the productions in the theatre's current season and reviewing workshops are held to help young critics formulate and structure their reviews. To find out more details email newvoices@oldvictheatre.com and include 'reviewers club' in the subject heading.

The Old Vic *103 The Cut, Waterloo Road, SE1 8NB (0870 060 6628/www.oldvictheatre.com).*

708
Go to Portugal for the day

The Portuguese population hits around 50,000 in Lambeth – that's nearly one in every five residents of the borough – and on 10 June (or the nearest weekend if it falls on a weekday) there's a celebration of all things Portuguese in the 'Little Portugal' area that surrounds Kennington Park. With live *fado* (among other music) and numerous seafood stalls selling *bacalhau* (salted cod), it's lusophone laughs all round.

709-718 *Try martial arts*

Martial arts are some of the best-value sports to get involved in. Classes rarely cost more than £10, while many clubs and centres offer membership schemes that make regular training even cheaper. And if you want to try before you buy, most offer a free trial session if you call or email in advance.

Battodo

Battodo is the Japanese 'practice of the sword' used to develop co-ordination, concentation and equanimity. 'Batto' refers to a quick drawing and striking with the sword, 'do' means training for personal development. When students become proficient with non-bladed practice swords, then it's time to practise with real blades using straw and bamboo targets.
Classes St Paul's Church Hall, Camden Square, NW1 9XG (8533 5553). £10. See also www.battodo-fudokan.co.uk.

Brazilian jiu-jitsu

Originally developed from judo ground fighting, Brazilian jiu-jitsu has built up a reputation as a highly strategic martial art in which a variety of pins, locks and chokes are used to force an opponent to submit. Hugely popular with buff chaps in the fitness-obsessed cities of Brazil, its skills have played an important role in the development of mixed martial arts (the nitty-gritty hybrid form that has been popularised by the Ultimate Fighting Championship and Cage Rage).
Classes at the Tokei Martial Arts and Fitness Centre, Lion Court, 28 Magdalen Street, SE1 2EN (7403 5979/www.tokeicentre.org). £10.

Grappling

Many combat sports, such as judo, Brazilian jiu-jitsu, wrestling and mixed martial arts, incorporate grappling to some degree. Here, in a competitive but friendly environment, you can learn stand-up and ground grappling together with a variety of throws, joint locks and pinning techniques.
Classes at PL Gym, Unit 8, The Arches, Gales Gardens, E2 0EJ (07894 551559/ www.pancraselondon.com). £8.

Judo

Willesden Judo Club is one of Britain's top competitive clubs, but that doesn't mean that beginners and newcomers aren't welcome too. An Olympic sport since the 1960s, judo places a premium on grappling skills and the ability to perform clean throws. It's skilful and a great way to develop every aspect of your fitness.
Classes at Willesden Judo Club, Willesden Sports Centre, Donnington Road, NW10 3SQ (07702 322464/www.willesden judo.com). £4.

Kalarippayat

Kalarippayat is the martial art of Kerala and Tamil Nadu in India. It combines north and south Indian fighting forms, with strikes, kicks and grappling, but also draws influences from the equally ancient systems of yoga and Ayurvedic medicine.
Classes at The Place, 17 Duke's Road, WC1H 9PY (07812 416 009). See also www.kalarippayat academy.com. £55 for six weeks.

Karate

Karate is an exciting blend of kicks, punches, knee and elbow strikes and is popular as ever with kids. Guided by Sensei Linda Marchant, a 6th Dan black belt and former world champion, the structured programme of tuition here includes short sequences to allow you to practise defence and attack techniques with your partner but without the risks that are involved in free fighting.
Classes at Tooting Karate Club, Smallwood School, Smallwood Road, SW17 0TW (07771 932963/www.southwestlondonkarate.co.uk). £6.

Kick boxing

The Martial Arts Place teaches a form called *mo-gei-do* (meaning 'the way of no boundaries'). It's a combination of European and Eastern techniques including karate and boxing. Kick boxing is an excellent all-round fitness workout and is as popular with women as it is with men.

Beginners classes at The Martial Arts Place, 88 Avenue Road, NW3 3HA (7586 1222/ www.themartialartsplace.com). £10.

Kung fu

The Shaolin Temple in Tufnell Park offers a rare chance to train in authentic style with one of the 34th generation of fighting monks sent to this country by the abbot of the original Shaolin Temple in China's Henan province. Visit the website for details of classes here.

Classes at Shaolin Temple, 207A Junction Road, N19 5QA (7687 8333) £10; Ladywell Leisure Centre, 261 Lewisham High Street, SE13 6NJ (7687 8333/www.shaolintempleuk.org). £6.

Tae kwondo

Tae kwondo is an ancient Korean martial art that has evolved into a dynamic Olympic sport. The aim is to score points against an opponent's body using kicks and punches, or against their head using only kicks. Classes here are particularly convenient for those working in The City.

Classes at Easy Studio, 60-64 Kingsland Road, E2 8DP (7033 4660/www.bozdag-taekwondo.com). £8.

Wushu and Shaolin kung fu

These highly-rated beginners classes focus on traditional Shaolin-style training. Starting with stances, punching and kicking, you'll move on to learn a range of advanced fighting skills, followed by bare hand and weapons techniques.

ChanWuYi Culture Centre, 152-154 Blackhorse Road, E17 6NII (8509 2111/www.chinese gongfu.co.uk). £5.

719

Beautify yourself on a budget...

'It's better to be beautiful than to be good', claimed Oscar Wilde. But he wasn't living through a credit crunch. However, mindful of the sentiment, we recommend a trip to the Esthetique salon – part of the London School of Beauty, where students (under supervision of beauty therapists) will soothe away worry lines brought on by these troubled times. Eyebrow and eyelash treatments start at £5, a french manicure is only £8 and, although not eligible for this book, there's also a fantastially good value 45-minute facial (£15). Booking in advance is recommended as slots fill up fast.

London School of Beauty and Make-Up *Esthetique Student Salon, 48 Margaret Street, W1W 8SB (7636 1893/www.lond-est.com).*

720

...then get a cheap, chic haircut

There are also several places in London where you can have your tresses tended to for next to nothing. And if you like staring at yourself in the mirror for hours on end, then so much the better. Salon training schools such as Vidal Sasson and Toni and Guy need a constant supply of models for their students to practise on and trained stylists are always on hand to advise and deal with any mishaps. At Vidal Sassoon the standard haircut price is actually £12.50 (£5 if you're a student), but there are often special £5 offers available to entice more models when they have a high volume of students – check by phoning ahead or sign up for their newsletter. Every fourth haircut is also free. Mahogany Academy goes one better – the stylists are all pros from around the world, here to get some UK experience.

Mahogany Academy *22 Dering Street, W1S 1AN (7355 0910/www.mahoganyhair.co.uk). Free.*
Toni & Guy *71-75 New Oxford Street, WC1A 1DG (7836 0606/www.toniandguy.com). From £5.*
Vidal Sassoon *16 Davies Mews, W1K 5AA (7318 5205) and 19-20 Grosvenor Street, W1K 4QH (7491 0030/www.sassoon.com). From £5.*

721 Save yourself for 'Thirsty Thursday'

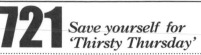

The American health food superstore Wholefoods Market on Kensington High Street offers wine and organic canapé sampling evenings every Thursday in an attempt to pull punters in to buy healthy goodies from the colourfully stocked shelves. But for just £5 you can try a selection of five seasonal wine and food combinations at different counters around the shop. In the past, the gourmet treats have included smoked eel with beetroot and horseradish crème frâiche paired with a sample of Codorníu cava clasico, and parmesan crisps with a snort of Taittinger Brut champagne. Five of these little babies should set you up nicely for the evening. Tasting from 5-8pm every Thursday.

Wholefoods Market *The Barkers Building, 63-97 Kensington High Street, W8 5SE (7368 4500/www.wholefoodsmarket.com).*

722

Turn your garden into a nature reserve

There are more that three million gardens in London – that's a whole lot of habitat for the capital's wildlife to take refuge in. As well as managing over 50 London-wide reserves the London Wildlife Trust is on a mission to get gardeners to turn their backyards into more inviting environments for plants and animals. They suggest planting mixed hedgerow and broad leafed trees to create more shade, buying drought resistant plants that are less water hungry, digging ponds to provide further habitat diversity and a place for animals to drink and bathe, and sticking compost on the roof of your shed to create a living roof and to allow further space for plants to grow. Visit the website to download their free 'how to' guides.

London Wildlife Trust *Skyline House, 200 Union Street, SE1 0LX (7261 0447/ www.wildlondon.org.uk).*

723
Tour Twickenham Stadium

England's rugby team are woefully inconsistent on the pitch – world-beaters one month, pub-team dawdlers the next – but a tour of their stadium can at least guarantee a positive experience. 'Twickers' now holds 82,000, and it's some ground. Tours take in the dressing room (ever imbued with the scent of Deep Heat) and the players' tunnel, as well as the view from the top of the North Stand. The ticket also includes admission to the World Rugby Museum, a diverting exhibition for anyone who's ever known the peculiar joy and beauty of spending frozen, muddy afternoons in a human heap.

Twickenham Stadium *Rugby Road, Twickenham, TW1 1DZ (8892 8877/ www.rfu.com/microsites/museum). £10.*

724
Visit Bermondsey's Fashion & Textile Museum

British designer Zandra Rhodes is known for her outlandish use of colour and so it comes as little surprise when you catch sight of the gaudy pink and orange façade of her brainchild (now run and co-owned by Newham College). As well as housing permanent exhibits by Rhodes, the Fashion and Textile Museum also has a changing programme of exhibitions (usually showcasing British designers), runs courses for both fashion students and businesses, and holds a series of fashion-related events and talks (many of which cost less than a tenner – see website for details).

Fashion and Textile Museum *83 Bermondsey Street, SE1 3XF (7407 8664/www.ftmlondon.org). Admission £5.*

725-733

Fabien Riggall

I have a soft spot for Gordon's Wine Bar (47 Villiers Street, WC2N 6NE, 7930 1408, www.gordonswinebar.com). There are few better places to hole up with friends and a bottle of wine on a dreary Sunday afternoon.

Or if it's a sunny Sunday afternoon, take your bottle of wine to the Serpentine and get your friends to row you around.

Nag's Head Market (opposite Odeon Cinema, Holloway Road, N7 6LJ, 01992 717198, every Saturday) is a fab place to offload junk from home and pick up the odd gem of new junk to replace the last lot with.

Victoria Park is my favourite London park. It's hard to beat a jog here on a crisp weekday morning. I also love cycling along Regent's Canal.

32 Old Bailey (32 Old Bailey, EC4 7HS, 7489 1842, www.32oldbailey.co.uk) is a wonderful Romanian enclave in the city. It's a great place to come for hearty food and enthusiastic Roma music and dance.

I'm always on the lookout for interesting London venues for Secret Cinema and Future Cinema film nights but for some reason it took a Rock'n'Roll cinema event at the Hackney Empire (291 Mare Street, E8 1EJ, 8985 2424, www.hackney empire.co.uk) for me to realise what a beautiful old place this is.

Another beautiful place, which we have just used for a Secret Cinema event is the Royal Horticultural Halls (80 Vincent Square London, SW1P 2PE, 0845 370 4606, www.horticultural-halls.co.uk). The Lawrence Hall is a stunning, high glass-ceilinged art deco space – we blacked it out and put on a Ghostbusters night.

I'm a keen swimmer and lucky to have London Fields Lido (London Fields Westside, E8 3EU, 7254 9038) – the only heated outdoor pool in town – as my local.

Fabien Riggall is the founder of Future Cinema as well as the Secret Cinema and Future Cinema film events.

734

Look a million dollars for less than a tenner

It can be tough to pull off a look on an evening when the purse strings are tighter than a David Hasselhoff perm, so we asked London's fiercest trendonistas how to concoct DIY club couture on the cheap.

Jodie Harsh, socialite and DJ, suggested that the best shop for obscure items is So High Soho on Berwick Street: the fancy dress shop to end all fancy dress shops. 'I've bought rainbow-coloured false lashes, light-up sunglasses and random bits of jewellery there. You can put a whole look together for a tenner.'

The fashion designer Nova Dando goes to the stall outside Sainsburys in the Kingsland Shopping Centre in Dalston, which sells assorted earrings and hair bobbles for cheap.

Club kid Joshyou Are says: 'John Lewis' fabric section is great for upholstery fringing, or hit up B&Q for chains for necklaces or handbag straps .'

The alt. performance artist Scottee can often be found roaming around bargain basement bins in Shepherd's Bush's fabric and haberdashery stores. 'They're cheaper than Soho's and you're more likely to find something a bit,weird.' He also suggests the 'bits and bobs' lady at Goldhawk Road Market. Everything's rounded down to the nearest pound.

735

Get your gaff painted by street artists for free

Add potential value to your home by drafting in an angsty street artist to do up the side of your crib. Non-profit arts organisation Blank Expression run a kind of clandestine introductory agency for wall-hungry artists looking for public spaces to work on. If you're feeling adventurous you can add your pad to the register at by logging on to www.blankexpression.org.

736

Mix it up at Salvador & Amanda's cocktail classes

At Spanish bar and restaurant Salvador & Amanda they like to keep the weekend vibe going all week long, and Monday evenings are for catching up on the delicate art of mixology. Watch the experts make three cocktails (and yes, you do get to drink them) then take your turn to get behind the bar and have a go yourself. After your session, which lasts around an hour, you'll be shaking and stirring like a true son of Tom Cruise. There's no denying that this is office/hen party territory, but with its Latino vibe, gorgeous seating areas and tasty tapas menu, come with an open mind and a lined stomach and there's a whole world of shakin' and stirrin' fun to be had.
Salvador & Amanda *8 Great Newport Street, WC2H 7JA (7240 1551/www.salvadorandamanda.com). Maximum group of eight, £10 per person.*

737

Take a tour round the pet cemetery in Hyde Park

A century before Stephen King's creepy cat Church scared us silly by clawing his way back from the dead in *Pet Sematary*, the Victorians, obsessed with death and mourning, were laying their dear-departed mutts and moggies to rest in this macabre little corner of Hyde Park. It started with Cherry, a Maltese terrier, in the 1880s and the last interment was in 1967. George Orwell described it as 'perhaps the most horrible spectacle in Britain' and while we wouldn't go that far, it's certainly a spooky spot, hidden behind the railings at Victoria Gate on the Bayswater Road. If you fancy a fright, visit at twilight and you might agree with Mr King's assertion that 'sometimes dead is better'.

738 *Dust off your crest at the College of Arms*

The Court of the Earl Marshal in the College of Arms is the 17th-century, wood-panelled HQ of the royal heralds, guardians of the right to bear arms (of the heraldic variety). If you ask to speak to the officer-in-waiting, one of the qualified genealogist heralds, pursuivants or officers-in-arms, he may probably be happy to explain his function for free, especially if there's a chance of his later being able to undertake research into your ancestors and whether or not they carry a coat of arms (for a fee). The College can also arrange for the examination of pedigrees and prepare heraldic artwork. Recent grants of arms include those to Loyd Grossman, who chose a polar bear for his crest, and the motto 'If not now when', and to Sir Christopher Frayling, Rector of the Royal College of Art, who, perhaps equally inexplicably, chose a dodo for his crest, three owls on his arms, and a cactus for his badge.
College of Arms *Queen Victoria Street, EC4V 4BT (7248 2762/www.college-of-arms.gov.uk).*

739 *Listen to the SOAS World Music series*

Want to expand your musical horizons? Then head to SOAS's series of gigs. Try north Indian Dhrupad, a classical vocal song dating back to the 15th century. And that's just the tip of the musical iceberg. How about hearing a master of the Middle Eastern *oud*, or watching a dab hand at the Afro-Cuban *batá* drums? There's exorcistic *salpuri* dance from Korea; Pontic lyre sessions; Argentinian *chacarera*, *candombe*, *zamba* and *chamame* dances; the *maqam* music of the Uyghurs; Judeo-Spanish *Ladino* song; or *seprewa* sounds from the Ashanti region of Ghana. The concerts are organized by the SOAS World Music Series and are free. You can't book, so you'll need to turn up in good time and even then there can sometimes be something of a crush at the door.
SOAS *Brunei Gallery Lecture Theatre, Thornhaugh Street, Russell Square WC1H 0XG (7898 4500/www.soas.ac.uk/concerts). All performances start at 7pm usually on a Tuesday, Wednesday and/or Friday.*

740

*Tree-filled Nunhead cemetery
(entrances on Limesford Road
or Linden Grove, SE15 3LP,
7732 9535, www.fonc.org.uk)
is a nature reserve and a maze
of Victorian statues with fine
views from its highest points.*

741-747 ...then pay some more at London's other great graveyards

Abney Park
If ivy-clad sculpture is your thing, head to this cemetery in Stoke Newington. A series of atmospheric, rambling walks takes you past the last resting place of William Booth, founder of the Salvation Army, whose massive headstone assures us that he has not died but been 'promoted to glory'. Further on, you'll see monuments to slavery abolitionists and missionaries as well as music hall stars.
Stoke Newington High Street, N16 0LN (7275 7557/www.abney-park.org.uk).

Bunhill Fields Burial Ground
Tucked away off City Road (near Old Street tube) is another atmospheric oasis of eternal peace. Used as a nonconformist – and therefore unconsecrated – cemetery from the late 17th century to the middle of the 19th, it features the graves of such notables as poet and mystic William Blake, John 'Pilgrim's Progress' Bunyan, some assorted lesser Cromwells, Thomas Hardy, Daniel Defoe and Susannah Wesley – mother of John Wesley, the founder of Methodism.
City Gardens Office, 65 London Wall, EC2M 5TU (7374 4127). Guided walks June, July 12.30pm Wed. £4.

Brompton Cemetery
Full of magnificent Victorian monuments, Brompton Cemetery has seen many of the great and the good laid to rest within its boundaries, not least among them suffragette Emmeline Pankhurst. And it's said that many of the names you'll see here inspired Beatrix Potter who lived nearby – look out for Jeremiah Fisher, Peter Rabbett, Mr McGregor and Mr Nutkins.
Fulham Road, SW10 9UG (7352 1201/www.royalparks.org.uk).

Highgate Cemetery
The fame of many of Highgate Cemetery's 'residents' makes this a popular visitor attraction and explains the entry fees (East cemetery £3; West cemetery, by guided tour only, £5). But with its angels, shrouded urns, broken columns and dramatic tombs, this is a delightfully atmospheric place to wander. The checklist of celebrated graves includes Christina Rossetti, Michael Faraday, Karl Marx and George Eliot. Both sites are closed during funerals, so call ahead to check before you visit.
Swain's Lane, N6 6JP (8340 1834/ www.highgate-cemetery.org).

Kensal Green Cemetery
Kensal Green Cemetery hides its fair share of notable figures behind its neoclassical gateway. It's particularly strong on 19th-century intellectuals – towering examples of which include Isambard Kingdom Brunel, William Thackeray, Anthony Trollope and Wilkie Collins – but don't forget to visit the grave of Charles 'the Great' Blondin whose high jinks on a tightrope above Niagara Falls way back in 1859 put David Blaine to shame.
Harrow Road, W10 4RA (8969 0152/ www.kensalgreen.co.uk).

Tower Hamlets Cemetery
Though the gravestones here may be a little light on famous names, Tower Hamlets Cemetery has a serene charm all of its own – an expanse of calm just off the busy Bow Road. You'll find 33 acres of beautiful woodland and meadow here, making it a much-needed green heart in the middle of the East End.
Southern Grove, E3 4PX (07904 186 981 office hours only/www.towerhamletscemetery.org).

West Norwood Cemetery
West Norwood cemetery in Lambeth, with its impressive gothic revival architecture, holds memorials to Mrs Beeton, Sir Henry Doulton, Dr William Marsden, Baron Julius de Reuter, Charles Spurgeon and Sir Henry Tate.
Norwood Road SE27 9JU (www.fownc.org).

748 *Visit Trinity Buoy Wharf*

Once a ship and buoy maintenance depot, Trinity Buoy Wharf has had many different incarnations over the years and now it's a thriving centre for the arts and creative industries. With spectacular views over the Thames and with Canary Wharf twinkling in the background, the site is home to exhibitions and performance venues, and houses what is probably London's smallest museum – a former docker's hut dedicated to 19th-century scientist Michael Faraday. Artists' studios are in old shipping containers that have been revamped and painted bright colours, forming an area known as container city.

The Wharf is also home to London's only lighthouse (there are great views from the top) and the Longplayer Tibetan bell sound installation: Jem Finer's 1,000-year-long musical composition has been playing since 31 December 1999 and should continue, without repetition, until the year 3000. It's open to the public at weekends.

Trinity Buoy Wharf *64 Orchard Place, E14 0JW (7515 7153/www.trinitybuoywharf.com). Free.*

749

Create a Spark

Tired of listening to celebrity self-publicity? Well, Spark is your chance to star – along with other 'ordinary people' – in your own tragi-comic story. Creator Joanna Yates explains that Spark is the place to hear and tell true stories. On the first Monday of every month at the Canal Café Theatre in Maida Vale performers – including teachers, car dealers, mothers and barristers – stand up in front of an audience and spill their beans. Each show is loosely structured around a theme (such as 'mistaken identity' or 'under the influence') and individual stories are (perhaps advisedly) limited to seven minutes. After the show, audience and performers float downstairs to the bar for a drink and a chat. Tickets are £6 (plus a once-yearly £1.50 membership fee to the Canal Café Theatre).
Canal Café Theatre *Delamere Terrace, W2 6ND (7289 6056/www.canalcafetheatre.com).*

750

Visit the 18th century at Dennis Severs' House

Journey through time at one of London's most magical houses in the heart of the old Huguenot district in Spitalfields. The 'still-life drama' that takes place here is the creation of American Dennis Severs who lovingly restored the decaying 18th-century building, with each room reflecting a different era of the house's past. The rooms are inhabited by the invisible (and invented) members of the Jervis family, silk-weavers and residents of the house between 1725 and 1919, who leave half eaten pieces of bread and murmur just out of sight as you drift from room to room on your dream-like tour. Silence and concentration encouraged on a trip that's not really aimed at children.
Dennis Severs' House *18 Folgate Street, E1 6BX (7247 4013/www.dennissevershouse.co.uk). £5-8.*

751 *Watch short films*

Short film screenings are thriving in London. The capital offers a variety of venues and festivals where audiences can enjoy anything from quirky music videos and short stories to animations and documentaries – and not necessarily in a traditional cinema setting.

The good folk behind Future Shorts (www.futureshorts.com) have taken it upon themselves to create a culture around the medium of short films. They're not afraid to take film out of the cinema and have previously let their reels loose in galleries, bars and clubs (such as Fabric where they showed *Metropolis*, with a band re-scoring the film), and a cave in Cornwall while on tour with the Guillemots. 'We want to change the way people watch short films and to create an immersive experience,' says founder and director of Future Shorts Fabien Riggall.

They group films by theme, so around Valentine's Day, for example, you'll see 90 minutes' worth of shorts from all over the world, each showing different interpretations of love. The team is also behind Secret Cinema (www.secretcinema.org, although this costs more than £10), a monthly event that invites people to a secret and often bizarre venue to watch a film (are you up for spending an evening in a five-star hotel car park?).

Short and Sweet (www.shortandsweet.tv) hosts weekly short film evenings. It's run by Julia Stephenson, a passionate enthusiast who single-handedly brings together both filmmakers and film lovers. As she puts it, 'the idea is to inspire all who attend, expose the best talent and ultimately celebrate film.' Interaction is also encouraged and it can be a great place to meet and network with people who are fanatic about film. Check out the Café 1001 coffee shop in the Old Truman Brewery on Monday nights; see the website for the location for Tuesday nights.

And finally, there's the London Short Film Festival (www.shortfilms.org.uk), set up in 2004, which runs over ten days each January in some of the city's best cinemas, and brings together excellent contemporary talent.

752 *Moonwalk*

A charity marathon walk held each year in aid of breast cancer research, Moonwalk is for the hard core. Yes, a 26.2 mile walk through London is doable – but try doing it sleep deprived in the dead of night, wearing a lavishly embellished bra. The shenanigans start at midnight and places get sold out fast, so book early. Register on www.walkthewalk.org.

753

Have a Friday Night Skate

It's been seven years since this weekend warm-up skate around town began, and it's still one of London's best free nights out. Open to rollerskaters (in-line and quad varieties both welcome) of all ages and levels, the evening kicks off every Friday at 8pm. Hundreds of individuals (many of them clad in lycra) bunch together, racing, socialising and rolling along to tunes pumped out by a boombox taped to an accompanying bike. The route (which changes every week) is between ten and 15 miles long with things getting more intense in the second half as the pace picks up for the serious skaters. Afterwards everyone usually piles into the nearest pub for a well-deserved pint. The skate starts at the Wellington Arch, Hyde Park Corner; see www.thefns.com for details.

Family fortunes

Riding the DLR, splashing in fountains, picnicking with llamas – there's a wealth of budget family fun to be had in the capital, says Ronnie Haydon, Time Out's London for Children editor.

London has an embarrassment of riches for the thrifty family. You only need the price of a travelcard, a packed lunch and a following wind to spend the whole day freely entertaining your children. Museums, galleries, parks, gardens, farms, dancing fountains and prancing minstrels await their pleasure.

Your travelcard will set each adult back (off peak) £5.60 for Zones 1 and 2 (£6.30 if you're after Zone 3 and 4 as well; £7.50 for 1-6), plus an extra £1 for each child aged 10-16 travelling with you. You must travel together, however. This is your ticket to all the free fun that London can offer. Just experiencing big red buses (Routemasters still operate on routes 9 and 15), trains and trams is a treat for the very young, especially those deprived darlings who don't ordinarily travel on public transport. The range of vehicles you can hop on and off using your travelcard is wider than in any other city. Choose your carriage: bus, tube, Docklands Light Railway (DLR), overground train, tram and riverboat (where you'll get a discount).

A pleasant overview of that excellent source of free entertainment, the South Bank, is afforded by the commuter/tourist bus number RV1. The clue's in the name. It takes you along past some great riverside sights – the London Eye, National Theatre, Royal Festival Hall, Tate Modern – on its route from Covent Garden to Tower Gateway. You could use it on a fun-filled self-guided tour starting at Covent Garden piazza, where crowds gather for the street entertainers on a daily basis, then on to Watch This Space, outside the National Theatre (7452 3400, www.nationaltheatre.org.uk), which has a free summertime arts programme (July to mid September) showcasing the best street, theatre, circus, music, art and dance from all over the world. After which you can stroll all the way along the South Bank to see what else is going on. If it's hot, the dancing fountains outside the Royal Festival Hall are a source of pure pleasure for children. Take a change of clothes and tempt them out of the water for a South Bank picnic in Bernie Spain Gardens nearby.

Discover the Story Centre

Angel Theatre

Take a moment to look in on the Clore Ballroom in the Royal Festival Hall (0871 663 2500, www.southbankcentre.org.uk, free) while you're promenading: this is often the site for free school holiday events, such as treasure trails, storytelling and quite bizarre performances.

The RV1's terminus at Tower Gateway will lead you to your next fun transport option – the DLR. Happy is the child who baggsies a front seat on these driverless trains. They love to pretend to be the driver and enjoy the swoops down the humpy track that takes you on to Docklands. Stop off at Canary Wharf for an ogle at the shiny tower blocks at One Canada Square and the various neat little gardens, pontoons and public art, then hop on to the DLR again and continue your journey.

If you take the southerly branch toward Lewisham, you can get down on the farm in the heart of the city at Mudchute City Farm (7515 5901, www.mudchute.org, free), one of the most rewarding of London's bumper crop of agricultural idylls. This is the only place in the city where you can picnic with llamas. Other animals grazing and rootling with the city's skyscrapers as their backdrop include ponies, poultry, sheep, goats, pigs and cattle. The Mudchute Farm Kitchen is plump with home-made cakes and cream teas, if your budget will allow. For a list of some of London's other city farms see p106.

The next DLR stop from here is Island Gardens, by the river. If you fancy a trip south, take the Greenwich Foot Tunnel (a spooky experience if ever there was one) under the river and emerge at Greenwich, to see how the *Cutty Sark* restoration is coming along, and visit one of the best free museums in the city, the National Maritime Museum (8858 4422, www.nmm.ac.uk), which has art activities and storytelling for children. If the weather's good, don't miss the chance to enjoy the airy heights of Greenwich Park and the Royal Observatory courtyard (8312 6565, www.rog.nmm.ac.uk, free), where costumed storytellers often hold forth during the school holidays. The Meridian Line here is the classic photo opportunity.

If you choose to travel north on the DLR from Docklands, you can stop off at Stratford to look in on preparations for London's Olympic jamboree in 2012. Better fun, perhaps, is Discover the Story Centre (8536 5555, www.discover.org.uk, free), which, although it has an admission charge for the indoor storybuilding centre, has a lovely – and free – little garden with a space ship, slides and willow tunnel that kid adore. It's a splendid place for a picnic too.

Back in town, the DLR links up with the Jubilee Line of the tube system, the most modern and attractive line. It'll take you to London Bridge, where several overground trains an hour can whisk you to Forest Hill and the most original and one of the best free museums in town – the Horniman (8699 1872, www.horniman.ac.uk) – where there's always something going on in the school holidays: summer sees wildlife art activites in the extensive, beautifully managed grounds and woods, and open-air shows in the bandstand. If the weather's iffy, take time to enjoy the music rooms and yet more arts-based fun inside this quirky museum. The Aquarium here is a fantastic floaty freebie, with mesmeric jellyfish, graceful seahorses and loads of variations on the Nemo theme.

If the children are keen to sample every form of public transport in the city, be prepared to fit in a tram ride – down in deep south London. Take a train from Forest Hill to East Croydon (provided you have a Zone 1-6 travelcard), from where you can pick up a tram to Wimbledon, an oft-neglected London outpost but an essential stop-off point for families because of the excellent children's theatre, the Polka (8543 4888, www.polkatheatre.com). You don't have to buy tickets for a show to enjoy spending time in the indoor and outdoor play areas, the super little café and at the teddy bear collection. You can also play the Teddy Bear Trail (£1 is the recommended donation).

From the Polka, Morden South tube station will whisk you a lot more quickly into town again. Get out at London Bridge and walk westward from Bankside to Tate Modern (7887 8888, www.tate.org.uk, free).

Smart arty programmes for children can be found here and at older sister Tate Britain (7887 8888). The former gives kids a pack called Start, which contains puzzles, art materials and an architectural trail (available on Sundays). You can also pick up Tate Teasers at the Family Zone on Level 3 and the Bloomberg Learning Centre on Level 5 has a variety of interactives. Once you've done the Modern you can float off to the Britain – on Damien Hirst's dotty Tate to Tate boat (with your travelcards it costs just £3.35 for adults and £1.65 for children). Tate Britain provides kids with the Art Trolley at the weekends, which is laden with a wide variety of make-and-do-ideas; other distractions include the new Tate Tales trail, a different kind of treasure hunt.

If you want to take in a show in the evening, a just-a-tenner artistic treat not to be missed (if your party consists of just one adult and one child) is Friday Fives at the Little Angel Theatre in Islington (7226 1787, www.little angeltheatre.com), where all tickets for the 5pm Friday performances cost just a fiver. This diminutive but legendary arts venue, (the only permanent puppet theatre in London), is an atmospheric place to take in a show, particularly around Christmas time.

Bear in mind that packing a picnic is essential if you're going to spend the day in London with the children without spending more than a tenner. With so many museums and galleries to explore the kids are going to fade fast without one. And we haven't even mentioned the big three: Science (0870 870 4868, www.science museum.org.uk, free), Natural History (7942 5000, www.nhm.ac.uk, free) and Victoria & Albert (7942 2000, www.vam.ac.uk, free) museums, all of which have a busy school-holiday programme of events for younger visitors. Also, in good weather there's nothing better than relaxing in the park with your lunch. Hyde Park and Kensington Gardens (7298 2000, www.royalparks.gov.uk) is your best bet, mainly for the excellent Diana, Princess of Wales Memorial Playground and for paddling in the Memorial Fountain, by the Serpentine. Most big museums have a picnic room too, so food brought from home can still be eaten in comfort even if the weather's foul.

Still, if you've forgotten to bring food or fancied treating everybody, and there's just one adult and one or two children to feed, you can just about do lunch for under a tenner. The Deep Blue Café in the Science Museum offers a good children's set meal; some places in Chinatown offer budget lunch deals, as do, of course, the Pizza Huts and McDonald's of this world. Belgo Centraal and Belgo Noord, in Covent Garden and Camden respectively (www.belgo-restaurants.com), go one better, however, and offer their mini menu for children (chicken, sausages, mussels or cod with frites, followed by ice-cream) free of charge if the accompanying adult orders a main course. However, in order to keep within the budget it means everyone has to settle for tap water. Sometimes it's hard to be a parent.

Take advantage of the capital's free music festivals

Who said festivals had to happen in leafy green fields in the middle of nowheresville? London's streets might not be paved with gold, but in the summer they are a hive of free musical and cultural activity. Here's our top ten.

The Big Dance

This week-long dance party is now in its fourth year and encourages all ages to get fit in toe-tapping fashion. It's organised by the Mayor's office although it's unlikely that you'll be treated to the sight of Boris shaking a tail feather. Instead you can get your jig on at hundreds of events. In the past these have included tango demos on the tube, performances in Oxford Street shop windows and alfresco shows in Regent's Park. It climaxes with a two-day dance-off in Trafalgar Square. *Various venues (www.london.gov.uk/bigdance). Jul.*

Hyde Park Music Village

Dedicated to showcasing the best in global beats, Music Village is an annual two-day

Paradise Gardens

event that offers the chance to absorb musical traditions from all over the world. With a carnival atmosphere, live shows and dance and spoken word events, you'll not be short of multicultural kicks. *Hyde Park, W2 (www.culturalco-operation.org). Mid July.*

London Jazz Festival

The London Jazz Festival continues to stretch its elastic definition of jazz, so an excitingly eclectic and top-notch line-up is guaranteed. Not only that, but LJF has now expanded out of its original central London bases like the South Bank and Ronnie Scott's to embrace far-flung venues across the capital, from Finchley's Artsdepot to Blackheath Halls. Many tickets are under a tenner and there's an amazing range of free events – a great opportunity to discover different jazz genres and a chance to join in a Big Sing with leading vocalists. *(www.londonjazzfestival.org.uk). Nov.*

London Mela

Dubbed the Asian Glastonbury, tens of thousands flock to Ealing for this exuberant celebration of Asian culture – contemporary and traditional. Garage beats play happily alongside traditional Qawwali and you'll also get an opportunity to check out innovative commissioned projects (such as a collaboration with Circus Space that brought Indian dancers together with aerial performers). As well as the music and dance, there are also bustling bazaars and tasty food stalls. *Gunnersbury Park, W3 (www.londonmela.org). Mid Aug.*

More Music

What could be better than music in the open air on a summer's day? Stroll down to City Hall in July and you'll find a diverse range of alfresco concerts livening up the outdoor Scoop amphitheatre. From big band swing to R&B, Latin beats and classic rock, you'll catch a few famous faces here alongside established

London Mela

performers and stars of the future, playing for free on the banks of the river.
City Hall, SE1 (www.yourlondon.gov.uk). July.

Paradise Gardens

Victoria Park is transformed into a musical wonderland for this family-friendly festival. Offering a modern take on the traditional village fête it boasts a cutting-edge line-up with the emphasis on ska, soul, Latin, folk and gypsy beats. With the demise of the popular Stokefest, this looks set to establish itself as the East End's top community bash.
Victoria Park, Grove Road, E3 (www.paradisegardens.org.uk). Mid June.

Portobello Winter Music Festival

Free music doesn't have to mean fun in the sun. This regular weekend-long bash helps kick off winter festivities with a seasonal soundtrack ranging from cutting-edge electro to pop to dub and reggae. Rough Trade Records host a stall, and there are also art, fashion and food stalls.
The Bridge, 4-8 Acklam Road, W10 (www.portobellowinterfest.com). Mid Dec.

Rise Festival

Europe's largest event celebrating cultural diversity aims to unite the capital through music. The last few years have seen over 100,000 people flock to Finsbury Park for a day of fun, sun (well, sometimes) and great live performances. Previous headliners have included the likes of CSS, Jimmy Cliff, Kelis, Beardyman and the Specials' Terry Hall. There's also a youth slam poetry competition and heaps of food and drinks stalls (not free, sadly).
Finsbury Park, N4 (www.risefestival.org). July.

Shoreditch Festival

London's hippest neighbourhood is transformed into one massive venue for this annual shindig. Aimed as much at families as trendies, it's packed with musical happenings and events. Past highlights have included Proms in Shoreditch Park, performances by the English National Ballet, tea dances, fireworks and the famed Shoreditch Bark Dog Show.
Shoreditch Park, N1 (020 7324 5117/ www.shoreditchfestival.org.uk). Mid July.

Watch This Space

The National Theatre takes the action outdoors in summer with this packed programme of cultural riverside events. Proceedings centre around the now familiar AstroTurf patch on the South Bank. The entertainment is a playful mix of gigs, club nights, dance, cabaret and street theatre.
Theatre Square, South Bank, SE1 (www.national theatre.org.uk/wts). End June to end Sept.

787

See a new piece of architecture every year at the Serpentine Pavilion

With its consistently acclaimed and thought-provoking exhibitions, the Serpentine Gallery has long been a great pit stop on a leisurely stroll around Hyde Park, but since 2000 there's been even more to entice you here each summer. The temporary summer pavilion, designed by a host of high profile architects, is now one of the most anticipated annual events in the architectural calendar. Past designers have included Frank Gehry and Oscar Niemeyer. **Serpentine Gallery** *Kensington Gardens, near Albert Memorial, W2 3XA (7402 6075/ www.serpentinegallery.org).*

788

Become a graduate of the School of Life

The School of Life is in the business of promoting ideas for us to live by. Its services, which include weekend philosophy courses (discussing themes such as love, politics, work, family and play), retreat holidays to unexpected locations and psychotherapy, may not come for under a tenner, but the sermons – lectures in modern living if you will – should stand any stressed out Londoner in good stead. Experts and specialists expound on a variety of everyday thorny issues such as 'pessimism', 'seduction', 'curiosity' and 'humour'; it's classic Alain de Botton territory – indeed, he is one of their several well-known 'preachers'. The sermons, which are held around six times a year, are designed to be entertaining and persuasive with an emphasis on performance, but you can also visit the shop for inspiration – their series of aphorism posters sell for £2 each. **The School of Life** *70 Marchmont Street, WC1N 1AB (7833 1010/www.theschooloflife.com).*

789 *Visit an artist's studio*

Whether you want to buy work, commission a piece or just gawp at the art (and the art crowd), open days – where artists, sculptors and artisans throw open the doors of their workspaces for a weekend – are great fun. Most studios open twice a year to the general public, often in December and also May. Arts Unwrapped (7274 7774, www.arts unwrapped.com) is Europe's biggest open studio event, involving 2,000 artists over three weekends in May and June. Shuttle buses ferry people from one studio to the next. Hidden Art (7729 3800, www.hiddenartlondon.co.uk) is a not-for-profit organisation that supports artists and holds open studio events in central and east London – check the website for details.

790 *Take a closer look at the Albert Memorial*

The overblown Gothic wonder that is the Albert Memorial, opposite the Royal Albert Hall in Kensington Gardens, was opened to public view 11 years after the premature death, from typhoid, of Queen Victoria's beloved Prince Consor in 1861t. At 176 feet tall, it's a shrine to the certainties of the Victorian age – and definitely worthy of closer inspection.

Surrounded by a microcosmic Empire and all its achievements – four continents, frozen life-size models representing the industries and the respected professions of the day – a 14-foot figure of Albert sits amid a fantastic sparkling shed of jewels, polished stones and glass, surmounted by four brightly coloured mosaics of the arts, an angel-strewn spire and a golden cross. It's as kitsch as anything you're ever likely to lay eyes on.

Stand and stare, and you'll soon find hidden wonders: a marble camel and bison, models of Native Americans, voluptuous Miss Asia and her elephant, as well as a 'hive' of industry. If you want to know more, tours are held every first Sunday of the month from March to December; they cost £4.50, and pre-booking is not required.

791

Sample Sampled

Are you a fan of dance but not of dance ticket prices? Or perhaps you're not inclined to blow money on an art form you know nothing about? Fear not, for internationally renowned dance venue Sadler's Wells is now planning to hold 'Sampled' weekends once a year, following the success of the first event held in 2007. The idea is to give people an opportunity to check out a variety of different dance styles – in manageable bite-size chunks, and all in the space of one evening. Pretty much everything is covered, from hip hop to flamenco, tango to classical ballet. Tickets are £10, £5 standing.
Sadler's Wells *Rosebery Avenue, EC1R 4TN (0844 412 4300/www.sadlerswells.com).*

792-795

Drink champagne

Bars selling champagne aren't rare, but a classy joint offering fizz for under a tenner is a less common occurrence. Here are a few of our favourites.

If you visit on the right night, the blood-red champagne and oyster bar at Boisdale of Bishopsgate (Swedeland Court, 202 Bishopsgate, EC2M 4NR, 7283 1763, www.boisdale.co.uk) is dead sexy. Sit at the marble-topped bar and sip one of 20 champagnes (house bubbly starts at £8.50 a glass). The new St Pancras Champagne Bar (St Pancras International Station, Pancras Road, NW1 2QP, 3006 1550, www.searcyst

pancras.co.uk), part of the £800 million refurb of St Pancras station, is the 'longest champagne bar in Europe'. A glass of Pommery Brut Royal or Henriot Rosé will set you back £9.50, but sitting at the impressive 300-foot bar, you can pretend you're at New York's Grand Central Station – until you step back out into the street. It's perfect for toasting new romances or celebrating the departure of the in-laws. Other good places to sip fizz are the beautiful 19th-century La Grande Marque (47 Ludgate Hill, EC4M 7JU, www.lagrandemarque.co.uk, from £10 a glass) popular with a well-heeled City crowd, and the elegant Kettners (29 Romily Street, W1D 5HP, 7734 6112, www.kettners.com), where class comes in a flute-shaped glass (from £8.95) and is accompanied by a pianist every evening.

796 Do the Docks

It's a shame so few tourists make their way any further east than the pub-, restaurant- and shopping-happy St Katharine's Dock close by Tower Bridge. A mere ten-minute walk away on Wapping Wharf there are whole streets of waterfront wharves prospering as flats, but still full of atmosphere with their stock-brick pavement arcades, deep-water inlets, old gantries, river stairs and lookouts.

For example, from next to the Town of Ramsgate pub (62 Wapping High Street, E1W 2PN), take the historic Wapping Old Stairs down to the Thames foreshore – make sure the tide's out, and don't wander too far – to explore the site of the old Execution Dock, marked with an 'E' on the pierhead façade. This is where the East End river pirates – known variously as Heavy Horsemen, Mudlarks and Scuffle Hunters – were chained and washed by tides in punishment for robbing an impressive 50 per cent of the Docks' spices, tea, butter, tobacco, tropical woods and coal. That was until the West India Dock Company began defending their new, stoutly fortified premises with cannon.

797 Watch a Bollywood film at the Boleyn Cinema

A beacon of charm amid fast-food shops on Barking Road, in Newham this ornate picturehouse screens a strict diet of Indian Bollywood blockbusters (£5, £3.50 Tuesdays). **Boleyn Cinema** *7-11 Barking Road, E6 1PN (8471 4884/www.boleyncinema.co.uk).*

798 Have a one-night stand

You may read short stories and watch short films, but how often do you go to see short plays? One Night Stand is a bi-monthly event showcasing six new, short plays written by emerging theatre talent. Tickets cost only £5; email onenightstandevents@googlemail.com for more details.

799-802 Start eco-clubbing

There's a new revolution in clubland. This time there are no white gloves, mercifully few whistles and more recycling boxes than record crates. London's clubland is going green for the first time, with eco-warriors trading in picket lines and protests for fun-filled nights on energy-generating dancefloors.

At the helm of this carbon-saving craze is Surya, London's first official eco-disco, which launched with much fanfare in summer 2008. The brainchild of the mysterious Dr Earth (aka eco-entrepreneur Andrew Charalambous), it aims to turn carbon-guzzling hedonists into climate-conscious campaigners. Central to its green credentials is the high-tech dancefloor, which supposedly provides 60 per cent of the club's electricity by harnessing clubbers' kinetic grooves. It also boasts solar panels, a wind turbine, low-flush toilets, energy-saving disco lights and eco-friendly air-conditioning. And, of course, organic beer is on offer at the bar.

Surya might be London's greenest club but others are also busy doing their bit. New superclub Matter encourages punters to reject carbon-emitting transport and use the boat bus to get to their Greenwich location. There's also a wave of club nights promoting eco-awareness spearheaded by the likes of Luminopolis (formerly the Synergy Project) and Fish Seeks Bicycle. What these nights lack in green technology, they make up for in activism, engaging with organisations such as Greenpeace and inviting them to give talks, run stalls and programme parts of their festival-style events. Recycling is also encouraged, with clearly labelled bins for partygoers to chuck their empty beer and water bottles into. Saving the planet has never been so much fun. **Surya** *156 Pentonville Road, N1 9JL (8888 2333/ www.club4climate.com). £5 or free if you take public transport to the venue.* **Matter** *O2 Dome, Peninsular Square, SE10 0DY (7549 6666/www.matterlondon.com). Early bird tickets usually £10.* **Luminopolis** *www.luminopolis.org. £15 – but free to those prepared to help out on the night.* **Fish Seeks Bicycle** *www.fishseeksbicycle.com. £10 in advance.*

A few of my favourite things

803-808

Emmy the Great, musician

You can go to London Zoo for free if you just walk around it on the outside. I take all my friends when they come over from America. The bigger animals live on the outskirts, and if you go in the afternoon they all come out of their stables. You can see the llamas and the giraffes, and of course all the birds that have long necks, like emus. I've got a route: start at the Parkway end of Regent's Park in Camden Town and begin with the birds and work clockwise. Go after lunch – the best time is around 2pm, around feeding time and before nap time.

At Borders (122 Charing Cross Road, WC2H OJR, 7379 8877, www.borders.com), I work through all the floors and get all the books and magazines I want to read, then I go to Paperchase upstairs and buy a pen and notepad, and then I sit in Starbucks, which, convieniently, is also in the shop. I can spend a whole day reading and making notes and the total cost of that experience is about £2.50 (for one cup of tea). I don't get any funny looks because everybody there is doing the same.

The Roundhouse (Chalk Farm Road, NW1 8EH, 0844 482 8008, www.roundhouse.org.uk) has a great youth programme for under-25s. If you sign up you can use one of their rehearsal rooms for £1 an hour. Most people use it to practice DJing or for band rehearsals, but I go in there and pretend I have an office. I write all my songs there. The Roundhouse café has free Wi-Fi too.

Next door to the Roundhouse there's a nice branch of Japanese restaurant Feng Sushi (Adelaide Road, NW3 3QE, 7483 2929, www.fengsushi.co.uk). Sushi is not cheap usually but they do something called 'the power lunch' for £7. It's a lot of food, everything you could possibly need to get you through the day – raw fish, soya beans, seaweed, brown rice, avocado and pomegranate. You're like: 'every bite of this lunch is adding a year to my life.'

The V&A Museum of Childhood (Cambridge Heath Road, E2 9PA, 8983 5200, www.vam.ac.uk/moc) is kind of weird. There are all these really creepy Victorian toys, and then lots of screaming children. It would be even better if only the adults were allowed in. My favourite exhibit – it's really ridiculous – is just a plinth, and the sign says 'Use your imagination and imagine there's a toy on this plinth.' They must have run out of funding or something.

In the mornings I help my friend walk his dog, a mongrel called Maggie, on Hampstead Heath. It's really fun because you meet all the dog owners – and all the retired people on benches who are out waiting for the dog owners to go past. Walking is way, way more fun with a dog. You don't even have to think of proper things to say to each other, you can just go, 'oh look, she's done a poo.' 'She did a poo yesterday too.' 'No way!'

809

Yodel!

Since 1967, Joseph, with the help of his lederhosened lads and dirndled lasses, has been providing an impressively high-camp version of Austrian hospitality in this cellar venue. The likes of David Walliams, Elle McPherson and Kate Moss have descended the stairs to this basement restaurant – along with countless stag nights and works parties: and we're pretty sure they didn't come for the bratwurst. It's the floorshow of yodelling, cowbells and accordian-accompanied singalongs that keeps the place packed out. A meal would cost around £20 per head (reservations are recommended), but you can squeeze in at the tiny bar and wet your whistle on a few Dortmunder Unions for a tenner. You might even be persuaded to belt out to a few tunes from *The Sound of Music*. **Tiroler Hut** *27 Westbourne Grove, W2 4UA (7727 3981/www.tirolerhut.co.uk).*

810 *Learn to box*

Attention, Rocky Balboa wannabes. Boxing
London serves up sweaty, seedy glamour,
from the rickety weight machines to the
well-thumped bags. And the training is Rocky
intense: the coach is Enzo Giordano, a one-time
super-middleweight contender. The vibe is
friendly and good-humoured, though, and the
punters are of both sexes and all ages – from
child prodigies to comeback kings, out-of-shape
actors to East End wide boys. Classes cost £8
each, or £70 if you book ten.
Boxing London *20 Hazelville Road, N19 3LP
(07956 293768/www.boxinglondon.co.uk).*

811

Hula Hoop!

Of all the retro crazes that have come back – from neon to knitting – hula hooping is the most fun, not to mention the best for your waistline. Hula hoop guru Anna Drury has developed quite a following for her classes – light-hearted, sociable occasions, perfect for those who want to work out in an atmosphere more *Flashdance* than *Fitness First*. Call 07523 448 484 to book.

812 *Walk the Jubilee Walkway*

Pity taxi drivers. London is a colossal patchwork rug of a city, and even long-term residents find it tricky to gain an understanding of how its various districts stitch together. The Tube map might be a design classic, but those linear patterns and handy spacings bear little relation to things at ground level – the average street lay-out in an A to Z is cartographic spaghetti.

The Jubilee Walkway, then, offers a dual function: meaningful exploration for newcomers to the city and a refresher course for those who call it home. Just as important, though, is the fact that it's a great walk. Initially created to celebrate the Queen's Silver Jubilee in 1977, the route has since been honed and enlarged to provide a pavement-pounding 14-mile loop through some of the centre's more absorbing pockets. You'll get your fair share of postcard sights – Big Ben, the Tower et al – but you'll also get a genuinely enlightening look at London in its various guises: old and new, hushed and chaotic, grand and grotty.

The 'official' starting point is Leicester Square, although in our view it makes more sense to begin with the stretch between Lambeth and Tower bridges – it's the only section south of the river and a view-packed hors d'oeuvre for what's to follow. From there it's over the water into St Katharine Docks, across into the Square Mile and on to the Barbican before winding back down to St Paul's. Then, head along Fleet Street, up into Holborn and hard north to St Pancras, at which point the route plunges back through Bloomsbury and Covent Garden, touching St James's and heading on into Westminster and Lambeth. Easy.

There are metal 'Jubilee Walkway' sign-plates embedded in the pavement at regular intervals, although if you'd rather not stare down at your feet all day you'd do well to pick up a dedicated map beforehand (see www.jubileewalkway. org.uk). The loop can be done in a full day but it's a fair trek, so many choose to split it over two or three days. It can be whatever you make of it – a history tour, a photographic walk or even the mother of all pub crawls. And the beauty lies not in the classic set pieces but in the finer details: the architectural quirks, the sense of ages gone by, the stately calm of backstreet Bloomsbury, the suit-and-tie mêlée of St Paul's, the sheep of Coram's Fields and the pelicans of St James's Park.

Potential pit-stops are countless, and a big part of the fun – the route passes some of the best cafés, museums, shops, pubs and galleries that London has to offer – but we'd cherry-pick the following: the madcap interior design at Sir John Soane's Museum (13 Lincoln's Inn Fields, 7405 2107, www.soane.org); an arthouse flick at the Renoir Cinema (the Brunswick, 0871 7033 991, www.curzoncinemas.com); a pint in Victorian opulence at the Princess Louise (208-209 High Holborn, 7405 8816); then head over to Monmouth Street, where you'll find boutiques aplenty along with Covent Garden caffeine stalwart Monmouth Coffee House (27 Monmouth Street, 7379 3516, www.monmouth coffee.co.uk). Finally, walk to Cecil Court (www.cecilcourt.co.uk) and a have a browse through its antiquarian bookshops.

813

See deep space in Hampstead

The capital's would-be astronomers may think of Greenwich as the ultimate place to star gaze in London – or they may not bother at all, given the city's light pollution – but Hampstead's observatory, with its six-inch Cooke refracting telescope, opens up the night sky to curious beginners and keen amateurs alike. Located at the highest point of London, on a clear night there are fascinating views of not just the moon, but also planets, stars, double stars (like Alpha Centauri), as well as eclipses and comets when they occur. The observatory is open to the public on clear nights and visits are free. It's run by the Hampstead Scientific Society charity and a member is always on hand to help navigate visitors round the sky.

Hampstead Observatory *entrance on Lower Terrace, by Whitestone Pond, NW3 (www.hampsteadscience.ac.uk).*

814

Browse the Petrie Museum with a torch

While the British Museum's Egyptology collection is strong on the big stuff, we love the Petrie for its focus on the minutiae of ancient life. Set up in 1892 by eccentric traveller and diarist Amelia Edwards, it's named after Flinders Petrie, one of the indefatigable excavators of ancient Egyptian treasure. Borrow a torch from staff and explore the gloomy Second Gallery (dimly lit for conservation purposes) and shine it into old-fashioned glass cases housing all manner of everyday items, including the world's oldest tunic (a 5,000-year-old linen dress), tools, cosmetics (kohl pots, combs) and – hurrah! just what you need to complete the Indiana Jones fantasy – human remains in a pot (a 4,000-year-old female skeleton).

Petrie Museum of Egyptian Archaeology *University College London, Malet Place, EC1E 6BT (7679 2884/www.petrie.ucl.ac.uk). Free.*

815

Tower over the city atop Westminster Cathedral

Often overlooked in favour of the more famous Westminster Abbey, Westminster Cathedral is spectacular in its own bizarre way. Looking like a wedding cake with a stick of rock stuck on the side, this neo-Byzantine confection – finished in 1903 – has incredible views from the four-sided viewing gallery in its 273-foot bell tower. The bell's inscription reads, 'While the sound of this bell travels through the clouds, may the bands of angels pray for those assembled in thy church.' Don't worry about aural assaults though, the public aren't allowed in while the bell is being rung. Access (by lift) costs £5, £2.50 reductions.

Westminster Cathedral *Victoria Street, SW1P 1QW (7798 9055/ www.westminstercathedral.org.uk).*

816

Watch Scene and Heard

Scene and Heard is an unusual and inspiring theatre trip. Based on New York's similar 52nd Street Project, it's a scheme that was set up ten years ago to encourage and challenge – emotionally and creatively – disadvantaged children from the Somers Town area south of Camden Town. The kids, all aged between nine and 11, write a short play and are then united with a dramaturg, a director and two actors – all of whom are professionals. The result is an often hilarious, heart-warming and hugely impressive piece of theatre, proving that children have a lot to teach us about imagination and clarity of vision. Performances are held at Theatro Technis, and are endorsed and attended by many well-known faces; donations are appreciated.

Theatro Technis *26 Crowndale Road, NW1 1TT (7388 9008/www.sceneandheard.org).*

817 *Check out the Thames Barrier from all angles*

The Thames Barrier has saved the city from watery catastrophe some 70 times since its construction in the early '80s. It's also a fantastic sculptural presence on the river that's worth travelling to see. Ideally a visit should be timed to see it in action – you can find out when that is from the Information Centre.

One approach is via Charlton station (from Charing Cross or Cannon Street) followed by a ten-minute hike up Anchor & Hope Lane, then right along Nagasaki Walk and Hiroshima Promenade. Alternatively, take the DLR to Pontoon Dock, which is set in the freshly landscaped Thames Barrier Park on the north side. Designed by Allain Provost, of the Parisian landscape architecture practice Groupe Signes, the park opened in 2000 and

offers superb views of the Barrier. You can also check out the east side of the barrier from the Woolwich Free Ferry (8921 5965) – just hop back on the DLR for a couple of stops to King George V, from where it's a short walk south to get to the ferry.

Alternatively, and for perhaps the most amazing views, visit Greenwich Yacht Club (084 4736 5846, www.greenwichyacht club.co.uk) after 8pm on a Tuesday. Their clubhouse is on the river a few hundred yards upstream from the barrier. Of course, come the flood, they'll be okay on their boats.

**Thames Barrier Information
& Learning Centre**
*1 Unity Way, SE18 5NJ (8305 4188/
www.environment-agency.gov.uk/thamesbarrier).*

818-827 Listen to free lunchtime recitals

Robin Saikia spends his lunch hours in some of the capital's most lovely churches listening to sublime music – for next to nothing.

Listening to live classical music in London can often be an expensive pastime but there are several churches around town where astonishingly good recitals can be heard and you'll come away with change from a fiver. At most of the venues mentioned here, recitals and concerts are free but if this is the case, a donation will be appreciated.

The Church of St James's, Piccadilly (197 Piccadilly, W1J 9LL, 7734 4511, www.st-james-piccadilly.org) offers a holy grail of free recital programming with its free 50-minute concerts every Monday, Wednesday and Friday at 1.10 pm. The suggested £3 donation is well worth paying for concerts that routinely include – and this is taken from the running order for one month alone – works from the likes of Bach, Chopin, Rachmaninoff, Beethoven, Glinka, Janaceck, Faure and Ravel.

St Martin-in-the-Fields (Trafalgar Square, WC2N 4JJ, 7766 1100, www.stmartin-in-the-fields.org) hosts a popular programme of music (from Franck and Parry, Mozart and Gershwin for example) at its free lunchtime recitals at 1pm every Monday, Tuesday and Friday. For a concert in such a magnificent church, the suggested donation of £3.50 is a snip – and the money goes towards the church's continuing renewal programme.

There are free lunchtime recitals too in St Paul's, Covent Garden (Bedford Street, Covent Garden, WC2E 9ED, 7836 5221, www.actorschurch.org) known to Londoners as the Actors' Church on account of the many thespians interred or commemorated here. The recitals are usually held on Thursdays and Fridays but check the website before you turn up.

The tiny St Olave's Church in the City (Hart Street, EC3R 7NB, 7488 4318), is the burial place of Samuel Pepys and his wife Elizabeth and is also one of very few medieval churches still standing in London (it dates from around 1450). Lunchtime recitals are held here at 1pm on Wednesdays and Thursdays.

At St Giles-in-the-Fields Church (60 St Giles High Street, WC2H 8LG, 7240 2532, www.stgilesonline.org) the organ dates from 1678 (there's an appeal fund currently working to raise money for its restoration) and there are free concerts every Friday afternoon from 1.10 to 1.50pm. The church also has strong American connections and is the burial place of the second Lord Baltimore, proprietor of Maryland.

Around the corner at the Swiss Church (79 Endell Street, WC2H 9DY, 7836 1418, www.swisschurchlondon.org.uk) there is an ongoing programme of free music – and, lately, free cinema screenings. The church also collaborates closely with the Dutch Church (7 Austin Friars, EC2N 2HA, 7588 1684, www.dutchchurch.org.uk) in the City. Check both churches' websites for forthcoming events.

St Anne's Lutheran Church (Gresham Street, EC2V 7BX, 7606 4986, www.stanneslutheranchurch.org) is another City church that holds free lunchtime recitals – every Monday and Friday at 1.10pm. Watch out for Bach, Telemann and Buxtehude in particular.

In addition to a busy calendar of lectures, seminars and exhibitions, Southwark Cathedral (London Bridge, SE1 9DA, 7367 6700, www.southwark.anglican.org) has an impressive musical programme. As well as the free organ recitals on Mondays there are also other classical recitals on Tuesdays. Again, check the website for details.

Finally, don't forget that there are free organ recitals at Westminster Abbey (7222 5152, www.westminster-abbey.org) every Sunday evening from 5.45pm to 6.15pm. If you are lucky you may hear the Abbey organist, James O'Donnell, one of the finest musicians in Britain.

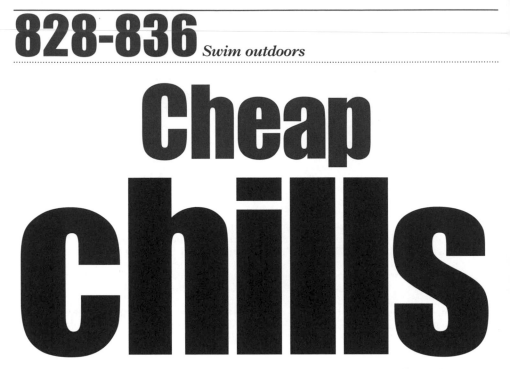

Cheap chills

In freezing December weather, Annie Dare plunges headlong into London's outdoor swimming pools.

Iceland's financial collapse, in the summer of 2008, was a surreal demonstration of the start of the global recession. In its wake, shocked Icelanders, noted the BBC, distracted themselves by attempting a little submersion of their own: in November Reykjavik harbour (at 3.5° centigrade) was bobbing with unprecedented numbers of swimmers, up by more than 300 per cent since the start of the banking crisis that had caused monthly job losses of 5,000. Observers saw a direct correlation between the crash and the soaring attendance levels, as people took drastic measures to forget their economic woes. As Britain's economy starts to tank, would more Londoners do well to take the plunge too?

It is a cold white morning. People are stomping their feet at Gospel Oak's bus stops, exhaling breath plumes. Up on Hampstead Heath, a series of terriers wear tartan gilets and some hockey lads lazily jog round goalposts in an attempt to keep warm. On the brick ledge encircling Parliament Hill Lido (Parliament Hill

Fields, Gordon House Road, NW5 2LT, 7485 5757), a troop of pigeons have puffed out their feathers so hard that you can't even see their necks. Their bird eyes follow the figures of bobble-hatted humans bounding beneath them. At the water's edge, a small group dressed in fleeces traces the slow arc of a martial arts sequence. Behind, as a pep-talk draws to an end, a crowd in swimming caps and Speedos suddenly breaks apart, towels are flung off shoulders and feet move fast, like children's, towards the pool's edge. With 'Two widths minimum!' as our only requirement, on the count of three, we're told, we are to jump into the December water. This is the Outdoor Swimming Society's December Dip at Parliament Hill Lido and the goose-bumped bodies have been gathered here by its high priestess, Kate Rew, as part of a crusade to reconnect Britons – and today Londoners in particular – with nature by way of water.

Standing on the brink, strangers giddily swap stories and the line of people sways with excitement; thighs jog in trepidation, toes are dipped into the freezing meniscus, ice drops are dribbled onto the backs of necks. Then, on three, 100 or so ragtag swimmers jump into four degrees of pool, more or less instantaneously.

I see the tall man next to me power away in a front crawl. Then I realize that I'd be close to having an out of body experience, were it not for the acute lightening rod sensations running through the cavity of my belly and around my chest. I didn't realize shock had a physical expression, but it does, and it is this that is now stabbing up and down my legs and arms, scything at my pelvis and ribs. It is masochistically fun. Around me, people laugh and yell, frantically front- and back-crawling, and quite forget who, and where, they are – apart from the near-cardiac arrest sensations.

After 90 seconds, for me at least, it's over. A few stalwarts swim on, gently gliding to and fro. But most are quickly wrapped up in towels, whooping, comparing notes on pain and invigoration, eyes bright as they surge towards the queue for hot chocolate and mince pies.

The popularity of outdoor swimming in Britain predates the current testing economic times. The empassioned writing of the late environmentalist Roger Deakin was a key catalyst. His 1999 book *Waterlog: A Swimmer's Journey Through Britain* galvanised people to use swimming outdoors as an expression of anarchic delight in the natural world. Rew is one of a handful of new evangelists to follow in his slipstream.

While the OSS's new recruits shudder and chat at the pool's margins, a handful of men and women are nonchalently stripping off and plopping into the water to do unhurried laps.

Members of Parliament Hill's local swimming fraternity, they greet each other with a familiar, if a little staccato, bonhomie and there's some friendly bragging about the natural beauty of various British swimming sites, recent swims and friends' attendance levels. Among them is Frank Chalmers, a daily swimmer at the lido, but whose spiritual home is Ye Amphibious Ancient Bathing Association on Scotland's River Tay. Chalmers, who is writing a book about cross Channel swimmers, has notched up a few remarkable dips since taking up outside swimming in the run-up to his 40th birthday: for example the four-hour swim he made across eight treacherous miles in high seas (temperature 12°) off the coast of Scotland, and the 'unnavigable' whirlpool he braved between two Hebridean islands (famously taken on by George Orwell's brother-in-law, drenched in sheep fat, in the 1940s). 'This is where it starts,' he nods knowingly towards the glacial lido. 'Next thing you know, you'll be down at Dover Sands and training for the Channel.'

'Under your toes fish are teeming, while grebes, herons and swans float above'.

The next day in Gospel Oak, it's another ghostly pre-dawn. Past brambles and under the canopies of ancient trees are two beautiful, and altogether more solitary, swimming wildernesses. Mallards skud low across the limpid swell of Highgate Men's Pond (7485 4491) – a spartan mirror of water to swim in – and crows, seagulls and magpies caw and hop unperturbed under the trees. At the end of a lane past a further tangle of bush and briar, bullrushes sway around Kenwood Ladies' Pond (7485 4491), a popular summer shangri la for many Londoners, however at this time of year you can count on swimming with maybe two or three ladies, and seldom more than ten.

Margaret Hepburn, who is 87 and has been swimming on the Heath since 1946, has just had her morning dip. Her father-in-law, a free-spirited Scot, once led midnight swimming

expeditions to the Heath's ponds during the summer, but she herself joined the cold-water swimming minority when her husband's health began to falter 20 years ago. 'I began getting up early and swimming regularly, creeping away silently with the dog. The people at the pond were so supportive, and kept saying 'see you tomorrow'. That's when it became a habit. Having done one winter I just kept it up. You come out physically feeling better, it makes your joints looser, and you've let go of things mentally. I'm of sanguine temperament, but for some people it is something akin to therapy.'

Jane Shallice, chair of the Kenwood Ladies' Pond Association, has been swimming here since she came to London after university in 1964. She only started to swim during the winter when she retired nine years ago and explains that being ringside to a particular part of the heath is an inextricable part of the appeal of year-long outdoor swimming. 'By going throughout the seasons, you get to know a small area in a very intimate way: which trees lose which buds, when the catkins come. You become very, very conscious of the surroundings.' Here, then, wild swimming is about holding a deep reverence for nature. Under your toes fish are teeming, while grebes, herons and swans float above.

Today she lasted seven minutes in the 4° centigrade pond, and emerged feeling invigorated – and incredibly privileged.

It's a privilege Shallice doesn't take for granted. The Corporation of London has maintained the facilities since the demise of the GLC and, four years ago it introduced a highly contentious charging scheme, which is largely flouted by swimmers to the ponds, who see access as a historic entitlement. 'It was such a contentious proposal', says Shallice, 'that they created a charging system that is wonderfully unobtrusive. No one's going to chase you for payment, there's a real elegance to the way they've resolved that whole battle with us.' But this elegance (voluntary machines, no barriers) has resulted in a huge shortfall in funding: the ponds cost £500,000 to maintain a year, and the charging scheme raised just £13,000 of a projected £80,000 contribution to the cost last year. The issue of funding is sure to raise itself again, particularly given the current turmoil in the City, which is likely to impact the Corporation's coffers: it has already announced that it is reviewing future spending pledges.

Conversely, these straitened times could represent a real opportunity for the advocates of outdoor swimmers. The London County Council engineered the last great lido building programme between 1920s and 1939, during the Great Depression to provide working class leisure facilities. Many closed during and after the 1980s (58 to date) and London now has just 12 outdoor swimming venues left.

Janet Smith, who swims at London's oldest built pool the Tooting Bec Lido (Tooting Bec Road, SW16 1RU, 8871 7198, www.slsc.org.uk), is also the author of *Liquid Assets*, a paean to Britain's outdoor swimming pools and an elegy for those which have already closed. She argues that if the government is to meet its pledges for swimming pool provisions, resurrecting lidos would be a cost-effective way of doing so. 'They are cheaper to build: you build less. The great lido boom of the 1930s which followed the great crash, came under the government policy of work projects as a scheme to give the unemployed a job and to build facilities for the benefit of families afterwards. Possibly the coming crisis and high unemployment could provide an opportunity for similar buildings.' She points to the successes of campaigns to reinstate London Fields and Brockwell Park Lidos, both of which were the subject of vigorous campaigning on the part of their local communities and are now finding favour with a new generation of swimmers.

It's a sentiment echoed by the Rivers and Lakes Swimming Association (www.river-swimming.co.uk), which says cash-strapped local authorities should stop subsidising swims at pools and instead reverse restrictions that overzealous interpretations of health and safety directives have imposed on outdoor swimming in lakes. 'There'd be no heating bill to pay.'

Other outdoor swimming fans argue it's not just cost-effective: beyond the act of swimming itself, the hardship and adrenaline associated with cold water swimming keeps morale up. As Smith sums up: 'There's a very high feelgood factor for swimming in the open air. It appeals to people's current desire for simplicity. It makes a great contrast to our stressful complicated working lives to wind down with a swim outdoors. It gives a sense of freedom and liberation you simply don't get in an enclosed building. And the common devotion to a lido is quite a bond.'

Enthusiasts are also proudly egalitarian. Smith talks of the 'incredible spectrum' of people who swim together as part of the South London Swimming Club in Tooting Bec. Meanwhile, on the south shore of Hyde Park's Serpentine lake (Serpentine Lido, Hyde Park, www.serpentineswimmingclub.com) Sir Anthony Cleaver, the chairman of the Nuclear Decommissioning Authority, is bounding towards the changing rooms just as a fellow member lowers himself off the jetty, fresh from his shift as a night porter. A 24-year-old visiting American student, who is training to swim the Channel, remarks that the comradeship is what binds her to the pond. 'I was also taken aback,' she says. 'You hear so much talk about the English class system. Here, you get a total cross section of society, and a really strong sense of community.' '£20 a year' beams the secretary, her pen poised over a spiral bound notebook as she tries to sign me up for membership and record the latest heats in the Club's handicapped winter series. A flock of swans flies low over the horizon. 'The cheapest annual sports membership fee of anywhere in London, and we'll throw in a cup of tea too.'

London's lidos

Brockwell Lido Brockwell Park, Dulwich Road, SE24 0PA (7274 3088/ www.brockwell-lido.co.uk). £5.20.

Charlton Lido Shooters Hill Road, SE18 4LX (8856 7180/ www.gll.org). £3.25.

Hampstead Heath Ponds Hampstead Heath, NW5 1QR (7485 4491/www.cityoflondon.gov.uk). £2.

Hampton Heated Open Air Pool High Street, Hampton, Middx TW12 2ST (8255 1116/ www.hamptonpool.co.uk). £5.50.

London Fields Lido London Fields Westside, E8 3EU (7254 9038/ www.hackney.gov.uk). £4.

Park Road Lido Park Road, N8 8JN (8341 3567/www.haringey.gov.uk). £4.75.

Parliament Hill Lido Hampstead Heath, Gordon House Road, NW5 1QR (7485 5757/ www.cityoflondon.gov.uk). £4.30.

Serpentine Lido Hyde Park, W2 2UH (7706 3422/www.serpentinelido.com). £4.

Tooting Bec Lido Tooting Bec Road, SW16 1RU (8871 7198/ www.wandsworth.gov.uk). £4.50.

837 *Play fives*

Similar to squash but played on smaller, oddly shaped courts and with the use of a gloved hand rather than a raquet, fives is a sport indelibly linked with the public schools that it originated in (Winchester, Eton and Rugby). However, that doesn't mean it's elitist. You can play the Eton version (sloping walls, split-level floor, no back wall and a buttress known as a 'pepperpot') on four purpose-built courts at Westway Sports Centre. Small group or private tuition is available, after which you can pay a £3 registration fee then book a court for £6-£8 per hour or test your skills in tournaments and leagues.
Westway Sports Centre *1 Crowthorne Road, W10 5XL (8969 0992/ www.westway.org/sports/wsc/fives).*

838

Inspect (but don't lie on) Freud's couch

Sigmund's family home is preserved as it was when he died – and as his previous house was when he fled Vienna in 1938 (he had written down the position of everything in his study, so it could be recreated in London). The centrepiece of the museum is Freud's library and study; check out his collection of Greek, Roman and oriental antiquities, along with the Couch – such a surprisingly inviting and comfortable looking piece of furniture, piled with cushions and a lush Persian rug, it's a shame you're not allowed to lie on it.
Freud Museum *20 Maresfield Gardens, NW3 5SX (7435 2002/www.freud.org.uk).*

839 *Get up early to see the deer in Richmond Park*

The park opens at 7am (7.30am in winter). See www.royalparks.gov.uk for more on the deer.

840

Volunteer in a charity shop

Although you won't be paid (unless you become a manager – and even then we're hardly talking big bucks), time spent working in charity shops is nevertheless rewarding. Firstly, there's the warm glow you'll get from doing something worthwhile and helpful – and secondly, chances are you'll get first dibs on everything that gets donated, which can be anything from Moschino dresses to rare vinyl. For your nearest shop see www.charityshops.org.uk.

841

Watch Tower Bridge opening

Long before it was a tourist landmark, Tower Bridge was a dazzling feat of engineering. Unveiled in 1894, it still thrills when its bascules swing into action. Watching it work its magic, one can understand why London was once the most technologically advanced city in the world. The Tower Bridge Exhibition, meanwhile, spells out the history, but the highlight (in every sense of the word) is the walk along the top tier of the bridge – just revel in those river views. Check the website to see when the bridge opens (which it does around 1,000 times a year).
Tower Bridge *SE1 2UP (7940 3985/www.towerbridge.org.uk). £6.*

842

Join the Fight Club

For blood, sweat and tears, and plenty of raw, unadulterated testosterone, watch East End bruisers punch each other's lights out in the unreconstructed surroundings of York Hall in Bethnal Green (Old Ford Road, E2 9PJ, 8980 2243, www.gll.org). The professional fights command prices of up to £100 a ticket, but on amateur night (usually held once a month), tickets are only a tenner.

843 *Visit the Hoxton Pony about tea time*

Cocktails in china tea cups? No this isn't Prohibition-era Harlem, it's just the way folk round these parts like their tea. As well as the self-cooling infusion jars dispensing 'tea', you'll find berry muffins, cinnamon cherry cake and, of course, an assortment of sandwiches. Served for groups of 4, 8 or 12, prices work out at £10 per head. Booking ahead is recommended.
Hoxton Pony *104-108 Curtain Road, EC2A 3AH (7613 2844/www.thehoxtonpony.com).*

844 *Hang out at the bar of the Theatre Royal Stratford East*

Never mind the performances on stage, check out the free ones seven days a week in the bar. As well as a diverse roster of musical performances, the bar also hosts comedy nights (every Monday, and on the last Sunday of the month) and poetry nights (every second Sunday of the month). And of course food and drinks are available, too.
Theatre Royal Stratford East
Gerry Raffles Square, E15 1BN (8534 0310/www.stratfordeast.com).

Theatre Royal Stratford East

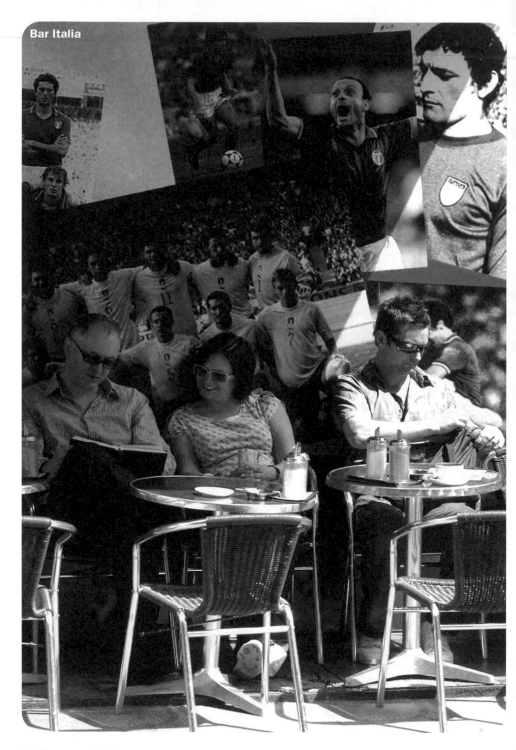

845-852

Have a proper cup of coffee in the West End

Amid the West End's sea of crappuccino merchants there are some very special coffee shop gems. Here we pick out the best places to fuel up on quality caffeine.

Bar Italia

When in Soho … do as the Romans (and other Italians) do and head to Bar Italia if you're in need of a short, sharp caffeine hit. The macchiato is all toffee richness, the dab of creamy foam smoothing the bitterness of the Italian-style blend produced by former neighbours Angelucci Coffee.

22 Frith Street, W1D 4RF (7437 4520/www.baritaliasoho.co.uk).

Caffè Vergnano 1882

You know that this classic Italian company is serious about coffee when you first clap eyes on the formidable retro Elektra Belle Epoque espresso maker that's the centrepiece of the Charing Cross branch (there's another one on the South Bank). It's cosy too – the little alcove at the back is much coveted.

62 Charing Cross Road, WC2H 0BB (8922 6308/www.caffevergnano.com).

Fernandez & Wells

The baristas at Fernandez and Wells work their magic by way of textbook-perfect crema served at the just the right temperature and cappuccinos on which the foam stands proudly several millimetres above the cup rim – the mark of an expert indeed. With its hard metal stools and long slabs of wood on the walls serving as 'tables' this may not be a place to linger for hours but sit yourself at a window seat and, in true Italian coffee drinking tradition, people-watch in style.

73 Beak Street, W1F 9SR (7287 8124/www.fernandezandwells.com).

Lantana

This airy space is ideal for a quiet morning spent reading the paper. The Australian proprietress Shelagh Ryan has chosen what she calls the 'coffee super-couple' to create her brews: Monmouth beans and a La Marzocco espresso machine –as she points out, it's 'sexier than Brad and Angelina, better pedigree than Peaches and Pixie'.

13 Charlotte Place, W1T 1SN (7637 3347/www.scramblingeggs.blogspot.com).

London Review Cake Shop

Books, newspapers and magazines are strewn about this sun-filled room. Monmouth beans are used and cakes are sourced from small, independent producers. The room, and the communal table, is perfect for literary chin-wagging. Despite its proximity to the British Museum we've rarely seen (or heard) any tourists amid the civilised nattering and clinking of teaspoons.

14-16 Bury Place, WC1A 2JL (7269 9030/www.lrbshop.co.uk/cakeshop).

Milk Bar

The Milk Bar gets everything right. The espresso (made from Square Mile Coffee Roaster beans) melds seamlessly into the thick, cashmere-soft layer of foamed milk creamed with microscopic bubbles. Everything – from the charming, mellow baristas to the ever-changing art on the walls – exudes a certain cool.

3 Bateman Street, W1D 4AG (7287 4796).

Nordic Bakery

The cappuccino served amid Scandinavian warehouse design is strong and sturdy, much like the Ikea-esque cup it comes in – and the cocoa dusted on top is smooth and bitter, not Nestlé-sweet. A word of caution: you won't find sugar on the table, nor will sachets be presented on your serving tray – welcome to coffee purism.

14 Golden Square, W1F 9JF (3230 1077/www.nordicbakery.com).

Sacred

Creative beatniks are the regulars at this 'Southern Hemisphere' café, staking out the sofas and downing ethical espressos (made from Fairtrade beans, blended in-house) under the mindful eye of a stone Buddha and other religious motifs. Rather fitting, considering their almost-evangelical attitude to promoting good coffee.

13 Ganton Street, W1F 9BL (7734 1415/www.sacredcafe.co.uk).

853

Remember the Winchester Geese at Crossbones Graveyard

At 7pm on the 23rd day of every month, a group, loosely collected under the banner 'Friends of Crossbones' and led by local Southwark playwright and historian John Constable, gathers outside the iron gates of an unprepossesing Transport for London storage lot on Redcross Way, SE1. They are here to honour the memory of the 'Winchester Geese' – prostitutes who were given a licence to work in the area by the Bishop of Winchester (this part of London being under his – let's call it *liberal* – jurisdiction). Eventually closed in 1853 once it was 'completely overcharged with dead', Crossbones Graveyard was an unconsecrated burial ground dating back to the medieval period and was used for disposing of people not considered fit for Christan burial.

Each month candles are lit, flowers, ribbons, notes and other memorial tokens are tied to the gates, poems are recited – and gin is poured on the ground in tribute to the fallen ladies' favourite tipple. As well as this monthly get together, each Hallowe'en sees performances from the *Southwark Mysteries*, an epic cycle of poems and mystery plays written by Constable and inspired, he says, by the spirit of a Winchester Goose who first visited him on 23 November 1996 on Redcross Way. Check the website for Hallowe'en performance venues. *www.crossbones.org.uk*.

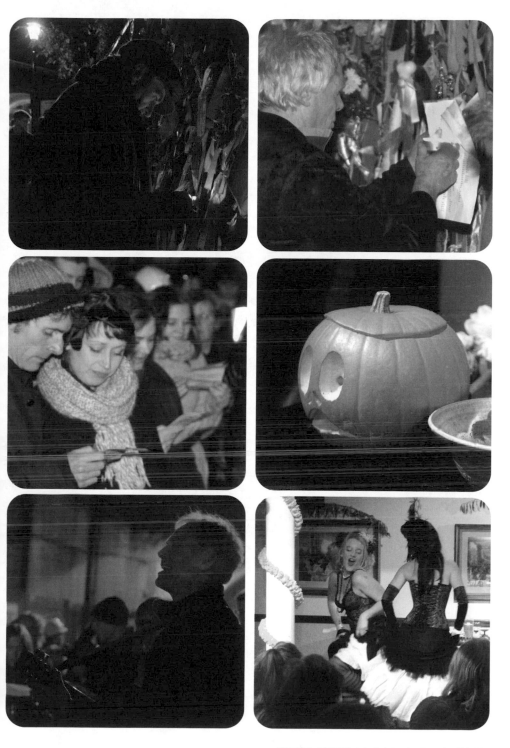

854-861

See Americans in London

Every patriotic American, and quite a few others besides, might well want to track down some of the monuments to their illustrious countrymen scattered around London. And it won't cost them a dime. Abraham Lincoln has just risen to his feet in Parliament Square, SW1, to hold forth in fine democratic style.

You'll find an even older father of the nation, Captain John Smith, first governor of Virginia, next to the St Mary-le-Bow Church on Cheapside, EC2, in the City. He was created by Charles Rennick in 1960. George Washington's likeness stands proudly in front of the National Gallery; it was presented by the 'Commonwealth of Virginia' in 1921. The great American philanthropist and pioneer of affordable housing, George Peabody, holds court at the Royal Exchange, EC3, in the heart of the City. His statue is by WW Story and was erected in 1869, the year of his death.

More famously, in Grosvenor Square, W1, the statue of Franklin D Roosevelt by Sir William Reid Dick was unveiled by his wife in 1948, three years after his death. It was paid for with 200,000 donations of five shillings each, apparently raised in a single day, from grateful Brits. Also in the square, Dwight D Eisenhower, Allied Commander during World War II and 34th President of the United States, was sculpted by Robert Dean in 1989.

A fine bust of John F Kennedy overlooks Marylebone Road, NW1, near Regent's Park tube. It was made by Jacques Lipchitz, unveiled in 1965 by Bobby and Edward Kennedy, and paid for by £1 donations from 50,000 readers of the Daily Telegraph. And finally, nearby at 84 Hallam Street, off Great Portland Street, a blue plaque acknowledges that flat No.5 was the home (from 1938-46) of the legendary World War II CBS broadcaster Ed Murrow.

862 Deliver a speech at Speakers' Corner

See www.speakerscorner.net for a list of illustrious past orators.

863

Dodge bullets in Pickering Place

Down the side of Berry Brothers wine merchants (3 St James's Street, SW1A 1EG) is a rare surviving timbered passageway, dating back to 1730. Ducking through, the warped and crooked wainscoting draws you into the quiet of gas-lit Pickering Place, site of the last duel ever to be fought in London. Fittingly, a plaque at the alley entrance proclaims the 19th-century site of the Texan Embassy.

864

Take a tour of the Globe

If you're not up for being a groundling at the late Sam Wannamaker's faithfully reconstructed Elizabethan playhouse (see p221) then fear not: the Bard's world is also brilliantly brought to life at an exhibition and tour of the theatre. Here, you can reacquaint yourself with England's greatest playwright through displays of costumes, music, dance and rehearsal performances as well the plays themselves. The Globe have very kindly offered readers of this book £2 off the exhibition and theatre tour, bringing prices under a tenner at £8.50 for adults, £6.50 for seniors/students and £4.50 for children 5-15 (make sure you bring the book along with you, and the discount is valid for up to four people).

Tours begin every 15 to 30 minutes but when the Globe theatre is not available (usually because there's a matinee performance in progress), visitors are taken instead along Bankside to the excavated Rose theatre (see p123), Bankside's earliest theatre and the place where Shakespeare learned his trade. Tickets for entry here are £7.50 for adults and reductions apply.

Shakespeare's Globe *21 New Globe Walk, SE1 9DT (7902 1500/www.shakespearesglobe.org).*

865-867

Eat old-school sweets

The realisation not only of the owner's but also many other people's long-held dreams, Hope and Greenwood is a proper, old-fashioned sweet shop which opened its doors to a grateful local clientele in East Dulwich in 2004 and now has a branch in Covent Garden. Adults yearning for cola cubes, sherbert pips and rosy apples won't be disappointed and we're pleased to see (although their parents might not be) that children also bundle in every afternoon for a sugar fix. Over in Soho, Mrs Kibble's Olde Sweet Shoppe is a very handy source of liquorice twists, clove rock and swirly lollipops.

For a different confectionery vibe, try CyberCandy, which stocks a range of sweets from all over the world – perfect if you're a US national craving a Hershey Bar or you just need some Hello Kitty Candy in a hurry.

Cybercandy *3 Garrick Street, WC2E 9BF (0845 838 0958/www.cybercandy.co.uk).*
Hope and Greenwood *20 North Cross Road, SE22 9EU (8613 1777) and 1 Russell Street, WC2B 5JD (7240 3314); www.hopeandgreenwood.co.uk.*
Mrs Kibble's Olde Sweet Shoppe *57A Brewer Street, W1F 9UL (7734 6633).*

Hope and Greenwood

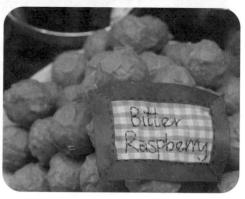

868-876

Drink in some history

What's the strangest, most historical watering-hole in all London? To locals and visitors of a certain disposition, it's a hotly debated question (in a casual, leaning-on-the-bar, giving it the large opinion after four pints kind of way). So, for argument's sake, here's our must-sample 'rub-a-dubs' to set you on the right road to an unforgettable knees-up – especially if you manage to crawl round them all in one go.

When it comes to layer upon layer of atmospheric history, the waterfront Town of Ramsgate (62 Wapping High Street, E1W 2PN, 7481 8000) takes some beating. This was once Captain Bligh and Fletcher Christian's local, pre-Mutiny. The cellars were at one time fitted with shackles for drunks in the process of being press-ganged. From the tiny Thameside patio, you look out directly on to Execution Dock and Wapping Old Stairs, where Captain Blood was nabbed making off with the Crown Jewels. In the panelled bar, 'Hanging' Judge Jeffreys was spotted dressed as a woman as he tried to escape England in 1685. The Bloody Assizes' hard-liner's local was actually the 16th-century Prospect of Whitby (57 Wapping Wall, E1W 3SH), five minutes downriver, where a dangling noose marks his memory. There's also a 400-year-old flagstone floor, London's last pewter bar and a smashing hoard of antique seafaring knick-knacks.

Directly over the river in Rotherhithe is the Mayflower (117 Rotherhithe Street, SE16 4NF, 7237 4088), whence local skipper Christopher Jones carried the Pilgrim Fathers to America in 1620. The rickety wooden terrace over the river is highly recommended, and don't forget to send a card – the pub is licensed to sell British and American stamps.

Off Borough High Street, near London Bridge, lies the National Trust-owned George Inn (George Inn Yard, 77 Borough High Street, SE1 1NH, 7407 2056), London's sole remaining galleried coaching inn, handily positioned just down the road from what was then London's only bridge. Just a third of the rebuilt 1676 structure survives, but there's still a

Mayflower

Prospect of Whitby

wonderfully creaky atmosphere which evokes the pilgrims, travellers and theatre players who've crowded the cobbled courtyard over the centuries.

Moving across the river into the City, you can find the tiny Mitre Tavern (1 Ely Court, EC1N 6SJ, 7405 4751) down an alley between Hatton Garden and Ely Place. Built in 1547 as a London base for the servants of the Palace of the Bishops of Ely, until recently this pub was officially considered to be part of Cambridgeshire, and therefore became a regular loophole refuge for thieves escaping the frustrated City police. The recently deceased tree built into the wooden frontage is said to have been used as a maypole by Elizabeth I.

Meanwhile, although the Viaduct Tavern (126 Newgate St, EC1A 7AA, 7600 1863) gin palace stands right opposite the Old Bailey (once Newgate Prison), it features a landlady's token kiosk aimed at preventing staff thievery. Its cellars boast four vaulted, barred cells from the long-gone Giltspur Street Compter debtors' prison.

Over in the West End's theatreland, the Salisbury (90 St Martin's Lane, WC2N 4AP,

7836 5863) is even more magnificently showy. All cut-glass chandeliers and eyecatching mirrors, with fabulous light fittings decorating the bar, it's a Victorian art nouveau gin palace that manages to mimic the experience of walking directly into your great gran's jewellery box.

Down on Millbank, the cells in the cellar of the riverfront Morpeth Arms (58 Millbank, SW1P 4RW, 7834 6442) remain an intriguing mystery. Now the neighbour of Tate Britain, this was once the site of the miserable Millbank Penitentiary megastructure, to which the pub cells are supposedly related. However, hard fact on the subject seems to be as scarce as the long-rumoured tunnels linking the pub, prison and foreshore.

Finally, a change of pace up at the Spaniards Inn (Hampstead Heath, NW3 7JJ, 8731 6571), effectively a wood-beamed and -floored country pub in zone three, knee-deep in Dick Turpin 'lookout' legends and a full set of Romantic ex-locals in the form of the poets Shelley, Keats and Byron. It's great for Hampstead Heath and the garden is heaven on a sunny summer afternoon.

877

Get out of the house at the London Gaming Festival

This celebration of all things video game related provides geeks with an exciting week of consumer events and product launches and a rare incentive to get out of the house. 2008 featured the launch of Guitar Hero World Tour with a Battle of the Bands – a glorious convocation of rock nerds letting it all hang out at this air guitar/karaoke contest. www.londongamesfestival.co.uk

878

Chill in St Pancras Crypt Gallery

Under the watchful gaze of the caryatids of St Pancras Parish Church, young, emerging artists exhibit their work in what used to be the last resting place of the local Bloomsbury gentry back in the 1800s. Opened as an exhibition space in 2002, the Crypt Gallery's echoing corridors, low ceilings and uneven cobbled floor are constant reminders of the building's past, but despite being chilly and a little damp, it avoids being too creepy thanks to some soft lighting and almost no trace of its former occupants. In fact the musty alcoves now act as enclosures for individual artworks: paintings, installations and sculptures whose inspiration is often the setting itself. The gallery hosts a year-round programme of group shows which rotate frequently and are often curated by the artists themselves, so opening times may vary.

St Pancras Church *Euston Road, NW1 2BA (7388 1461/www.cryptgallery.org.uk). Free.*

879 *Walk a city ley line*

Regardless of your views on paranormal energy fields, walking a ley line through London's backstreets is a great way to explore the hidden city and a neat medieval antidote to the 21st-century world of corporate finance. Follow in the footsteps of Alfred Watkins – who first defined leys as prehistoric sighting lines conceived from high viewpoints and maintained by ground-level markers – by grabbing a map, drawing a straight line from St Martin-in-the-Fields in Trafalgar Square to Arnold Circus in Shoreditch, and walking the roughly two-and-a-half mile (as the crow flies) Strand Ley. The line spookily falls through three other City churches (St Mary le Strand, St Clement Danes and St Dunstan-in-the-West) before finishing up at the Victorian bandstand in Arnold Circus in the grand Victorian Boundary housing estate.

880 *Get the real deal at Ridley Road Market*

While so many markets go trendy and/or upscale, Ridley Road in Dalston has hung on to its roots. It is gloriously cheap: fresh fruit and vegetables sold in giant buckets go for a quid a throw and the fresh red snapper is the cheapest you'll find this side of Billingsgate. Whether it's watch straps, giant snails or saucepans you need, there's sure to be someone flogging them for next to nothing. Conclude your visit with a wander round Turkish superstore TFC – the onsite bakery is particularly tempting.

Ridley Road Market *Ridley Road, E8.*

881 *Watch classic films for free*

A hi-tech peep show for the capital's cineastes, the British Film Institute's Mediatheque offers the chance to explore the entire digitised National Film Archive for free. Users are given their own private booth in which to browse hundreds of British films from David Lean's *Brief Encounter* to Shane Meadow's *Dead Man's Shoes*. Check out the monthly updated Pandora's Box collection, an oddball mix of celluloid quirks. It includes a 1920s shock drama about STDs and what are thought to be the first words ever recorded on film: a bashful Alfred Hitchcock toying with Anny Ondra, the Czech-Polish star of his 1929 thriller *Blackmail*.

BFI Mediatheque *BFI Southbank, Belvedere Road, South Bank, SE1 8XT (7928 3232/www.bfi.org.uk).*

882 *Invest in a Wedge Card*

Save money and help keep your favourite independent shops independent with this loyalty card. It costs £10 (£5 of which goes to various different charities) and entitles you to a multitude of discounts from traders across London. Partcipating businesses include everything from trendy Soho hairdressers to hip Hoxton sex shops, along with larger institutions such as the Barbican and Cargo. See the www.wedgecard for a full list.

883 Get kitted out with some lovely lashes

Glam up instantly for less than a tenner with a pair of MAC false eyelashes. Buy a pair at the MAC store on the King's Road and get them professionally applied too.

MAC *109 King's Road, SW3 3PA (7349 0022/ www.maccosmetics.com). Lashes £7.50.*

884 Knit for nowt

A fun yet (potentially) frugal pastime, and one that's easy to turn into a social event, whether you want to learn to knit or simply enjoy knitting in a convivial environment. The new generation of modish yarn shops are friendly and inclusive in a way that seems to be typical of the craft. All the ones we list here offer advice, drop-in sessions and a sense of community (as well as classes, though these usually break the £10 barrier – an exception is the crochet taster sessions on Wednesdays at All the Fun of the Fair in Soho); they also tend to be run by self-confessed knitting fanatics. I Knit London in Waterloo describes itself as 'a shop and a sanctuary' and the same ethos is true of east London's Prick Your Finger, Stash Yarns in Putney, and Islington's Loop (which runs a drop-in SOS clinic once a month – check the website for date). There's even an informal Tuesday Knit Club at south London florist and café You Don't Bring Me Flowers. Have a look at www.castoff.info, www.knitchicks.co.uk or www.stitchnbitch.co.uk for an idea of the number and variety of events out there.

All the Fun of the Fair *Unit 2.8 Kingly Court, off Carnaby Street, W1B 5PW (7287 2303/ www.allthefunofthefair.biz).*
I Knit *106 Lower Marsh, SE1 7AB (7621 1338/www.iknit.org.uk).*
Loop *41 Cross Street, N1 2BB (7288 1160/www.loop.gb.com).*
Prick Your Finger *260 Globe Road, E2 0JD (8981 2560/www.prickyourfinger.com).*
Stash Yarns *213 Upper Richmond Road, SW15 6SQ (8246 6666/www.stashyarns.co.uk).*
You Don't Bring Me Flowers *15 Staplehurst Road, SE13 5ND (8297 2333/www.youdont bringmeflowers.co.uk).*

Loop

885

Get out of town

Despite soaring rail fares, there are still places you can get to from London for less than a tenner that really do feel like they're a world away (rather than just at the end of the northern line). The train stations listed below all cost less than £10 to get to if you travel at off-peak times (after 10am Mon-Fri and all day at the weekend).

Coulsdon South station (£6) is less than 30 minutes from London Bridge or Victoria, so you'll soon be walking in unspoilt country, in particular the belt of ancient hedgerow (home to more than 20 different tree varieties) and Farthing Down, designated a Site of Special Scientific Interest.

From Marylebone station, the village of **Great Missenden** (sometime home of both Roald Dahl – his house is now a museum – and Robert Louis Stevenson) is around 40 minutes away (£9.50). Nestled in a valley in the Chilterns, it makes a great starting point for walks. Maps and routes are available from www.chilternsaonb.org.

The dormitory town of **Oxted** in Surrey is half an hour from both London Bridge and Victoria stations (£7.70) and a good jumping off point for walks on the North Downs. We recommend walk No.2 from the reliable Saturday Walkers Club – one of many free downloadable walks (www.walkingclub.org.uk).

Purfleet in Essex is within walking distance of the RSPB reserve Rainham Marshes where you can spot all manner of wading species as well as the odd peregrine falcon. Purfleet is around 30 minutes from Fenchurch Street station (£8).

For something a little less rural, discover what a garden city is all about by making your way to **Welwyn Garden City** in Hertfordshire. The mile-long stripe of green at its centre, known as Parkway, has been described as one of the world's greatest urban vistas. A tad far-fetched? You decide – it's 25 minutes on the train from King's Cross station (£9.50).

886

Splash out at Hunga Munga

'Make stuff, make friends, make a mess!' is Hunga Munga's motto. This rag-tag art collective organises evenings of monthly mayhem and alternative creativity usually at the Bethnal Green Working Men's Club, which it transforms into an arty wonderland. It's a bit of a handmade cabaret night – with dancers, performers, a game show, paint-a-thon and raffle as well as quirky bands, DJs and some temptingly inexpensive drinks (not mention free scones!). While you watch, use the arts table to create a your own masterpiece. Anything goes.

Organiser Lloyd Ellis says, 'there are art clubs that take themselves too seriously and there are others that encourage people to splatter paint around everywhere. We're somewhere in-between … not too messy, not too boring … just right.' *www.hungamunga.co.uk. From £6.*

887

Take some tapas with your burlesque at the Gore Hotel

With its chichi, fin-de-siècle charm, there are few places more suited to hosting an evening of burlesque than the Gore Hotel's seductive, mahogany-panelled Bar 190. Regular soirées here are the perfect induction for anyone yet to experience the capital's still-roaring alt-nightlife scene. For a £10 cover charge you'll get four performances through the evening, which is hosted by glam cabaret doyenne Miss Polly Rae and her naughty Hurly Burly Girlys. There's a complimentary cocktail on arrival (check out the drinks list – there are 53 cocktails for starters) and a chance to sample the tapas menu, which includes classics such as chorizo al vino, patatas bravas and gambas pil-pil (prawns sizzling in garlic and chilli). Booking is essential.

Bar 190 *The Gore Hotel,*
190 Queen's Gate, SW7 5EX
(7584 6601/www.gorehotel.com).

888 *Visit William Blake Country*

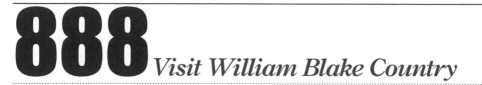

Across the road from North Lambeth tube is a plaque marking the sometime home of William Blake, the writer, artist and rebel of the Romantic age. Until recently, this was the only evidence of Blake's presence in Lambeth, despite him spending ten productive years living and working in what in his time was a 'new suburb'. Today, as well as an exhibition at Tate Britain scheduled for spring 2009, Blake is finally getting some recognition in South London with the help of the Southbank Mosaics and the William Blake Heritage Project.

Blake always wanted his works enlarged and put on the streets where the public could see them and it seems that he's finally getting his wish: on the brick walls of the railway bridge running over Centaur Street and low enough for you to be able to touch, Southbank Mosaics have already replicated several of his artworks such as his haunting vision of God *The Ancient of Days*. There will eventually be 24 mosaics hung here. You can also learn how to make mosaics out of ceramics, glass, marble and found materials in its studio in St John's Crypt in Waterloo, under the guidance of artistic director David Tootill. Everyone is welcome and, once you've got the hang of it, you'll be let loose on one of the next Blake works to go up under the bridge. (Tootill is also happy to let you create your own mosaics – each 10cm square costs just £3.)
www.projectblake.org and
www.southbankmosaics.com.

889

Trace the New River

The New River was constructed in the early 17th century to bring fresh water into London from Hertfordshire. Designed by Hugh Myddelton – commemorated with a statue on Islington Green – and some 20 miles long, it was the first fresh water supply of its type in the city, and most of its route can still be walked, courtesy of Thames Water.

In Islington itself, where it has been covered over in most parts, the Council have constructed a lovely sliver of a park along a half-mile open stretch: New River Walk runs from Canonbury Road (near Essex Road station) upstream to St Paul's Road, where the river disappears beneath Wallace Road and Petherton Road. A small section of it can also be seen further north in Clissold Park, where it has been converted into a duck pond in front of the café.

Back nearer Highbury, as it winds its way behind ranks of gentrified mansions, the walk along the river park can easily include a diversion to Canonbury Square – once home to George Orwell (No.27B) and also Evelyn Waugh (No.17) – or even the Estorick Collection of Italian Art (No.39A). The maintenance of the waterway is undertaken by the Friends of the New River Walk who can be contacted via the Secretary, Mr John Tasker, 3 Hope Close, Wallace Road, N1 2YS.

890

Save on interior design fees at the Geffrye Museum

The Geffrye, housed in a set of converted almshouses, is a quite marvellous physical history of the English interior. It recreates living rooms through the ages – from refined Georgian drawing rooms to cool Stateside-style 'living spaces' beloved by local Shoreditch DIY-obsessives. If you can't afford an interior designer, this is the perfect place to steal ideas. There's also a series of lovely gardens designed on similar chronological lines. Special exhibitions are mounted throughout the year.

Geffrye Museum *Kingsland Road, E2 8EA (7739 9893/www.geffrye-museum.org.uk). Free.*

891

Tour Wilton's Music Hall

Wilton's Music Hall is the world's oldest and last remaining grand music hall. It was built in Graces Alley, not far from Tower Hill, by John Wilton in 1858. In its heyday it crammed in as many as 1,500 people to see the talk of the town acts (including George Leybourne aka Champagne Charlie) and still has a programme of classical concerts and opera performances (some of which are under £10). Visit sooner rather than later, though, because unless this Grade II-listed building gets the funding it requires, it will have crumbled into such state of dereliction as to be completely inaccessible (only 60% of the building was in use at the time of writing). As well as attending the concerts, you can also tour the place – a great many of the original Victorian features, especially in the auditorium, remain intact. Tours cost £5 per person – if you are impressed you can give your remaining fiver to the Help Save Wilton's fund.

Wiltons Music Hall *Graces Alley, off Ensign Street, E1 8JB (7702 2789/www.wiltons.org.uk).*

892

Eat at one of Brick Lane's oldest curry houses

Successive waves of immigration have shaped Brick Lane, and any walk from north to south is pungent with the fragrance of different cuisines – most famously the curries. The restaurants can be hit and miss, but because pretty much all are BYO and most will offer you decent discounts to get you through the door, it's easy to keep the bill low. The Aladdin has been around for a while, and even got a look in from Prince Charles when he toured the East End.

Aladdin *132 Brick Lane, E1 6RU (7247 8210).*

Wilton's Music Hall

Transports of delight

Peter Watts rides the buses – each and every one.

London is unimaginable without its buses. They flow through the city's veins like little red blood cells, travelling along more than 500 different daily routes, dispensing Londoners around every limb and organ of the city. A couple of years ago, in a moment of recklessness, I decided to travel every single one of them, in order, end-to-end, starting at No.1 Tottenham Court Road to Canada Water and finishing at No.499, the Gallows Corner loop service via Becontree Heath. After that there are the weekday-only Red Arrow services (507, 521, 549), the school bus services (600-699) and the mobility buses (900-999) that take OAPs to local shopping centres. When you take into account all the night buses and the letter-prefixed local routes, from A10 (Heathrow Airport-Uxbridge) to X68 (West Croydon-Russell Square express service), it looks like i'll be kept on the move by the bright red behemoths until the day I die from excessive exhaust fume inhalation.

As a Londoner, I've always been a fan of buses, but I became particularly attached to them during a period of fallow employment, when I was cash poor and time rich, and therefore happy to pay a quid to take an hour to travel from A to B rather than £1.50 for the faster, more direct Tube. Travelling above ground, seeing how London unfolds and how postcodes knit together, was a key part in my London education. Every Londoner carries about in their head a mental map of the city, with the unexplored bits, usually those between Tube stations, left blank. The bus fills in the gaps. Cheaply.

London's routes cover plenty of ground and offer different things for different users. So if you are serious about buskateering, you need to be prepared. Start with the London Transport Museum (Covent Garden Piazza, WC2E 7BB, 7379 6344, www.ltmuseum.co.uk) or Ian Allen's transport bookshop in Waterloo (45-46 Lower Marsh, SE1 7RG, 7401 2100) to get Quickmap's *London By Bus* map, which shows you every London bus route for a bargain £2.95. From the same venues, you should also get the *Greater London Bus Map* (£1.50), which isn't quite as pretty, but has a very handy list of destinations, from 1 to X68, for every route on the reverse (Quickmap doesn't list routes, it only shows them on the map, so it can be difficult picking out individual routes from the mass of figures that march cheerfully across the page). Finally, crucially, get yourself a one-day bus pass for £3.50 (or the Oyster pay-as-you-go version, capped at £3). Now you're ready to ride.

EMERGENCY EXIT
TO OPEN

76
MUDCHUTE

London's busy morning buses are hellish for the unprepared, but one thing we'd heartily recommend is swinging by Waterloo – there are numerous usable routes – at around 8am to see the old-fashioned British queue in all its glory. Gaze down from the top deck as commuters, fresh off the train from the sticks, line up in sober crocodiles waiting for their bus to the City. You won't see neater queues outside of the Post Office and it's interesting to speculate on why they occur here of all places – the bus stations outside London Bridge and Victoria stations, by contrast, are screaming scrums of Metro-wielding ne'er-do-wells, and have none of the decorum and 1950s after-you-isms of the Waterloo brigade. Such good behaviour was clearly set in stone by commuters many years previously and has never been unbuilt by the generations that followed.

The top floor of the London bus is great for this sort of people-watching, and makes the double-decker London's answer to European café culture. Ride any of the dozen buses that shuffle along Oxford Street like scarlet pachyderms and, if you're lucky, you might see one of the great British scams in progress. It works like this: an Arthur Daley type sets up a trellis table on the pavement selling boxes of shady perfume. He starts up his patter and attracts a middle-aged woman, who, after some toing-and-froing, hands over a twenty to pay for a couple of bottles of the stuff. This initial purchase then convinces a further flurry of buyers to give up their hard-earned, and between them fill Arthur's suitcase with lovely lolly. Watch from a bus backed-up in Oxford Street traffic, though, and you'll have a bird's eye view of the fiddle in action as you catch the initial buyer – the woman that prompted the gold rush in the first place – returning to the vendor as soon as things have quietened down. She returns the perfume and cash to her partner, and then they'll both get ready to start the process again. If the traffic is really bad, you can watch the dodgy duo work the scent scam in tandem a couple of times before the police get wind of it.

The bus is also the perfect place to see the finer, forgotten points of London architecture, such as the impeccable first-floor detailing you find in the older parts of the City. Try the 21 or 43 north along Moorgate and you'll see a succession of delights: a carved lighthouse on the side of a Swiss bank; the bas-relief of two Tube trains entering a tunnel above a doorway; an old fire insurance plaque on the corner with London Wall; the fine stained glass window of the City campus of the London Metropolitan University; and, where the street feeds into Finsbury Square, the strident art deco Triton Court with its secular spire topped by the statue of a man, standing astride a globe, with one arm raised to shield his eyes from the sun as he stares into the distance. Most central London streets conceal similar treats.

'Their functionality is unquestionable, but nobody would catch a bendy bus for pleasure.'

Top decks are also the best place to witness another London ritual: school going-home time. In his recent transport policy document, the Conservative Mayor Boris Johnson argued that 'Free travel for kids has brought a culture where adults are too often terrified of the swearing, staring in-your-face-ness of the younger generation', but it's really not as bad as all that, and 'free' has nothing to do with it. For decades, schoolchildren have gone home by bus and in exactly the same manner – they swarm on, stampede upstairs, then spend the short duration of their journey shouting at each other about pop music and clothes, fighting and snogging, and occasionally waving wildly/gesticulatingly crudely to their peers who are doing exactly the same thing on the top decks of neighbouring buses. Sure, it might get a bit noisy, but it's only intimidating if you've never been a schoolchild on a London bus. So, ignore Boris's nannying and catch any London bus at around 3pm (the No.4 is particularly exciting) – you will, if nothing else, be able to impress your friends with some sensational new slang. You might even be pleasantly surprised: I was recently on a 68 when a gang of hoodies slouched on and stomped towards the back of

the bus. Commuters nervously eyed each other – was this the dreaded 'in-your-face-ness' Boris had warned them about? However, teenage gang war on the 8.47am to Euston seemed increasingly unlikely as the kids started an enthusiastic discussion about the best way to present a Thai green curry – they were catering students, threatening nothing but our tastebuds.

Most tourists won't go anywhere near buses that serve the inner-London schools though; they'll be too busy getting gushy over the Routemaster. Yes, these still survive, rattling along two 'heritage' routes, the 9 and 15. Both buses serve tourism hotspots – the 9 covers South Kensington and the West End, while the 15 goes from the Tower of London to Trafalgar Square. Tourists love them – and who can blame them? Boris Johnson wants to introduce a new generation Routemaster to replace the articulated 'bendy buses', and Londoners wait with interest to see whether he makes good on his promise. The bendies themselves are not as bad as people make out, and regular commuters seem to actually prefer them because of their increased capacity and ease-of-boarding, but for our purposes, they disappoint. No top deck means no chance to get above the London streets, while their impersonality tends to nullify conversation – one of the great features of single-deckers and lower decks on normal buses. Their functionality is unquestionable, but nobody would catch a bendy bus for pleasure.

Which leads us to the big question: what buses should you catch for pleasure? One of the best for seeing the sights is the 11, which goes from Fulham Broadway to Liverpool Street, taking in everything from the boutiques of Sloane Square to the national monuments of Westminster and the City. The 360 is a good way of getting from the museums of South Kensington down to the brilliant Imperial War Museum, albeit by entertainingly circuitous means. The 73, although now a bendy, is a London icon, being one of the capital's most regular services. The 214 is the most scenic way of getting from central London to Hampstead Heath. The 3 will take you down south to London's magical Crystal Palace Park. And the 22 allows you to finish your journey in the charming surrounds of the Spencer Arms on Putney Common, where the tables are big enough for you to get out your maps and contemplate your next voyage on London's best and cheapest form of transport.

894

Cheer, boo and hiss at a Mystery Play

For the last decade, the pale cream walls of St Clement's in the heart of the City have served as a backdrop for medieval Mystery Plays given a new lease of life by voluntary drama group the Players of St Peter. Back in the 15th century, the plays, which could go on for as long as 20 hours, were performed in the streets of London by guildsmen and craftsmen on pageant wagons that were moved around the city, each company or guild performing a different play. Based on biblical texts, the plots range from the story of Creation to the Last Judgment. These days, having tweaked the language just a bit, the Players select scenes from the plays and edit them to form an Advent production. They tell the story of the birth of Christ right through to the Ascension.

Dressed in elaborate and lovingly crafted costumes which resemble those originally worn in the 15th century, the audience is transported back to medieval London. 'We don't use any materials that wouldn't have been used originally', says Edward Weedon, stage manager and bit-part actor in the production. 'Even our stage hands are in costume.' The scene from the Shepherds' play features an excellent and very life-like sheep, while the shepherds themselves sup on 'a sheep's head soused in ale' (actual sheep's head not included).

Members of the audience are encouraged to join in with the performance: make sure you hiss and boo at the bad guys (that's Satan and his helpers) and clap and cheer on the good (Christ and Mary). With 50 volunteers involved in each production every year, the Players welcome new members. The entrance fee to the productions costs £6 and all profits from the venture go to the church fund.
The Players of St Peter *PO Box 3040, E1W 3TQ (www.theplayersofstpeter.org.uk). St Clement Eastcheap, Clements Lane, EC4N 7AE.*

895 *Browse under Waterloo Bridge*

Stroll along the South Bank and before long you'll find the second-hand book fair under Waterloo Bridge, a venerable London institution and a great place to browse for literary classics, out-of-print books and old magazines and prints (many of which you'll get for less than a tenner).

896

Taste vintage wine at the Sampler

Wannabe wine buffs need look no further than the Sampler in Islington, an independent wine shop that offers 80 of its more than 900 wines for you to try, whether it's an inexpensive Chardonnay from Australia or a fancy bottle of Château Latour from Bordeaux. The wines are rotated every two to three weeks so there's always something new to savour, starting at just 30p for a slug of fino sherry. Browse at your own pace or get some expert help from the staff.
The Sampler *266 Upper Street, N1 2UQ (7226 9500/www.thesampler.co.uk).*

897 *Marvel at the boat that made it to South Georgia*

Tucked away in a corridor of grand Dulwich School in south London, the James Caird might look like any old boat, but this 8 metre whaler is the one in which Sir Ernest Shackleton and five companions sailed over 800 miles to South Georgia during the Antarctic winter of 1916 in a bid to rescue their men from Elephant Island. They took stores to last one month, reckoning that if it took longer they would be dead anyway. In fact they reached their destination after 16 days – a voyage 'of supreme strife among heaving waters', Shackleton recalled. Amazingly, all members of the expedition were saved. To view this piece of history at Shackleton's old school, get a visitor's pass from reception.
Dulwich College *Dulwich Common, SE21 7LD (8693 3601/www.dulwich.org.uk). Free.*

898 *Follow the Artangel*

Londoners generally consider themselves spoilt when it comes to art shows but they have Artangel to thank for some of the bolder exhibitions in the capital. Working with a range of different artists, the production company (not a gallery in itself) stages one-off projects in temporary spaces around the city, placing priority on powerful concepts. Anything goes – thousand-year musical compositions, detritus sculptures, recreated battles between miners and police and most recently Roger Hiorns' extraordinary copper sulphate crystalline installation *Seizure* in a derelict building near Elephant and Castle.

Artangel *(7713 1402/www.artangel.org.uk). Usually free.*

899 _Brush up your Polari_

Hosted by author and _Time Out_ Gay Editor Paul Burston, this 'gay evening of words and music' recently celebrated 12 months of literary loucheness. Attracting a truly mixed crowd of all ages, from 18 to 70, there are different guest authors each month (Neil Bartlett, Stella Duffy, Christopher Fowler and Will Self have all graced the stage) and each evening is uniquely themed (for example, Dandy Night and Dirty Books Night). Readings are followed by a question and answer session and a book signing. Then it's over to DJs Dom Agius and Paul Burston himself and their mix of lounge sounds and dandy disco.

Polari _Freedom Bar, 60-66 Wardour Street, W1F 0TA (7437 3490/www.freedombarsoho.com). Third Wed of month, 7pm-midnight. Free._

900

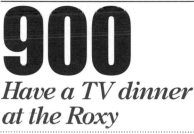

Have a TV dinner at the Roxy

OK, this may not be the dinner of a couch potato's dreams (you have to leave your house for starters) and 'dinner' does in fact mean 'lunch', but this is nevertheless a very cosy way to spend an hour or so and perfect for those yet to splash out on a new 60-inch flat screen. Order your panini (or a bowl of soup) and a drink and settle down to an episode or two of classic TV shows such as _Frasier_, _Blackadder_ or _Peep Show_ which are projected onto the big screen at the end of the bar. As well as the lunch deals, the Roxy Bar & Screen also has an interesting programme in the evenings (some screenings are free, others cost just £3) with a few thought provoking choices (a double-bill of David Lynch shorts, for instance), unusual independent feature films and a healthy smattering of footie thrown in for good measure.

Roxy Bar & Screen _128-132 Borough High Street, SE1 1LB (7407 4057/www.roxybarand screen.com)._

901 _Think positive in the West End_

Rubbing shoulders with trendy hair salons and minimalist boutiques, Covent Garden-based meditation centre Inner Space offers the kind of spiritual free lunch we're told doesn't exist: you can take courses in Raja Yoga meditation or try workshops in effective stress resistance, heightened self-esteem techniques and progressive relaxation methods. Alternatively, drop in to their curious, mood-lit quiet room, listen to piped Zen music and sit among London's enlightened ones.

Inner Space _36 Shorts Gardens, WC2H 9AB (7836 6688/www.innerspace.org.uk). Free._

902 _Get the most out of your Mac_

If you've splashed out on a Mac it makes sense to take advantage of the free in-store after care and to learn more about getting the most out of your investment. Check the website for details of the frequent workshop sessions.

Apple Store _235 Regent Street, W1B 2EL (7153 9000/www.apple.com/uk/retail/regentstreet)._

903 _Visit the eighth wonder of the world_

The closure of the East London line isn't entirely bad news, as it means for the first time in 140 years you can visit the grand entrance hall of the Thames Tunnel at the Brunel Museum. Built by the father and son team of Marc and Isambard Brunel, it was hailed as the eighth wonder of the world when completed in 1843 and Isambard held probably the world's first underwater dinner party here – complete with 50 guests and tunes from the Coldstream Guards. Access varies as museum expansion works go ahead. There is a suggested donation of £5.

Brunel Museum _Railway Avenue, SE16 4LF (7231 3840/ www.brunel-museum.org.uk)._

Baishakhi Mela

Pohela Boishakh (Bengali New Year) happens in Bangladesh on April 14 but its London incarnation isn't celebrated here until the second Sunday of May. The main thrust of this vibrant, cross-cultural event is a grand street procession and party in the heart of the East End's buzzing Banglatown. Food, rather than alcohol, is central to festivities and many of the curry houses bring their kitchens onto the (pedestrianised) streets to offer samples of their native cuisine. For the most authentic head towards the smaller cafés such as Meraz (56 Hanbury Street, E1 5JL, 7247 6999) or Naz Express (16 Brick Lane, E1 6RF, 7377 0643) where a proper home-style Bengali menu is served in place of the tired Anglo-Asian tikka masala-type fare. Finish with a trip to traditional Bangladeshi sweet shop Madhubon (42 Brick Lane, E1 6RF, 7655 4554) for some jalebis (deep-fried orange sugar spirals) or rasgullas (soft, spongy balls).

Chinese New Year

Based on the lunar and solar calendar, the date of this festival ranges from late January to mid-February and usually coincides with the capital's annual China in London festival. Flagship events include a parade of contemporary arts and traditional lion dance across the West End and a spectacular fireworks display in Leicester Square. Fortunately, the Chinese haven't installed their own version of a western-style midnight countdown piss-up – rather, celebrations are spread out across the restaurants and bars of Soho and Chinatown which are adorned with low-slung lanterns and duilián. For Chinatown on a budget try Baozi Inn (25 Newport Court, WC2H 7JS, 7287 6877) for satisfying noodles, dumplings and feather-light 'dragon' won tons.

Diwali

Diwali

This five-day 'Festival of Lights' is celebrated in October and is one of the most important religious occasions for Hindus, Jains and Sikhs. Trafalgar Square usually plays host to a day of lively festivities and is typically closed with traditional prayers and a moving and tranquil lamp lighting finale (known as Aarrti). But by far the best celebration is at the celestial Neasden Shri Swaminarayan Hindu Temple (*see p210*) where thousands of Londoners queue to enter the grand prayer hall to see a kaleidoscopic display of over 1,000 artisanal vegetarian dishes known as an annakut. Alternatively, head to Ealing Road in Wembley, a unique hub of Indian shops and cafes. The best budget meal here is at Sakonis (129 Ealing Road, Wembley, Middx HA0 4BP, 8903 9601), always heaving with local Gujju families. Try the masala dosa or dahi wada – and don't expect to pay much for it.

Nowruz

Iranian New Year lands on March 21-23 on the Gregorian calendar and is best celebrated in London's little Middle East – Edgware Road. Home to a large number of the capital's Arabic population, a variety of languages, including Farsi, can be heard outside the street's many kebab shops and shisha lounges. Persian New Year here can feel like a central Tehran bazaar. For some of the cheapest and most authentic cuisine head to Patogh (8 Crawford Place, W1H 5NE, 7262 4015). It doesn't stand on ceremony – the decor is basic, the menus laminated and main courses come served on simple metal plates. Try starters of freshly baked Persian bread with masto khiar (yogurt with cucumber and mint) or masto musir (yogurt with diced shallots) or houmous followed by lemon and saffron-marinated chicken or lamb kebabs. The fact that no alcohol is served is not only in keeping with the native tradition but another let-off for the wallet – though you can always bring your own.

Russian 'Old' New Year

The Soviet Union adopted the Gregorian calendar in 1918 but Russians still celebrate 'Old New Year' (that is New Year according to the Tsarist calendar) which falls on 13-14 January. Since 2005, an annual Mayor of London-sponsored Russian Winter Festival has taken place in Trafalgar Square and includes a free bill of dance and entertainment. It serves as a neat excuse, should any be needed, to get into Russian pop music. Traditional food on offer includes blinis, borscht and piroshkis (small pies). After that, head to Clerkenwell vodka bar Potemkin (144 Clerkenwell Road, EC1R 5DP, 7278 6661, www.potemkin.co.uk) and try one of 130 seductively sweet flavours of the Russkii national tipple or head north to East European bolthole Trojka (101 Regent's Park Road, NW1 8UR, 7483 3765, www.troykarestaurant.co.uk) where violinists or accordion players are sometimes on hand to further liven up the party atmosphere.

Chinese New Year

Ronnie Scott's main stage may be prohibitively expensive these days, but that's not to say that there are no London venues catering to the hard-up jazzer – far from it. Here are ten of the best.

Boat-Ting at the Yacht Club Embankment
London's only free jazz session based on a boat. With two monthly sessions Boat-ting has established itself at the best weird-yet-wonderful, free jazz/poetry night in town. Featuring three off-kilter combinations of cello/voice/guitar/laptop/drums/bass each night, the bizarre but friendly atmosphere is enhanced by poetry readings from Zolan Quobble or curator Sybil Madrigal.
Temple Pier, Victoria Embankment, WC2R 2PN (7836 1566).

Charlie Wright's International Bar
A newly refurbished jazz bar in the heart of trendy Hoxton, Charlie Wright's has quickly established itself as one of the most exciting new jazz venues in the capital. London's equivalent of New York's legendary 55 Bar,

this is very much a 'players' club, attracting a new generation of jazz virtuosos, as well as quite a few international heavyweights, both in the diverse modern jazz programme and also at its high energy late night jam sessions.
45 Pitfield Street, N1 6DA (7490 8345).

Crypt in Camberwell
There's something both magical and mysterious about walking into this basement jazz club, situated under an imposing church a stone's throw from the centre of Camberwell. Attracting a loyal, and knowledgeable jazz audience this charming, quirky venue hosts many high calibre (and often cutting edge) jazz and world music acts. The no-nonsense food is a real plus, as is the well stocked (and cheap) bar.
St Giles Centre, 81 Camberwell Church Street, SE5 8RB (7701 1016).

Lord Rookwood, East Side Jazz Club
This lovely, atmospheric pub venue has consistently booked big jazz names from the UK scene. Yet the USP here is seeing the likes

of Acoustic Ladyland's Pete Wareham playing 'straight ahead' jazz without any post-modern irony in a relaxed 'pick up' band setting.
314 Cann Hall Road, E11 3NW (8519 0785).

Octave Jazz Bar

A boisterous jazz bar located near Covent Garden, the Octave makes up for what it lacks in sophistication with a good atmosphere and a decent nightly jazz programme that favours retro-jazz styled singer/pianists such as Tina May and Jonathan Gee, and hard blowing bebop saxophonists. A good alternative to the average city pub but not the best place to actually 'listen' to jazz.
27-29 Endell Street, WC2H 9BA (7836 4616/ www.octave8.com).

Ritzy Cafe Brixton

The beautiful Ritzy cinema is further enhanced by a well designed, upstairs café area that offers an intimate space for a huge selection of jazz-orientated (and mainly free) music nights. The likes of Mercury-nominated Polar Bear drummer Seb Rochford and Portico Quartet have been regulars among the constant stream of emerging talent passing through.
Brixton Oval, SW2 1JG (7326 2617).

Ronnie's Bar, Upstairs at Ronnie Scott's

Once destined to be an exclusive member's bar under the old management regime, this is now the hippest late-night hang out in central London thanks to the club's new, inclusive attitude. With its plush decor and funky vibe general admission is a steal at £5. Musicians can get in free on the now-packed jam nights, while themed vocal, Latin and funk jazz nights make up a lively late night weekly programme. Expect to queue if you arrive late.
47 Frith Street, W1D 4HT (7439 0747/ www.ronniescotts.co.uk).

606 Club

Now over 30 years old the 606 relocated from 606 King's Road to Lots Road and is still run by flautist/saxophonist Steve Rubie (who took over in 1976). As well as retaining its original street number it's also hung onto its intimate but swinging atmosphere. Programming mainly classic hard bop jazz artists such as sax greats Peter King, Bobby Wellins and Mornington Lockett, the club also features fine blues, soul and funk artists such as ex-Average White Band guitarist Hamish Stuart.
90 Lots Road, SW10 0QD (7352 5953/ www.606club.co.uk).≈

Spice Of Life

Another stalwart of London's soho music scene, the Spice has been around for more than 60 years, taking in blues, funk and trad jazz (with a regular Friday afternoon big band session) It's also nurtured many of the new generation of jazz musicians via Jazz Jamaica bassist Gary Crosby's acclaimed Tomorrow's Warriors and Nu Troop jam sessions.
6 Moor Street W1D 5NA (7437 7013/ www.spiceoflifesoho.com).

Vortex

Widely regarded as London's hippest jazz club this cosy, 100-capacity Stoke Newington venue puts on the cream of today's contemporary jazz scene. While international luminaries such as Tim Berne, Vinicius Cantuaria and John Taylor have all played here, the imaginative and eclectic nightly programme ensures speculative visits are rewarded with a rich and diverse selection of artists from the top drawer of the jazz spectrums.
11 Gillett Street, N16 8JN (7254 4097/ www.vortexjazz.co.uk).

919-922
Get some wickets

London landmarks such as White Conduit Street in Islington, Lincoln's Inn Fields and, of course, Lord's are key locations in cricket's venerable history. However, until recently the game was almost extinct in inner London (though a common sight out of the city). Things only began to change when the charities Cricket 4 Change (www.cricketfor change.org.uk) and Capital Kids Cricket (www.capitalkidscricket.co.uk) started campaigns to restore the game to urban areas. You'll now find thriving cricket leagues in Regent's Park and Victoria Park, with many inner-city schools involved. See the websites for details.

Club cricket remains, on the other hand, quintessentially suburban. The sport is organised on a county basis, and top clubs play in Premier Leagues where recreational and professional teams compete. The season runs from late April to mid-September and games are free for spectators, plus there's usually a bar to help jolly the afternoon along. For all the details of both clubs and fixtures, consult the following websites: Essex League (www.essexcricket.com), Middlesex League (www.middlesexccl.com), Kent League (www.kcl.uk.net) and Surrey Championship (www.surreychampionship.com).

If you're after something more bucolic, simply head off into the countryside around the capital. You won't have to go far before you find a village green with two sets of stumps pitched – and possibly even a welcoming pub on the corner.

The following are all good grounds within London at which to catch matches:
Wanstead Cricket Club *(Essex) Overton Drive, E11 2LV (8989 5566/ www.wanstead.hitscricket.com).*
Blackheath Cricket Club *(Kent) Rectory Field, Charlton Road, SE3 8SR (8858 1578/www.blackheathcc.com).*
Finchley Cricket Club *(Middlesex) East End Road, N3 2TA (8346 1822/www.finchley.play-cricket.com).*
Dulwich Cricket Club *(Surrey) Burbage Road, SE24 9HP (7274 1242/www.dulwichcc.com).*

923-924
See (bits of) Buckingham Palace

The State Rooms and garden of Buckingham Palace cost more than £10 to see *and* they're only open in August and September. However, throughout the year two lesser known, and in some ways more rewarding, bits of the Queen's official London residence can be visited – each for less than a tenner.

The Royal Mews are the Queen's stables (and garage), complete with Georgian riding school and magnificent horses, as well as a pungent saddlery, impressively sumptuous state carriages and the odd customized Rolls Royce (aka Her Majesty's motor). The Queen's Gallery, erected in the 1950s on the ruins of the palace's bomb-damaged private chapel, and recently renovated at great expense, shows changing selections from the Royal Collection of fine art, sculpture, furniture and porcelain. Exhibitions in 2009/10 include the world's finest display of Sèvres porcelain, acquired between 1783 and 1830 by George IV and Conversation Pieces, a show dedicated to informal portraits of high society life over the last few hundred years.
Royal Mews and Queen's Gallery *Buckingham Palace, SW1A 1AA (7766 7301/www.royal.gov.uk). £7.50 and £8.50 respectively.*

925
Rethink science at the Dana Centre

Think science and scientists are dull, irrelevant and best confined to labs? Think again. An evening spent at the Science Museum's Dana Centre, an adult-only venue exploring issues in contemporary science through dialogue, performance and art, should be enough to convince you otherwise. Every night the creative minds behind this innovative venture roll out something different: from haute couture catwalk shows, video gaming cabaret nights and stand-up comedy to no-kids-allowed fun and games in the Museum's Launchpad gallery. Come with an open mind, prepare to participate and enjoy a drink or two at the café-bar.
Dana Centre *165 Queen's Gate, SW7 5HD (7942 4040/www.danacentre.org.uk). Free.*

926-930 *Indulge in tea and cake*

Tea at the Ritz and other 'ritzy' London hotels will set you back anything up to £40 – here we pick some of our favourite tea rooms where you'll come away with change from a tenner.

Bea's of Bloomsbury

Dusky blue walls and plush velvet chairs add a glamorous contrast to the bakery that sits at the back of this friendly café. Teas from prestige specialist Jing (earl grey, english breakfast, green tea and a couple of herbal options) are offered alongside excellent coffee and chai lattes made with Cordon Bleu-trained Bea's own concoction of organic Darjeeling tea and spices. Cakes are in the French and American traditions: chocolate truffle, cheesecakes, red velvet and exceptionally pretty cupcakes.

44 Theobald's Road, WC1X 8NW (7242 8330/ www.beasofbloomsbury.com).

High Tea of Highgate

Tea cosies illustrated with dogs, hearts and Union Jacks, cow-shaped milk jugs, cute aprons, porcelain jelly moulds and bags of humbugs provide a colourfully retro take on the traditional village tea room in this most traditional of London villages. You can hear the hand-mixer whirring away behind the counter as owner Georgina Worthington whips up a fresh victoria sponge or carrot cake. Organic butter and eggs are used in the baking.

50 Highgate High Street, N6 5HX (8348 3162/ www.highteaofhighgate.com).

Orange Pekoe

A pretty tearoom huddled neatly among the boutiques of Barnes, Orange Pekoe offers pleasing river views and a shop boasting over 100 high quality teas. Owner Marianna Hadjigeorgiou uses teapots with a removable filter, so you can brew your tea to the perfect strength. Spectacular cakes are provided by esteemed bakery Konditor & Cook, but check out the big, warm own-made scones too.

3 White Hart Lane, SW13 0PX (8876 6070/www.orangepekoeteas.com).

Sketch

At styled-within-an-inch-of-its-life Sketch on Conduit Street you won't get much for a tenner but in the decadent and eccentric parlour, between 3pm and 6.30pm, you can take cream tea. There's not a huge range of teas available but some perfectly acceptable as well as pretty pots of english breakfast, earl grey, camomile and mint varieties are served with scones, jam and clotted cream, all for £9.50.

9 Conduit Street, W1S 2XG (7659 4500/www.sketch.uk.com).

Tea Smith

Spitalfields' premier tearoom – with its distinctly Japanese aesthetic – might not have the homely charm of some of its contemporaries, but it is undeniably stylish. Owner John Kennedy sources exquisite teas direct from the Far East and brews them with precision. The pâtisserie's offerings (mostly innovative, fusion combos such as jasmine truffles or dark chocolate infused with oolong tea) come from leading pastry chef and chocolatier William Curley – keep an eye out for their tea and chocolate matching sessions.

8 Lamb Street, E1 6EA (7247 1333/ www.teasmith.co.uk).

931

Why limit fireworks viewing to fifth November? Other pyrotechnical highlights of the capital's calendar include Diwali, Chinese New Year, the Lord Mayor's Show, the Thames Festival and, of course, New Year's Eve on the river.

932

See the poetry in modern architecture

The heart of the City doesn't necessarily feel like the most auspicious spot for a poetic experience, but if you sit on the stone benches that circle the base of the 'Gherkin' (30 St Mary Axe, EC3) that is exactly what you'll have. Incised on each bench, one line at a time, is 'Arcadian Dream Garden' by eccentric, neo-classical Scottish modernist Ian Hamilton Finlay. Could he have been thinking about the Gherkin itself when he wrote: 'A slender stone vase…', 'A tree, pierced right through by a bronze arrow'?

933

Rise with the birds

London's bird-lovers have taken to International Dawn Chorus Day with enthusiasm since it was initiated for the UK (in Birmingham) back in 1984. There are two approaches to the event, neither of which need cost a brass razzoo. Those who can already tell a tweet from a twitter often go it alone in their local park or back garden, then feed their findings back to the official website (www.idcd.info). Sociable coves and the blissfully ignorant can set the alarm early on the designated Sunday in early May (check the website for this year's date) and head out to one of London's organised events. The prime location (the London Wetland Centre) is out of our price range, notwithstanding the group breakfast, but many local reserves – notably Tower Hamlets Cemetery Park and Roundshaw Downs Local Nature Reserve – are enthusiastic participants, offering free tours. You'll probably have to be up at 4am… but you can always go back to bed afterwards.

934

Play in Coram's Fields

You have to be accompanied by a child to gain entry to Coram's Fields in Bloomsbury. Set up in 1936 as London's first public children's playground, the seven sprawling acres of playgrounds and park are exclusively for use of children living in or visiting London. There are massive lawns for free play and family picnics, sports pitches, a paddling pool, sandpits, a flying fox and other slides, a pets' corner (sheep, goats, ducks and hens), a sensory play area designed for children with disabilities and a branch of lovely Austrian café Kipferl. **Coram's Fields** *93 Guilford Street, WC1N 1DN (7837 6138).*

935

Send ten squids up in smoke

Still puffing? If so, you can destroy your lungs in style after a visit to G Smith & Sons (74 Charing Cross Road, WC2H 0BG, 7836 7422). Established back in 1869 (and pretty much unchanged since then), this was the first shop on Charing Cross Road and is bound by a 'condition of lease' that states the site can only ever house a tobacconist. You can buy 20 Marlboro if you must, but G Smith is really a place for the aficionado: invest your tenner in something special – perhaps a Zippo bearing a picture of the shop (£9.99) or their own-blend snuff (£6.60).

936
Stand at the pagan heart of the City

Set low in the wall of a sports shop opposite Cannon Street Station is a strange glass case protected by an ornate wrought iron grille. It contains the bare stump of a stone which once stood tall, a pagan menhir at the centre of the Roman city from which all measurements in the land were once taken. It said that if the stone ever leaves London, the city will fall.

A few of my favourite things

937-944

Anna Robertson, market trader

I love Borough Market (7407 1002, www.boroughmarket. org.uk) because pretty much everyone who comes there – the sellers and the buyers – are complete foodies. And despite its image, it's still an inexpensive place to get your fruit and veg. I buy mine from a stall called Ted's Veg. Their seasonal stuff tastes like it comes straight out of the ground and into your hand – the freshness is amazing. Last week they had some beautiful pink, orange and gold beetroots. The one you should really look out for is called chioggia beetroot, which has pink and white spirals. I just made a salad with it and it looked stunning.

One of my favourite veggie restaurants is the Rootmaster (Elys Yard, Hanbury Street, E1 6QL, 07912 389314, www.root-master.co.uk), which opened about a year ago on an old routemaster bus on Brick Lane. They've transformed the upstairs of the bus into a seating area and downstairs into a kitchen. They do really good, traditional veggie and vegan food, all of which is great value for money. Last time I was there we had a homemade tart with purple sprouting broccoli and an amazing dessert of baked banana dipped in chocolate and wrapped in pastry. Out of this world.

If you're ever in town late at night and want to grab a cheap veggie takeaway, go to Maoz (43 Old Compton Street, W1V 6SG, 7851 1586, www.maozveg.com) in Soho. You get falafel in pitta bread and there's also a whole salad bar with things like couscous, chilli carrots, fresh vegetables and sauces which you can pile on top. It's absolutely gorgeous – and feels quite healthy for fast food.

There's a wonderful vegan restaurant near Old Street called Saf (152-154 Curtain Road, EC2A 3AT, 7613 0007, www.safrestaurant.co.uk). It's quite expensive for dinner, but you can get their Buddha Bowl, which is a bowl of tofu, rice and vegetables, for £9.50. And if you go there at lunchtime it's even cheaper. They do all kinds of foods that you would never imagine could be vegan – I love the beetroot ravioli, which has beetroot instead of the pasta and, inside, vegan cheese made with nuts and herbs. I wouldn't normally go anywhere near vegan cheese, but their cheesecake is also quite possibly the best I've ever had.

We live near Hither Green, and really try and keep everything as local to there as possible. One place we go to a lot is Royal Teas (76 Royal Hill, SE10 8RT, 8691 7240, www.royalteascafe.co.uk), a vegetarian coffee shop in Greenwich. They do classics like eggy bread, but they just do them really well. All the cakes and juices they serve are made on site and every day there's a special soup of the day.

Another local favourite is a nice little Lebanese café called Levante (11 Lewis Grove, SE13 6BG, 8355 3522), in Lewisham. They do a vegetarian special which has falafel, houmous, tahini, salad and olives.

Also nearby is the Greenwich Picture House (180 Greenwich High Road, SE10 8NN, 0870 755 0065, www.picture houses.co.uk). It's £9 to see a film on a Monday night and they show everything from blockbusters to world cinema and children's films. There's a bar there too and you can buy drinks and take them into the cinema, with its comfortable, relaxing chairs.

When we were starting up the business, I went everywhere by bike, and I still have a lot of fun cycling around London. One of my favourite cycle rides is around Greenwich Park (8858 2608, www.royal parks.org.uk). There are paths throughout, which means that there are always lots of other people cycling, rollerblading and skateboarding here. And because it's on a hill you have fantastic views over the whole of London.

Anna Robertson is the owner of the Veggie Table market stalls.

945 *Let off steam at Kew*

For those who usually associate steam engines with the railways, it may come as a surprise to learn that they were also used to supply water to the city. The Victorian pumping station at Kew, now Kew Bridge Steam Museum, is a significant piece of industrial architecture in its own right but it is now also home to an extraordinary collection of different engines and is one of London's most engaging visitor attractions – particularly at weekends when the great pieces of machinery are in steam. The museum illustrates how the rapidly expanding city met the challenge of delivering water to its citizens – and of removing their effluvia. With plenty of hands-on exhibits for children, including a small steam train, the stars of the show remain those beam engines – four of them in all – gleaming behemoths whose mighty pistons and whirring wheels fill the building with an unearthly, rhythmic whooshing sound.

Kew Bridge Steam Museum *Green Dragon Lane, Brentford TW8 0EN (8596 4757/ www.kbsm.org. £9.50.*

Art for art's sake

Mindful of our ten pound budget, Robin Saikia takes a tour round the West End's finest – and most expensive – galleries.

Spending time visiting the lush lairs of London's leading art dealers, either for private views (easier than ever to gatecrash, *see p156*) or simply in search of warmth and edification, is a time-honoured pursuit of the cash strapped Londoner. It may require a steely frame of mind to ignore the sometimes withering glances of the starchy front-of-house concierges in Bond Street, but the effort is well repaid, because London's leading commercial galleries and auction houses routinely exhibit works of art that are as good as – if not better than – the art on show in the national collections. The West End (for our purposes, both sides of Piccadilly) remains the core of the art world and the following itinerary is easily walkable and manageable within a day (two, if you're taking your time).

Choose a busy auction house as your first port of call – they're slightly less daunting than an intimate and dimly lit old master gallery. Saunter purposefully into Sotheby's (34-35 Old Bond Street, W1Y 9HD) or Christie's (8 King Street, St. James's, SW1Y 6QT) and disarm the resident ice maiden by asking her what's 'on view' – it could be next week's sale of Old Master paintings or next month's sale of Oriental Art. Unless you resemble a Texan oil magnate or a Russian oligarch, refrain from making loud and disparaging remarks about the prices or quality of the goods on offer. Instead, muse your way thoughtfully around the exhibits, pausing to inspect the occasional lot. If there is, say, a marvellous piece of Fabergé locked in a cabinet, you may ask to see it or handle it. Don't drop it or steal it.

One of the grandest, most civilised and most welcoming galleries in London is Philip Mould (29 Dover Street, W1S 4NA). Mould specialises in museum-quality portraits of important people from the Tudor period to the present day, and a visit to his gallery is every bit as instructive as a visit to the National Portrait Gallery. There is always a chance (if you're lucky) that Mould will have made one of his now celebrated 'discoveries' of a long-lost portrait and that it will be on view. The frisson afforded by these twice- or thrice-yearly unveilings is nothing less than addictive: past triumphs have included a fire-damaged Charles II, Elizabeth I in the first flush of youth, Bonnie Prince Charlie's brother, Cardinal Henry, and a

Philip Mould

sensitive early portrait of Henry VIII, yet to become the harsh, unbending tyrant of later years. Next door at 27 Dover Street, W1S 4LZ is the affable Andrew Wyld, formerly top dog at Agnew's and now a leading dealer in British and Irish paintings. 'Nothing over £5,000' is a down-to-earth watchword of one of this gallery's annual exhibitions.

On the other side of Piccadilly, in St James's, is the Portland Gallery (8 Bennet Street, SW1 1RP), representing the unimpeachable face of British contemporary art. Here, the pictures and sculpture are unlikely to frighten, unnerve or annoy you; instead a visit should prove an appropriate antidote, should one be needed, to the hurly-burly of the YBA scene – and a cost-effective alternative to tea in Fortnum and Mason. Expect masterly London scenes by Nick Botting, glimmering and glittering visions of Venice by Alexander Creswell, sexually charged couples by Jack Vettriano, and meditative seascapes by Sophie Macpherson.

Nearby is Peter Nahum at the Leicester Galleries (5 Ryder Street, SW1Y 6PY), an extremely energetic and knowledgeable dealer who exhibits important 19th and 20th century art – gorgeously pale and irredeemably chaste pre-Raphaelite maids, petal-strewn courtesans in the palace of Heliogabalus by Lawrence Alma Tadema and unsettling visions of the hereafter by Theodor Baierl. There is often unusual and exciting contemporary art at the Leicester these days – notably by the child prodigy Pejman Ebadi.

Diagonally opposite is Chris Beetles (8 & 10 Ryder Street, SW1Y 6QB), a leading specialist in British watercolours and illustrators. There is always entertaining work to be seen here: a drawing of a steely and self-assured Kenneth Clark by Ronald Searle, for instance; genially mad contraptions by Heath Robinson; pop-eyed cats playing golf by Louis Wain; dashing Italian views by Brabazon and Winnie the Pooh as Roman emperor by EH Shepard. In recent years Beetles has shown photography too: some elegant work by Snowden (Jack Nicholson, David Bowie, the Queen, Anthony Blunt) and Terry O'Neill (Frank Sinatra, Robert Redford, Pierce Brosnan, Bowie again, Bridget Bardot and a strikingly provocative Marianne Faithfull).

Arguably the best dealer in Dutch old masters in the world is Johnny van Haeften (13 Duke Street, SW1Y 6DB). Here you can enjoy Brueghel's skating peasants, drink-crazed boors or desperate alchemists by Teniers or a magnificent tulip by Bosschaert. Next door is Derek Johns (12 Duke Street, SW1Y 6BN) who deals in important Italian, Spanish and French old masters – there is a fair chance of seeing work by Canaletto, Guardi, Francesco Zanin, Tiepolo, Goya, Murillo and Ingres.

Finally, on the other side of Piccadilly again, there are about two dozen galleries in Cork Street, a location which has successfully managed to preserve its reputation as a cradle for contemporary art. Favourite galleries include the Mayor Gallery (22a Cork Street, W1S 3NA), the Medici Gallery (5 Cork Street, W1S 3LQ) and Waddington Galleries (11 Cork Street, W1S 3LT). At the Mayor you can see the latest multi-million pound art phenomenon – contemporary Chinese art by painters such as Chang Xugong and Chen Weimin. Medici have at any given time a selection of solid and pleasing figurative work by Alan Kingsbury (the thinking man's Jack Vettriano), Dylan Lisle (stimulating nudes) and Ray Donley (who has acquired a cult following through painting, with startling effect, like an old master). A visit to the unassailably cosmopolitan Waddington's should give you a firm grounding in most of the things that really matter in the art world on either side of the Atlantic: Picasso, Moore, Robert Indiana, Barry Flanagan (refer knowingly to his 'hares', for under no circumstances are they rabbits), Josef Albers (yes, very like Rothko) and many more.

Chris Beetles

958

Take in the calm of Chiswick House and Gardens

For a gasp of earthly paradise amid West London's urban bustle, head to graceful Chiswick House and Gardens. This is the birthplace of the English landscape movement, which bulldozed formal gardens in favour of sweeping elegance. The magnificent neo-Palladian villa was conceived as a kind of giant cabinet to display its owner's art and book collection and the garden's grand vistas and hidden pathways influenced designs as far afield as New York's Central Park. Lord Burlington, who completed the villa in 1729, entertained such luminaries as Handel, Alexander Pope and Jonathan Swift, while in the Swinging Sixties the Beatles filmed promos for *Paperback Writer* and *Rain* here. Why not join them?

Chiswick House *Burlington Lane, W4 2RP (8995 0508/www.chgt.org.uk). £4.20.*

959

See the future at the bottom of a cocktail glass...

Twelfth House (35 Pembridge Road, W11 3HG, 7727 9620, www.twelfth-house.co.uk) is a bar with a mystical twist. Though having your tarot cards read by owner Priscilla will set you back £30, there are other cheaper astrological options on the menu: such as having your basic star chart printed for £5 or picking your 'tarot card of the day' for £3. Simple food – from burgers to salads to pasta – is all own-made, though most people plump for something on the long drinks menu, where you'll find 'astrological cocktails' (£7) made from ingredients selected on the basis of the drinker's zodiac sign.

960

...or the past

The art deco-styled restaurant and late night bar Lost Society pays homage to the tipples of the '80s each Tuesday when it wheels out some old favourites – complete with umbrellas on sticks, sparklers and maraschino cherries – for a reasonable £4.25.

Lost Society *697 Wandsworth Road, SW8 3JF (7652 6526/www.lostsociety.co.uk).*

961-962

Check out London's mosques

There's no mistaking the London Central Mosque in Regent's Park with its golden dome and stout 140-foot minaret. The main prayer hall is as grand as one might expect – lush red carpets, mosaics and an impressive chandelier – but this centre for British Muslims also houses a library, offices, an events venue and a bookshop. Its history goes back to World War II when Churchill's War Cabinet put aside £100,000 for the site, but the mosque was actually built in the 1970s.

Up to 50,000 Muslims visit during the two main Islamic festivals, or Eids, and at lunchtime on Fridays, the main day of worship, the mosque is usually overflowing. Visitors are allowed in any time the mosque is open, though women must cover their heads (headscarves are available from the bookshop) and both sexes must cover their legs to below the knee. Guided tours are also available if you call ahead.

Also impressive is the towering complex of the East London Mosque in Whitechapel – one of the biggest mosques in Britain. Building work began in the 1980s and it has continued to grow steadily since – the latest part, London Muslim Centre, opening in June 2004. If you'd just like to visit the building, ring ahead first.

London Central Mosque & Islamic Cultural Centre *146 Park Road, NW8 7RG (7724 3363/www.iccuk.org).*
East London Mosque & London Muslim Centre *46-92 Whitechapel Road, E1 1JX (7650 3000/www.eastlondonmosque.org.uk).*

Why work from home (wandering aimlessly from room to room then grazing on the contents of your fridge) when some of London's most impressive cultural centres, quirky little cafés and world-class museums are more than happy for you to pitch up, log on and generally make like their gaff is your very own office for the day? And, what's more, most won't charge you a penny.

Barbican Centre

Accommodating hordes of culture vultures during weekends and evenings, the Barbican Centre is often eerily empty on weekdays – working here can seem like stepping on to a near-deserted Kubrickian film set. Nevertheless, you'll come across the odd writer, a few creative types and students as well as businessmen and women. A word of warning though: the complex lies within a Wi-Fi hotspot, but because its walls are six feet of solid concrete, the signal can sometimes be unreliable (the library on the second floor has internet terminals if you get stuck). *Silk Street, EC2Y 8DS (7638 4141/ www.barbican.org.uk).*

Camden Arts Centre

The Camden Arts Centre's café is light and airy and has free Wi-Fi and big tables. There's also a gallery and bookshop stocked with quirky little publications that you'll struggle to find anywhere else. The café tends to be populated by twenty- and thirtysomething creative types but there's also usually a healthy smattering of gossiping pensioners to liven things up. The café opens on to a garden, where you can work among the various temporary artworks. *Arkwright Road, NW3 6DG (7472 5500/ www.camdenartscentre.org).*

Camera Café

Idiosyncratic Camera Café near the British Museum is a perfect example of many quirky little cafés around town that love having people pitch up for the day but won't hassle you to keep buying coffees. In the front there's a shop selling secondhand cameras (lovely old Leicas and restored Hasselblads), out back is a cosy café with photographs covering the walls. For £1 you can use the Wi-Fi all day and you'll no doubt run into a character or two.

44 Museum Street, WC1A 1LY (7831 1566/ www.cameracafe.co.uk).

Leon

At this Spitalfields branch of Leon there's free Wi-Fi and a massive table if you need to spread out. It attracts including City folk, art directors and copywriters from the nearby advertising agencies as well as young artists. It tends to get very busy at lunchtime but before noon and after 3pm you'll have the place pretty much to yourself. Bear in mind a rumour we once heard: arty types sit to the right, suits to the left…

3 Crispin Place, E1 6DW (7247 4369/ www.leonrestaurants.co.uk).

Peyton and Byrne

This bright, airy branch of Peyton and Byrne on the ground floor of the Wellcome Collection is great for a light lunch or an indulgent afternoon tea. You can potter away on your laptop using the free Wi-Fi while enjoying superb scotch eggs, pastries, pork pies and salads or sticky cakes, sponges and crumbles made fresh daily. If you're lacking inspiration have a wander round the (free) museum.

Wellcome Collection, 183 Euston Road, NW1 2BE (7611 2138/ www.peytonandbyrne.com).

Royal Festival Hall

The Royal Festival Hall has a little more hustle and bustle than the Barbican. The ground floor next to the windows overlooking the Hayward Gallery is a popular spot as this is where the building's free Wi-Fi signal is strongest. However, if the constant onslaught of classical music and the glare from all those pristine white Apple laptops gets too much, you'll find the very peaceful Saison Poetry Library on the sixth floor, complete with workstations.

Southbank Centre, Belvedere Road, SE1 8XX (0871 663 2501/www.southbankcentre.co.uk).

969-970
Collect bits of old London Bridge

The medieval, 19-arch London Bridge, once cluttered with houses, shops and heads on sticks, was finally demolished in 1831 but you can still catch a glimpse of a few of its ancient fixtures and fittings. Most incredible of all of them is the royal coat of arms which adorns the front of the King's Arms pub in Newcomen Street, off Borough High Street. It was salvaged from the stone gateway which stood at the southern end of the old bridge until 1760, and duly shows the arms of George III.

From 1762 comes a collection of stone alcoves, which were installed at regular intervals on the bridge to prevent pedestrians being trampled under hoof by the traffic when the last of the teetering buildings were cleared from the bridge. Needless to say, they were quickly pressed into alternative service by dossers, beggars, footpads, thimble-riggers and their dog-eyes, street hawkers and tuppenny molls. Two of them survive in Hackney's Victoria Park, and you'll find another closer to its original home in the grounds of Guy's Hospital.

971
Eat at the home of Reggae Reggae sauce

Super charismatic marinade maverick and *Dragon's Den* slayer Levi Roots opened his own restaurant in Battersea in 2007. Definitely one for the frugal, the Papine Jerk Centre offers a small but uncomplicated menu of Caribbean staples: Jamaica's national dish, ackee and saltfish (£3 per portion) is a crowd-pleaser (expect queues at lunchtime), or try the richly seasoned mains of jerk chicken, curried goat or oxtail (£5 small, £6 large), with a side of fried plantain or saltfish fritters (£1 per portion). The Guinness punch (£1.50 small, £2.50 large) is also a big draw, as, of course, is the entrepreneurial chef himself – real name Keith Graham – who you'll sometimes see here.
Papine Jerk Centre *8 Lavender Road, SW11 2UG (7924 2288/www.papinejerk.com).*

972
Reconnoitre the City's less familiar Wrens

There'll be a lot written about St Paul's over the next few years, what with the restoration reaching its glorious completion and the cathedral's 300th anniversary celebrations in 2010. However, Sir Christopher Wren was a notably prolific architect and there are many other fine churches in the vicinity that can be visited for free. If you start on the west side of Ludgate Circus and look up to St Paul's, the black spire to the left of the dome is St Martin Ludgate, while St Bride's is hidden behind. The latter's steeple is the tallest of any Wren church and was supposedly the model for tiered wedding cakes. Turn right in front of the Cathedral and you pass through Temple Bar, another Wren creation. It originally stood at the western end of Fleet Street to mark the boundary between the Cities of London and Westminster, but now it marks the entrance to the new Paternoster Square. Cross the square, emerging on Newgate Street, and Christ Church is opposite. Almost destroyed during World War II, the ruined nave is today a lovely rose garden. Head east to Gresham Street for the Wren motherlode: first, St Anne and St Agnes, with its leafy churchyard; then a glimpse of the tower of St Alban, Wood Street; next you pass St Lawrence Jewry, the church of the Corporation of London; and finally, when Gresham Street becomes Lothbury, St Margaret Lothbury. This has one of the loveliest interiors of any Wren church, and the impressive wood screen is by Wren himself.

Over at Bank tube station, take the Mansion House exit and turn left for St Stephen Walbrook, Wren's most grandiose church, a mass of creamy stone with a soaring dome, fabulously bulbous pulpit and a slightly incongruous modern altar by Henry Moore. Near Cannon Street station on Abchurch Lane you'll find St Mary Abchurch, a real gem with a shallow, painted dome and a beautiful carved reredos by Grinling Gibbons. It was shattered into 2,000 pieces by a wartime bomb but painstakingly pieced together again afterwards.

973 *Bob on Apple Day*

Despite sounding like more like an ancient pagan ritual, or perhaps a corruption of the Christian harvest festival, this celebration of apples, orchards and locally grown food actually only dates from 1990 (though bobbing for apples has been around for much longer). There are events all over the country and in London with Borough Market (7407 1002, www.boroughmarket.org.uk) a great place to dunk, bob, eat and drink this quintessentially English fruit, in all its many varieties. It all takes place around the nearest Sunday to the 21st October.

www.commonground.org.uk/appleday

974-983 *Follow some vintage advice*

In search of cheap thrills from an earlier era, Derek Hammond plunders some old London guidebooks.

The *London Spy* was London's first ever guidebook, published in 1703 to shout up the pleasures of dog-tossing, gaming and baiting lunatics in Bedlam. But it isn't just the long-disappeared aspects of Dickensian/Swinging/Thatcher's London that stand out when you pick up an old guide for pennies from a secondhand bookshop – there's also a surprisingly broad swathe of places, possibilities and things to do that remain strangely constant – and affordable.

Pop in to the Anchor, Bankside

'What more would you have than a tankard of ale where the greatest of all Englishmen used to have his?' demands HE Popham in his brilliantly swashbuckling *Guide to London Taverns* (Claude Stacey, 1927). 'If you prefer a West End hotel, with gold-laced flunkeys to bow you in, and a drink that costs five shillings a glass, for goodness sake leave us here and take yourself westward in the first cab that you can find, or swim up river if you prefer it. We don't care. We are for a game of darts with our riverside friends in the taproom'. Shakespeare may be no more likely to turn up now than he was 80-odd years ago but, on the plus side, the Anchor has added a smart new(ish) drinking area right by the river that's glorious on a summer's day.

Gaze through misty glass at a 'Roman' curio

'At 5 Strand Lane is an antiquarian's mystery,' teases Harold F Hutchinson, author of London Transport's *Visitor's London* (1954), 'and no reputable authority will vouch for its latinity. But it is an interesting relic'. It remains a thrill to dodge down this dingy alley off the Strand and shade your eyes in order to see into this spring-fed plunge bath – still in working order, and handling around 2,000 gallons of fresh spring water a day. 'The oval lead overflow pipe is considered to be genuinely Roman,' Harold stuck his neck out, 'but the bricks are more probably Tudor.'

Buy your own hanky on Petticoat Lane

'Thousands pack into Petticoat Lane between the sweatshops and bomb sites on Sunday morning, and it is the nearest thing London can offer to an Oriental bazaar.' So reckoned VS Pritchett in 1962, when Harvest published *London Perceived*. 'They used to say that you could walk through this market and see your own handkerchief on sale on a stall by the time you got to the end. I was brought up on scandals of a similar kind sold at the dog market in Bethnal Green: you met your own dear Airdale painted black and offered as a retriever'.

Get into ironwork at Leadenhall

'Leadenhall Market is solid and reassuring, and it asserts the Victorians' belief in the virtues of cast iron. The entire market with its adjoining alleys is of the greatest interest to the London virtuoso...' Londonologists don't come any more cultish than the great writer/sketcher Geoffrey Fletcher. *The London Nobody Knows* (Hutchinson, 1962) was his debut outing and subsequently made into a documentary film starring James Mason. Leadenhall Market features in both: 'The ironwork is highly elaborated with ornament and the griffins which support the City's coat of arms... discreetly sober. One of the most attractive buildings is the Lamb Tavern, with its large hanging lamps and engraved glass. All is Victorian here, apart from the human element and the delivery vans.'

Let's all go down the Strand... on the green

'A picturesque stretch of tree-lined riverside walk with Georgian houses, a boatyard and a couple of pubs. The City Barge was granted a charter for 500 years by Queen Elizabeth I, and the river entrance has to be sealed up with clay and boarding during high tides'. Brilliantly grumpy American tourist Betty James went for a stroll down Strand on the

Green in Chiswick the very year the Beatles filmed scenes from *Help!* in the City Barge pub. Her *London on £1 a Day* (Batsford, 1965) is truly evocative of the times – and timeless. 'The Bull's Head has an underground tunnel to an island known as Oliver's Eyot. It is said that this tunnel was used by Oliver Cromwell and his Roundheads, which is decidely peculiar because, as everybody knows, they didn't drink.' Actually, there are three more-than-decent riverside pubs on Strand on the Green, and it's the Bell and Crown that has come to the fore in claiming the tunnel myth today and Oliver's Eyot is now a haven for herons and cormorants.

Be very scared... at a cult leader's spooky Gothic house

'At 12 Langford Place, sheer horror: a Francis Bacon shriek in these affluent, uncomplicated suburbs at the end of Abbey Road. It looks like a normal St John's Wood villa pickled in embalming fluid by some mad doctor...' That's how Ian Nairn described the Victorian charlatan John Hugh Smyth-Pigott's pad in his witty, opinionated architectural bible, *Nairn's London*. The book was published by Penguin in 1967, but he could have written this particular entry yesterday.

Take a perfect London photo

Len Deighton's *London Dossier* is the essential guide for clawing back the mood of London in 1967. Len's own chunks are masterly, but the book also benefits from the multiple perspectives of specialist buddies roped in to write odd chapters – like Adrian Flowers on photography: 'Some foreigners are most struck by the effect of twilight,' he wrote. 'Certainly some of London's special moments are at this time, as the artificial lights slowly take over... All along the Embankment is good for night shooting, especially the Victoria Embankment and the promenade between Westminster and Lambeth Bridges on the south side.'

Tune in, drop out

Nicholas Saunders was an anarcho-hippy self-publisher with plenty of vital information to pass on about drugs, dole, sex and squats in his psychedelic-covered *Alternative London*, from 1972. 'There are millions of things you can do in London,' he wrote, 'like yelling at people in Speaker's Corner, climbing every tree in every park, flying kites just about anywhere, but it's best in the middle of Oxford Street or outside Buckingham Palace... See the second half of any play for free, simply by walking in at the interval... Drop in for free entertainment when the light is on over Big Ben: the entrance is the arch in the car park: you can leave your car where it says "Peers only"...' Saunders went on to found Neal's Yard wholefood empire and later wrote another underground classic, *Ecstasy and the Dance Culture* (1995).

Go 'window shopping' at an auctioneer's

The high-tension atmosphere of auction houses is great fun to drop in on, whether you're bidding on outlandish art yourself – or just watching others sweat it out. 'But they have their own set of rules,' warned Martin Lightfoot in his *Visitor's Guide to London Shopping* (Martlet, 1982), 'and it is well to know roughly how they work before venturing into them. If you watch an auction you will often find it difficult to see who is actually bidding, one reason for this being that the auctioneer may have recorded bids by people not actually present, and is therefore pushing up the bidding by taking a slightly higher bid 'off the wall', as they say. There are horror stories of someone sneezing or scratching his ear and finding himself with a £20,000 lot. These stories are complete myths.'

Visit the birthplace of Indie

Richard Jobson was the singer in punk band the Skids before he drifted into TV, and so to novels and directing films: no wonder he dealt in muso mythology with a lasting quality. 'The most independent record shop in Britain, Rough Trade was the place where the alternative music scene, born off the back of punk, really matured,' he wrote in the Virgin *Insider's Guide To London* (Virgin, 1993). 'Covered with posters from seminal punk and post-punk releases and gigs, the Rough Trade shop is the meeting place for people interested in new music. Now that CDs seem to have taken over completely, it's one of the few places you can get new releases on vinyl.'

984-993

Buy brilliant British beer at London's finest real ale pubs...

We know, we know: it's hard to spend less than £4 on a pint in central London these days, but at least at the following places your money will buy you a great British gourmet treat.

Greenwich Union

The Greenwich, flagship pub of Alistair Hook's laudable Meantime Brewery makes the most of the training and recipes its founder gleaned at age-old institutions in Germany. Meantime produces London Stout, Pale Ale, Helles, Kölner and Union, plus strawberry and raspberry varieties, all on draught and at reasonable prices. *56 Royal Hill, SE10 8RT (8692 6258/ www.greenwichunion.com).*

Jerusalem Tavern

Located in the alleys behind Farringdon station, this creaking and cosily tatty little pub serves the sought-after ales of Suffolk's St Peter's Brewery. Almost hidden between timber divides, the bar is backed by barrels, their names and ABVs chalked on a board: Suffolk Gold, Grapefruit, Cinnamon & Apple, Organic. A rag-tag and decidedly loyal crowd muses over the *Evening Standard* crossword or tucks into their moreish haddock and salmon fishcakes. *55 Britton Street, EC1M 5UQ (7490 4281/ www.stpetersbrewery.co.uk).*

Lamb

Founded in 1729, this Young's outpost in Holborn found fame as a theatrical haunt when the A-list included Sir Henry Irving and assorted music hall stars; they're commemorated in old photos and surrounded by well-worn seats, much polished wood and a few vintage knick-knacks. Punters range from discerning students to Gray's Inn barristers, supping from half a dozen pumps – expect real ale from Young's and Wells (the two breweries combined operations in 2006), plus a guest beer (perhaps St Austell Tribute).

94 Lamb's Conduit Street, WC1N 3LZ (7405 0713).

Market Porter

Few market bars stock this range of beers. In an invariably cramped main bar area – there's more room in the back, but the bustle can be off-putting – Borough Market traders and sundry other regulars gather around the likes of Okell's Maclir, Vale Brewery Best, Acorn Brewery Kashmir, Harveys Best and Lund's Bitter. There are choices from Meantime Brewery too.

9 Stoney Street, SE1 9AA (7407 2495/ www.markettaverns.co.uk).

Pembury Tavern

Drinking in this vast, overlit Hackney bar room feels like rattling round a youth hostel canteen, but the 16 handpumps – mostly fine real ale from Cambridge's Milton Brewery (Pegasus, Jericho, Cyclops and their stout Nero on our last visit) – are a delight. Bar billiards and a red-baize pool table on one side give way to bookshelves and boardgames on the other. Beer festivals take place in March, July and November.

90 Amhurst Road, E8 1JH (8986 8597).

Royal Oak

The Royal Oak off Borough High Street seems wonderfully trapped in time, complete with its unused hatch for off sales. Serving the great works of Lewes brewery Harveys, the ales – Mild, Pale, Old, Best and Armada – are all under £3, and a felt-tipped menu offers classics such as rabbit casserole and Lancashire hotpot. Music hall stars Harry Ray and Flanagan & Allen, celebrated in framed hand bills, would have tucked into the same.

44 Tabard Street, SE1 4JU (7357 7173).

Sultan

In the backstreets of south Wimbledon lies an ale-drinking nirvana, named after an 1830s racehorse. A much-loved, if rather antiseptic locals' boozer, the Sultan is the only London pub owned by Wiltshire's Hop Back Brewery; on the weekly beer club evenings, chattering middle-aged locals enjoy the delights of GFB, Entire Stout, Summer Lightning and Quad Hop for the princely sum of just £1.90 a pint (carryouts are also available).

78 Norman Road, SW19 1BT (8542 4532).

Wenlock Arms

From the outside, the Wenlock doesn't look like much. To be honest, it doesn't look like much inside either, but god forbid it should ever tear out its carpet or gastro-up its menu of doorstep sarnies. On any given night, you might find yourself sitting next to a table of beer-bellied ale-hunters going through the excellent and ever-changing range of beers and, of course, the eccentric, ever-talkative regulars.

26 Wenlock Road, N1 7TA (7608 3406/ www.wenlock-arms.co.uk).

White Horse

This stupendously popular stalwart does what it does best exceptionally well: it serves a fantastic, even mind-boggling, array of beers. There are 60 (count 'em) available at any one time, including 30 on draught, eight of them cask ales (the likes of Harveys Sussex Best, Adnams Broadside and rotating guests). And there's always a cask mild, stout and porter on offer, as well as regular beer festivals.

1-3 Parsons Green, SW6 4UL (7736 2115/ www.whitehorsesw6.com).

Ye Olde Mitre

Its secluded location requires you to slink down an alleyway just off Hatton Garden, and as you do so you're transported to a parallel pub universe where the clientele are friendly and the staff (in pristine black and white uniforms) briskly efficient. A Monday-to-Friday joint, it opens for just one weekend a year – happily that's to coincide with the British Beer Festival. Ales are certainly the speciality – Deuchars and Adnams are regulars, with frequently changing guest beers beside them – but the proprietors don't turn their noses up at wine either. Historic, but never dusty.

1 Ely Court (Ely Place side of 8 Hatton Garden), EC1N 6SJ (7405 4751).

994 ...or the city's best beer shops

Since the migration online of Pitfield Street's excellent Beer Shop, Twickenham residents have been the only Londoners with a local beer specialist: the Real Ale Shop (371 Richmond Road, TW1 2EF, 8892 3710, www.realale.com) sells around 100 beers, ales, ciders and perrys, including bottle-conditioned varieties which are as close as the home-drinker can get to cask ale flavour without installing handpumps in their kitchen. Even better, you get 500ml of most bottles for less than £3. From Thursday to Saturday, the Utobeer stall in Borough Market sells hundreds of different beers from all over the world. Alternatively, go direct to the brewer: the Griffin Brewery (Chiswick Lane South, W4 2QB, 8996 2085, www.fullers.co.uk) sells the full Fuller's range.

997 Spot secret creatures at the Natural History Museum

The 70 million specimens housed in the Natural History Museum's galleries – from immense pickled squids to tiny lichens pressed by Charles Darwin – are, of course, mind-boggling: but when did you last look at the building itself? Monkeys scamper up arches in the central hall, huge columns resemble fossilised trees, and outside there are more statues of animals and plants (the extinct above the east wing, the living to the west). In a final flourish, beautiful paintings of gilded plants – many chosen for their economic value to the Empire – look down from the high, broken-arched ceiling.
Natural History Museum *Cromwell Road, SW7 5BD (information 7942 5725/switchboard 7942 5000/www.nhm.ac.uk).*

995 Hear a free steel band concert

Do yourself a favour and avoid Notting Hill Carnival crowds by heading instead to the incredible steel drumming of the National Panorama Championship. Every year on the Saturday before carnival (which is always on the August Bank Holiday weekend), an enthusiastic crowd converge in Hyde Park to watch the cream of UK steelpan talent battling it out to be named national champions. The music begins at midday, with the contest proper kicking off at teatime and running into the evening.

996 Check out the MPs' secret tunnel

In the grand baroque lobby of the St Ermin's Hotel in Westminster, it's easy to overlook the small door given unusual prominence halfway up the grand staircase. Down a tight spiral staircase lies a vaulted four-metre tunnel – now definitively blocked – which once carried MPs to and from the Houses of Parliament, some 600 metres distant. The Division Bell still sounds in the hotel when it's time for members to return to work and cast their vote.

998 Enter a government office

Want to see London government in action? The 25 London Assembly members call Boris to account once a month at Mayor's Question Time – and anyone can watch: check www.london.gov.uk/assembly/assembly_meetings.jsp to find out what's next up for discussion. Even if the hurly-burly of live politics doesn't appeal, Lord Foster's motorbike helmet of a building might. The first two floors of City Hall are, subject to a security search on entering, open to the public from 8am to 8pm on weekdays, as well as some weekends. You can walk up the spiral ramp to visit the temporary exhibitions and view the Assembly Chamber, or descend to the café and – best of all – the London Photomat. Most recently updated in April 2008 (although some source photos date to summer 2006), this is a walk-on aerial photo of the whole of Greater London, at sufficiently high resolution for you to be able to identify your own house. London's Living Room, located on the top floor and offering fabulous views, is also occasionally open too.
City Hall *Queen's Walk, SE1 2AA (www.london.gov.uk/gla/city_hall/index.jsp).*

999

Take it all in at Somerset House

You can see all of Somerset House for less than a tenner if you plan things right: the trick is to turn up on Monday between 10am and 2pm when entry to the Courtauld Gallery is free.

Start from the river side of the building and head downstairs from the new Embankment Galleries – which replaced the Hermitage Rooms and Gilbert Collection in early 2008 (although the latter can be seen for free from autumn 2009 at its new home at the V&A). You'll find a free exhibition on the history of Somerset House, complete with ceremonial Thames barge and the strains of Handel's *Water Music*. Next, explore the Studio and Terrace Rooms, which hold intriguing temporary exhibitions: we particularly enjoyed Richard Bryant's London photographs, shown in the Terrace Rooms in 2009. Done? Then it's time to make your first investment: cough up £8 to get into the Embankment Galleries themselves, where changing exhibitions highlight the connections between art, architecture and design under inviting titles like 'Wouldn't it be nice…: Wishful thinking in art and design'.

Once you've had your fill of the contemporary, cross the brilliant fountain court – lingering among the choreographed water jets in summer or laughing at the tumbling ice-skaters in winter – and head into the Courtauld Gallery (7848 2526, www.courtauld.ac.uk/gallery). This is one of the country's best collections of paintings – diverse and compelling, yet on a more manageable scale than, say, the National Gallery. Sensational Old Masters, Impressionists and Post-Impressionists are displayed in atmospherically creaky rooms, alongside prints, drawings and sculpture. Key works include Cranach's *Adam and Eve*, Manet's *Bar at the Folies-Bergère*, Van Gogh's *Self-Portrait with Bandaged Ear* and Gauguin's *Nevermore*.

When you're thoroughly cultured out, take the stairway all the way to the basement and invest your remaining two quid in something restorative from the tiny café.
Somerset House *The Strand, WC2R 1LA (7845 4600/www.somerset-house.org.uk).*

1000 *Get to the top…*

… of the Monument (Monument Street, EC3R 8AH, 7626 2717, www.themonument.info). The recent recipient of an impressive £4.5 million refurbishment, Sir Christopher Wren and Robert Hooke's memorial to the Great Fire of London is the world's tallest free-standing column and unlike other high points in the city (such as the London Eye or St Paul's Cathedral, to name just a couple) it'll only cost you three quid to get to the top. Scaling the internal spiral staircase with its 311 steps may make you a little tired and dizzy, but what the hell – you'll have London at your feet.

A-Z index

Thematic index

Advertisers' index

Please refer to relevant sections for addresses and / or telephone numbers
When you have run out of things to do why not visit...